Exceptional Experience and Health

Exceptional Experience and Health

Essays on Mind, Body and Human Potential

Edited by CHRISTINE SIMMONDS-MOORE

McFarland & Company, Inc., Publishers
Jefferson, North Carolina, and London

LIBRARY OF CONGRESS CATALOGING-IN-PUBLICATION DATA

Exceptional experience and health : essays on mind, body and
    human potential / edited by Christine Simmonds-Moore.
         p.   cm.
      Includes bibliographical references and index.

      ISBN 978-0-7864-5966-7
      softcover : acid free paper ∞

      1. Mind and body therapies.   I. Simmonds-Moore,
    Christine, 1971–
    RC489.M53E93 2012
    615.8′528—dc23   2012004957

BRITISH LIBRARY CATALOGUING DATA ARE AVAILABLE

Cover image © 2012 Getty Images; front cover design by TG Design

Manufactured in the United States of America

*McFarland & Company, Inc., Publishers
    Box 611, Jefferson, North Carolina 28640
       www.mcfarlandpub.com*

Table of Contents

Preface

Let me begin by defining exceptional experiences. The *Collins English Dictionary* states that exceptional refers to "someone or something that has a particular quality, usually a good quality, to an unusually high degree" or to events that happen infrequently, i.e., are unusual or extraordinary. Readers may also be aware of Rhea White's term "exceptional human experience," which spans a variety of experiences, and has been defined as "an umbrella term for anomalous experiences that transform the individual who has them so that they are engaged in a process of realizing their full human potential, which makes the experience an exceptional human one." The term has been applied here as it allows for many types of experiences to be considered in one volume. It has also been employed for its neutrality in terms of the ostensible veridicality of such experiences.

In this book, the term *exceptional* is used to describe anomalous healing effects, placebo healing effects, hypnotic healing effects, paranormal, mystical, religious and transpersonal experiences and creative experiences. The essays herein explore how beliefs, intentions and the nature of "mind" interface with exceptional experiences and both physical and mental health.

In recent years, it has become increasingly acceptable (at least in the United Kingdom) to study exceptional experiences and beliefs. For instance, there are currently fifteen British universities where one may study anomalous or paranormal experiences as part of a psychology undergraduate degree. Another research unit (at the University of York) focuses on understanding exceptional experiences from a sociological perspective. In addition, British high school students are now learning about exceptional experiences as part of the psychology Advanced level[1] qualification. This is likely to lead to a greater demand for university level education in the coming years.

Recently, several serious academic discussion groups have also emerged, with a focus on understanding these experiences from a variety of perspectives (e.g., one is *Exploring the Extraordinary*, based at York University). New journals (e.g., *Paranthropology*) and conferences (e.g., *Exploring the Extraordinary*) dedicated to topics relevant to exceptional experiences have also emerged in recent years.

1

In the United States, alternative or non-western approaches to medicine and *spirituality* have become valid topics for academic and applied consideration.[2] In terms of other exceptional experiences (e.g., the subject matter of parapsychology) it is noteworthy that an introductory online course — examining exceptional experiences and classes at undergraduate and masters levels are being run by two academic institutions.[3] However, the exploration of exceptional experiences is a semantic mine field. Researching (and the teaching of) *some* exceptional experiences (for example, extrasensory experiences) are often associated with stigma. One reason is that if they are real, they would challenge the current scientific status quo. However, such experiences are clearly part of the human experience, and as such, there is a need to study them and understand them. This is particularly the case where they are experienced in an applied context — i.e., where they interface with health and mental health.

In putting together this book, I have tried to capture something of the clinical and academic zeitgeist, in order to move forward in thinking about the nature and potential of mind and exceptional experiences and how they might be applied to health and mental health. For instance, it is becoming increasingly clear that the mind has a role in healing. It is also increasingly clear that clinical psychology and parapsychology are close cousins and can and should be moving forward together.

The chapters that comprise this book were originally presented as papers at a conference that took place in Liverpool, England, in September 2009. Taken together, they reflect the contributions of many minds who are each working in diverse areas, but whose research, clinical practice, and thoughts and insights allow us to further understand the complex interactions between *mind, exceptional* experiences and beliefs, and physical and mental health.

The project was conceived in the hope that a variety of disparate disciplines might come together to further understand how human consciousness, beliefs and intentions (conscious and less conscious) can impact the physical body in terms of healing; how practices and experiences such as meditation and creativity can impact mental health and exceptional human experiences, and to develop greater understanding as to how and why unusual experiences can relate to transcendence and mental health as well as psychopathology. The focus may therefore be summarized as an aspect of Positive Psychology — how the mind and exceptional experiences can be involved in better physical and mental health. We hope to normalize experiences that are often pathologized, and recognize that exceptional human experiences can and do have value for physical and mental health.

Contributors were invited to allow for a triangulated approach toward understanding these complex interactions. In the Introduction, Christine

Simmonds-Moore presents an overview of the current research and practice with regard to the mind and body relationship. This includes discussion of the various strands of research which have explored the role of the mind in healing; spiritual and religious beliefs, placebo effects, the role of metaphor and imagery in healing and research in parapsychology. It also includes an overview of the history and current state of play with regard to clinical approaches to exceptional experiences and is designed to whet the reader's appetite for the essays that follow.

The book is organized into two parts. The first contains four essays grouped under the title "Belief, Mind and Body." This begins in Chapter 1 where John Gruzelier presents a thorough examination of his recent research into hypnosis and mental imagery and the ways that they influence mental and physical health. He later describes how two energy healing practices, Johrei and Reiki, affect mental and physical health, looks at how personality interacts with hypnosis and healing practices with regard to health outcomes, and considers the mechanisms by which bioenergy healing methods may succeed. In chapter 2, David Luke explores altered states of consciousness and the mental imagery associated with such states and their possible outcomes on health. Luke focuses mainly on dreams and states of consciousness and shamanic experiences associated with the drug Ayahuasca, and explores how the fascinating imagery evoked during these states might facilitate healing.

In chapter 3, Carl Williams, Diane Dutton and Chris Burgess present the results of a phenomenological study which explored energy healing. This included the verbal and non-verbal interactions between the healer and the healee. The authors observe that the healing process includes shared and embodied metaphors symbolizing ailments, by both the healer and the healee. Healing might therefore be understood socially, and the co-constitution of shared representation and meaningfulness of the ailment may allow for health changes in the healee. In Chapter 4, Eve Binks presents some of her recent research findings pertaining to the role of religious belief and practice in Northern Ireland. Binks demonstrates that religious affiliation appears to act as a buffer against the pathologizing impact of exposure to traumatic events; illustrating a role for belief and shared social identity in terms of health outcomes.

The second part of the book focuses on how exceptional experiences affect health and mental health. In Chapter 5, Stefan Schmidt gives an excellent overview of meditation and its impact on health, mental health and the possibility of non-local awareness/influence (psi). Drawing on a range of research studies, it is clear that meditative practice has great value for both physical health and mental health, but also allows for non-local or psi effects, which challenge the mainstream view of consciousness. In Chapter 6, Nicola

J. Holt explores the relationship between creativity and anomalous experiences, and how this relationship influences mental health. She presents a fascinating exploration of research in creativity and a range of different anomalous experiences and how both relate to health. The nature of the association between these variables is explored, and it is concluded that creativity is often associated with healthy rather than less healthy anomalous experiences.

In chapter 7, Christine Simmonds-Moore presents an overview of what is understood by *anomaly-proneness* and how our knowledge of the traits associated with healthy and less healthy anomaly-proneness might inform researchers and clinicians interested in advising people about methods which might encourage more anomalous experiences, or attenuate or eliminate unwanted experiences. In Chapter 8, Isabel Clarke describes the bipolar nature of psychotic experiences, i.e., how they can lead to either spiritual or transformative experiences *or* to experiences which are more destructive. She applies insights from theory (Interacting Cognitive Systems), her own work as a clinical psychologist and discusses methods she has employed to harness the positive potential of what she describes as the "transliminal" (after Thalbourne).

In Chapter 9, Eberhard Bauer and Martina Belz present an overview of the work of the IGPP (Institut für Grenzgebiete der Psychologie und Psychohygiene) in Freiburg, Germany, one of the few existing centers where research and clinical practice have proceeded hand in hand. In Chapter 10, we hear more about the work of the IGPP in Martina Belz's insightful discussion of clinical approaches to the exceptional, and the differences between exceptional experiences (ExE) that are associated with pathology and those that are associated with health.

In the final chapter, Ian Tierney discusses clinical approaches to exceptional experiences in the United Kingdom, informed by his own practice as a clinical consultant at the Koestler Parapsychology Unit in Edinburgh, and from recent research which has investigated the clinical requests made of research units specializing in parapsychology/the psychology of anomalous experiences. Tierney also introduces his ongoing research which explores one spontaneous experience (Recurrent Spontaneous Psychokinesis) from a clinical perspective, testing Von Lucadou's *Model of Pragmatic Information.*

This collection expands current awareness of consciousness and the mind with regard to its potential for healing and to help further the expansion of current global clinical practices with regard to exceptional experiences, which are too easily labeled as pathological. For further reading on these topics, we have included one Bibliography at the end of the collection, which has combined references from each essay.

This book would not exist if it were not for Rhea White and Professor Robert (Bob) Morris who have both played prominent roles in the recent history of research in these areas. They have also provided personal inspiration to the editor. Rhea White's work has encouraged the neutral study of exceptional human experiences as a valid topic for modern researchers. The late Professor Bob Morris propelled the academic acceptability of these experiences by nurturing many academic careers, particularly in the United Kingdom. His philosophy was to combine normal with "paranormal" and by so doing, equip future students of exceptional human experiences with the skills to plant their feet firmly in mainstream research, and to find employment within the psychology departments of universities. Bob Morris had great insight, and it is of note that during his last conference, in Vienna in 2004, Bob shared that he felt that clinical approaches were an excellent line of development for parapsychology; the future of parapsychology, I hope that this book inspires more research and application of findings from research into exceptional experiences.

Notes

1. This is a two-year qualification which is completed between ages 16-18, prior to entering university.

2. For example, researchers in Boston have explored yoga and at Duke University in North Carolina, there is a center for complementary medicine and spirituality as part of the medical center.

3. The Rhine Research Center now offers an introductory course on parapsychology and plans to introduce certificate and degree programs in the next few years, in addition, the University of West Georgia includes a parapsychology course at undergraduate and postgraduate levels, in addition to a certificate in integrative health.

Introduction

Overview and Exploration of the State of Play Regarding Health and Exceptional Experiences

CHRISTINE SIMMONDS-MOORE

The essays in the first half of this collection are presented under the title "Belief, Mind and Body." These contribute to the currently blossoming literature which provides evidence for an expansion of our concept of mind and body, supports the notion that both normal and exceptional experiences are by nature *embodied*, and explores how mind, beliefs and experiences influence personal experiences and the experiences of others in our social world. These essays also return value to the often dismissed *placebo* phenomenon, which clearly indicates a role for belief in health outcomes, and a pivotal role for the mind in one's own healing processes (and those of others in the shared social world). Findings from research on distant healing will also be discussed in terms of their implications for understanding the capacity of the mind for healing.

The essays in the second half of the collection are presented under the title "Exceptional Experiences and Mental Health." These reflect topics pertinent to the growing field of clinical parapsychology (or clinical approaches to exceptional human experiences). This field has been in existence for a number of years, but unfortunately still remains on the fringes of clinical psychology and psychotherapy. This is despite the fact that many people in the general population experience unusual phenomena. Although not everyone experiences problems, it is clear that there *is* shared variance between exceptional experiences and pathology (but also with transcendence). For a number of years, clinical and counseling approaches have existed at the heart of transpersonal psychology in the U.S., and many people working in mental health professions, who are also aware of research in academic parapsychology, understand the need for an expansion of existing clinical approaches.

There has also been a recent surge in personality research focusing on the psychology of the *anomaly-prone* personality (with a particular focus on the personality types Positive Schizotypy and Transliminality) and how these relate to psychopathology. In recent years, research has found that there are different types of anomalous experience; a healthy and less healthy form. By further understanding the differences between healthy and less healthy unusual experiences, it may be possible to learn how to harness the healthy and diminish the less healthy in the general population and among clinical groups. By managing the products of such experiences, it may be possible to enable greater productivity, increase access to non-local mind, and so on. Healthy versus less healthy anomaly proneness and suggestions of ways in which it might be possible to control experiences, and to learn to switch them on or off, are considered in Simmonds-Moore's essay (chapter 7).

The Mind-Body Connection

Health and Mental Health

In this collection "mind" will refer to non-physical aspects of the self and include a range of conscious experiences, beliefs and mental practices (including ways of cultivating certain states of consciousness, and harvesting the products of dreams and other mental imagery). The essays attempt to illustrate some of the ways in which mind may influence physical and mental health.

If one looks at recent history pertaining to the relationship between belief systems (religion and spirituality) and mental health, throughout much of the 20th century it is clear that there was a reticence toward exploring these areas, which were often considered to be old fashioned or even pathological by mental health practitioners (see Moreira-Almeida, Neto & Koenig, 2006). As Belz notes in her essay, the inclusion of religious and spiritual problems in the *DSM-IV* (*Diagnostic and Statistical Manual of the American Psychological Association*) may have partially contributed to a shift in this perspective. Today, the idea that "mind" and body are not actually separate from one another is attracting more and more attention in the health disciplines (e.g., Jessop, 1998; Taylor, Goehler, Galper, Innes, & Bourguignon, 2010). Indeed, the idea that other (non-physical) aspects of the self can affect recovery from illness and surgery are noted by many physicians and other health professionals. For example, it is clear that practices (or belief systems) that result in a reduction in stress are of benefit to health, and that researchers should be exploring the substrates of these mind-body therapies (see Taylor et al., 2010). The study of "spirituality" is now highly acceptable in the health arenas, and a literature search on spirituality returns many hits for journals associated with the work of nurses in particular. In addition, Duke University has a Center for Spirituality housed within its medical department. The same university frequently runs courses on Mindfulness-based Stress Reduction, an application of a mental discipline to stress, which has known outcomes for health (See chapter 5).

Although the literature is somewhat mixed in terms of positive or negative outcomes, when the whole database is considered, spirituality and religiosity generally seem to have positive impacts on both physical and mental health (e.g., George, Larson, Koenig & Mccullough, 2000; Moreira-Almeida, Neto & Koenig, 2006). However, it is important to further understand the parameters of these effects, as they appear to work more robustly amongst those who are undergoing some form of life stress (e.g., those who are elderly, those who have disabilities or those suffering from medical illnesses, Moreira-Almeida et al., 2006). In addition, it is not yet clear exactly how and under which circumstances these effects actually manifest.

In recent years, psychometric measures have been developed for the measurement of "Spirituality" (including Piedmont's Spiritual Transcendence Scale, 2001 and Cloninger's Self Transcendence Scale, Cloninger, Svrakic & Przybeck, 1993) which appear to stand up as robust personality measures.[1] However, in stark contrast to the relationship between health and medicine, there are few psychology departments within universities which include the academic study of spirituality or the psychology of religion. Although there are several universities (mostly in the United Kingdom and Europe) where it is possible to study subjective paranormal experiences and beliefs as part of a degree in psychology, this is unfortunately still at the edge of the mainstream, despite the likelihood that such experiences and beliefs can also be associated with health benefits. In addition, there is relatively little exploration of the mechanisms by which unusual beliefs and experiences may facilitate health and mental health. The problem may lie in the compartmentalization of many psychology departments and people working on only one aspect of the phenomena. Indeed, psychologists may focus on the nature of beliefs while medical practitioners might focus on the application. Progress in this area would undoubtedly be propelled via research collaborations between those interested in both the social structure and purpose of believing and those who are open to exploring exceptional human experiences and neurobiological processes. In fact, such collaborations are beginning to emerge. For example, the proposed International PsychoSocial and Cultural Bioinformatics Project would combine a variety of approaches to create "a new neuroscience of mind-body communication, brain plasticity, memory, learning, and creative processing during optimal experiential states of art, beauty, and truth" (Rossi, Rossi, Yount, Cozzolino & Iannotti, 2006, p.1).

The Placebo Effect

The placebo effect is a very powerful healing effect which is observed when patients *believe* that they are receiving a certain treatment for a physical or mental condition, often presented as inert sugar pills. Interestingly, the effect occurs for a range of disorders, including those whereby certain pathways in the brain are damaged (e.g., placebo induced release of dopamine in Parkinson's disease; see de la Fuente-Fernandez et al., 2001). In addition, recent research has indicated that the effect works even when the person is informed that he is receiving a placebo pill (Kaptchuk et al., 2010). Moerman and Jonas (2001) have observed that the placebo effect has received renewed academic interest in recent years, including articles, books and a conference called "Science of the Placebo" (sponsored by the U.S. National Institutes of Health). They note that placebo effects should be re-conceptualized as an effect of *meaning* on health outcomes, as by nature a placebo is inert, and cannot directly cause anything.

Humphrey (2002) has noted that the capacity for self-healing must be part of our human makeup, but that it may function within evolutionary and biological constraints. The mainstream (psychoneuroimmunologic) interpretation of the placebo effect is that it reflects the role of belief or expectation on the activation of certain neural circuits (in particular the prefrontal cortex and limbic areas of the brain) which in turn instigate a biological chain of events that result in a physiological outcome. This may not allow for all observations in placebo literature. Radin and Lobach (2007), for example, note that other authors have proposed weak quantum models to explain placebo observations which result in double blind experiences. These imply that "non-local" effects (a term from quantum physics which suggests that following entanglement, effects on one system may impact on another system at a distance, i.e., non-locally) may sometimes also enter the placebo picture. Radin and Lobach report some evidence which supports their suggestion that belief or expectation,

> act(s) to focus our attention on our potential future states, and allows us to "select" favorable future paths to pursue.... If gaining information from our future were possible, then in principle we might be able to navigate through potential futures to achieve a desired outcome [p.734].

Whatever their etiology, placebo effects are one of many examples of mind-body interactions which visibly occur among many people. Such effects may well be at the core of some of the observations discussed herein. These include observations that certain altered states, holding certain beliefs and the results of certain practices (e.g., healing practices, shamanic ritual, religious ritual, the quiet focusing ritual of meditation) all have an impact on health and mental health.

Embodied Metaphor and Social Meaning

Other effects should also be considered in terms of the interaction between mind and body. For example, Lakoff and Johnson (1999) have presented a thesis regarding the nature of mind as fundamentally metaphorical and *embodied.* There is an interaction between our biological systems and the sensory and social world from which we automatically develop primary and secondary metaphors, only some of which are linguistic in nature. As such, we usually experience the world relationally; between ourselves and our social and perceptual worlds. The way that we think and experience mental imagery is also representational. In an earlier work (Lakoff & Johnson, 1980) metaphors are presented as inherent in our everyday thinking, such as that person is *down* today, time is *flying,* etc. If we consider this in relationship to health, the mind and body are already fundamentally entwined.

In this collection, Gruzelier discusses the use of imagery in self-hypnosis; and asks participants to imagine sharks (later dolphins) who consume pathogens as a metaphor for white blood cells attacking pathogens. This is a clear example of health and body-related metaphors being employed successfully for health benefit. Luke also explores the role of imagery (particularly arising in altered states of consciousness) on healing. For example, he notes that shamanistic practices can result in the production of creative symbolic products (healing artwork — weaving a certain pattern which is associated with the removal of a certain illness and "singing" an illness away) which are employed for the elimination of poor health. Thus, the symbols of altered states are represented in the shared social world and may work as shared symbols which allow for change. Williams and Dutton's observations on how healing emerges as an embodied shared experience indicate that the mind is important in the healing process, which is a human social-embodied interaction using metaphor and physicality for healing the self.

The social aspect of healing might also partially explain Gruzelier's interesting findings of a difference between self-hypnosis and two different forms of energy healing — Johrei and Reiki. Although self-hypnosis was found to be more effective than relaxation, Johrei (in particular) and Reiki healing supersede self-hypnosis in the up-regulation of the immune system. Both systems include a healer and a healee — a social interaction which may lend insight into why these methods differ in their outcomes.

The social nature of healing is also touched upon by Binks, who found that religious belief can enable better protection against the affect of traumatic experience. This may be via belonging to a social group, as well as the impact of the believing practice itself. The importance of belief, intentionality, and perhaps more essentially *meaning,* emerge as pivotal in the healing process. The mind is involved in healing, in a complex manner pertinent to the social nature of human beings. As such, even without touching upon the non-local potential of mind, these essays indicate that mind is not restricted to one person's brain and functions in interesting ways to engender healing. Western ways of seeing should continue to be supplemented by insights from other world views. This has already begun, with the impact of mindfulness on mental health and health, the existence of Reiki as an alternative healing method, and the growing influence of Chinese medicine. Whether funding and public health policy will follow these insights is another matter, although the increasing presence of academic papers in mainstream journals can only be positive, even if this is a gradual process.

Unconventional (PSI and Bioenergy) Interpretations of Healing Effects

This discussion would not be complete without consideration of the psi, or "non-local;" and bioenergy alternatives to the previous discussions regarding the relationship between the mind and body. A full discussion of thinking on the idea that mind can interact with physical matter in a healing capacity is beyond the scope of this introduction (see Leder, 2005). However, there has been much research which has explored whether mental intention (e.g., of a healer) can impact the physiology of a healee, ruling out all normal physical interactions between healer and healee, as "distant healing intention" (see Schwartz & Dossey, 2010 for a recent review and Schlitz, Radin, Malle, Schmidt, Utts & Yount, 2003 for research guidelines). Although one meta-analysis on prayer did not find an overall effect which differed from zero (Masters, Spielmans & Goodson, 2006), two meta-analyses have found evidence for small but significant overall effect sizes for a series of studies which have explored the effects of intention on psychophysiology (Direct Mental Interactions with Living Systems research) and staring studies, both analogues of distant healing (Schmidt, Schneider, Utts, & Walach, 2004). Other research has explored whether healers are able to use psi in the diagnosis of certain physiological ailments (see Benor, 2002). Some healers, for example, report synesthetic-like color and other sensory impressions that are interpreted to indicate that a certain area of the body of the healee needs healing. In addition, many healing traditions have considered healing as involving energy, as the bioenergy model (see Levin & Mead, 2008 for a review). Gruzelier notes that many healing practices involve the phenomenal experience of light energy which comes to the healer from a universal source, and is employed for the purposes of healing. After consideration of a number of normal explanations, Gruzelier considers a bioenergy interpretation for his findings that healing practices are particularly efficacious for a number of physical and psychological ailments. There is some evidence for the emission of light from healers (see Baumann, Joines, Kim, & Zile, 2005). In addition, Joines is currently pursuing a similar research program (funded by the Bial foundation), which is further investigating the claim that healers emit light energy. It is clear that this is an area which warrants further attention, given that non-traditional healing methods do appear to facilitate both mental and physical health.

Exceptional Experiences and Health

The Mainstream Approach
to Exceptional Experiences and Health

At present, many clinicians treat exceptional experiences including subjective paranormal experiences as examples of pathology. It is clear that there are overlaps (see next section, and Belz, this collection). Indeed, several contributors note the need for the expansion of clinical psychology to delineate what is pathological from what is actually healthy. Unfortunately, with the exception of some spiritual and religious experiences (now acknowledged by the DSM, see Belz); the current dominant cognitive neuroscientific paradigm often reduces many exceptional experiences to biological anomalies—a deviation from the norm — which is equated with pathology. For example, recent theorizing on the out of body experience (OBE) summarizes these experiences as resulting from disturbances in bodily multisensory integration (mostly in the right temporo-parietal cortex) (Blanke and Arzy, 2005). This observation may well be true at a physiological level, but this fails to acknowledge the possibility that this type of dissociative experience can lead to unusual (e.g., extrasensory) perceptions and that they are often very meaningful. In fact, Twemlow found that those reporting OBEs were significantly more healthy than a group of psychiatric inpatients and outpatients, as well as a group of college students (Twemlow et al., 1982). In addition, the OBE is associated with positive changes to the life of many who have experienced it (Alvarado and Zingrone, 2003). Similar patterns are actually the case for a range of other exceptional experiences.

To date, a lot of research which has explored unusual experiences has also been designed from the perspective of pathology. For example, research with paranormal belief has often explored the Cognitive Deficits Hypothesis— the idea that those who are prone to believe in paranormal and related phenomena are less intelligent and have other cognitive deficits as compared to other people (see Irwin, 2009). In fact, recent research does not find a difference in terms of critical thinking (see Roe, 1999) and paranormal belief is a heterogeneous variable (see Irwin, 2009) with some individuals exhibiting signs of pathology, and others exhibiting rationality, intelligence and good mental health (see Goulding, 2004). It is also the case that research has mainly focused on the reasons for *believing* in the paranormal, at the neglect of studying why other people may strongly *disbelieve* in paranormal phenomena.

Exceptional Experiences as Bi-Polar

There are clear overlaps between the range of exceptional experiences and psychopathology. This is explored in more detail by Belz, and touched upon by Clarke (2001, and this collection) in terms of psychosis and spirituality. Indeed, clinical groups are often more likely to report paranormal beliefs (Greyson, 1977; Thalbourne and Delin, 1994; Thalbourne, 1998) and in addition, paranormal beliefs actually form part of an older version of the DSM classification of schizophrenia (DSMIII). Following a review of the literature, Irwin (1993) summarized that there is "a clear association between a wide range of paranormal beliefs and proneness to psychosis. Many skeptics presumably would rest their case at this point; people who believe in [and experience][2] the paranormal are simply crazy" (p.o,25).

However, not all research finds more paranormal belief among schizophrenics (e.g., Williams and Irwin, 1991). It is also true that some spiritual and paranormal experiences have been mistaken as signs of pathology (e.g., Kundalini awakening experience, see Ossoff, 1993).

Transpersonal and other theorists about the nature of consciousness have previously noted this bi-polarity. Andras Angyal (1965) for example noted that "all our experience comes in two forms— an adaptive, integrative aspect in the context of hope and optimism or with the very same function, a negative, defensive side of despair and dread" (in Hunt, 1995, p.45). There are similarities in the subjective experience associated with the negative experience of psychotic onset and the positive experience of meditation (Hunt, 1995) and it may be that "altered states provide an axis point for either disturbance or growth" (Parker, 1975, p.124).

This may be conceptualized as a shared variance between a proneness toward unusual experiences and transcendence and personal development. A recent survey highlights that although some subjective paranormal experiences can indeed be associated with conflict or personal trauma, others are life-enhancing and positively assimilated into one's life (Montinelli and Parra, 2000). This is the approach of those who are working in "clinical parapsychology," that those presenting with distressing experiences can be helped, and that only a proportion of them require the label of psychopathology.

The relationship between anomalous experiences and psychopathology is clearly rather complex. Berenbaum et al. (2000) note that there are three possibilities which would explain the relationship; firstly that pathology and anomaly-proneness are the same; secondly that anomalous experiences are implicated as part of the etiology of psychopathology; thirdly that psychopathology might contribute toward anomalous experiences. A fourth option is also possible, that there may be a (common) factor which contributes toward both psychopathology and anomalous experiences. This is the view taken by recent researchers who are exploring the idea of the "happy schizotype"; a person who is adjusted and healthy in spite of, or because of, their anomalous experiences and beliefs. Recent research on schizotypy indicates that being prone to anomalous experiences per se may well be neutral in terms of pathology, and other factors impact on pathology (e.g., Goulding, 2004). [See chapter 6 and chapter 7 by Simmonds-Moore and Holt herein for further discussion of the differences between types of believer.]

Here, "exceptional human experiences" will be taken to include creativity, spiritual/transpersonal experiences, as well as experiences indicating the "non-local" nature of mind. Such experiences can be cultivated (perhaps by meditation and other intentional altered states of consciousness) but they can also arise spontaneously in other altered states of consciousness and by those experiencing psychotic states. If there is a huge potential for both growth (which may include access to non-local mind) and destruction, Clinical psychology (as it stands) should embrace and further understand the polarity, and work with these experiences in a more open-minded manner.

Semantics and the Study of the Exceptional

Several contributors will discuss semantics and clinical approaches toward exceptional experiences (in particular, see the essays by Clarke, Belz, and Tierney, respectively). Belz (2009), for example, has argued for the use of the term "clinical psychology for exceptional experiences" (or what she defines as ExE), rather than "clinical parapsychology."

The term parapsychology is often misapplied, and attributed toward anything of an occult and New Age nature. Indeed, some people who are practicing as mediums and psychics have labeled themselves "parapsychologists," and the New Age section in bookshops is full of texts which use the term erroneously. Often parapsychology is mistakenly considered to be the subject matter of those who believe in paranormal and occult phenomena. In addition, the terms paranormal and parapsychology are also often used interchangeably, when one is a hypothetical process and the other is a scientific field which studies subjective experiences from a variety of empirical perspectives and is skeptical in the true sense of the word; being driven by the data.

Many scientists simply do not know about the large body of research in these fields. This may partially result from research being housed in journals which are particularly designated as parapsychology journals and may therefore not be read due to pre-existing biases. It is likely that many people working within clinical practice may also be ignorant of this body of research, even when clients may not easily fit into the usual diagnostic categories.

These biases and semantic issues may be ameliorated by the employment of a more neutral term such as exceptional experience (or anomalous, extraordinary). Expanding the research focus beyond paranormal phenomena to a range of other related exceptional experiences may also help to normalize how experiences are perceived by mainstream academia. The use of normalizing language and the consideration of paranormal experiences among others may allow for greater acceptance of this field within mainstream clinical psychology and the mental health disciplines.

A Brief History of Clinical Parapsychology

At this juncture, I will provide a brief history of "clinical parapsychology," a term coined by Montague Ullman in the 1970s. The literature of both academic parapsychology and transpersonal psychology include many papers which explore the relationships between clinical psychology and subjective paranormal experiences. Belz (2009) provides an excellent summary of the etiology of this field, which may be traced back to the shared interests of the early psychical researchers who focused on psi phenomena and other anomalies of consciousness, including multiple personality, hysteria, somnambulism and hypnosis. The field continued into the twentieth century as those working as psychoanalysts noted psi experiences occurring as part and parcel of the therapeutic relationship, often occurring on the part of the therapist and the client. Carpenter has noted that this follows neatly from the predictions of his First Sight model of ESP phenomena (e.g., 2004). As such, clinical parapsychology emerged partially from those working at the forefront of mental health.

Jung's concept of synchronicity also influenced the idea of clinical experiences, as acausality. The observation of synchronicity and related phenomena including psi experiences occurring in a clinical context was recently explored by Nachman (2010). She provides several examples whereby distress might occur in association to psi experiences into particular, e.g., the precognitive experience. She also explores a range of possibilities for the incorporation of synchronicities and apparent psi experiences into the therapeutic process, and gives an excellent summary of the nature of the shared variance between psychopathology and psi.

Belz (2009) goes on to note that the origins of the IGPP (Institut für Grenzgebiete der Psychologie und Psychohygiene e.V.), one of the key players in clinical approaches to exceptional experiences, was pre-empted by the work of Hans Bender at Freiburg University, who adopted a clinical approach in his work with mediums (see chapter 9 by Bauer and Belz for further discussion of the history and work undertaken by the IGPP and chapter 10 by Belz for a discussion of research which has emerged from this program).

Another key player in the history of clinical parapsychology is the field of transpersonal psychology, which allows for exceptional experiences to emerge as part of one's personal development. Belz notes that several counseling approaches toward paranormal experiences were developed in the 1980s. This notably includes the approach of Arthur Hastings (1983) who has interests in transpersonal psychology and parapsychology. Hastings considers that therapists who are interacting with those with distressing paranormal experiences should possess both therapeutic skills in addition to an awareness of the research literature in parapsychology. The therapist should approach each interaction with a working hypothesis that psi phenomena do exist but that each case should be evaluated individually (some pertaining to genuine psi, whilst others may be examples of psychopathology). He notes that "effective counseling may provide ways of integrating the psi processes into a healthy personality, as well as reducing the disruptive effects that often occur as people encounter psychic experiences" (p.165), and in so doing there might be a cross-fertilization of knowledge between the clinical and academic disciplines. [In chapter 11, Tierney presents Hastings' 7 steps for working with people with psi experiences].

In 1985, William Roll convened the first Parapsychology Association (PA) panel discussion on the topic of clinical parapsychology (see Roll et al., 1986). This included a contribution from Stanley Krippner on the idea that psychotherapy may be provided by some practitioners working in folk healing traditions alongside the deployment of a range of psi phenomena. Montagno discussed clinical psychology in terms of the Spiritist (mediumship) model in Brazil, where Spiritist methods are combined with psychiatry and appear to be having interesting therapeutic effects. Cynthia Siegal discussed her observation of six patterns of typical responses that people have when experiencing distressing paranormal experiences. In her presentation, she discussed each reaction pattern in turn, and offered clinical suggestions for each (see also Siegal, 1988).[3] Sharon Solfvin discussed the relationship between clinical issues and academic parapsychology. Julian Isaacs discussed psychotherapeutic intervention in laboratory experiments exploring training of PK (psychokinesis) ability and finally, Jeannie Lagle Stewart discussed crisis-intervention counseling in the context of families who are experiencing disturbing haunting experiences.

In 1989, the Parapsychology Foundation (PF) convened an entire conference to explore this issue. The event was held in England and explored approaches to counseling individuals who experience psi phenomena, multiple personality and definitions of "normality" and "paranormality." The papers presented at this event were published as a volume on clinical parapsychology (1989). Unfortunately, it is not clear to what extent this publication has been read by those outside of academic parapsychology. However, the PF also provides a comprehensive list of references pertaining to clinical parapsychology on their website. Presumably, clinicians who have encountered an unusual case and who are naturally more open-minded may be able to find this resource relatively easily.

In 1995, a second PA panel was dedicated to the topic of clinical parapsychology (Solvin, 1995). This centered around the idea that clinical parapsychology might be a key feature of the parapsychology of the 21st century. It included several presentations, including one from the late Professor Robert Morris who discussed how parapsychology might contribute to mainstream clinical psychology training and a presentation from Martine Busch who presented a summary of a suggested approach toward counseling those experiencing disturbing subjective paranormal experiences. It also included four papers from those working at the Rosebridge Graduate School of Integrative Psychology, focusing on how to approach subjective paranormal experiences, and the education of future parapsychologists and clinical psychologists on the topic of clinical parapsychology. Finally, Jerry Solfvin discussed research approaches that should be adopted within this area of parapsychology. More recently, the topic has picked up, with researchers also exploring clinical practice. For example, Montanelli and Parra (2004) found that a humanistic approach to group therapy for those experiencing distressing anomalous experiences was highly effective. This included three stages— emotional support, intellectual and emotional processing and group closing and interpretation of the experiences (by group members). Other work has also explored how spiritual guidance and the use of expressive arts in a group context can facilitate the integration of the after-effects of a near death experience into the self (Rominger, 2009). Other work has explored how traumatic experiences may interact with ESP —for example, the psychiatrist Theo De Graaf explored how trauma may make clients more psychically sensitive to trauma-related information (De Graaf and Houtkooper, 2004), which simultaneously adds to the body of research in academic parapsychology and clinical psychology.

In 2007, a clinical parapsychology expert meeting was held in Naarden in the Netherlands. This meeting explored perspectives on clinical parapsychology and included participants from 8 countries. The presentations from this meeting were published in 2012 (and include contributions by Bauer and Belz, contributors to this book).

In 2009, the Parapsychology Foundation convened a conference (Utrecht II) designed to chart the future of parapsychology. Martina Belz (2009) presented an excellent summary of clinical approaches toward exceptional experiences during this event. In September 2009, this author convened a conference on exceptional experiences, health and mental health, which resulted in the publication of this book.

In addition, a third panel was convened by this author at the 2010 convention of the Parapsychology Association to enable greater awareness of this growing area of parapsychology, and to draw attention to the need to further develop this field, particularly outside of western Europe (e.g., in the U.S.). The panel consisted of presentations from those who have experience undertaking clinical practice with those who have exceptional experiences including Eberhard Bauer, Ian Tierney and Renaud Evraud, in addition to presentations from those who are researching anomalous experiences from a non-clinical background, such as Stefan Schmidt, Christine Simmonds-Moore and Nicola J. Holt. In 2010, a second clinical psychology expert meeting was held by the original Naarden group, under the direction of Eberhard Bauer. A U.S.-based conference which attempted to encourage a greater awareness of the need for the integration of mental health practice and exceptional experiences was held in March 2012 by the RRC and the University of West Georgia. ASCISTE will host a conference in 2012. Another similar event is being planned for 2013. It is clear that this is a subject of growing interest.

The Current State of Play Re: Clinical Parapsychology

Unfortunately, the topic of clinical parapsychology is only just beginning to be taken seriously, despite its importance. For example, in academic psychology, the psychology of anomalous experiences has become something of a hot topic in recent years, with several researchers exploring the personality dimension of positive schizotypy and how this relates to the tendency to experience and believe in exceptional phenomena. Research on anomalous experiences and mental health is ongoing at several universities in Europe, including the United Kingdom (e.g., Nicola J. Holt at University of the West of England, and Thomas Rabeyron and Caroline Watt at Edinburgh University) and Sweden (Etzel Cardeña and Devin Terhune at Lund and Adrian Parker and Anneli Goulding at Gothenburg). There are also other centers of integration of mental health practice and exceptional experiences, and yet other centers where academic research in this area is alive, for example in Argentina (Alejandro Parra — many studies focusing on clinical aspects of parapsychological experiences), in Brazil (Wellington Zangari and Alexander Moreira-Almeda) and in the U.S. (Arthur Hastings and Charley Tart at ITP, Stanley Krippner at Saybrook University and Christine Simmonds-Moore at the University of West Georgia).

Indeed, academic research centers that are overtly undertaking research on subjective paranormal phenomena clearly attracts people who may sometimes be distressed by their experiences (Coelho, Tierney, and Lamont, 2008). Coelho et al. (2008) note that this is therefore a first point of contact for help, and that there is much need for research units to develop their own protocols for dealing with experiencers, ideally in collaboration with those who are clinically trained. There are currently some research units in existence which do have clinical references set up. For example, Tierney (see chapter 11) has worked in collaboration with the Edinburgh unit for a number of years. At the Rhine Research Center, the director emeritus of the center is a retired clinical psychologist (Sally Rhine Feather) and another faculty member (Jim Carpenter) is a practicing clinical psychologist. Other clinicians may also be open-minded, but it is currently difficult for academic researchers, not trained as clinicians, to know how to locate active clinicians who are open to exploring paranormal experiences in a neutral or at least non-dismissive manner. However, a number of individual practitioners do exist around the world. For example, a few clinicians who are currently working in the U.S. include Jan Holden, David Lukoff, Alan Kubler, Mitchell Kossak (among others) and those currently working in the United Kingdom include Ian Tierney and Isabel Clarke. The compilation of an extensive list of practitioners would clearly benefit many academics and experiencers.

There are a number of centers around the world which specialize in clinical approaches to exceptional experiences; one of the main ones being the IGPP in Freiburg, in Germany, with a second, the Parapsychological Counseling Office, also in Germany, existing under the direction of Walter Von Lucadou. Recently, clinical psychologists and researchers Renaud Evrard and Thomas Rabeyron co-founded the Center d'information de Recherche et de consultation sur les Experiences Exceptionelles (the Center for Information, Research and Counselling on Exceptional Experiences) in Paris (see http://www.circee.org/). Other centers and organizations with a focus on clinical approaches to the exceptional also exist.

The problem potentially lies in where one might receive training in clinical approaches to exceptional experiences. John Klimo (1998) ran a training program at Rosebridge Graduate School of Integrative Psychology (called the

American Schools of Professional Psychology, San Francisco), which focused on clinical parapsychology, however it is not clear that this is still in existence. The American Center for the Integration of Spiritually Transformative Experiences (ACISTE) has recently been set up, with a focus on the near death experience. The center provides both support for those undergoing experiences (and their families) but also provides a training program for mental health practitioners.

Currently, the IGPP also offers some training courses, which are always popular, even though they are funded by the practitioners themselves, who recognize the need to expand their awareness on this aspect of their practice. In the U.S., one can study clinical psychology from a transpersonal perspective at the Institute for Transpersonal Psychology and Saybrook University (both in California) and undertake a master's degree with a clinical focus at the University of West Georgia. These incorporate subjective paranormal experiences within them, approached from a transpersonal perspective (i.e., that experiences can be transformative).

Recently, more serious academic interest has focused on understanding differences between healthy and less healthy anomaly proneness within the non-psychiatric population. This volume seeks to represent the input from those working at the forefront of mental health practice, and those who are actively engaged in research.

The Future of Clinical Approaches to the Exceptional

In light of the discussion emerging from recent conferences, there are clear gaps in the established mental health systems for supporting people experiencing problems associated with anomalous experiences in both the U.S. and the U.K. (taking two examples). With the continuation of existing training programs and the establishment of new ones, it may well be that more clinicians working within the system might become aware of the need for an established clinical parapsychology practice for exceptional experiences. However, at present a lot of support is coming from charity-based organizations and organizations set up by those who have experienced problems and returned to full health.

In the United Kingdom, organizations such as the Spiritual Crisis Network (http://www.spiritualcrisisnetwork.org.uk/) and Hearing Voices Network (http://www.hearing-voices.org/information.html) have been set up, and may currently be serving to fill the gap. The SCN is an organization which provides support for people experiencing problems by those who have experienced a spiritual crisis and emerged from their experience. There are a number of people who are professionally involved in mental health who are also affiliated with this group (including Clarke, chapter 8). The website provides advice for people going through spiritual crises, and includes normalizing experiences, such as grounding the self. The Hearing Voices Network is a coordinated organization, which provides support (in the form of self-help groups), information and advice for people who are hearing voices. It includes a statement that hearing voices is not necessarily indicative of mental health problems and that a new approach is emerging which explores the meaning of the content of the voices, rather than voice hearing per se. The site notes that voices are "similar to dreams, symbols of our unconscious minds. Although the Network is open to many diverse opinions we accept the explanation of each individual voice hearer." These two organizations are not part of the mental health system and may well serve as another first point of contact for those experiencing problematic anomalous experiences.

In the U.S., the Spiritual Emergence Network (http://www.spirituale-mergence.info/), "provides individuals that are experiencing difficulties with psychospiritual growth a therapist referral and support service that is staffed by trained graduate students. In a culture which has not understood issues surrounding spiritual development, the gift of being heard and understood by a knowledgeable and supportive listener can be life-altering. We can provide referrals to licensed mental health care professionals (often in the caller's area) who may be of ongoing assistance. All members of SEN's National Referral Directory are licensed and insured and specialize in or have been trained to deal with many psychospiritual issues." As such, this group helps to put people in touch with open-minded therapists.

The results of conference discussions also touched on differences in the way in which the therapy should be approached. This might be summarized as two main camps for clinical approaches toward exceptional experiences—one favoring a transpersonal perspective and the other favoring a symptom-based treatment perspective (which is more neutral in terms of the content of the experiences themselves). The transpersonal approaches reflect the idea that experiences may function as a pivot or stimulus for spiritual transformation. This is a predominantly American perspective as highlighted in the work of Stanislov and Christina Grof (see Holder, Vanpelt-Tess and Warren, 1999, for a discussion of the idea of spiritual emergency). The alternative perspective, which is predominantly found in Europe, explores (distressing) exceptional experiences as a symptom for other underlying problems. As such, clinicians who are at the forefront of this field differ slightly in their outlooks. It is also not clear to what extent the therapist should believe in or be open to the possibility that the phenomenological phenomena being explored are genuine. Both approaches may serve to help the individual in terms of the basic aims of the therapist — to heal. It is clear that the integration of exceptional experiences (when approached more spiritually) may take longer to seep into the (mainstream) mental health system than the more neutral approach. The future of the field may lie in a fusion of the approaches, which might help a person deal with distress, but also provide support for the integration of the experience into the spiritual self.

Conference discussions also centered on the measurement and assessment of distressing exceptional experiences. The current version of the DSM does not include paranormal phenomena directly within its definitions, but does include cultural context for the assessment of beliefs and experiences. The new DSM is due to come out in 2012, and it is rumored that there will be more integration of the exceptional within it. Researchers and practitioners differ in terms of whether the DSM should include specific paranormal and other exceptional experiences within it. On one hand, it might highlight to clinicians that these experiences are part of the human experience. On the other hand, it may be impossible to state clearly what is pathological versus what is not (vis a vis the bipolarity of these experiences, see also Belz, chapter 10). Neppe (1988) has suggested that it is necessary to address experiences themselves to understand what features are *pathological* and what are "psychic" and not associated with psychopathology. He has formulated a multi-axial classification system for the classification of the phenomenological dimensions of anomalous experiences on the understanding that some will be genuine psi, others may be associated with psychopathology and others still may be associated with non-psi anomalous experiences. This was later amended and updated, and proposed to be employed alongside the current version of the DSM (Neppe, 2009). However, this is published on the Parapsychology Association website, and therefore not readily available to clinicians who are not already members of the PA.

It may well be that a separate published clinical manual for exceptional experiences would be more useful. Interestingly, in 2009 the INREES group (Istitut de Recherche sur les Experiences Extraordinaires) published a clinical manual of extraordinary experiences, the *Manuel Clinique des expériences extraordinaires* (Bernstein and Allix, 2009). This volume is written in French, and includes chapters on what is an extraordinary experience, psychopathology, near death experiences, nearing death awareness, subjective experiences with the deceased, out of body experiences, lucid dreaming, drug-induced extraordinary experiences and states of consciousness, psycho-spiritual experiences, experiences of possession and extrasensory or psi experiences.

This is an excellent addition to the existing literature on the topic of clinical parapsychology and is designed for those working with clients. This is a European project and at the time of writing this volume, the INREES manual is only published in French. This decision was made as it was felt that the information already exists in the U.S. This is certainly true, but the existence of a volume labeled in this way could allow for wider awareness of the subject matter of parapsychology and research on exceptional experiences to those working as clinicians. In order to move this field forward, there is a great need for expanding awareness of clinical approaches to exceptional human experiences. It is hoped that this book will help to achieve this goal.

Notes

1. However, it may be that there are 4 rather than 5 subscales comprising the self transcendence scale (see MacDonald & Holland, 2002).

2. This author's addition.

3. These are: 1. the fear that they may personally be hurt; 2. that they are going crazy; 3. they have a sense of responsibility or fear of someone else being hurt; 4. a fear of losing control; 5. they have special or divine gifts; 6. some are seeking to develop their abilities.

4. Since September 2010, Simmonds-Moore has been based in the U.S.

PART ONE

Belief, Mind and Body

1

The Mind-Body Connection and Healing

John Gruzelier

Abstract

This chapter explores the mind-body connections inherent in diverse interventions aimed at benefiting well-being, immune function and health, and evaluated through randomized controlled trials. These included self-hypnotic immune visualization, most recently assisted with 2D and 3D animation, and extended to biofield therapies including Johrei and Reiki. Hypotheses about individual differences in efficacy arose from cognitive and neuroscientific considerations about cognitive flexibility and cortical efficiency, and about brain hemisphere functions in relation to immune regulation, bipolarity of mood, positive versus negative schizotypy, hypnotizability and hypnosis, as well as empirical relations with absorption and openness to experience. Putative biofield energetic mechanisms are also discussed, while preliminary EEG studies shed light on process. Finally the author argues that training with EEG-neurofeedback may enhance and facilitate the productivity of abilities currently appraised as exceptional.

Hypnosis and Exceptional Experiences

Hypnotic Susceptibility

The facility to enter a deep hypnotic state is an exceptional experience for it involves an unusual alteration of brain organization and behavior which is not typically an everyday occurrence. This has an impact on attention, perception and memory, together with heightened responsiveness to suggestion and instruction. Hypnosis may have profound clinical applications such as hypnotic analgesia, permitting invasive surgery without anesthetic, and act directly on skin disorders (Mason and Black, 1958, Geiben & Chalmers, 1959;

Fry et al., 1964; Dennis & Philippus, 1965; Liossi, Santarcangelo & Jensen, 2009). In more disreputable contexts, hypnosis may induce uninhibited and bizarre behavior for stage entertainment, sometimes with tragic consequences (Gruzelier, 2001). Hypnosis is typically delivered via verbal suggestion by the hypnotist to the participant alone or in a group, and it can be done via a recording, where following instruction, and with practice, the participant can put themselves into hypnosis; this is termed self-or auto-hypnosis. The mechanism underpinning hypnosis has engaged names in the history of psychology, to include Pavlov, Freud, Hull and Hilgard, to name a few.

However, not all of us have the facility for hypnosis. Historically, individual differences in hypnotic susceptibility have been apparent since the earliest demonstrations of hypnosis (Braid, 1846). The eventual development of scales of hypnotic susceptibility enabled large scale investigations of hypnotizability which have shown an approximately normal distribution, often with a positive skew and a second peak denoting exceptional susceptibility accompanying virtuosic hypnotic ability (Hilgard, 1965). Through high retest reliability over 25 years, hypnotizability has appeared as a stable personality trait (Hilgard, 1986), though as every hypnotherapist knows, low susceptibility is modifiable, and there have been experimental attempts including recent ones (Batty et al., 2006).

Personality Correlates of Hypnotizability Including Positive Schizotypy

The search for correlates of hypnotizability has been something of a holy grail, and is one which still eludes us. Correlates have included perceptual alteration, vividness of imagery, fantasy proneness, absorption, imaginative involvement and creativity, with absorption the best candidate to date accounting for up to 20 percent of variance only. All of these features relate to processes underlying many of the exceptional experiences referred to in this collection of essays including positive schizotypy.

Three investigations conducted in London and Rome (Jamieson & Gruzelier, 2001; Gruzelier et al., 2004) found positive correlations between items from a schizotypy scale and hypnotic susceptibility measured with the Harvard Group Scale of Hypnotic Susceptibility, Form A (HGSHS:A, Shor & Orne, 1962) and the Stanford Hypnotic Susceptibility Scale, Form C (SHSS:C, Weitzenhoffer & Hilgard, 1962). The assessments of each domain were obtained in independent contexts, where neither the participant nor the experimenter were aware of any future analysis of interrelations between domains, and therefore were free from contextual bias which may increase the likelihood of hypnotic behavior (Kirsch & Council, 1989). The disclosed relations belonged essentially to the positive syndromes of schizotypy (Gruzelier, 1996), and encompassed unreality experiences and cognitive activation as well as a nonspecific factor, social anxiety.

The main features of schizotypy that were associated with hypnotic susceptibility were (1) having a deeply vivid quality to thoughts and perceptions—"my thoughts are so strong sometimes I can almost hear them"; (2) belief in the supernatural and other psychic phenomena; (3) a rapid, free flowing association of thoughts such as going off on tangents, using words unconventionally, being flooded by thoughts and possibilities, and saying one thing and meaning another; (4) perceptual alteration in visual, auditory and olfactory modalities; (5) social anxiety which is a pervasive but non-specific aspect of schizotypy. Similarly Kumar et al. (1996), found positive correlations between hypnotic susceptibility (HGSHS) and both the Dissociative Experience Scale and the Phenomenology of Consciousness Inventory (Pekala, 1991), while features of unreality have included a range of alterations including body image, meaning, perception and time sense (Pekala & Nagler, 1989). Among this repertoire we find anomalous experiences, another major theme of the collection.

Hypnosis may offer unique insights into mechanisms underlying schizotypy and other exceptional experiences. Before outlining our investigations—using self-hypnosis to mediate the mind-body pathway with the aim of improving mood, immune function and health, which then led to exploring the biofield interventions Johrei and Reiki—cognitive neuroscience considerations will be briefly outlined. These guided hypotheses and the choice of measurement parameters. Indeed, cognitive neuroscience considerations allow for a unification of the dynamics of hypnotizability, positive schizotypy and immune up-regulation.

Flexibility, Efficiency and Hypnotic Susceptibility

The premise that hypnotic susceptibility is a trait underpinned by neurocognitive and biological flexibility is supported by cognitive and neurobiological evidence (Crawford & Gruzelier, 1992). Hypnotizability has been associated with the flexible control of sleep, such as the ease of falling asleep and staying asleep, while the ability to respond to suggestion in REM sleep was found to correlate positively with both hypnotizability and the facility for falling asleep in the laboratory (Evans, 1991). The latter phenomenon is noteworthy because it signifies dissociative control outside of awareness and volition, integral to the nature of sleep. The flexibility concept was extended by showing that the facility for random number generation was associated with high hypnotic susceptibility (Evans & Graham, 1980), while Shames and

Bowers (1992) theorized that both hypnotizability and hypnosis are associated with an ability to prime wider networks of association between cortical representational networks. It will later be seen that connectivity is a key neurophysiological dynamic of hypnosis.

Flexibility has been an explanatory construct when reviewing both the cognitive and neurophysiological findings that have differentiated high from low hypnotic susceptibility (Crawford, 1989, 1994; Crawford & Gruzelier, 1992). Highly hypnotizable individuals were better able to shift from analytic to holistic strategies (Crawford & Allen, 1983), were more responsive to visual illusions and reversible figures, and were more susceptible to autokinetic movement, all in keeping with a more flexible perceptual system (Miller, 1975; Wallace et al., 1976; Wallace, 1986, 1988; Atkinson & Crawford, 1992). Psycho-physiological evidence has included prior to instructions of hypnosis both greater task-related hemispheric specificity, followed by neuropsychophysiological changes after instructions of hypnosis (Karlin, 1979; MacLeod-Morgan, 1979; MacLeod-Morgan & Lack, 1982; Meszaros et al., 1978; Morgan et al., 1974; Moore et al., 2004). Such dynamic changes in neurocognitive function have been consistently demonstrated by the author in keeping with alterations of anterior-posterior and lateral brain axes favoring posterior over anterior processing, and right over left hemispheric processes according to behavioral instruction and challenge (for review see Gruzelier, 1998, 2000b, 2004, 2006). Evoked potential and fMRI/EEG studies (Gruzelier et al., 2002; Egner et al., 2005), have supported Crawford's (1994) thesis of stronger attentional filtering abilities in highly hypnotizable subjects.

Regarding brain mechanisms, in an fMRI investigation (Egner et al., 2005), we found that selective attention measured with a Stroop–like conflict resolution task known to involve left frontal and cingulate functions (Macdonald et al., 2000), disclosed less activation prior to hypnosis in hypnotically susceptible subjects compared with those with low susceptibility, while relations between the groups were reversed with hypnosis. Hypnosis placed greater demands on metabolism in the hypnotizable subject who ordinarily required less metabolism. Additionally in hypnotizable participants hypnosis produced an uncoupling of left lateral and anterior cingulate cortex. This disconnection is compatible with evidence of frontal hypofunction as a result of hypnosis, releasing posterior cortical process from frontal control. The metabolic differences at baseline are compatible with *higher cortical efficiency* in the hypnotizable, who do not require the same metabolic demands as those with low hypnotizability outside of hypnosis (Gruzelier, 2006). Conceivably this may contribute to the trait of neurocognitive flexibility.

Hypnotic Susceptibility, Schizotypy and Hemispheric Asymmetry. The positive relations between schizotypy on the one hand and hypnotic susceptibility inventories are also paralleled by neurocognitive affinities between them. Similarities between the Activated schizotypy syndrome and high hypnotic susceptibility have been found in investigations of hemispheric functional asymmetry. The Activated syndrome was originally distinguished (and delineated) from a Withdrawn syndrome by classifying unmedicated schizophrenic patients on the basis of lateral asymmetry in electrodermal orienting responses, putative indices of left versus right fronto-limbic hemispheric influences. These were in the direction of a leftward activational preference in the *Activated* syndrome and a rightward preference in the *Withdrawn* syndrome (Gruzelier, 1984). This finding was replicated with other psychophysiological and cognitive measures (Gruzelier, 1999; 2003). All patients shared a third *Unreality* syndrome consisting of hallucinations and delusions of first rank; indeed these symptoms were necessary for the schizophrenia diagnosis. The Unreality syndrome was associated with an equivalence of hemispheric activation. Noted that lateral imbalances will have differential consequences for cognitive asymmetry depending on the arousal level of each hemisphere, in line with the inverted–U relationship between arousal and performance (Kinsbourne, 1982). This feature is overlooked in simplistic left versus right, up-down interpretations.

A similar three-fold syndromal structure was found in university students assessed with schizotypy questionnaires (Gruzelier, 1996, 2002a). Initially this was found with cognitive asymmetries in verbal and non-verbal recognition memory (Gruzelier & Doig, 1996), measures that had been applied to schizophrenic patients (Gruzelier et al., 1999a, b), and subsequently with perceptual indices (Richardson & Gruzelier, 1994), and self-report activation scales (Gruzelier & Doig, 1996). Interestingly prospective evidence from a class assessment disclosed in one healthy medical student an extreme outlying face/word recognition memory asymmetry (a right/left hemisphere profile) that was predictive of a Withdrawn/Unreality syndrome in their later development of two episodes of schizophrenia (Gruzelier & Doig, 1996).

The same left hemispheric activational preference characterizing Activated schizotypy was found in highly hypnotizable subjects outside of hypnosis (Gruzelier, 1998) with measures including bilateral electrodermal orienting responses, unimanual haptic discriminations and controlled verbal fluency and design fluency tasks (Gruzelier et al., 1984; Gruzelier & Brow, 1985; Gruzelier & Warren, 1993; Gruzelier, 2000b; Moore et al., 2004). As Cognitive Activation has been characterized by a functional asymmetry favoring the left hemisphere, and the same neurophysiological profile has often characterized highly hypnotizable subjects, positive schizotypy may share processes associated with hypnotisability. We note that Cognitive Activation in the normal population is highly correlated with Unreality, the second positive syndrome.

A Three-Step Model of Hypnotic Inductions. Functional brain imaging studies have confirmed the earlier neurophysiological and neuropsychological evidence of the existence of wide ranging alterations following the induction of hypnotic relaxation and challenges such as analgesia and hallucinations (Rainville et al., 1999, 2000; Kosslyn et al., 2000). The author had translated the neuropsychophysiological evidence of "neutral hypnosis," i.e., the traditional hypnotic relaxation without challenges, in a three-stage working model of the induction process (Gruzelier, 1998, 2006). Oakley et al. (2007) has provided validation through investigation of the three-stage temporal process for depth of hypnosis in an fMRI scanner.

The first stage of the three-step model involves the instructions to fixate on a small object and to listen to the hypnotist's voice. Here was posited a directed-attention network including a thalamocortical attention control system requiring left hemispheric frontotemporal processing that underpins focused, selective attention.

The second stage replaces eye fixation with eye closure, with suggestions of fatigue at continued fixation, and tiredness together with deep relaxation. It is proposed that this sets in motion frontolimbic inhibitory processes with dissociative or uncoupling consequences, left-sided in particular, and encompassing orbitofrontal and dorsolateral frontal regions and limbic structures such as the amygdala, hippocampus and cingulate. These underpin the suspension of reality testing and critical evaluation, and the handing over of executive and planning functions to the hypnotist; in other words the flexibility underpinning the "letting go" component of the hypnotic induction. This letting go is accompanied by a lateral shift towards a right hemispheric preference.

The third stage involves instructions of relaxed, passive imagery leading to a redistribution of functional activity and an augmentation of posterior cortical activity, particularly of the right hemisphere in the highly susceptible subjects. Simplifying the vocabulary and message of the induction text may also facilitate right hemispheric processing as does emphasizing past experience and emotion.

Participants with low susceptibility fail to show engagement of left frontal attentional control mechanisms, or if there is focal attentional engagement, the subject with low susceptibility fails to undergo the "inhibitory," letting go process. Accordingly this provides two reasons for ostensibly willing subjects to remain unhypnotised — a failure to focus attention and a failure to let go. Letting go requires reassurance about the lack of unwanted consequences of hypnosis, such as a loss of control or failure to come out of hypnosis, which may preoccupy naïve subjects. Alleviation of these worries through practice with self-hypnosis may account for some of the beneficial effects in participants with low hypnotisability in our immune studies (Gruzelier, 2002b, c).

It is important to note that the relaxation that accompanies hypnosis is mental relaxation not physical relaxation. This follows our demonstration of neurocognitive changes with hypnosis while pedaling a stationary bicycle that are similar to those hypnotized while reclining (Cikurel & Gruzelier, 1990). In fact deep relaxation in a flotation tank did not produce the same cognitive and neuropsychological changes found with hypnosis (Raab & Gruzelier, 1994). For while flotation produced cognitive changes in line with a shift to right hemispheric processing, it did not produce the left anterior hypofunction that is characteristic of hypnosis.

In summary, the focusing of attention and absorption that initiate hypnosis engage left anterior attention systems, enabling the "letting go" stage, cardinal to hypnosis, and with an inhibition or disconnection of selected frontal functions from posterior and sub cortical networks. This leads to the giving over and the placing of the executive and planning functions under the hypnotist's influence, and to the suspension of critical evaluation and reality testing, as well as to alterations in the control of the supervisory attention system (Gruzelier, 1990, 1998; Crawford & Gruzelier, 1992; Woody & Bowers, 1994; Woody & Sadler, 1998).

Functional hemispheric asymmetry also underpins up- and down-regulation of the immune system. The immune system has been our chosen domain with which to exemplify the role hypnosis has in elucidating mind-body connections relevant to health, the central theme of this chapter. As yet, no invasive brain imaging procedure has involved self-hypnotic immune visualization, an important question for future research.

Self-Hypnosis Training and Up-Regulation of the Immune System, Mood and Health

Brain Asymmetry and the Immune System

Persuaded by the neurophysiological evidence that enabled lawful neurobiological predictions about hypnotic susceptibility and the hypnotic process (e.g., Gruzelier, 1998), in a series of studies, the efficacy of self-hypnosis training in up-regulating the immune system and mood, and ultimately health, was explored first in medical students, and then in patients with viral illnesses. Hypnosis provides direct access to a mind-body pathway if we consider its well documented analgesic effects.

The choice of the immune system as a neurobiological pathway also followed considerations of the importance of functional brain laterality for up- and down-regulation of the immune system demonstrated in animals and man. In rodents opposite effects on immune parameters were found to be dependent on the laterality of unilateral neocortical ablations including Natural Killer (NK) cell activity, IgG plaque forming cells and mitogen induced splenic T-cell proliferation (Bardos et al., 1981; Renoux et al., 1983a,b; Neveu et al., 1986). These parameters were found to be enhanced with an intact left hemisphere and were compromised with an intact right hemisphere. Lower NK cell activity has also been associated with left paw preferences (Betancur et al., 1991), and similarly a model has been proposed linking left handers in man, who in the majority have a greater reliance on right hemispheric processing, with an increased incidence of autoimmune disorders (Geschwind & Behan, 1984; Geschwind and Galaburda, 1985; Lindsay, 1987). Furthermore reduced NK cell activity has been found in nurses with preferential right frontal EEG activation compared with those with the opposite asymmetry (Kang et al., 1991).

The writer proposed an heuristic model integrating the evidence of lateralized influences on the immune system with hemispheric specialization theories of mood and behavior. This aligned left hemispheric immune up-regulation with left hemispheric specialization both for approach behavior and for positive affect, and aligned right hemispheric immune down-regulation with right hemispheric specialization for withdrawal and negative affect (Gruzelier, 1989). A test of the model was afforded by a longitudinal assessment of asymptomatic men with HIV infection (Gruzelier et al., 1996). In correspondence with the model, both the EEG and neuropsychological asymmetry patterns assessed at study onset were found predictive of CD4 counts two to three years later. Patients with a left hemispheric functional preference on first assessment had higher counts than those with a right hemisphere functional preference at the end of the study up to three years later, and vice versa. Subsequently Clow and colleagues reported theoretically consistent asymmetries in salivary IgA and free cortisol concentration following lateralized trans-magnetic stimulation of temporo-parietal occipital cortex (Gruzelier et al., 1998; Evans et al., 2000).

The Text of the Self-Hypnosis/Visualization Induction

Visualization of a healthy combatant immune system was incorporated in the text of the hypnotic induction. This imagery had been said to be successful with oncology patients (Simonton et al., 1978). Following traditional instructions of deep relaxation, of increased confidence and ability to concentrate on exam preparation, and of preparation to counter life's difficulties, "immune visualization" imagery was inserted two thirds of the way through the hypnotic induction. It involved metaphorical instructions of a healthy immune system combating invaders. In the first study sharks patrolling the blood stream were visualized and in all subsequent studies sharks were replaced by friendly dolphins.

Immune and Mood Up-Regulation Study

Design. In the first report (Gruzelier et al., 1998; 2001a) there were 31 medical students with whom immune and mood parameters were obtained prior to training which was four weeks before the exams and then repeated during the exams. As a requirement for participation volunteers agreed to practice three times a week in order that frequency of practice was controlled. This was recorded in diaries and checked by telephone. The hypnosis group contained subgroups of high and low hypnotically susceptible participants, who were compared with a nonintervention control group. The lymphocyte subpopulations measured included CD4+ T helper and CD8+ T cytotoxic cells, CD3+ total T cells, CD19+ B cells and CD56+ NK cells. Plasma cortisol was also assayed and a life style questionnaire recorded exercise, sleep, consumption of alcohol, coffee, tea and cigarettes, medication and major life changes. The latter included health, however, there were too few reported illnesses to make evaluation of illness possible on this occasion. Mood was assessed by the Speilberger State Anxiety scale (Speilberger, 1970) and by the Thayer Activation-Deactivation checklists (Thayer, 1967) consisting of Calmness, Energy, Tiredness and Tension, while personality was assessed with Activated and WithDrawn schizotypy scales developed through the research on personality and hemispheric functional specialization. The schizotypy scales were relevant to evidence of lateralized influences on the immune system, with the prediction that the cognitively activated students would respond advantageously to self-hypnosis training while the withdrawn individuals would be less responsive.

Natural Killer Cells and Helper T-Lymphocytes. As expected, NK cell counts and CD8 counts were found to decline in the non-intervention control group, for this has been well documented with the stress of exams. Importantly this decline did not occur in the hypnosis group, for hypnosis was successful in buffering both the decline in NK and CD8 cell counts and their proportion relative to CD4 cells. All immune effects were independent of life-style factors. There were additional benefits from hypnosis on mood in the face of the stress of exams which increased anxiety and tension for participants as a whole. Energy ratings were higher, while increased calmness after hypnosis correlated positively with increased CD4 counts. The mood and immune domains were interrelated. The exam counts of NK cells correlated positively with energy and negatively with anxiety. As the changes in the immune parameters themselves were also significantly correlated, this suggested that there was an integrated pattern underpinning the students' resilience, and suggesting the reliance on an inter-related underlying process. Hypnotic susceptibility was not found to be a moderator in this student study.

Cortisol. Interestingly cortisol, often regarded as a stress hormone, increased with hypnosis, whereas there was no change overall in the control group. In exploring the significance of this positive correlations were found between the increase in NK cells and increases in both cortisol and CD8 cells, suggesting that the humoral-mediated changes indexed by cortisol accompanied the cell-mediated changes indexed by the lymphocytes. Correlations with the mood ratings shed further light. In line with the negative effects of cortisol due to stress, only in the control group did cortisol correlate positively with tiredness at exam time, as was shown by the correlation between their increase in cortisol and increase in anxiety. However, these negative relations were not found with self-hypnosis; apparently hypnosis brought about a dissociation of the negative effects of cortisol on mood, as will be seen to be replicated in studies below. The goals of the intervention were an important consideration when interpreting cortisol up-regulation. While relaxation imagery aimed to reduce stress, the immune-specific imagery encouraged the fighting off of infection through the hypnotic instructions to actively mobilize resources for increased alertness and energy. This chimes with cortisol's everyday metabolic properties such as the need for a sufficient level of cortisol for optimal function, shown by the substantive increase when one wakes from sleep (Evans et al., 2000). An increase in cortisol appears consistent too with the activated, coping-spirit goals of the immune-specific imagery training. Although long-term cortisol elevation is associated with a number of deleterious effects, short-term elevation of cortisol may be beneficial (Di Padova et al., 1991).

Individual Differences. Turning to individual differences in personality, for the group as a whole the Activated personality scale score predicted up-regulation in the full range of lymphocytes, as well as their levels at exam time. This was in line with the laterality hypothesis—the left hemisphere underpinning immune up-regulation and the activated, agential personality. These relations could largely be seen to be a function of the Cognitive Activation component. This correlation in the total sample of participants was despite the fact that the hypnotic intervention by elevating lymphocyte numbers would be expected to mask somewhat the relation; indeed correlations between Cognitive Activation and lymphocyte counts were of the higher statistical significance in the control group who did not receive hypnosis. The

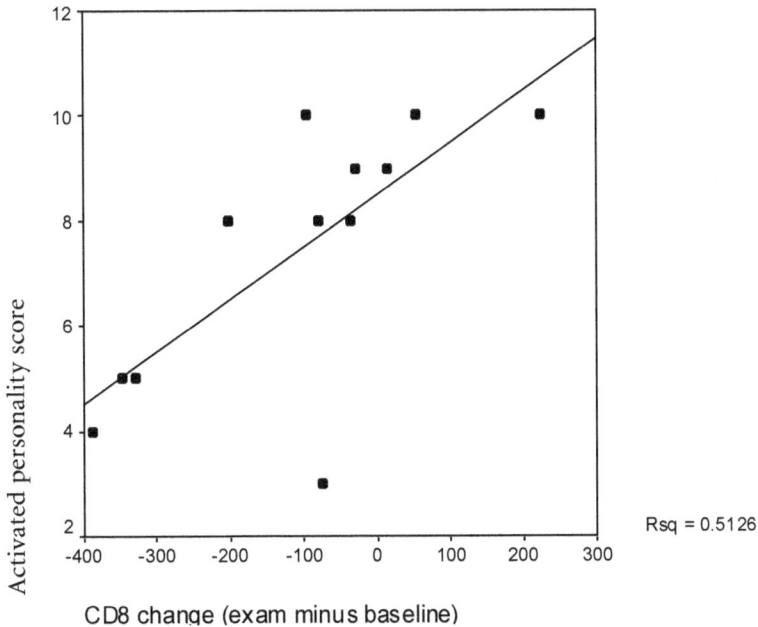

Figure 1. The greater the immune up-regulation in CD8 helper lymphocytes, the higher the activated personality score.

correlation in controls between the Activated personality score and the change in CD8 counts, is shown in Figure 1.

Imagery, Health, Immune and Mood Up-Regulation Study

The two studies that followed (Fox et al., 1999; Gruzelier et al., 2001b; 2002) both succeeded in demonstrating that the beneficial effects of self-hypnosis training did in fact carry over to improvements in health. One study involved medical students at exam time which took place the subsequent winter when viral infections were more prevalent (Gruzelier et al., 2001b). The other involved patients with the chronic medical condition Herpes Simplex Virus-2, a form of genital herpes (Fox et al., 1999; Gruzelier et al., 2002). Though the studies were small in scale, they represent an important step for the psycho-neuro-immunological field, because the translation to health validates the changes in immune function resulting from the psychological interventions; bidirectional changes in immune parameters are ambiguous.

In the first study we set out to replicate the beneficial influence of self-hypnosis in buffering the decline in natural killer cells and T–lymphocytes normally resulting from stress. Could we also replicate the integrated pattern of immune-up-regulation to include up-regulation of cortisol, a pattern also integrated with the elevation of mood? Did these effects translate to health benefits? Was visualization of the immune system necessary, or was the deep hypnotic relaxation responsible?

Design. In order to elucidate the importance of the type of imagery, whereas one hypnosis group received imagery of the immune system, e.g., "imagine your immune system as strong healthy dolphins swimming around the blood stream destroying germ cells," another had the imagery of the immune system replaced by imagery of deep relaxation. Otherwise all aspects of the induction were identical. The same immune parameters were assayed, but the design differed by counterbalancing the order of baseline and treatment conditions with the baseline assessment taking place after the exam for half of the students.

Lymphocytes. As before hypnosis buffered the decline in CD8 cells, as well as their percent of total lymphocytes, and the CD8 ratio relative to CD4 cells. This was a highly reliable differentiation for individuals within groups. In answer to the question whether the type of imagery training was important, results confirmed those of Olness et al. (1989). Crucially, as shown in Figure 2, it was only the training in imagery of immunity that was successful in buffering the compromise in lymphocytes. Thus relaxation imagery per se failed to halt the stress-induced decline in both total lymphocytes and lymphocyte subsets, whereas immune visualization successfully buffered the decline in all lymphocytes. Visualization of the immune system was critical.

Health. Eight students reported illnesses around the exam period. Importantly fewer of the students in the immune imagery group fell ill — 2/11 (18 percent) compared with 6/9 (67 percent) of the controls and 5/11 (56 percent) of those with relaxation imagery. The difference between the immune imagery and the other groups was highly significant. Furthermore in those that became ill there was a highly significant decline in CD4 counts, whereas the decline was not significant in those that remained well.

This evidence of resilience in the face of an influenza epidemic assisted with the validation of the efficacy of self-hypnosis/visualization. Furthermore imagery of a combatant immune system did provide advantages over relaxation imagery.

Mood and Cortisol. Mood ratings confirmed that students as a whole felt less calm at exam time. Correlations were then examined between cortisol and the Thayer scales of Tension and Tiredness before and after hypnosis training in view of the dissociation with hypnosis found previously between cortisol and negative mood. Whereas Tiredness correlated positively with the baseline cortisol as expected, there was a negative correlation between the

DECLINE WITH EXAM STRESS

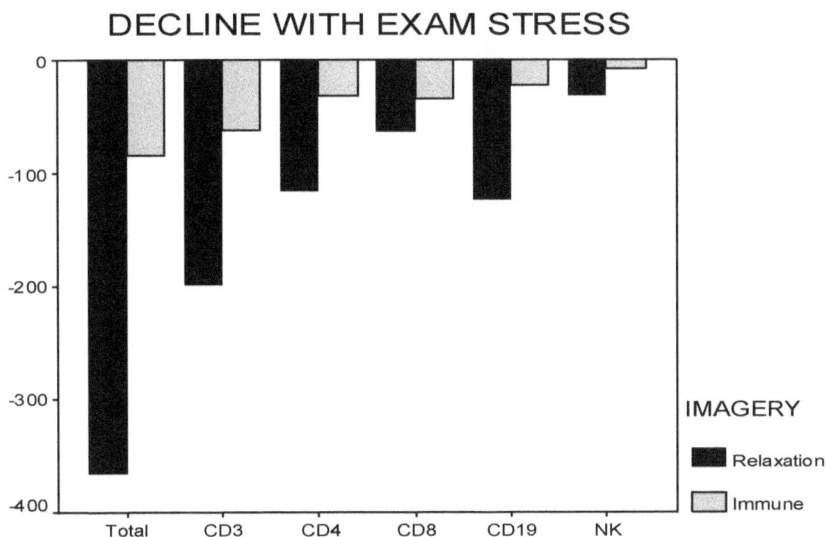

Figure 2. There was a decline in lymphocytes in participants receiving hypnotic relaxation imagery not seen in those with hypnotic immune imagery.

changes in Tiredness and cortisol following hypnosis; the more that tiredness increased the less was the increase in cortisol. In other words on this occasion the relation between cortisol and adverse mood, following hypnosis training went beyond the null relation found in our first study to a reversal, i.e., the higher the cortisol the lower was the negative affect after hypnosis, and consistent with this, any increase in tiredness following hypnosis was associated with a decrease, not increase, in cortisol. In order to elucidate further the relation with mood, the 10 subjects in the hypnosis group who showed a decline in cortisol were compared with the eight who showed an increase in cortisol. In support of stress raising cortisol, those students characterized by the increase in cortisol had the higher levels of Tension at baseline when compared with those with a decline in cortisol.

In summary, while there was clear evidence that cortisol was positively related to negative affect outside of hypnosis, hypnosis altered this relation and attenuated the negative relation between cortisol and mood.

Patients with a Chronic Viral Illness

A third intervention study aimed for validation in a more challenging context. This concerned patients who presented chronically with the herpes simplex virus HSV-2 (genital herpes), and who had a high frequency of recurrence. This is a distressing condition shown by persistently elevated levels of anxiety (Carney et al., 1994), often profound psychosexual morbidity (Mindel, 1993) and compromised psychological well being and quality of life (Goldmeier et al., 1982). An association between psychological distress in the form of depression and reduced resistance to HSV was first reported by Lycke et al. (1974). In reviewing a decade of evidence, Green and Koscis (1997) observed that in many patients the psychological impact of the disorder overshadowed the physical morbidity.

Given its diversity this was an ideal cohort with which to examine personality predictors, for it was likely to include socially withdrawn patients, a personality not present amongst the medical students who volunteered for self-hypnosis.

Design. The 20 patients recruited were due to discontinue prophylactic antiviral medication for a trial period or were reluctant to take the medication. They were examined at baseline and after a six-week course of self-hypnosis, which was delayed by six weeks for half of the cohort to provide a baseline. After a group hypnosis session they were given self-hypnosis cassette recordings to take home and were recommended to practice a minimum of three times a week, a total of 18 times with a mean of 17 sessions. Hypnosis involved instructions of relaxation, immune imagery, cognitive alertness and ego strengthening, as for the student studies.

A wider range of immune measures was assayed. Immune parameters included the numerative measures as before including plasma cortisol, CD3, CD4, CD8 +ve T–lymphocyte populations, CD19+ B cells and CD16+ NK cells. In addition functional NK cell activity was assessed including peripheral blood mononuclear cell (PBMC) non-specific NK cell cytotoxic activity, HSV specific NK cell cytotoxic activity of PBMCs infected with HSV–1, HSV specific cytotoxicity following stimulation with interleukin-2 (termed LAK cell activity) as well as HSV specific antigen dependent cellular cytotoxicity (ADCC). NK cells, macrophages, CD4 and CD8 lymphocytes, INFα and INFγ, IL-2 and leukocyte migration inhibitory factor were all significant in protecting against HSV (Rinaldo and Torpey, 1993). Psychometric measures consisted of the Thayer Activation-Deactivation checklist, the Hospital Anxiety and Depression Scale (HADS), and the Activated and Withdrawn personality dimensions.

Health and Well-being. The self-hypnosis intervention had beneficial effects on genital herpes. The number of recurrences fell with hypnosis by a remarkable 40 percent, reaching 48 percent with the exclusion of two patients who experienced highly stressful life events— a bereavement and a relationship break-up in the course of the six week intervention. The median number of occurrences in the six weeks before was 2 (range 0–6) and in the six weeks of self-hypnosis was 1 (range 0–3). Thirteen patients (65 percent) showed a reduction in recurrences (responders). The results could not be attributed to demographic or clinical factors, hypnotic susceptibility or frequency of practice. In fact non-responders tended to practice more perhaps due to their visible lack of improvement in herpes recurrence.

The beneficial effect on health coincided with an enhancement in mood. Importantly this was not restricted to clinical responders, for in participants as a whole there was a reduction in HADS Anxiety and Depression. In other words participation in the study had a beneficial effect on anxiety and depression, whether or not there was clinical improvement. Notwithstanding, relief from anxiety was associated with additional clinical benefits, as shown by a significant positive correlation between reduced frequency of recurrence and reduced anxiety.

Immune Function. Along with the clinical advantages there were demonstrable benefits for natural killer cell function in the direction of immune up-regulation. In the case of NK cell numbers, there was a significant increase in clinical responders whereas nonresponders on average showed a fall. Furthermore there was striking evidence of specificity of action when plasma was exposed to the herpes virus. Functional NK cell activity in responders showed significant changes in HSV specific NK cell cytotoxicity, and HSV specific cytotoxicity following stimulation with interleukin-2.

Personality. Turning to individual difference predictors, of particular significance was the finding that Cognitive Activation correlated positively with clinical improvement. In line with theoretical hypotheses, herpes recurrences during the six weeks of hypnosis training were fewer among those with higher personality scores. In view of the absence of confounding relations with baseline herpes recurrences or frequency of tape use, which did not differ between clinical responders and non-responders, this relationship could be interpreted as independent of motivation and other extraneous factors, and could be interpreted as a demonstration that Cognitive Activation predicted the better clinical response to hypnotherapy.

Cognitive Activation also correlated positively with the improvement in Natural Killer cell parameters. This was seen with NK cell cytotoxicity. This included a decrease following hypnotherapy in HSV specific cytotoxicity and in HSV specific LAK activity, as well as a positive correlation with post-hypnosis levels of HSV specific cytotoxicity. There was also a positive correlation with some baseline levels, namely HSV specific cytotoxicity, as shown in Figure 3, and HSV specific LAK activity. Consistent with the bipolarity of activity-withdrawal, the Withdrawn scale also correlated negatively with NK cell activity at baseline, i.e., the opposite direction to Cognitive Activation, as predicted.

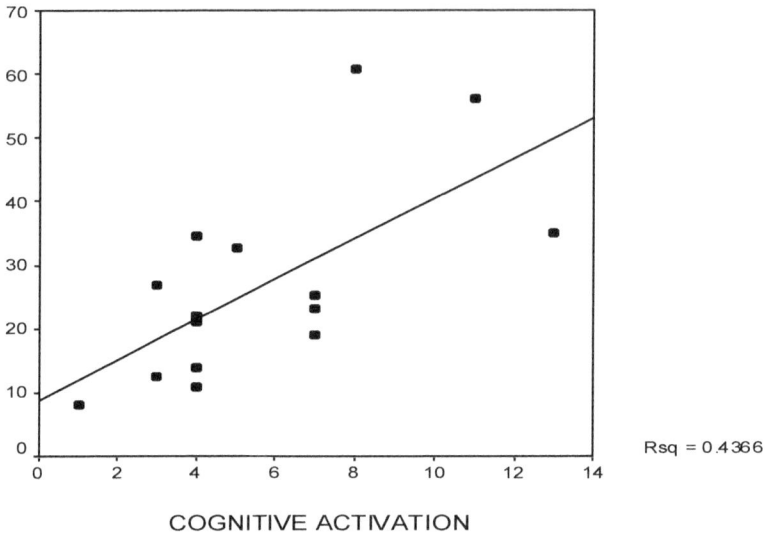

Figure 3. The higher the cognitive activation score the higher the baseline functional naturalKiller cell activity for the herpes virus.

In patients hypnotisability was found to be associated with up-regulation of immune function and mood. Immune parameters included changes in NK CELL percent and HSV specific LAK cell cytotoxicity, the post hypnosis CD8 count, and baseline CD3, CD4 and CD8 lymphocyte counts, while mood parameters included reduction in Tiredness and Depression.

Outcome. The clinical outcome was promising, and in the year following the study some patients remained off medication and experienced very little recurrence of HSV. While the clinical benefits require confirmation in a controlled clinical trial, advantages of self-hypnosis with directed immune imagery training for immunity, well-being and importantly the translation to health, replicated the student studies, as did the predictive ability of the personality factor Cognitive Activation.

Openness to Experience and 2D Animation-Assisted versus Traditional Spoken Self-Hypnotic Visualization

Animation. More recently we undertook two studies to explore whether an animated immune scenario incorporated within the self-hypnotic induction might facilitate the visualization process (Thompson et al., 2009,2010) In the first exploratory study, which incorporated 2D animation, we randomized Psychology freshmen either to our conventional verbal self-hypnosis immune visualization scenario (N = 13), or to an animation assisted self-hypnosis visualization group where the passage of spoken immune imagery was replaced this time by animated immune imagery (N = 11), or to a non-intervention control group (N = 11). The animated imagery consisted of 3, 11/2 minute sequences depicting white blood cells gradually destroying germ cells until none remained. All images were symbolic representations, and participants were asked to visualize the schematic animations as healthy white blood cells destroying weak germ cells. The immune parameter was cortisol.

Personality. Openness to experience was examined, which is one of the "Big Five" inventory personality dimensions, and broadly represents an individual's openness to novel experiences and ideas (Costa & McCrae, 1992). We hypothesized that openness may lead to greater engagement with the novel animation. Further, openness to novel experiences in general has been associated with hypnotizability, creativity and with image generation (Lynn & Sivec, 1992). These associations were reflected here in the Fantasy and Esthetics subscales which encompass items about a vivid imagination and appreciation of artistic images, while the Ideas subscale reflects intellectual curiosity and energy and had affinities with the Cognitive Activation scale.

Outcome. We found no overall group advantage for self-hypnosis training as before, and it was only after Openness was taken into account that a beneficial effect of training was disclosed. Those high Openness scorers who received traditional verbal imagery showed the up-regulation of cortisol, predicted by our medical student studies. Similarly a reduction in Tiredness was found only in the same high Openness subgroup. The relation between changes in cortisol and Tiredness was consistent with our previous studies.

Subscale analyses suggested that Esthetics (appreciation of art and beauty), Fantasy (receptivity to the inner world of imagination) and Feelings (openness to inner feelings and emotions) may be the crucial components of Openness, along with Ideas, all of which could be important in assisting creative mental imagery generation. In support of this, recent neurological research has linked Openness to Experience with greater dorsolateral prefrontal cortex activity, possibly via increased dopaminergic activation (DeYoung, Peterson, & Higgins, 2005). Increased dopaminergic activation in this region has been linked to improvements in creative thinking and memory (Ashby, Valentin, & Turken, 2002).

Absorption & Engagement and 3D Animation-Assisted versus Traditional Spoken Self-Hypnotic Visualization

Hypotheses & Design. In the subsequent study we explored whether the superior immersive properties of 3D, when compared with the 2D animation of our previous study, would prove to be more efficacious (Thompson et al., 2009). As a measure of immersion we constructed an Engagement scale with items pertaining to psychological immersion, vividness of imagery, freedom from distraction and sustained concentration (Cronbach's alpha ranged from $\alpha=.80-.92$). We also especially focused on whether we could help those participants who may have difficulty becoming absorbed in imagery, and in this regard included an Absorption scale (Tellegen and Atkinson, 1974). Could virtual reality (VR) technology enhance the effects of self-hypnosis visualization of a healthy immune scenario, particularly for those participants low in imaginative trait absorption? A randomized controlled study was performed ($N = 35$) involving 10, 20 minute laboratory sessions of either self-hypnosis visualization training using VR imagery, or visualization training using traditional verbal imagery, or guided relaxation. Outcome variables were pre-and post-assessments of sleep quality, salivary cortisol and mood, with the measures of Engagement and trait Absorption administered.

Mood & Personality. To some extent the greater immersive properties of 3D animation were found to be beneficial. First there was no suggestion that wearing the head mounted display to view the immune scenario had any deleterious effects on hypnotic relaxation; there were comparable increases in calmness and reductions in arousal with self-ratings of Energy and Tension (Thayer, 1967) in both visualization groups across the ten sessions. This had also been the case with our 2D scenario. Thus visualizing with eyes open assisted by animation instead of imagining the scenario with eyes closed posed no apparent disadvantage.

VR and traditional imagery training resulted in significantly lower Tiredness ratings than relaxation training for those who were high scorers on trait Absorption. Specifically, while the relaxation control group showed an increase in Tiredness as examinations and course assessments drew closer, along with the accumulated pressures of the fresher academic year (Whitehouse et al., 1996), both VR and verbal visualization groups showed no such increase in Tiredness. There were corresponding advantages for cortisol which approached significance. Thus these results confirm trait Absorption as an important moderator of visualization training, and extend previous findings of positive moderated effects on immunity and anxiety (Gregerson et al., 1996; Kwekkeboom et al., 1998) to include relief from tiredness.

Those with low trait Absorption did benefit from VR imagery. They reported higher Engagement ratings for VR relative to the traditional method, although this did not translate to outcome improvement. Specifically, while traditional imagery resulted in a mean immersion rating of 4 ("moderate" absorption), the mean VR immersion rating was 5.5 (with 7.0 representing the highest rating possible). This finding was apparent on the first training session, suggesting an immediate advantage of VR imagery. In contrast, when trait Absorption was high, there were no gains in immersion afforded by the VR over the traditional imagery. Perhaps this was because high Absorption scorers already preferentially tend to use internal imagery in mental processing (Nadon et al., 1987), and therefore might be expected to be affected less by manipulations of external imagery.

The pattern of results is generally consistent with the previous study (Thompson et al., 2009) where high levels of Openness to Experience, a trait conceptually and empirically related to trait Absorption (Glisky et al., 1991), facilitated the effects of imagery training on Tiredness. Importantly, however, whereas in the current study both the VR–assisted animation and verbal imagery visualizations resulted in less Tiredness with high Absorption when compared to the control procedure, in the previous study only the verbal imagery and *not* the 2D screen animation proved beneficial. This exploratory study suggested that for those low on Absorption, VR animation did provide a more immersive method for self-hypnotic visualization than traditional methods, and may therefore warrant further investigation for its potential to enhance therapeutic efficacy.

Summary of Self-Hypnosis and Immune Function

We have provided validatory evidence that self-hypnosis training can indeed advantage health by strengthening the immune system and enhancing mood, and that these influences may occur independently implying separate but interacting pathways (Gruzelier, 2002c). Self–hypnosis made otherwise healthy medical students resilient in the face of a winter influenza epidemic, and reduced recurrences by half in patients with a chronic virulent genital herpes. There were advantages from engagement with the imagery of a healthy immune system combating invading viruses, widely termed "visualization" in clinical practice, over simple, deep relaxation imagery. We explored the use of technical aids to imagery in the form of animation-assisted visualization, and though this is at an exploratory stage greater engagement with the imagery was afforded to participants with low Absorption scale scores.

In examining individual differences beyond the conventional scales of hypnotic susceptibility, Absorption, the best correlate of hypnotic susceptibility to date, was associated with improved mood and cortisol up-regulation. Openness to Experience, one of the established five basic personality dimensions, was also associated with both mood and immune up-regulation following self-hypnosis/visualization. While this inventory has not been examined before in the hypnosis context, engagement with novel experiences has been linked with hypnotisability and with creative image generation. Our subscale analyses suggested that Esthetics, Fantasy, Feelings and Ideas were the responsible components of Openness, all obvious aids in the generation of creative imagery. Openness to experience has affinities with Cognitive Activation, a scale arising out of our schizotypy research, and a scale which had been associated with the efficacy of self-hypnosis/visualization.

The schizotypy association was made initially on the basis of considerations of underlying neurophysiological mechanisms involving hemispheric asymmetries of function, and a model of immune and mood up-and down-regulation (Gruzelier, 1996). The first medical student study provided support through the association of Cognitive Activation with up-regulation of the full range of T-lymphocytes assayed. The study with herpes patients provided a better opportunity in view of the inclusion of withdrawn patients along with the activated personality. Withdrawn patients showed evidence of immune-down-regulation, in contrast to the activated patients who also showed up-regulation. Relations extended beyond immune up-regulation to symptomatology in the form of reduced recurrences of the virus in the cognitively activated patients.

Before considering the nature of self-hypnotic healing mechanisms, studies on a second domain of healing practices will be outlined in which self-hypnosis and relaxation training have often been incorporated in the randomized controlled intervention designs.

Biofield Therapies: Johrei and Reiki

Comparative Studies of Johrei, Hypnosis and Guided Relaxation

Johrei is a Japanese method of healing representing one of the energy healing methods arising from the East. Johrei literally means "purification of the spirit," and originated in the first half of the 20th century being introduced by Mochiki Okada. While developed in Japan it is widely used as a daily exercise, mainly in Japan, Brazil and Thailand. During a Johrei session, the channeller imagines a universal healing light entering the body and beamed through the palm of a gently outstretched cupped hand directed towards the head and torso of the participant. In our procedure the practitioner, without touching the recipient, slowly moved their hands from the head down to the kidney area, front and back. Typically the roles of practitioner and receiver are interchanged: when in the role of practitioner concentrating on the transmission of subtle energies through the hand via the metaphor of light, and when in the role of recipient visualizing images of light received. Johrei is also based on the concept that "one can heal oneself by healing others" and has its own philosophical background. Aside from healing it has two other main tenants: the importance of esthetics for spirituality and health, and the use of natural, uncontaminated food. Thus the experience of Johrei is one of a self-contained time to be quiet, mindful and kindly, concentrating on the recipients' benefit as well as one's own. Our study of efficacy in combating exam stress demonstrated remarkable benefits.

Exam Stress in Medical Students. *Design.* A month before examinations 48 students, most of whom were studying medicine, were randomly assigned to attend four weekly training sessions over a four week period. and subsequently to practice at home either Johrei or self-hypnosis, or were to experience 8 sessions of relaxation induced by mock alpha/theta neurofeedback (Egner et al., 2002).

Johrei training was undertaken by a medical practitioner who had practiced Johrei in Japan. The four training sessions involved an introduction to Johrei practice and philosophy which emphasized the importance of harmony, balance, esthetics, pure food and natural farming practices. Administration took approximately 15 minutes and was mostly silent. Participants were requested to practice Johrei daily with a partner, and self–Johrei was introduced as a supplement if a partner was not available. Diary evidence showed a mean level of practice of about once a day, falling off somewhat over the 4 weeks of training.

Self-hypnosis training differed from our previous visualization induction in a number of ways. Firstly it began with a Spiegel–type eye-roll for "instant" relaxation which could then be combined with specific immune imagery (Spiegel, 1972). Participants were taught breathing control for acute anxiety (Laidlaw, 1994) and the interrupt distraction technique (Laidlaw, 1999) for worries and change in beliefs, both to be used on an *ad hoc* basis. As before, all were provided with a standard tape recording using a relaxation induction that included the immune imagery description. The students chose their preferred method, and were requested to use self-hypnosis three-times a day for the first fortnight and once a day after that. Diary data indicated that most practiced their self-hypnosis more than once a day at the start, somewhat falling off towards the end of the study.

The relaxation control group had eight, thirty minute sessions of mock alpha/theta neurofeedback training, two per week. This has been shown to produce a valid experience of relaxation as measured by Thayer Activation and Deactivation self-report ratings (Egner et al.,, 2002). Control participants with eyes closed listened to sounds through headphones: a babbling brook and sounds of the sea breaking on the shore. In the mock neurofeedback the sounds were pre-recorded from someone else's contingent feedback session and were not contingent on their own alpha and theta waves. Though not comparable to the other interventions which involved daily practice, it did address the placebo effect arising from engaging in a stress intervention.

The students had exams at two different times: within a few weeks of finishing their training, when they practiced almost daily, and at follow-up about three months post-training when many subjects had stopped practicing. 26/48 were available for the follow-up assessment.

Mood. After the formal month of training preferential benefits were found from Johrei and self-hypnosis training when compared with the relaxation control group. In controls, despite lower anxiety at baseline there was an increase in State Anxiety (Speilberger) in contrast to a fall in Anxiety with Johrei and self-hypnosis. In controls there were also increases in Tension and Depression measured with the Profile of Mood States (POMS, McNair et al., 1971) not seen in the other groups, while at the follow-up assessment there was an elevation in overall distress in all groups. This was more pronounced in controls on assessments of State Anxiety, POMS Total, Depression, Confusion and Loss of Vigour. Considering the relative merits of Johrei and self-hypnosis, Johrei buffered the effects of exam stress on State Anxiety to a greater extent than occurred in both other groups, while hypnosis showed preferential benefits on mood according to self-report diary records. There were also some indications that Johrei may have subtle superiorities that require further examination, such as reducing Depression and Anger.

It is noteworthy that the advantages to Johrei and self-hypnosis had mostly occurred independently of the beliefs the students disclosed about the efficacy of treatment, both on entry and after completion, other than a tendency for an association between increasing anxiety and a decline in their beliefs in Johrei. Interestingly Absorption scores were 10 points lower in those disclosing low efficacy.

Immunology. For the group as a whole, aside from an increase in Perceived Stress Scores, there was a decrease in NK cells as well as in NK cytotoxicity, in support of the ecological validity of the examination stressor. This is in keeping with the well-documented decline in NK cells and cytotoxicity under conditions of exam stress, such that NK cell percentages and activity are often used as stress benchmarks (Dopp et al., 2000; Levy et al., 1989; Schedlowski et al., 1993; Whitehouse et al., 1986). CD4 counts on the other hand increased, an increase correlating positively with Perceived Stress and negatively with NK cell counts. In the face of such evidence of distress and immune compromise, Johrei's efficacy was remarkable for the following reason. Whereas previously we had shown that self-hypnosis had been successful in buffering the decline in NK cells, all but one of the Johrei subjects (14/15) actually showed an increase in their NK cell percentages (mean change = 3.22;

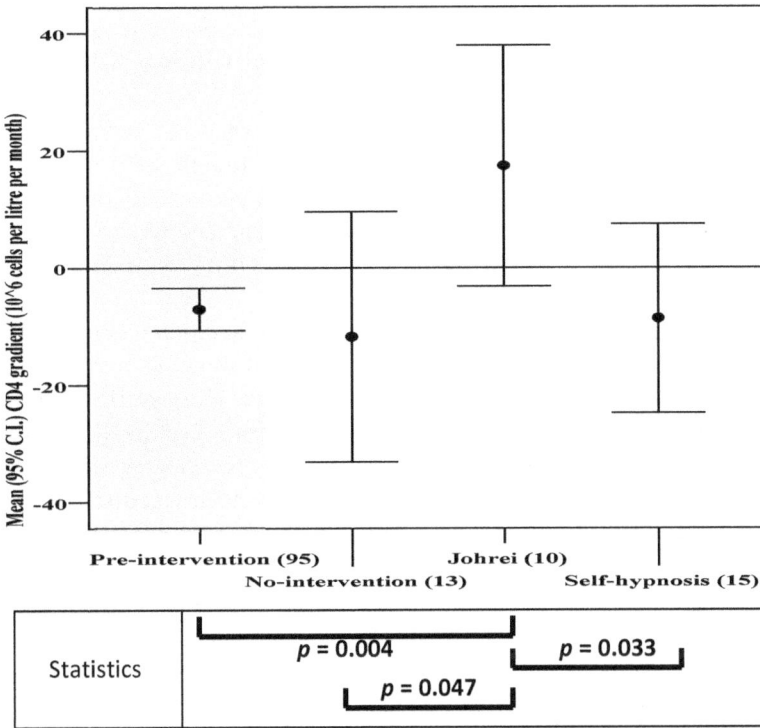

Figure 4. Mean (95 percent C.I.) CD4 gradients over the four months study period in the Self-hypnosis, Johrei and No-intervention (control) groups; and twelve month pre-intervention.

$p = 0.003$). There were no consistent effects with the other interventions, whereas previously self-hypnosis maintained NKC levels (mean = -0.36) and the control group showed a non-significant decline (mean = -2.14). The results are shown in Figure 4. Accordingly, Johrei was superior to both relaxation ($p = 0.005$) and hypnosis ($p = 0.016$). Following Johrei there was a decrease in CD4 percentages, which in this experiment was associated with a reduction in Perceived Stress.

The buffering of the decline in NK cells with self-hypnosis was examined further by a median split on the basis of the Perceived Stress Scores of the hypnosis group. This disclosed that buffering occurred in the non-stressed participants, but not in those with high stress scores. In contrast, CD8 percentages were not only maintained with hypnosis, in replication of previous results, but significantly increased. The more eclectic approach to stress reduction in the techniques offered in this study, whose repertoire extended beyond hypnotic relaxation/immune visualization, had no impact following hypnosis on the NK cell reduction in the highly stressed participants, in contrast to the previous studies, but hypnosis was successful in elevating CD8–helper T–lymphocytes in the highly stressed participants.

The relaxation controls had higher levels of CD4 percentages post-training, here a lymphocyte associated with stress. Although their NK cell percentages were the lowest, the decline in NK cell percentages did not reach significance, suggesting that relaxation could be contributing to the maintenance of NK cell percentages during exams as has been found in other studies.

Summary. By the time of the exams the immune markers of the Johrei participants successfully combated exam stress in showing increases in NK cell percentages and decreases in CD4 percentages. This was the opposite to the stress pattern disclosed by the participants overall. Remarkably, following Johrei practice, all participants maintained their NK cell levels, with 14/15 showing an increase. In contrast participants who learned self-hypnosis increased their CD8+ percentages, shown to decline with exam stress in previous studies, and on average maintained NK cell percentages, though these advantages were not found in those participants with high Perceived Stress. By comparison with the Relaxation group the differences were sufficient to support the impression there is more to hypnosis and Johrei than relaxation, nor is Johrei an elaborate form of hypnosis.

The participants' expectations about the efficacy of the various interventions either before or after training were unrelated to mood or lymphocyte subpopulation outcomes.

Metastatic Breast Cancer. A small pilot study whose overriding aim was to maintain health and well-being was conducted with metastatic breast cancer patients whose cancer had returned (Laidlaw et al., 2005; Bennett et al., 2006). Johrei was compared with self-hypnosis and a wait-list control group. Several psychological variables have been associated with increased survival times in metastatic breast cancer: better appetite, good physical and role functioning, as well as less fatigue. Anxiety alone has been found to be a significant predictor of the clinical response in breast cancer (Walker, 1999). Whether there is an impact on the disease per se is controversial (Spiegel, Bloom, Kraemer & Gottheil, 1989; Edelman, Craig, & Kidman, 2000; Edwards, Hailey, & Maxwell, 2004).

Design. Initially thirty-seven women were randomly assigned to 4 weeks of training in self-hypnosis or Johrei or to a wait-list group for three months. The Johrei program had health at its basis and involved daily practice. Self-hypnosis included specific suggestions for immune enhancement, health and vitality, and was presented in immune-oriented, audio self-hypnosis CDs that were to be used daily. Of the 16 who completed their training, data were obtainable for 14 women, 7 receiving self-hypnosis, 4 Johrei and 3 controls (1 of whom subsequently trained in self-hypnosis). Patients were examined with quality of life and mood scales on two occasions prior to training, and again three or more months later (Laidlaw et al., 2005).

Eight agreed to be interviewed about the meaning and experience of living with breast cancer which had returned after conventional treatment (Bennett et al., 2006). The focus of the interview was on how the process of learning and applying a specific psychological intervention guided their coping. Six received self-hypnosis and two Johrei. Interviews were recorded, transcribed and then analyzed using interpretative phenomenological analysis.

Mood. Following both Johrei and hypnosis patients were more Composed and less Anxious (POMS) than controls. Energy levels, a variable important to increased survival, were increased by hypnosis while Johrei maintained them. There was a reduction in Anxiety and a general improvement in other mood scores, predictive of a better quality of life.

Interview. From the interview the major themes that conceptualized living with the return of breast cancer were self-identity, self-blame, social isolation and feelings of being constrained (Bennett et al., 2006). Themes relating to the psychological intervention were gaining a sense of control and empowerment, *normalizing* and re-attribution. Furthermore "They had something in the tool bag" for dealing with the actual cancer. There was also a clear message of approval that neither involved any pharmacological products.

HIV Infection. *Background.* HIV infection is a life-long biological and psychological stressor. High stress levels have been shown to contribute to detrimental outcomes associated with HIV disease progression, with a less rapid decrease in the key immunologival marker with HIV, CD4 T–cell numbers, in patients with low stress levels (Catalan et al., 1995; Nott et al., 1995; Cole et al., 2003). We conducted an open study in which treatment-naïve HIV patients were randomized to training with Johrei, self-hypnosis or to a no-intervention control group.

Design. A total of 63 HIV patients were recruited: 60 males and three females with a median age of 37 years (range 27–58 years). Patients were free from HIV-related symptoms and had more than 200×10^6 CD4 T–cells per liter of their peripheral blood. Patients were followed for four months after which the non-intervention group (n = 24: wait-listed controls) was randomly re-assigned to Johrei (28) or to self-hypnosis (34) training. The study continued for a further twelve months during which there was a four month training of the controls and post training assessments for all. In addition, patients acted as their own controls by comparing the historical results over the preceding twelve months with the prospective results obtained during the intervention and follow-up. Furthermore, a total of 49 case-matched database controls were selected from the same HIV patient database during the equivalent period. This selection was performed blind by an independent researcher in order to match the study participants using the same inclusion criteria and requiring more than two assessments both twelve months prior to and after training commenced.

Those assigned to Johrei were encouraged to practice Johrei at least four times a week with a partner. Because of the concept of paired practice participants were recommended to bring their Johrei partner with them to one of the four Johrei training sessions. At the end of training, self–Johrei techniques were introduced as supplementary tools so that participants could also practice alone. The self-hypnosis procedure was the same eclectic approach outlined for the student exam stress study. After the one month training period, each participant practiced Johrei or self-hypnosis at home, attended at least three follow-up sessions held monthly, and was encouraged to continue to practice.

Psychological well-being was assessed by questionnaires including the Perceived Stress Scale (Cohen et al., 1983) and Speilberger State and Trait Anxiety Scale, Locus of Control (Furnham and Steele, 1993), and the Mental-Components-Summary in the SF–36 which together with the Pittsburgh-Sleep-Quality-Inventory (Buysse et al., 1989) assessed quality-of-life. All scales were administered at recruitment and four months later. CD4 T–cell counts were obtained through the patients' routine clinical assessment. 95 subjects (46 study participants and 49 Database controls) had sufficient assays to calculate a gradient over time. Regarding the initial four month intervention period, only 38 of the 63 participants (13/24 Non–intervention, 10/16 Johrei and 15/23 Self-hypnosis) attended sufficient blood collection sessions.

Immunology. In line with established findings (de Wolf et al., 1997), there was a steady decline in CD4 counts over the twelve month period preceding the study with a mean loss of 7 ± 4 million CD4 T–cells per-litre-per-month. Following training for the 38 participants who attended two or more CD4 assessment sessions (15 self-hypnosis, 10 Johrei, 13 No-intervention controls) with Johrei there was a significant reduction in the rate of decline and indeed a reversal with a mean gain of 17 ± 11 million cells per-litre-per-month, compared with self-hypnosis with a mean loss of 9 ± 8 million cells per-litre-per-month and the no-intervention groups with a mean loss of ±8 million cells per-litre-per-month. The finding that Johrei practice delays or halts the decline in CD4 T–cell counts from the initial four month intervention (Figure 4) was further supported by the twelve-month data sets and by the comparison with the preceding twelve months' historical data.

Psychology. While neither intervention significantly affected the psychological assessments obtained across the four month intervention period (N = 32), correlational analysis with the CD4 T–cell gradients showed relations with Locus of Control in the direction of an internal locus of control and improvement ($r = -0.39$, $p < 0.028$), with quality of life measured with the MCS SF-36 ($r = 0.32$, $p < 0.076$) and with Sleep Quality ($R = -0.33$, $p < 0.063$).

Hypnotisability. At an early stage of the study, 9 participants receiving Johrei and 13 receiving self-hypnosis practice were examined for possible relations between hypnotic susceptibility and the change in CD4+ counts following four months of training (Laidlaw et al., 2004). When the highly hypnotisable subjects were compared with those of lower hypnotisability, CD4 counts were significantly higher in those who were hypnotically susceptible. This was due to a non-significant increase in the highly hypnotisable subjects while the CD4 counts of the less hypnotisable subjects declined significantly ($X = -79.4$). Thus hypnotisability may assist in predicting immunological response to psychological interventions with HIV.

Summary: Johrei, Hypnosis, Relaxation. In both the student and patient investigations comparing Johrei with self-hypnosis, Johrei produced benefits in the immune parameters superior to both self-hypnosis/visualization training and relaxation. Whereas in students self-hypnosis and relaxation did buffer the typical decline with stress in T–lymphocytes, Johrei not only maintained NK cells and functional activity, but in 14/15 participants their levels were raised ($p<0.0001$). This should have made the field sit up, but it has largely gone unnoticed. In the HIV study with asymptomatic patients who had early stages of HIV infection in advance of cognitive signs such as AIDS–related dementia, Johrei reversed the decline in CD4 T–lymphocytes ($p<.04$). The reversal was not found with self-hypnosis. In the case of influences on mood, both hypnosis and Johrei were equally beneficial, though there may be subtle differences between them. Turning to the outcome of the various relaxation control groups the value of both self-hypnosis/visualization and Johrei was in addition to relaxation, though relaxation provided a foundation for their effects, as is likely for Reiki considered in the next section.

The outcome with students can be compared with our previous studies of self-hypnosis/visualization for the designs were virtually identical except that a more diverse and eclectic approach to hypnosis was adopted in the studies comparing hypnosis with Johrei. In the earlier two student studies self-hypnosis with immune visualization, buffered the decline in NK cells and CD8–T lymphocytes and in the second study also maintained health in the face of a winter influenza epidemic. In the subsequent Johrei study self-hypnosis similarly maintained NK levels, as did relaxation, but here hypnosis was successful in raising CD8 counts, but not NK cell activity.

Two controlled studies with Reiki will be reviewed before further consideration of the promising outcome with Johrei and the differential outcome with self-hypnosis, and in turn possible mechanisms underlying these effects. Reiki has interesting affinities with Johrei and at the same time has striking differences.

Reiki

Reiki is a biofield therapy similar to Johrei and may be practiced with or without physical contact. Unlike Johrei the practitioner requires attunement by a Reiki master, a ritual believed to facilitate connection to the universal energy source. Hitherto evidence consisted of case reports, descriptive studies, and controlled studies with small sample sizes. For example Wetzel (1989) reported oxygen-carrying changes in hemoglobin and hematocrit values over 24-hours in 48 essentially healthy adults. They were compared with 10 healthy medical professionals who disclosed no changes, but the study was without control for placebo expectancy effects or relaxation, nor was there random assignment. Rubic *et al.* (2006) examined the effect of Reiki on overnight cultures of heat-shocked Escherichia coli K12 bacteria in vitro which were compared with untreated control cultures. Practitioners administered Reiki to a patient suffering pain before treating the bacteria. Cultures treated with Reiki produced more bacteria than control cultures. Baldwin and Schwartz (2006) compared the effect of Reiki, or sham Reiki involving an attuned practitioner mimicking Reiki, on rats exposed to excessive white noise and control rats exposed to noise without Reiki. Reduced microvascular leakage only accompanied Reiki.

A Controlled Study on the Health and Mood of University Students
Design. We carried out a randomized controlled single-blind study with 35 healthy Psychology undergraduate freshmen (Bowden et al., 2009). They were randomly assigned to Reiki or sham Reiki in 10, 20-minute administrations over two and a half to 12 weeks. Within each of the two groups participants were further randomized to one of three guided imagery relaxation procedures which had the effect of diverting attention away from Reiki. The experimenter, a Reiki master, directed Reiki by holding her hands 3–30 inches above the head or towards the back of the participant. The participants wore headphones and were either blindfolded or wore a VR head-mounted display headset. During the no–Reiki sessions the experimenter sat impassively. Illness symptoms, mood, sleep and salivary cortisol were assessed pre and post intervention.

Health and Mood. Whereas there was a substantive increase in the no–Reiki group in illness symptoms on a 20-item questionnaire, the Reiki group disclosed a tendency towards a reduction in symptoms, leading to a highly significant advantage for Reiki. Accompanying the improvement in health the Reiki group had a comparative reduction in stress measured with the Depression, Anxiety and Stress Scale (DASS), although they also had significantly higher baseline stress and illness symptoms. Before their sixth intervention session and again at post-assessment, participants completed a tailor made Reiki blinding and expectation questionnaire which asked whether they believed they were receiving Reiki and whether the intervention was positively affecting their well-being. This disclosed that the Reiki blinding was successful, and at post-assessment more of the Reiki participants reported benefits for well-being. Thus the results are suggestive that Reiki buffered the substantive decline in health in the course of the academic year seen in the no–Reiki group.

A Controlled Study of Students with Anxiety/Depression. *Design.* A constructive replication was conducted involving a randomized controlled trial where 40 participants were selected on the basis of high versus low Anxiety/Depression DASS scores (Bowden et al., 2010). Half of those with high depression and/or anxiety and half with low depression and/or anxiety were randomly assigned to Reiki or to a no–Reiki control. Participants experienced six 30-minute sessions over a period of two to eight weeks, and were blind as to whether non-contact Reiki was administered with their attention absorbed by a guided relaxation CD also providing a control for relaxation. As before the efficacy of the intervention was assessed pre-post intervention by self-report measures and additionally there was a five-week follow-up.

Stress and Anxiety. There were beneficial effects with the DASS favoring Reiki, and these were sustained at follow-up. Here the benefits which took the form of a reduction in Anxiety and Stress scores were specific to those with high negative mood and were not found in the corresponding control group; all but one of the participants who received Reiki showed an improvement in Stress, whereas 5/8 control subjects showed an increase in stress at follow-up. The improvement in Stress had a counterpart in reduced Anxiety post-treatment and at follow-up, whereas the controls with high negative mood showed an increase in Anxiety at follow-up.

All participants benefited to some extent. In keeping with the guided relaxation that all participants received, the cohort as a whole disclosed improvements on the patient Hospital Anxiety and Depression Anxiety scale, while the Activation-Deactivation checklist disclosed improvements in Calmness, Tension and Sleep, though Tiredness was unchanged and Energy was significantly reduced. None of the benefits common to the group as a whole were sustained at follow-up, and on these indices there were no advantages to Reiki. There was no impact on Illness symptoms as in the previous study.

Thus the main sustained benefit of the study favored Reiki and was seen in participants with high Anxiety/Depression on the DASS scale. The lack of an effect on all the participants receiving Reiki, as in the first study, may have been due to the fewer sessions—6 compared with the 10 in the previous study. Number of treatment sessions has been positively associated with favorable psychological outcome. The method of blinding was again successful.

Conclusion. The focus in the Reiki studies was on energy transmission. The mental state of all participants was absorbed with guided relaxation imagery, allowing control for the impact of relaxation with Reiki, while Reiki was administered from behind without any interpersonal interaction (as occurs with Johrei). The outcome of both Reiki studies was more than suggestive of an influence of bioenergy. Although there was no impact on salivary cortisol in either study, there was an improvement in mood—particularly stress and anxiety—for both studies. There was also an important health advantage in the first study. A further study has been conducted examining the impact of Reiki and mock Reiki on the growth of seeds. This was a double blind design and involved five experienced practitioners. Some advantages for Reiki were disclosed (Bowden, 2010). Therefore all three controlled studies support the proposition that the transmission of subtle energy has efficacious results, mechanisms for which are now considered.

Mechanisms

Johrei as a Therapeutic Procedure

What could be responsible for the superior efficacy of Johrei on the immune system? While there are numerous differences between Johrei and self-hypnosis practice, there are a few central ones. With Johrei, as with Reiki, there is no verbal instruction guiding the intervention moment by moment, and imagery in Johrei is incidental, if it is present. With Johrei, not only is the participant a recipient, but perhaps crucially, the participant takes the active role of practitioner. Depending on the circumstances of healing, roles are interchangeable. Conceivably, the agential role in Johrei may be a critical one. This would be compatible with our finding in both the student and herpes patient studies that it was the Activated personality that was the personality associated with the positive outcome on immune up-regulation and health. The importance of an agential personality may also be at work in the "fighting spirit" that has been linked with recovery from breast cancer (Greer, 1983). The interpersonal dynamic in Johrei is surely fundamental where the practicing partner provides support and encouragement. In contrast, self-hypnosis is practiced alone and is without this support. The importance of a symbiotic, sympatique relationship in hypnotherapy (and in psychotherapy generally) is becoming increasingly recognized. In addition, the Johrei philosophy involves thoughts of "spirituality" where bonding via the ethereal healing-light provides the Johrei practitioner with a sense of support and connectedness to the partner.

A further distinction involves the direction of attention and alertness. Whereas attention is directed inwards in the case of guided immune imagery, the interpersonal partnering of Johrei (especially in the role of practitioner, but also in the role of recipient who directs attention outwards to the partner) heightens perceptual awareness and the feeling of energy transmission. Participants enter a meditation-like state and with practice there is a sensitization to experiences such as variations in temperature between the recipient and practitioner. There is inner-directed attention with both hypnosis and relaxation and outer-directed attention with Johrei. We went on to explore this with EEG analysis.

Resting EEG before and after Johrei, Self-Hypnosis, and Relaxation Training

In the student stressor study, resting topographical EEG was examined before and after the four week intervention in order to shed light on putative differential effects of the three interventions. Incidentally, this was the first EEG study to examine the outcome of a course of self-hypnosis training; traditionally, EEG studies of hypnosis have examined the hypnotic induction itself (Crawford & Gruzelier, 1992). It was of interest to determine whether there were spectral differences such as higher EEG spectral power in Johrei and with an increase in fast wave activity that might accompany a more cognitively activated state.

EEG monitoring from 28 electrode derivations was undertaken with conventional eyes closed and eyes open conditions together with a four minute period of relaxation with eyes closed. Spectral amplitude values were derived from artifact-free EEG recorded in 47/48 participants and then aggregated into different frequency bands: Delta (1–3.9 Hz), Theta (4–7.9 Hz), Alpha (8–12.9 Hz), Beta1 (13–19.9 Hz) and Beta2 (20–30 Hz).

As hypothesized, following Johrei training, there were increases in fast frequency activity (beta 1 and 2) in the central region, following hypnosis there were elevations in slower frequency activity (alpha and theta), while following Relaxation training there was a decrease in beta 1 centrally, the opposite pattern to Johrei. Consistent with the apparently alerting effect of Johrei signified by the increases in beta activity, the Johrei group was also distinguished by an absence of increases in theta power in the temporal lobe shown with Hypnosis and Relaxation. We had previously associated elevations in theta during hypnosis with relaxation, for they occurred independently of hypnotic susceptibility (Williams & Gruzelier, 2000).

EEG Complexity and Mutual Information
Analysis Between Practitioner and Recipient

Topographical EEG was recorded from both practitioner and recipient simultaneously in order to elucidate the process of administering Johrei. This involved a controlled two-session study of thirty-five medical students with the standard 28 electrode derivations. Johrei or Mock Johrei were scheduled in a counterbalanced order, each for ten minutes in both sessions, and administered from behind the participants by one of three experienced Johrei practitioners. Participants were blind to order of conditions. In the mock condition the practitioners' attention was drawn inwards as they silently performed a self-paced mental arithmetic task with eyes closed. For the purposes of this study the EEG spectral power was submitted to complexity analysis (Tononi et al., 1994) and mutual information analysis (Darbellay, 1999).

Complexity analysis provides a metric of the intricacy of the spatio-temporal dynamics of neuronal populations at a gross, mass-action level. Reduced complexity reflects strongly coupled networks and the inactivation of previously active networks (Lutzenberger et al., 1995). It follows that the more widely distributed the engagement of diverse neural assemblies, the higher the complexity will be. Recent findings include a reduction in twenty experienced meditators over midline central and anterior regions along with an increase in theta and low alpha power which was interpreted as follows: "It is suggested that meditative experience, characterized by less complex dynamics of the EEG, involves "switching off" irrelevant networks for the maintenance of focused internalized attention and inhibition of inappropriate information" (Aftanas & Golocheikine, 2002). Conversely complexity is increased by tasks involving wider versus constrained networks such as creative divergent versus convergent thinking (Molle et al., 1996) and functional thinking versus both predictive thinking and mental relaxation (Molle et al., 2000). Complexity has shown hemispheric equivalence in participants with paranormal ideation, (Pizzagalli et al., 2000) [see also the Unreality syndrome of the 3-syndrome model of schizotypy (pages 30–31)]. Importantly complexity increases with the intensity of emotions, especially positive emotions (Aftanas et al., 1998). Reduced complexity has been related to the greater depth of anesthesia (Zhang et al., 2001), and is reduced in the vegetative state (Sara & Pistoia, 2010). However, interpretation is complicated by the finding that reduced complexity is also associated with greater effort in attention

(Aftanas & Golocheikine, 2002), at least in anterior regions, and Elbert et al. (1994) concluded that complexity is higher over areas that are uninvolved in cognitive processing.

What would one predict the differences to be between the practitioner and recipient in Johrei? In both Johrei and mock Johrei the recipient is in a relaxed state with a passive, receptive, diffuse, outer-directed attention style, with limited cognitive involvement, and with the intention of receiving Johrei. The practitioner on the other hand while relatively relaxed throughout is in an active, focused mode in the Johrei condition and with the intention of transmitting energy, while in the mock Johrei condition is engaged in cognitive processing through the mental subtraction task. The recipient role would be more akin to the state of loosened attention, imagery, and divergent thinking associated with higher EEG complexity (Aftanas & Golocheikine, 2002b).

Complexity analysis did in fact disclose higher complexity in total power in receivers than practitioners (p <0.001) seen at both extremes of the EEG spectrum. In alpha, whereas receivers did not differ between the two conditions (they were blinded as to condition), practitioners showed an increase in complexity with Johrei and a decrease with Mock Johrei ($p < 0.001$) which would be consistent with more diffuse attention in Johrei compared with the mental subtraction task.

Mutual Information Analysis has typically been used to measure the dynamic coupling within systems such as brain areas, independent physiological channels, and concurrently applied imaging techniques. The transmission of information between systems is termed cross mutual information (Gaens et al., 1991), and to our knowledge this was the first application where transmission is between people. Mutual information was higher with Johrei than Mock Johrei in total power (p <0.007), particularly in alpha ($p < 0.001$ and gamma ($p < 0.009$), both of which have been involved in alterations of consciousness (Vaitl et al., 2005). But the result may simply mean greater commonality between the states of the recipient and practitioner when the practitioner was administering Johrei than when engaged in mental subtraction. Notwithstanding this analytic approach is worthy of further investigation.

Therefore the state of receiving Johrei is certainly not a passive one, as disclosed by the recipients' higher complexity, and in keeping with the raised EEG power shown in the study described above. Thus when receiving Johrei one's state is unlike meditation and relaxation, and if Aftanas and Golocheikine's (2002) interpretation is correct the higher coherence found in receivers signifies a freer attentional and imaginative state (see also Schupp et al., 1994).

Johrei and Reiki: Energetic Fields

Johrei and Reiki, which originated in Japan contemporaneously, share the theory that the practitioner is a conduit of universal energy enabling a spiritual connection with the recipient. One hypothesized explanation for the energy transmission has invoked biomagnetic fields. These fields surround the body and are generated by electric currents throughout the nervous system, especially from the heart and the circulatory system which can be measured at a distance of fifteen feet. In the brain the healing process is served by perineural cells, which constitute more than half of brain cells. When an injury occurs an electrical potential is generated at the injured site which alerts the perineural system which orchestrates repair cells at the site through direct current, rebalancing the electrical potential and resulting in wound healing. The biomagnetic fields may be measured with magnetometers, and each organ has a unique frequency range which changes with illness, and which may be regulated through pulsation jump-starting the healing process (Frölich, 1978). This is well known for bone healing where the optimal frequency range is 7–8 Hz.

The perineural system is very sensitive and responsive to externally applied magnetic fields. Not only may the currents be in phase within the body creating electrical fields, as measured by the EEG, but coherence may occur between people, demonstrated by the synchronization of menstrual cycles in women sharing accommodation (Oshmann, 2000). Individual differences in biomagnetic fields have been disclosed such that fields surrounding healers' hands were 1000 times the strength of nonhealers' hands in a study by Seto et al. (1992). How this arises is unclear, for while attunement by a Reiki master may be posited, Johrei requires no such attunement, and as we have demonstrated, important effects may result from novices administering Johrei (Naito et al., 2003).

However, biomagnetism does not readily account for healing at a distance, for which there is evidence from a number of rigorously designed studies (Abbot, 2000). Biomagnetic fields decrease rapidly in strength over distance. Here we speculatively turn to the perspective of quantum physics acknowledging, as did Einstein, that the universe is one indivisible, dynamic whole, which involves an integration of independent energy fields entangled in a meshwork of interactions (Lipton, 2005). As Lipton (p. 111) notes:

> Specific frequencies and patterns of electromagnetic radiation regulate DNN, RNA, cell differentiation, morphogenesis (the process by which cells assemble into organs and tissues), hormone secretion, nerve growth and function. Each one of these cellular activities is a fundamental behavior that constitutes to the unfolding of life.

Hundreds upon hundreds of other* scientific studies over the last fifty years have consistently revealed that "invisible forces" of the electromagnetic spectrum profoundly impact every facet of biological regulation. These energies include microwaves, radio frequencies, the visible light spectrum, extremely low frequencies, acoustic frequencies, and even a newly recognized form of force called scalar energy.

Rand (2000) has theorized that scalar waves may mediate healing at a distance. These waves are created when two magnetic fields of equal frequency and half a wavelength out of phase cancel each other out maintaining the potentials of the waves and the effects of the fields. Scalar waves can propagate to any distance without decreasing in strength. Importantly Rein (1998) has shown that scalar waves can affect the immune system and promote healing. Applications with healers are awaited.

New Directions: Enhancement Training

The final questions to be addressed briefly are whether individual differences in traversing the mind-body pathway can be facilitated. In particular whether healing may be facilitated by EEG–neurofeedback. Neurofeedback has been the primary focus of the author's research over the past decade in applications as diverse as schizophrenia, social withdrawal, and surgical, music, dance and acting performance (Gruzelier, et al., 1999, 2006, 2010; Gruzelier, 2009; Ros et al., 2009). Others have investigated inter alia memory, sleep and intelligence (Cortoos et al., 2009; Hansylmayer et al., 2000; Kiezer et al., 2010).There have been wide ranging clinical applications, especially attention deficit hyperactivity disorder (Monastra et al., 2005; Arns et al., 2009). Neurofeedback involves learning to control electrocortical activity by making the activity to be controlled contingent on the occurrence of environmental stimuli. In conventional slower EEG–frequency band training the participant with eyes closed will hear attractive sounds, but only if their theta and alpha activity increases, so that they learn to adjust their mental state to hear the sounds more often. With faster rhythm training visual stimuli are presented on a computer screen and events occur when the target rhythm, such as low beta or the sensory motor rhythm lying between alpha and beta in the EEG–spectrum, increases in amplitude and concurrent slow theta activity and faster high beta is reduced.

In the context of exceptional experiences, there are several main reasons why this training may be beneficial. The sensory motor rhythm induces a relaxed and sustained attentional focus in university students (Egner & Gruzelier, 2001; 2004), and has shown proven usefulness with children with attention deficit hyperactivity disorder (Arns et al., 2009; Monastra et al., 2005). It has also induced a more efficient and modulated performance in the micro surgery skills of trainee eye surgeons (Ros et al., 2009), while acting performance has been improved along with the actors' experience of flow when training screens and training contexts such as a virtual reality environment have been made ecologically relevant, e.g., a theater auditorium (Gruzelier et al., 2010). Conceivably neurofeedback may facilitate hypnotic susceptibility in those who find difficulty in focusing their attention, the first prerequisite in inducing hypnosis. It will facilitate absorption, which also plays an important role in Johrei and Reiki.

Turning to the slower rhythms the alpha/theta neurofeedback paradigm induces a hypnogogic state (Gruzelier, 2009), one which has been associated with creativity (Koestler, 1966). Elevations in theta and low alpha are commonplace in hypnosis, meditation and in deep states of relaxation (Vaitl et al., 2005), and as was disclosed in our hypnosis study with medical students. We confirmed its impact on creativity with musicians and dancers (Egner & Gruzelier, 2003; Raymond et al., 2005). Alpha theta training may also enhance well-being as shown in addiction (Peniston & Kulkowsky, 1989; Scott et al., 2005), and as we have found in socially withdrawn medical students with high negative schizotypy scores (Raymond et al., 2005b) and has assisted in the recovery from post-traumatic stress syndrome (Peniston & Kulkowsky, 1991). This protocol may facilitate the letting go requirement of hypnotic susceptibility, receptivity to the healing properties of Johrei and Reiki, and openness to paranormal experience.

Green and Green (1977), in their foundational work with this protocol found serendipitous evidence of PSI phenomena as a result of training to include subjects not well disposed to PSI phenomena. Three out of eight colleagues had ESP–type experiences during lab sessions, while ESP events were also found in three out of twenty-six college students trained in hypnogogia. The first three experiences were of the remote viewing type, and included E. Green as subject in one instance, as were two of the other experiences in the subsequent study. The third example in that study was of a student who has a series of experiences including both remote viewing and clairvoyance.

In conclusion, a body of validation studies is being published on a range of healing methods, not all of which can be accounted for by Western neurobiology and cannot easily be dismissed by skeptics. Validation is growing too for approaches within the realms of conventional neuroscience, such as hypnosis, both from a mechanistic perspective through functional brain imaging and through controlled clinical trials. Both domains of evidence will encourage further applications within conventional medicine (Liossi et al., 2009).

I predict that erstwhile exceptional abilities will come increasingly under focus and will enter the mainstream. An example of this potential osmosis is seen in spirituality which is currently under debate as a possible sixth personality dimension to compliment the Big–5 consisting of neuroticism, extraversion, conscientiousness, openness to experience and agreeableness (Piedmont, 1999; Unterrainer et al., 2010). Vulnerable abilities such as those of positive schizotypy have been aligned with facets of creativity (Claridge, 1985) and actualization such as described by Jung, Maslow, Csikszentmihalyi. Given the proposition that not only schizotypy but also a large proportion of the schizophrenia spectrum are modifiable (Gruzelier, 2002), healing approaches such as Johrei, Reiki, self-hypnosis, and especially EEG–neurofeedback may assist vulnerable individuals achieve resilience (Raymond et al., 2005b; Santarcangelo and Sebastiani, 2004), and so allow them to actualize or make productive their exceptional abilities. In this way ESP abilities may be trained (Shiah, 2009) and brought within the realm of the useful, and not merely appraised as exotic. To my mind the prospects are tantalizing.

2

Altered States
of Consciousness,
Mental Imagery and Healing

DAVID LUKE

Abstract

In this chapter, the relationship between mental imagery (in particular, those evoked from a variety of altered states of consciousness) and healing are explored. It is noted that the long-standing practice of using mental imagery for healing is virtually inseparable from the use of techniques for altering states of consciousness, be it through hypnosis, ingestion of psychoactive substances, breathing, chanting, dancing, drumming or any other means. Altered states, generally, give rise to increased mental imagery. This chapter considers the use of two specific types of altered state — dreaming and those states brought about through the use of psychoactive substances — to explore ancient and contemporary uses of mental imagery in healing, in both the so-called Old World (Afro-Eurasia) and New World (Australia and the Americas).

The Old World: Dream Incubation

Dreaming is one of the earliest documented types of altered state used to induce imagery for the sake of healing. In order to practice dream incubation to cure sickness the ancient Greeks, for instance, constructed dream temples, called *asclepions*, sacred to Asclepius, the God of healing. Over 400 asclepions thrived all over Greece, particularly at sites such as Cos and Epidaurus, and, later, in Rome, for about a 1000-year period between 600 BC and 400 CE (Meier, 1989). The Romans spread the practice as far as Britain and there are at least two sites in the United Kingdom now considered to have been dream temples: the Temple of Nodens, near Lydney in the Forest of Dean, and a temple on a site near Thistleton in Rutland (Trubshaw, 1995).

Patients would typically enter the temple after a period of ritual and "lie upon" (literally *incubate*) a couch on a sacred skin called a *klínè* (from which the term "clinic" is derived). During the patient's dream, under auspicious circumstances, the god was believed to appear to them and heal their sickness directly. According to the sources, including the greatest physician of the Roman era, Galen, the patient was always cured if Asclepius appeared to them during incubation, such as in his theriomorphic form as a serpent. Snakes were sacred to Asclepius and the god is depicted with a single serpent around his staff, probably as a development of his Egyptian origins as Osiris, known as Serapis, the god who carries the *thyrsus* — a staff entwined by two serpents and bearing a pine cone at its summit. A similar motif is found in Indian tantra, where the staff represents the spinal column and the serpents represent the kundalini energy rising up the body and culminating at the ajna chakra, an etheric point of the body whose physiological counterpart is the pineal gland in the brain (Roney-Dougal, 1991). The pineal gland is an organ that is shaped like a pine cone and is seemingly also represented by the pine cone at the top of the ancient Egyptian thyrsus, with the staff of the thyrsus representing the spine (Luke, 2008a). In some ancient depictions, the staff of Asclepius also appears to be topped with a pine cone, though in modern times this adornment is absent despite the staff and the entwined serpent still being used widely today as the symbol of medicine and health care, no doubt because the ancient Greek physician, Hippocrates, the father of "Western" medicine, was an initiate of Asclepius apparently, as was the Roman physician, Galen (Meier, 1989). The ancients explained the association between serpents and healing as the power of the snake to shed its skin and rejuvenate itself (Meier, 1989).

As well as being a god of healing, Asclepius was also the father and, sometimes, husband of Hygieia (from where the term "hygiene" is derived) and Panacea too, so it is only fitting that the modern medical symbol utilizes his emblem, but, unlike modern therapeutic interventions, healing in the Asclepian tradition was conducted through sacred dreams alone. Nevertheless, the word "therapy" itself derives its name from the attendants at the ascepions, the *therapeutēs*, who became dream interpreters in the latter days of the dream temples when the original concept of incubation began to decay, especially in the Roman Empire. Dreams at the asclepions in this later era became healing oracles, which prescribed for the illness, rather than delivering direct contact and healing from Asclepius himself. Nevertheless, in the early period of the asclepions the Greeks regarded the dream as something that really happened and believed that the effectiveness of incubation lay in the fact that only when dreams were highly valued could they exert a healing influence. In some cases healing wasn't granted, but Ascelpius was also reputed to help the dying, and it was believed he would cure them of "the fever called living" (Meier, 1989, p.56), and so he was psychopomp too, much like healers in the shamanic tradition.

Shamanism: The Union of Altered States, Imagery and Healing

Shamanism, strictly speaking, comes for the Tungusic word *šaman* and, according to Eliade (1972), it is pre-eminently a religious phenomenon of Siberia whereby the ecstatic state is considered the religious experience par excellence and so, in its simplest sense, shamanism is the mastery of techniques of ecstasy. Shamanism also utilizes religious, magical, spiritual, healing and trance aspects but is not essentially just any one of these things (Eliade, 1972), but has been described as comprising "a group of techniques by which practitioners deliberately alter or heighten their conscious awareness to enter the so-called "spirit-world," accessing material that they use to help and to heal members of the social group that has acknowledged their shamanic status" (Krippner, 2000, p. 98). However, Achterberg (1985, p. 6) considers healing as integral to the practice such that, "shamanism *is* the medicine of the imagination." Nevertheless, the use of techniques for altering states of consciousness is paramount and virtually all shamanic healing rituals make use of these techniques to produce imagery (Wade, 1996), which Noll (1985) suggests are integral to shamanism. For Noll (2001, p. 249), in essence, "Shamanism is an ecstatic healing tradition which at its core is concerned with the techniques for inducing, maintaining and interpreting the vivid experiences of enhanced mental imagery that occur in the deliberately induced altered states of consciousness in the shaman."

The New World: Shamanic Dreaming

Much like the activities within the Greek *asclepions,* traditional shamanic cultures still in existence use the imagery of dreams in various ways to assist in healing. Unlike the ancient Greeks, however, the imagery of the dream is usually used indirectly in the shamanic healing process, such as an aid in the discovery of power objects or animals and healing songs, in the spontaneous calling and initiation of shamans, or prophetically, in prescribing for an illness or guiding the actions of the community to circumvent harm. For instance, Harner (1980) recounts a Pomo Indian shaman's reception of her first power song in a dream, and Handelman (1967) retells a Washo shaman's experience of being initiated via a dream in which a snake spoke to him. In this sense, then, the dream of the German organic chemist, August Kekulé, in which he intuited the molecular shape of the benzene ring, might be viewed as an act of shamanism. Whilst dreaming, Kekulé saw a snake eat its own tail and thereby understood the perplexing ring shape of the carbon atoms of benzene (Kekulé, 1890). This dream alone was probably one of the most important events in modern medical pharmacology because the benzene ring structure is fundamental in the formation of many organic chemicals, such as neurotransmitters and, therefore, also medicines. So on one level the imagery of Kekulé's dream had a massive healing effect generally, albeit indirectly.

The Brazilian Guaraní and Xavante shamans are inveterate dreamers too, but they also believe that *everybody* can have important dreams and consequently they practice communal dream sharing, so that even young children's nocturnal visions may guide the activities of the community, and in this manner Krippner (2009) suggests that everyone who dreams partakes in shamanism. No doubt the Guaraní and Xavante would approve of Kekulé's dream discovery. Their neighbors in Chile, the Mapuche people, categorize dreams according to four different types: (1) Dreams from the unconscious that represent memories of life experiences, (2) Dreams evoked by external factors such as physical nocturnal disturbances, alcohol or food, (3) Dreams of telepathic or clairvoyant origin, and (4) precognitive dreams that foretell the future (Krippner, 2009). The latter two categories are valued the most. The Mapuche are also known to use dreams to diagnose illness (Krippner, 1995), which, if these diagnoses are correct, the dreams may come under the category of a psychic dream, i.e. one that utilizes so-called extrasensory perception (ESP: either telepathy, clairvoyance or precognition). When the experimental parapsychological research on dream ESP is reviewed the evidence for the genuine reality of such psychic dreams is highly favorable (Sherwood & Roe, 2003), and it is also a fairly common phenomenon because between 33–68 percent of spontaneous cases of ESP are reported to occur during dreams (Van de Castle, 1977).

Plant Shamanism, Imagery and Healing: The Case of Ayahuasca

Psychic diagnosis via the mental imagery of an altered state, such as through dream, would be a more direct method of shamanic healing, were it genuine, than those methods discussed above, however there may be a number of other means by which healing can occur directly through shamanic imagery. These other methods of shamanic healing may include suggestion, ordeal and catharsis, revelation, psychic healing, energy manipulation, synesthetic singing or the use of mediating entities. These methods may also be brought about through the use of techniques of altering one's state of consciousness other than via dreaming. The use of psychoactive plants, for example, is one technique that is both ancient and widespread. Archaeological evidence suggests that such practices have existed the world over for millennia (Devereux, 2008), incorporating numerous plants (Schultes & Hofmann, 1992) and virtually every culture ever studied anthropologically (Dobkin de Rios, 1990).

One such plant-based shamanic psychedelic that is receiving growing academic attention is the Amazonian jungle decoction *ayahuasca*. Used widely in the Amazon basin and across much of South America, ayahuasca, which means "the vine of the spirits" in Quechua, is usually a combination of at least two plants, one of which contains harmala alkaloids—such as the ayahuasca vine (*Banisteriopsis caapi*)—and the other of which contains *N*,-*N*-dimethyltryptamine (DMT), such as the chacruna bush (*Psychotria viridis*) (Shanon, 2002). Harmala alkaloids and DMT are also thought to be made in the pineal gland where they regulate dreams in much the same way that the melatonin made in the pineal gland regulates sleep (Callaway, 1988), indicating that ayahuasca potentially mimics the nocturnal chemistry of the pineal gland, and in turn the pineal gland can be considered to make a kind of *endohuasca*—ayahuasca from within (Callaway, 1995). In this sense ayahuasca provides a kind of waking dream (Luke & Friedman, 2009) and the pineal gland, supposedly so important to both dream and ayahuasca, is then aptly represented by the pine cone crowning the serpent entwined staff of Asclepius, the god of dream healing.

The ancient use of the ayahuasca vine goes back to at least 500–1000 C.E. in Andean Chile, as confirmed by archaeological hair samples (Ogalde, Arriaza, & Soto, 2008), although its Amazonian use has been suggested to be as old 8,000 years (Dobkin de Rios & Rumrill, 2008). In ayahuasca healing rituals the shaman always consumes the psychedelic brew and is often accompanied in this by the patient, because it may assist in their healing (Dobkin de Rios, 1972). The production of mental imagery, i.e. visions, is "undoubtedly the most expected experience for people drinking ... ayahuasca" (Mercante, 2008, p. 1). Indeed, in one study, 63 percent of first time ayahuasca users reported seeing visual phenomena, which were defined as extraordinary visual experiences including kaleidoscopic lights, geometric forms, tunnels, animals, humans, and supernatural beings (Barbosa, Giglio & Dalgalarrondo, 2005). Nevertheless, the mental imagery encountered in shamanic states remains rather neglected as an area of scientific enquiry despite the increased Western interest in shamanism (Rock, 2006).

Suggestion

A number of explanations have been proposed to account for the apparent healing involved in shamanism, and where mental imagery is involved these often have paranormal or supernatural etiologies when explained by shamans, whereas many academics take a more mundane view of the possible healing process. In any event, one, some, all or none of the processes to be discussed may genuinely occur. Consistent with the proposition that all shamanic healing essentially occurs through placebo effects and hypnosis (McClenon, 2002), the anthropologists Dobkin de Rios and Rumrill (2008) take the view that ayahuasca and other psychedelics induce a state of hyper-suggestibility akin to that produced by hypnosis. If the patient drinks the brew, as they often do when they consult ayahuasca shamans (called *ayahuasqueros*), they are then supposedly highly susceptible to the shaman's healing suggestions, both implicit and explicit. This suggestibility "allows an individual to transcend reality, become cohesive with his social group, allow himself to discharge negative emotions, and turn away from himself—a good escape from trauma and irreconcilable conflict" (Dobkin de Rios & Rumrill, 2008, p. 15–16). With regard to the shaman's belief in the contact with animal plant familiars who may assist the shaman in diagnosing illness, discussed shortly, Dobkin de Rios and Rumrill suggest that the belief is merely self-deception, an illusion that provides a sense of security and a means of coping that supposedly immunizes people against depression.

For instance, in an interview with the Peruvian ayahuasquero, Don Hilde, he informed Dobkin de Rios how under the influence of ayahuasca he was able to see inside the patient's body, like an X-ray, and observe the source of illness. In this manner Don Hilde would *tell* the patient what their problem was, rather than *ask* them what the problem was as Western doctors do. As Mercante (2004) points out, ayahuasqueros attempt to find the causes, be they spiritual, psychological or physical, whereas Western medicine primarily attempts to treat just the physical or psychological symptoms, although clearly this is not an absolute rule for either party. Dobkin de Rios and Rumrill indicate that the veracity of Don Hilde's apparently paranormal power is not important but rather the degree to which the patient believes in the shaman's power is the salient factor. However, it would seem entirely logical that even the patient's belief in Don Hilde's power would be in direct proportion to how accurate he was, a point which is made by others studying these phenomena (e.g., McClenon, 1994), thereby highlighting an intellectual limitation in Dobkin de Rios and Rumrill's approach that is culture bound by the materialist-reductionism dominant in Western scientific thinking. For Dobkin de Rios and Rumril (2008, p. 18), "nature cures the illness, while the doctor [shaman] amuses the patient," which appears to be a rather dismissive and painfully ethnocentric view to take of the shamanic ontology, even if suggestion clearly has some part to play in ayahuasca healing, and indeed there is some evidence that it does (for a review see McClenon, 2002).

Ordeal and Catharsis

Counter to Dobkin de Rios and Rumrill's (2008) view that the ayahuasca experience affords escape from trauma, shamanic initiations are often characterized by ordeals and ayahuasca visions that can often be extremely challenging, even terrifying, such as Harner's (1980) highly fearful vision he had taking ayahuasca for the first time with the Conibo of Peru. During his *ordeal*, as shamanic initiations are rightly called, Harner encountered a race of ancient intergalactic dragons who said they had secretly enslaved humans ever since our species first evolved. The suffering experienced during the ritual may be seen as a result of previous misdeeds (Mercante, 2004) and as a process of purification that may culminate in a physiological catharsis through purging, which may manifest as vomiting, diarrhea and/or crying. Ayahuasca is often called "the purge" (e.g., Luna, 1984), and Mercante (2004) sees the experience of purging as a means of eliminating the spiritual mess someone has inside, and that the suffering leads to healing as a signal of salvation.

Revelation

In Brazil, modern syncretic ayahuasca churches, such as the *Santo Daime* and the *Barquinha*, often distinguish between a simple vision and a *miração,* the latter of which is stronger than a vision, is self-evidently different, may be multisensory, and can only occur when drinking ayahuasca (Mercante, 2004). The miração is the intense emotional moment when people receive the teachings of spiritual beings and behold the revelation that is the highest moment of the ecstatic experience and a source of knowledge and self-transformation. In this manner, through revelation, where perception and knowledge are intrinsically connected, the patient understands the root of their problems and makes significant headway in their ongoing healing process (Mercante, 2004).

Psychic Healing, Energy
Visualization, and Synesthetic Singing

A process of psychic healing, where the shaman reportedly heals the patient directly by psychic means, may be mediated by imagery that helps the shaman diagnose the patient's illness directly, such as via the supposed X-ray vision of Don Hilde. At other times the healing may occur through direct treatment with the visualized manipulation of the patient's "energy" field (Dobkin de Rios & Rumrill, 2008). Alternative means include the use of songs, often called *icaros*, that are reported to alter the shape of the unique colorful geometries that can be seen surrounding each organism or object when under the influence of ayahuasca. The Amazonian Shipibo-Conibo call these geometric patterns *quenés*. According to the Shipibo-Conibo shamans, asymmetrical and misshapen geometry is a manifestation and sign of illness and the shaman sings the *quenés* back into a harmonious symmetrical alignment (*quiquin*) through the profound synesthetic qualities of the ayahuasca vision. In the words of one shaman, "at first, the sick body appears like a very messy design [quené]. After a few treatments, the design appears gradually. When the patient is cured, the design is clear, neat, and complete" (Sayer, 2000, p. 129). However, the healing power of songs and imagery themselves are usually mediated by spiritual entities, like the visionary hummingbird that weaves the quenés together when the shaman sings (Sayer, 2000; Luna, 2008).

Mediating Entities

Aside from the use of altered states, shamanism is essentially a communication with the numen of the otherworld and an attempt to "dialogue with nature" (Narby, 2006, p. 16). In relation to the use of psychedelic plants in shamanism, like ayahuasca, often it is believed that it is the plants themselves who make their presence known to the shaman and teach them how to diagnose and cure illness, or else when the shaman adds a plant to the ayahuasca brew they can ask the plant itself which illness it is useful for (Dobkin de Rios, 1996). During the shaman's visions or dreams "plant teachers," which are always psychoactive or purgative plants, will also appear to the shaman and teach them to sing icaros, and it is through these plant teachers that ayahuasqueros learn most, or commonly all of what they know about shamanism (Luna, 1984). Such a belief in plant spirits is not restricted to shamans, however, and interspecies communication is a particularly widespread phenomenon among many Western researchers who end up taking psychedelic substances (Krippner & Luke, 2009). In one survey of psychedelic substance users, the sense of encountering the intelligence within the substance was the most prevalent type of a range of 17 *transpersonal* experiences (i.e., experiences beyond the usual boundaries and limitations of ego, space and time — Grof, 2009), however, this only occurred with non-synthetic plant-based psychedelics, such as ayahuasca, psilocybin-containing mushrooms, and *Salvia divinorum* (Luke & Kittenis, 2005).

The following account relays the Santo Daime *Padrinho* (priest) Sabastião's experience of drinking ayahuasca for the first time:

I drank the daime [ayahuasca], went to my corner and sat. After some time things started to happen, and I became fearful.... Then my old body hit the floor and there it stayed. I was outside my body looking at the old junk that was me. All of a sudden I saw two men who were the most beautiful beings I have ever seen in my life. They were resplendent, like fire! They began to take out my whole skeleton from within my living flesh without hurting anything. As they worked, they vibrated everything from side to side, and I, on the other side, was watching all they were doing. Next they took out my organs. One of them held my guts in his hands. Together they used a hook that opened, separated, and extracted from my guts three nail-sized insects, which were responsible for what I felt walking up and down inside me. Then the one who had been seated next to my prostrate body, which was still stretched out on the floor, came very close to me and said, "Here it is! What was killing you were these three insects, but now you will not die from them anymore." Then they closed my body (De Alverga, 2000, p. 74–75).

Sabastião was left with no scar from the operation but on other occasions some patients claim that they have such marks on their body corresponding to the site of the operation (Mercante, 2004). Mercante suggests that seeing the healing occur, as in Sabastião's experience, acts as a kind of proof of the healing process that the person is going through.

The Ontology and Epistemology of Shamanic Journeying Imagery

Having given an account of some of the ways in which healing has been reported to occur through the use of mental imagery — at least within the altered states experienced whilst dreaming or under the influence of ayahuasca — it is necessary to consider the reality of these accounts. One approach has been to induce mental imagery under experimentally controlled conditions and compare shamanic induction techniques with control conditions, and then to classify the type of imagery induced into different phenomenological categories (Rock, 2006; Rock, Casey & Baynes 2006). In doing so, a classification system has been derived in which the potential ontological origin of particular imagery may be discerned as being either: (1) Autobiographical, and derived from one's long term memory, therefore having an imaginal ontology; (2) Symbolic, if the image seems to perform a symbolic function without appearing to mentally represent a previous sensory experience (Rock & Krippner, 2008), and is therefore not imaginal; (3) Transpersonal, if it appears to have an origin independent of the person's mind-body complex (such as encountering a skeleton being), and so has a transpersonal ontology; and finally 4) Indeterminate, if the person is unable to isolate its origin (Rock, 2006; Rock, Casey & Baynes 2006).

It is noted, however, that this epistemological approach to discerning the ontology of shamanic imagery is marred by philosophical obstacles such as problems associated with induction and deduction, Wittgenstein's private language argument and the fallacy of reification (Rock & Krippner, 2008)— issues too lengthy to detail here. These obstacles constitute what Walsh (1990) calls the *ontological indeterminacy* of the shamanic worldview, and Rock and Krippner (2008, p. 17) add that it would not be an exaggeration to state that, "the fundamental nature of [shamanic] journeying imagery is currently unresolvable." Nevertheless, like many previous studies, Rock (1996) found further evidence in his shamanic journeying research that one's cultural cosmology or religious tradition to some extent shapes the phenomenological content of altered states of consciousness. However, this epistemological consideration does not automatically negate the potentially transpersonal ontology of the shamanic experience (Rock & Krippner, 2008) but neither does the phenomenological approach taken by Rock (1996) and Rock et al. (1996) support the opposite view by providing good objective evidence of the transpersonal ontology. To begin to do so one must look elsewhere, for example, to the experience of extradimensional percepts and shared visions, and to parapsychological research findings.

Extradimensional Percepts

The concept of shamanic mental imagery revolutionized intellectual thinking in the study of Palaeolithic rock art recently by positing a shamanic origin for this art, thereby stimulating a lively academic debate that has continued for over twenty years. The progenitors of this debate, Lewis-Williams and Dowson (1988) put forward a model of shamanic imagery in altered states whereby the visions have three distinct stages. Stage one (entoptic) is the observation of colorful geometric forms that are supposedly universal in their six (Lewis-Williams & Dowson, 1988) or seven (Dronfield, 1996) distinct types, and these are proposed to be *entoptic* (literally "from vision"), in that they originate from within the visual system of the eye and the occipital cortex of the brain. In stage two (construal) the entoptic forms are construed as being derived from memory as they begin to become recognized as iconic images, usually with geometric aspects to them still. Finally in stage three (iconic), often after passing through a tunnel or vortex like experience, the voyager moves into a state of experiencing full sensory "hallucinations," even synesthetic, whereby the things being seen are no longer considered to be imaginal by those perceiving them but become literal. Icons in this final stage may be therianthropic (part animal and part human).

Like Lewis-Williams and Dowson (1988), many other researchers debating in this area are content to assume that the mental imagery of these shamanic states is purely neuropsychological and not in any way transpersonal in origin. According to the neuropsychological model the shamanic visual imagery is either entopic, stemming directly from the visual system, or culturally mediated, stemming from memory, and in both cases is ultimately derived from the brain alone. One counter argument (Luke, 2010) to the materialist-reductionist ontological assumptions of this model draws attention to the extradimensional qualities of the geometric (stage 1) forms in a number of ayahuasca experiences and in an even greater proportion of experiences with DMT, one of ayahuasca's chemical constituents. It is also noted that people under the influence of these shamanic substances also report omni-directional experiences, in that they experience seeing things from every direction simultaneously, or being able to see in every direction simultaneously. Subsequently it is argued that a three-dimensional psychical brain structure and two eyes cannot give rise to perceptions of more than three spatial dimensions or the experience of vision in or from every direction at once, thereby supporting a transpersonal ontology for this mental imagery (Luke, 2010). Supposed X-ray vision too, like that of the ayahuasquero Don Hilde, is also reported to occur spontaneously with some psychedelics (e.g., Price & Lebel, 2000).

Encountering Discarnate Entities, Plant Spirits and Power Animals

For the shaman a great deal of shamanic healing is believed to be mediated through the "spirits" encountered in altered states, be they spirits of the dead, plant spirits or mythological beings particular to the shaman's cultural cosmology. As Winkelman (2007, p. 158) notes, "at the basis of shamanism is animism — the spirit world." Indeed, as already noted, even non-shamans consuming psychedelic plants are also liable to encounter plant spirits and other entities (Luke & Kittenis, 2005; Krippner & Luke, 2009). The use of ayahuasca — and particularly the use of one of its chemical constituents, the endogenous neurochemical DMT — are known to induce such entity encounter experiences (primarily visual, but also multisensory) with a high regularity (e.g., Strassman, 2001; Strassman, Wojtowicz, Luna & Frecska, 2008). Considerable debate exists concerning the ontological origins of these "DMT entities" (see Luke & Friedman, 2009), which some see as purely neuropsychological (e.g., Kent, 2005) and some take at face value as real "trans-dimensional" entities (e.g., Meyer, 1994). Other researchers have instead proposed that these entities cannot be considered either real or fictitious but might be better thought of as just a part of ourselves (Turner, 1995), nevertheless, Rodriguez (2007) has put forward an experimental protocol for supposedly proving or disproving the entities' existence.

Grossly simplified, Rodriguez (2007) proposes obtaining from the entities solutions to complex mathematics puzzles that are unknown to the DMT participant communicating with them. Regrettably, this ingenious method for testing the reality of DMT entity encounters is subject to a number of flaws aside from the huge assumptions involved in expecting our supposed hyper-intelligent beings having the desire to cooperate and make themselves "proven." The most crippling problem for Rodriguez' test, however, is what is known as the *super psi* hypothesis, which is an issue that has long proved difficult to surmount in parapsychological attempts to validate the existence of discarnate entities considered to be spirits of the dead, e.g. those apparently communicating via trance mediums. The problem is that, because clairvoyance, telepathy and precognition (collectively called *psi*) have no theoretical or even apparent limits, it remains a possibility that any information provided by ostensibly discarnate entities may actually be due to the "super" psi of the person (e.g., the medium) receiving the information directly from an earthly source (see Braude, 2002, for a comprehensive discussion).

One alternative approach to investigating the ontology of shamanic entity encounters considers similarities in independent reports concerning the characteristics of particular entities, especially those encountered naïvely and without any cultural context from which the characteristics of the entity could be derived (Luke, 2008a, 2008b). For instance, one such being that commonly appears to naïve DMT users is an entity consisting of multiple entwined serpents covered in multitudinous eyes, often forming a fibbonaci spiral-like geometrical shape not unlike that appearing on a pine cone. Obscure mythological references to a similar entity also exist in various cultural cosmologies possibly indicating the transcultural nature of this entity (Luke, 2008b), thereby posing questions as to whether the entity is culturally mediated — which seems unlikely given the obscurity of the cultural references — or a culture-free universal feature of DMT activation (naturally or artificially) in the brain, with possible transpersonal origins. A similar approach could fruitfully be made with other types of entities commonly encountered with shamanic plants, such as praying mantis (Luke, 2008c), to determine how statistically improbable is the preponderance of these shared visions. Such a methodology has its limitations, of course, nevertheless upon inspection of the literature it appears that such an approach has rarely been applied to the study of apparently shared visions.

Shared Visions

From an experimental perspective one of the best ways to discern whether people genuinely have shared visions with psychedelic substances, such as ayahuasca, would be to use participants completely blind to the effects and compare their reports once they had been administered the substance. One such experiment was conducted by Naranjo (1967, 1973), who used harmaline, a harmala alkaloid found in ayahuasca that is thought to cause visions by both potentiating the effects of the DMT present in the brain (and in the brew if taken as a mixture), and by activating the brain's production of DMT variants (Luke & Friedman, 2009). Upon giving the substance to 30 naïve urban elite Chileans, several of the participants inexplicably reported the same images of snakes and jaguars, or big cats, as are commonly reported in traditional ayahuasca visions in the Amazon jungle (Naranjo, 1987; Shannon, 2002). It's not clear how well controlled this experiment was but visions of jaguars and snakes after taking harmaline have also been reported elsewhere (Shulgin & Shulgin, 1997). Furthermore some of the participants in Naranjo's study were convinced they had seen these images by traveling out-of-body in time and space.

Similarly, Strassman (2001) also found that administering DMT intravenously induced a similar certainty of space-time travel and resulted in the inordinately frequent occurrence of images of DNA, an image which Narby (1998) also found commonly featured in the ayahuasca healing visions of Amazonian shamans, but which was most often represented by two intertwined snakes. It has recently been suggested, amid some controversy, that the geneticist Francis Crick was under the influence of LSD when he had a vision of the double helix structure of DNA in 1953, a discovery for which he was jointly awarded the Nobel Prize (Rees, 2004). Prior to this news report, which came after Crick's death, the anthropologist Narby (2000) took three molecular biologists to the Peruvian Amazon for their first trip there and for their first encounter with ayahuasca. The two female biologists both had encounters with plant teachers who they perceived as independent sentient entities, and all three scientists received valuable information from their visions that helped inform their research, and which ultimately changed their world view. For instance, "the American biologist, who normally worked on deciphering the human genome, said she saw a chromosome from the perspective of a protein flying above a long strand of DNA" (Narby, 2000, p. 302). Similarly, the biochemist, Kary Mullis, who received the Nobel Prize for inventing the polymerase chain reaction (PCR) that significantly advanced DNA research, said that taking LSD had been invaluable in helping him experience the mental imagery that allowed him to visualize sitting on a DNA molecule and watch the polymerase go by (Mullis, 1998). Like Kekulé's dream vision of the oruborous snake that lead to deciphering the shape of benzene, all of these accounts here of scientific discoveries through shamanic-like mental imagery have lead indirectly to human's increased capacity to heal, manifest as scientific breakthroughs in the development of Western medicine, such as via organic chemistry, particularly genetics.

Out-of-Body Perceptions and Psi

Further light may be shed on the possible ontology of these exceptional experiences with findings from parapsychological research into psi. Parapsychology is a scientific enterprise that does not *a priori* reject such experiences as do most other areas of science, which tend to be dominated by the materialist-reductionist philosophy. Rather, parapsychologists test the paranormal or transpersonal hypothesis empirically under tightly controlled conditions. The phenomena of clairvoyance, which literally means "clear seeing," is a feat of mental imagery that results in the "paranormal acquisition of information concerning an object or contemporary physical event ... [whereby] the information is assumed to derive directly from an external physical source ... and not from the mind of another person" (Thalbourne, 2003, p. 18).

One such clairvoyance-type category of research is known as *remote viewing* (or *remote perception*), which requires accurately describing the physical (usually visual) characteristics of a distant location by mental means only, without ever having visited the location. At one point during the 1990s both the CIA and the DIA in the United States joint-funded a $20million research project into remote viewing under the codename STARGATE, which returned highly significant results overall when reviewed by two independent scholars. Of which, one said the research provided good evidence of paranormal perception (Utts, 1995a, 1995b) whereas the other (particularly skeptical) scholar said that the highly significant results needed replicating (Hyman 1995). Other large-scale remote viewing research studies, however, have also returned positive findings (e.g., Targ 1994; Dunne & Jahn, 2003), so the evidence for genuine paranormal visual perception seems relatively good, albeit with a useful signal to noise ratio that is impracticably low. Further evidence for genuine paranormal mental imagery is also evident in reviews of research into dream ESP (Ullman, Krippner & Vaughan, 2002; Sherwood & Roe, 2003) and with research of image-guessing experiments into clairvoyance and "precognition" (literally "prior knowing," or seeing future events) (Honorton & Ferrari, 1989; Steinkamp, Milton & Morris, 1998). In such research, attempts are made to select a target image from among a range of decoy images based on the similarity of the selected image to the participant's mental imagery, either produced in dreams or through conscious intention. The participant is often in an altered state of consciousness in such research.

Returning to ayahuasca, the use of this mixture is frequently reported to be accompanied by out-of body experiences (e.g., Devereux, 2008) and ostensibly telepathic or clairvoyant visions (e.g., Luna & White, 2000), as is its chemical constituent DMT (Luke & Kittenis, 2005). For instance, the anthropologist Kensinger (1973, p. 12) reported that, "on the day following one ayahuasca party six of nine men informed me of seeing the death of my chai, "my mother's father." This occurred two days before I was informed by radio of his death." Surveys typically reveal that under the influence of psychedelic substances there is a distinct increase in the experience of paranormal events, such as ostensible clairvoyance and precognition, and out-of-body experiences (Luke, 2008d; Luke & Kittenis, 2005). Attempts to experimentally verify the genuine nature of this surveyed increase in psi brought about by psychedelics have so far been inconclusive when considered collectively — primarily due to poor methodology and a relatively small number of studies — however the results are at least suggestive of the genuine induction of psi with these substances (Luke, 2008d). Addressing the methodological problems of previous studies, research is currently underway to experimentally investigate the production of genuine precognitive mental imagery with the use of ayahuasca in a tightly controlled and systematic manner (Luke, 2009).

Contemporary Psychedelic-Assisted Therapy

Moving out of the ancient indigenous shamanic traditions and into the nascent Western scientific setting there has been some recent cultural transfer in the use of psychedelics for healing. Unlike shamanic treatment, however, the modern use of these substances has tended to focus primarily on treating only psychological and psychiatric problems, such as non-psychotic conditions like anxiety, depression and obsessive-compulsive disorder, and addictions, particularly to non-psychedelic drugs — psychedelic substances being non-addictive by definition (Grinspoon & Bakalar, 1998). The exception to this purely psychological treatment is the recent use of psychedelics in alleviating cluster headaches, which is speculated to be due to purely neurological causes (Sewell & Halpern, 2007). Such "Western" therapy with psychedelics began in earnest in the 1950s, following the discovery of LSD, and continued to grow until the late 1960s when global prohibition of psychedelics effectively stopped all therapy and research, although nearly 700 scientific publications on such psychedelic-assisted psychotherapy were produced in that period (Passie, 2007). A very slow and gradual renewal of that work began in the

1980's and research is now entering into a new "psychedelic renaissance" (Jerome, Mojeiko & Doblin, 2009).

There are many convergences and divergences between traditional shamanic treatment and modern psychedelic-assisted psychotherapy (Winkleman, 2007), but in terms of mental imagery the focus in the modern setting has often been on the production of psychological subject matter from the unconscious for use in forming the material substrate for classical psychotherapy. However, mystical and spiritual breakthroughs have been considered beneficial, particularly in treating substance abuse and immanent death-related anxiety (Passie, 2007), and the leading psychedelic psychotherapist of the 1960s and 1970s, Grof (2009), acknowledges the importance to therapy of transpersonal experiences, in which the individual feels that their "consciousness has expanded beyond the usual ego boundaries and the limitations of space and time" (p. 157). Such experiences regularly include psi phenomena and encounters with other entities (Grof, 2001, 2009). In such therapy, Grof (2001) would not only discuss with the patient the phenomena arising in their psyches, but would also encourage them to express their experiences in artistic forms, such as through paintings and mandala drawings. These were considered to have esthetic, cathartic, and documentary value, in addition to providing a deeper understanding of the session. Nevertheless, the earlier emphasis on transpersonal experiences, by psychedelic therapists like Grof, has seemingly shifted over the years to a more neutral and mundane medical tone focusing on the efficacy and effectiveness of the treatment and away from any non-material sounding factors, no doubt in order to gain crucial acceptance by the mainstream. Consequently the modern psychedelic therapy contexts appear increasingly divergent from their shamanic origins, despite the almost conclusive experimental evidence, much of it very recent, that genuine mystical experiences can and do occur with such substances (Doblin, 1991; Griffiths, Richards, McCann & Jesse, 2006; Griffiths, Richards, Johnson, McCann & Jesse, 2008; Pahnke, 1966).

Concluding Remarks

It has been shown that altered states of consciousness (such as via dreams or psychoactive substances) for the purpose of inducing mental imagery for healing have been used in both the ancient and modern world and across numerous cultures. The processes by which this healing has been said to occur, by those who have used such methods, often incorporate transpersonal elements, such as spirits and other mediating entities, and the transcendence of quotidian space and time. On the other hand, modern academics investigating these healing practices often assume a materialist-reductionist perspective that disregards the paranormal or transpersonal ontologies proposed by those engaging in these activities. This divergence in worldviews between the practitioners of these visionary healing arts and the academics who study them may rest on both ethnocentrism, on the behalf of the investigators, and what has been called *pragmacentrism*, which is theoretical speculation "based exclusively on experiences and observations made in ordinary states of consciousness" (Grof, 2001, p. 15).

As much as ethnographic fieldwork is supposedly the antidote to ethnocentrism, Tart's (1972, 2000) proposals for *state-specific sciences*— whereby the phenomenology of altered states are researched on their own terms— would seem a good starting point for combating the pragmacentrism inherent in Western approaches to the study of altered states. As Shanon (2003) notes, one cannot hope to talk knowingly about altered states if one has not experienced such states, just as much as one cannot hope to talk knowingly about music if one has not heard music. Disciplines such as parapsychology, transpersonal psychology and the emerging field of anthropology of consciousness appear more akin to a state-specific science than other fields, and the approach they constitute collectively would seem an open minded and sensitive means of investigating little-understood exceptional human experiences, such as those described in this chapter. Currently, the seeming occurrence of extradimensional, omnidirectional and X-ray-like percepts, genuine psi, and encounters with discarnate entities have not been sufficiently addressed by the mainstream scientific enterprise and constitute a range of exceptional phenomena arising from the shamanic experience that warrant further investigation.

Acknowledgments

Thanks to Etzel Cardeña for feedback on an earlier draft of this manuscript. Thanks also go to the Beckley Foundation, the Society for Psychical Research, the Parapsychological Association and the Parapsychology Foundation for funding the field psi experiments in South American healing rituals that provided the impetus for writing this chapter.

3

Excerpts of Intercorporeality: A Phenomenological Exploration of Energy Healing

CARL WILLIAMS, DIANE DUTTON
AND CHRIS BURGESS

Abstract

In this chapter, the authors discuss energy healing and present an alternative view of the healing process. Energy healing is largely seen from the received view of science as a dubious practice based upon pre-modern conceptions of the body and illness. Often employing a synthesis of subtle energy concepts, models of ethnophysiology and narrative approaches, it is seen as a placebo at best and quackery at worst. The authors present a different view of the energetic healing process as hinging upon intersubjectivity and inter-corporeality, and suggest that this kind of healing process can involve effective strategies for changing a person's lived experience of their illness. This perspective also has something important to say about how mind/body experiences are co-constituted. Using observational and interview data from a healing session, the processes and interactions involved and the strategies used by the healer to initiate change in the healee will be explored. These changes are made through a gradual sense of co-proprioception (a developing joint awareness between healer and healee about the body mind state of the healee) and a sense of inter-coherence (a movement towards a shared meaning which informs the body mind and provides an alternative stance on the problem that the healee is presenting with).

Energetic Frameworks of Healing

Much to the chagrin of skeptics (Colquhoun, 2009) and many mainstream medical practitioners (Ernst & White, 2000; Zollman & Vickers, 1999) public interest in energy healing seems to show no evidence of a decline. In fact there seems to be something of a dramatic expansion in energy therapies and a proliferation of practitioners. In terms of an overall explanatory framework, there are persistent underlying ideas which structure the practice and theory of energy therapies: that health is a natural process; that many illnesses derive from psychological origins which thwart the free flow of vital energy and create energetic blockages; and that the application of energetic healing techniques will remove these blockages, restoring a natural state of energetic flow and re-establishing health.

From a mainstream perspective, energy is seen as an outmoded framework for understanding health which draws on vitalistic theories considered redundant following the development of molecular biology. There are high levels of scepticism about some approaches in complementary and alternative medicine (Ernst, 2007; Lillienfield, Fowler, Lohr &Lynn, 2005), and there has even been a concerted effort by some to close down some university degree courses, such as those teaching about homeopathy (see Colquhoun, 2009). At the same time, however, there are new perspectives developing which place energy healing within the context of new holistic theories of physics (see for example, Weber, 1995). Ironically, it is perhaps this abstract mechanistic paradigm adopted by medical orthodoxy that guarantees that the concept of energy remains on the fringes of mainstream science, attracting the attention of those who are not enamored of such modernist frameworks. The concept of energy also has a natural appeal because it draws on lay theoretical and natural conceptual frameworks. People are well aware day-to-day of their subjective experiences of either possessing sufficient vitality (and being able to complete tasks and activities) or alternatively feeling drained of vitality and energy. There is some interest in capturing and documenting the role of subjective vitality in psychology (Gould, 1991; Ryan and Frederick, 1997) but largely this natural prehension of vitality or common sense (Heller-Roazen, 2007) is ignored in mainstream medicine. It is interesting to note that more formal concepts of energy which form the basis of modern discussions in physics drew metaphorically on the vigor that a person is aware of in their life (see Hoad, 1993).

This concept of energy is employed in most traditional cultures to describe the vivifying forces which enable good health (Edwards, 2008). The terms used often have etymological references to *breath* or *air* just as the terms *spirit* or *soul* do, indicating another possible reason for the dismissal of these kinds of ideas and practices. In Chinese medicine, which is probably the most well documented alternative approach to western medicine and physiology, there is a detailed account of energy. The term which corresponds to energy (or at least is commonly translated that way in English) is *Qi* 氣).

The ideogram is constructed from two characters which emphasize vaporous movement and a nutritive aspect. We will discuss this concept briefly because it informs a good number of energy healing modalities and is very pertinent to the case we will discuss shortly.

Qi is considered to be both energy and matter, or to be more precise, it is the pivot or hinge between both. It circulates in channels around the body, and points on these channels can be accessed through touch (acupressure) or through the insertion of fine steel needles (acupuncture). Each of the channels have some specific functions and relate to certain vital organs, however, ultimately they form an interconnected network which vivifies the body and is perhaps also responsible for informational changes in the body (Ho, 2008). Although this network of channels has been well documented in Asian medical practices for something like 5000 years there is no counterpart in western physiological accounts. There is an interesting difference in how western and eastern medical practitioners approached an understanding of the body, health and illness. Chinese medical practitioners assume that problems in these channels forewarn of physical illness and can be treated to offset its development. These problems (often experienced as indeterminate but subjectively significant sensations) are likely to be ignored as unimportant by western medical practitioners or attributed to a local structural problem such as nerve damage.

Ideas of energy based on Chinese medical theory have been absorbed into other alternative medical practices along with concepts from Indian yogic practices. Although there are some parallels between these different cultural products our discussion here will concentrate on the ethnophysiology of Chinese medicine and its employment in healing therapies such as thought field therapy (TFT) and emotional freedom technique (EFT). Callahan and Trubo (2001), by adding a good dose of field theory from physics to Chinese ethnophysiology, developed TFT to help with psychological problems such as phobias. Callahan found that by tapping a sequence of acupoints while thinking of the problem that was to be treated there was some amelioration of symptoms. This is typically gauged using the subjective units of distress scale (SUDS). Here the patient will attempt to assess the magnitude of their phobia by imagining themselves in the situation that provokes the phobia and measuring their distress on a scale from 0–10.

Typically, the tapping on each acupuncture point is accompanied by affirmations which are phrased specifically to reorient the attention of the patient towards a new way of envisaging the problem. The procedure is repeated until the SUD rating drops from a higher number to 0 or 1. Callahan reports high levels of success for these procedures in treatments for psychological problems such as phobias and PTSD. There is very little experimental evidence to support these claims. After complaining that journal editors were wary of accepting papers on TFT, Callahan enjoyed a non peer reviewed special issue on TFT courtesy of the *Journal of Clinical Psychology* in 2001 (Callahan, 2001). Responses to these papers were generally very critical, questioning whether this healing modality could work in any way other than that of a placebo. Typically, the results of such studies remain contested on the basis of lack of appropriate study design, standardized measures and long term follow-up.

The main problem with assessing the efficacy of healing modalities like TFT is that, like most complementary therapies, it is difficult to instantiate traditional double blind trials and to obtain more objective measures of a change in symptoms (Walach, Jonas & Lewith, 2003). The tendency to implement biomedical standards and approaches to assess traditional or alternative medical modalities reveals the modern western view of individuals existing in an almost Newtonian atomistic framework. A modernist view of the human strongly emphasizes the dualist nature of mind and body, subjectivity and objectivity. In biomedical practice subjective experience counts for little as diagnosis is more increasingly achieved through technological tests (e.g., Joyce, 2005). The patient him/herself is considered to play a minor role in bringing about health and is in a dependent relationship with the doctor responsible for them (Segal, 2005). In contrast to this dualistic approach, other philosophical perspectives such as phenomenology offer ways of bridging the abyss between the abstract concepts of subjective and objective.

An Embodied Approach
to the Healing Encounter

Merleau-Ponty notes that: "The communication or comprehension of gestures comes through a reciprocity of my intentions and the gestures of others, of my gestures and intentions discernible in the conduct of other people. It is as if the other person's intention inhabited my body and mine his. The gesture which I witness outlines an intentional object" (Merleau-Ponty, 1945/1962, p.185). This recognition of intercorporeality and intersubjectivity is a challenge to the conventional modern schemas of the self which tend to be atomistic and strongly bounded. While intercorporeality has been discussed in the disciplines of sociology (Weiss, 1998) and anthropology (Csordas, 1997, 2008) it has largely escaped the attention of psychologists except those following the more phenomenological approaches advocated by Merleau-Ponty (1945/1962), Heidegger (1927/1962) and Husserl (1913/1931). These approaches suggest that humans co-constitute their worlds and that social interactions may involve a merging of intention, action, thought and feeling which largely takes place preconsciously. A phenomenological framework provides an alternate view to "subjectivity as the description of the individual cogito" (Csordas, 2008) and stresses the roles of embodiment, social, cultural and environmental relationships in relation to the structuring of thought and perception. Within the holistic vision that frames energy healing there is an assumption that this sort of interpenetrability of intention takes place (see Jonas & Crawford, 2002).

Johnston and Barcan (2006) go as far as to suggest energetic therapies employ a model of the self and body which is inherently plural, consisting of different energetic levels and radically open to interaction or a state of interconnectiveness: — what we might consider as intercorporeality. Such models of the self and its relationships emphasize the embodied or incarnate nature of experience, and also its dynamic and indeterminate nature. The exploration of such subtle or intangible aspects of experience requires a more phenomenological approach, in which experience is characterized as being-in-the-world, co-constituted through the interactions of the self with others in a particular social and cultural context. This approach has already proved productive for the investigation of a range of holistic healing and self-cultivation practices, including yoga (Smith, 2007), qigong (Ots, 1994), and spiritual healing (Csordas, 1994, 1997). In the analysis presented here, we particularly draw on the work of Csordas (1988, 1994, 1997, 2008) in establishing a framework which situates embodiment at the heart of the subjective experience of healing, and which contextualizes the healing process as an expression of transformation and re-orientation of the self within a social and cultural context. From this perspective, the healing process acquires both structure and meaning as a result of its intersubjectivity; the bodily dialog between healer and patient functions as a transformative space within which the possibility of change may arise. Although phenomenology stands independent of objective science (see Garza, 2007), it is interesting to note that there is support for some of these phenomenological findings in the simulation and neuronal mirroring noted in neurological studies which has been linked to empathy ad intersubjectivity (Gallese & Lakoff, 2005; Gallese, 2006).

The Healer

Chris (69) has a background in business and is currently a director and national councilor for the Federation of Small Businesses. He has practiced martial arts since the age of 14, as well as qigong and acupressure for over 20 years. He currently runs his own business *Alterity* which specializes in stress and change management of the corporate sector. He also holds qualifications in hypnosis, Neuro-Linguistic Programming (NLP) and a range of other alternative therapies.

The Healees

Each of the five participants that took part in the study were recruited through Liverpool Hope University and were staff or students. Each of them had responded to a request for participants who had phobias or muscular problems (two types of problem in which Chris thought his healing techniques were particularly efficacious). We will examine the interactions of Chris the healer with one of the 5 healees who participated in the study. Jane (pseudonym) is 52 and asked to take part in the study hoping that she would be able to deal with a lifelong phobia of dentists. Following a childhood experience where she and her sister acted as models in a dentist school she has had an almost physical reaction to dental treatment, feeling nauseous even when faced with thinking about and imagining going to the dentist.

Method

After obtaining informed consent each participant was introduced to the healer, who worked with each of them for approximately 30 minutes. The healing interactions were observed in a observation laboratory and recorded on a dual camera CCTV and video system.

Semi-structured interviews focusing on the most memorable events in the session, and the participants' assessment of their feelings at the time and following the session, were carried out with the participants no more than 48 hours after their sessions. We used an adapted form of Brief Structured Recall (Elliot & Shapiro, 1988) to structure the interviews. This is a recording-assisted recall method and was developed primarily as a way of accessing clients' subjective thoughts and feelings following psychotherapeutic sessions; as such it is a useful way to analyze phenomenological data. A form of this method has been used successfully in earlier research by Csordas (1988) on experiences of Catholic Charismatic healing. In the context of replaying extracts of the video recording of the treatment, the interviewer asked the participant about their perceptions and thoughts at different times during the treatment process. The healer was also interviewed in the same way, using the video recordings as a prompt for clarifying intentions and actions.

The Healing Process

Observing the healing techniques used by Chris, we noted a process moving from developing rapport with the participants to evidencing therapeutic efficacy (see Figure 1). Initially the healer engaged in rapport development like any other practitioner; whether alternative or conventional. Upon recognizing the problem that concerned the participant the healer typically related it to his own experience, indicating that he, a patient or a member of his family had had similar experiences. He may also at this time reframe the problem in energetic terms, asking the participant to locate where in their body they had feelings of fear, anxiety or pain. He would employ the Chinese physiological model to relate their sensations to specific energetic areas of the body, either acupuncture channels or general energetic fields such as the sections of the body known as the three dantiens. Reframing would also sometimes involve the generation of analogical or allegorical representations of the problem in naturalistic or organic images. Along with physical touch (tapping acupoints), affirmation and suggestions these techniques would recur during the treatment process as ways of furthering the understanding between healer and healee and developing a co-constituted sense of the body and the current problem. We suggest the term *co-proprioception* for this development of joint awareness of the energetic basis of the healing encounter. With the development of co-proprioception there are likely to be moments of *intercoherence* where the healee starts to adopt the healer's assumption that the problem can be healed and a new symptom-free or symptom-reduced state can be adopted.

Starting the treatment process typically involved Chris tapping on a series of acupuncture points called an "algorithm" in the terminology of TFT and EFT. In synchrony with the tapping Chris had the participant repeat affirmations. These followed a particular pattern consistent with EFT practice but their context relied on the generation of novel phrases and images specific to the problems of each participant.

We have documented the general process of healing elsewhere (Williams, Dutton &Burgess, 2010) and here would like to focus more specifically on the

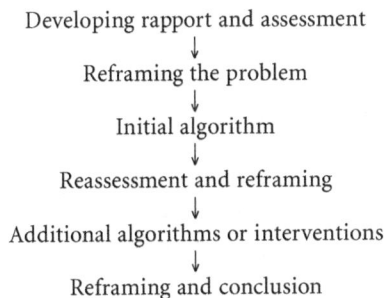

Developing rapport and assessment
↓
Reframing the problem
↓
Initial algorithm
↓
Reassessment and reframing
↓
Additional algorithms or interventions
↓
Reframing and conclusion

Figure 1. Representative stages of the healing process

main maneuvers used in the healing process. We argue that these maneuvers show that some of the efficacy of healing lies in the degree to which a healee or patient begins to accept the healer's view of the problem. Other conditions under which healing is efficacious involve the participant's experiences of spontaneous energy, and the extent to which they are prepared to negotiate further adaptation and change.

Talking about the Problem: Location and Form

Every consultation begins with some description of the ground to be covered, in terms of the history of a complaint, the relevance of the symptoms to day to day functioning and cognitive and emotional management of living with the problem. This mapping out of the problem reveals something of the patients conceptual understanding and perhaps encapsulates their general pattern of approaching life and engaging with their problem. This information grounds and shapes the healer's response to the patient's problem. A practitioner of any medical modality would naturally respond by representing the problem in terms of the conceptual system within which they operate. A "bad" arm would typically be reframed in western medicine as a structural problem, in terms of damaged bones, muscles or trapped nerves perhaps. Chinese medicine takes quite a different view from western medicine, emphasizing process over structure. The "bad arm" is perhaps a consequence of stagnation or congestion of qi and blood originating in initial trauma and worsened through subsequent stressing of the limb. Conveying the framework is important for joint negotiation of treatment and possible alleviation of the symptoms.

Chris as a healer uses relatively simple, naturalistic analogies to convey and structure his conceptual framework. A number of these analogies use spatial metaphors to indicate the location of the problem and emphasize the possibility of its relocation or removal. In this first example which took place in the initial consultation Chris identifies the automatic reactions of the brain (specifically the amygdala) as responsible for the maintenance of Jane's fear.

CHRIS: This works on *your* energy system, you have an energy system. Somewhere in the energy system something has got trapped about dentists. I tell you where it is trapped [points to forehead]. There is a thing here called the amygdala in the brain and that is an automatic fight or flight [system]. It is there to protect you ... it remembers [the trauma] as fear...

CHRIS: This dentist's room. Where is it?

JANE: Well, it's not here.

CHRIS: So where is it then?

JANE: It's in my mind.

CHRIS: It is your mind, yes.

CHRIS: This fear thing from years back, has got stuck in this [automatic] part of your mind ... it brings this horrible feeling back.

CHRIS: If I can shift it so that it's in your thinking part of your mind, so you think "dentists, so what?..." would that do you?

Identifying the locus of the phobia in terms of the brain and its natural functions frames the problem in terms of a lay psycho-physiological schema and opens up the possibility of removing it. Chris contrasts the "automatic" emotional nature of the amygdala with the "thinking part of the brain" and indicates that by "shifting" Jane's problem to this more rational part of the brain-mind, the problem might be resolved.

While tapping the sequence of points, Chris subsequently uses the image of fear as a block of ice melting, dripping, then flowing away and disappearing out to sea and over the horizon. These affirmations are repeated while Chris taps the acupuncture points. Jane is in a relaxed state and the rate at which she repeats affirmations seems to indicate that she is reacting in almost a hypnotized manner to these as verbal suggestions.

Another example occurs of Chris reframing Jane's problem later in the process. This time Chris likens the residual nature of Jane's childhood fear to a seed.

CHRIS: What it is ... you've got a seed and put it in the ground and it has grown and grown.... If you take the seed out and put it there, it can't grow, yeh? It's gone, finished, no fear, there's your fear gone.... If you leave a little bit in, a tiny bit there is a possibility of it growing....

The account is accompanied by gestures emphasizing the spatiality of the situation, the seed, when taken out, is placed by Chris at arms length to the side. The fear is a seed which can be located and moved outside the body-mind. However, a small fragment left in the body-mind is capable of re-establishing its influence.

Intercorporeality and Ethnophysiology

Communicating and negotiating the influence of the problem was also achieved by relating the location and form of the problem to the ethnophysiology of Chinese medicine — the acupuncture channels or meridians. The channels in Chinese medicine provide clues about local and distal problems, so headaches for instance can be treated with foot acupressure or acupuncture because the liver channel (which is often implicated in headaches) originates on the feet and tracks up the body, culminating at a point on the vertex of the head.

In her communication with Chris, Jane displayed some interesting gestures which seemed to provide Chris with useful information about how to proceed with treatment. These gestures also illustrate the way in which intercorporeality structures the exchange and develops through the course of the encounter.

When asked to describe her problem Jane reveals that when she thinks about going to the dentists, she experiences a paralyzing fear, accompanied by a sensation rising from her hands to her chest region. Chris immediately explains that there is a blockage in the chest region. As Jane attempts to ascertain the level of stress associated with thinking about a visit to the dentist she places her hands together close to her chest and moves them slightly to and fro, as if weighing up the sensation. This gesturing is a spontaneous somatic communication of where the problem resides; the fear is experienced bodily by Jane as a sensation in the chest, and verbally represented by Chris as trapped energy in the chest area.

Initially Chris identifies the problem more specifically with a blockage of the lung meridian or channel which runs on the radial aspect of the arm through the armpit and into the chest cavity. The feeling that Jane experiences when thinking about visiting the dentist ascends along the arms from the hands and seems to settle around the chest region. In classical Chinese medicine, each of the vital organs have an association with particular emotions. The lung is associated with sadness and Jane's symptoms of the ascending sensation along the arms to the chest match the route of the lung channel.

When beginning treatment Chris moves immediately to massage acupressure points on the hands, initially he uses the point named *LieQue* (Lung 7) on the radial aspect of the wrist. He massages *ZhongFu* (Lung 1) on the upper chest underneath the clavicle. Finally he massages both *ShaoShang* (Lung 11) points on the thumb, vigorously massaging these for a few seconds while looking in a silence at Jane. As Jane's sensations are experienced in the upper dantien (upper chest region of the body) using the lung acupuncture points on the thumb helps to move trapped energy in this area.

Chris then pulls his hands quickly away and synchronizes this with an outbreath. We see in this sequence a number of examples of the intercorporeality of the healer and healee in co-constituting the blocked energy, its path, and its removal from the channels. The *drawing out of energy* movement is common in clinical qigong practice (Johnson, 2000) and allows the practitioner to physically imagine and engage in the process of removing the energy, as well as indicating to the patient that something is being taken away. The gestures enact and co-constitute the location of blocked energies and the possibility of their removal.

Outbreathing while moving hands away from the body ensures that the negative energy is expelled from the healer as well. This technique is used in classical acupuncture when pathogenic qi is removed from a channel. It is likely to be an ancient approach to seeing illness as something that is foreign and invades the body (Williams, 2008) and which can be removed through this energetic exchange. It is also an example of the ancient assumption that energy and breath are corporeally equivalent.

Reaching Intersubjectivity: Towards a Co-constitution of Healing Efficacy?

The outline of the healing encounter as described above reveals a process by which social interactions within the healing exchange lead to intersubjectivity (defined here as an empathic sharing of cognitions and experiences) and subsequent healing efficacy. These shared cognitions and experiences are mediated in this study by a combination of gestures, narratives, image-based analogies and touch. The concept of "energy" is used as a way of grasping and communicating these shared impressions. However, energy is also shown to have a joint somatic presence, manifesting as spontaneous experiences which are focused upon for feedback about the problem and its alleviation through the healing process.

These changes in body-mind state influenced by gesture, touch, verbal reframing and affirmations occur as a result of a re-orientation of the problem the participant presented with. All participants in this study experienced a substantial drop in reported units of distress and in two cases (both participants who presented with phobias) there was a recognition that the problem seemed to have gone altogether. Checks with these two participants revealed that even a number of weeks later the effects of the session had been retained. In follow-up interviews the two male healees were less convinced that Chris had had an influence on their muscular problems, although both had provided low ratings on the scale by the end of the session. One of the two had been more skeptical of the healing event, admitting that he found the person of Chris as a healer to be quite different from what he had expected. These issues present an important insight into the success or failure of energetic healing and how this is mediated through the characteristics of the social situation.

We note a general process in the healing encounter which illustrates a gradual development of intersubjectivity and a growth of co-proprioception (the development of shared awareness about the patient's body and emotional state) through to the achievement of inter-coherence (the development of a state of shared coherence in terms of awareness of subjective experience). This is achieved through high levels of rapport, the various strategies and maneuvers used by the healer and the resulting spontaneous, and often shared, experiences of changed energy. The healee may feel somatic changes in the previously blocked energetics in terms of movement or quality of the sensations and the healer also feels changes in his experience of massaging or tapping the healee. On some occasions the healer also verbally noted changes in the location and flow of energy when he heard a cracking sound issuing from the healee's body, emphasizing to him that the healee's energy had moved.

This growing sense of intersubjectivity seems to play an important role in determining the efficacy of the healing process. When a healee was less involved in co-proprioception and inter-coherence it was also less likely that they would experience a reduction in levels of subjective distress. They were also less likely to agree that the problem they presented with was substantially changed for the better. An example of this lack of inter-coherence was seen in the culmination of an algorithmic tapping sequence, in which Chris gradually and gently presses down on the healee's hand to move it downwards in co-ordination with a drop in verbal tempo. One healee seemed to resist this, indicating perhaps a non-acceptance of this somatic *re-orientation*; in other words, the process of co-proprioception was only partial in this instance. With reference to this example, Chris suggested that this was a form of resistance and we interpreted that this could be a factor that mitigated the efficacy of the healing for some clients. In the case of other participants, Chris' suggestions were picked up quickly and a range of sensations of subjective energy accompanied the touch and suggestion, leading to the participant's recognition of changes and movements in spontaneous energy experiences.

In EFT, the healing strategies, actions and gestures are explicitly coordinated with the intention of bringing together what is conceptualized as a fractured self; a state in which somatic and mental aspects of the person are not communicating effectively. This new state of coordination, achieved through verbal, imaginal and gestural acts is a result of a relational process, the effectiveness of which is revealed by the extent to which both healer and healee share in the somatic and interpretational aspects of experienced energy. It is this empathic "merging-with" the bodily awareness of another (Finlay, 2005) that is the instrument by which the transformation of energy in the healing encounter occurs. This "melting of boundaries" has also been addressed from another perspective in terms of weak quantum theory (see Walach, Schmidt, Schneider, Seiter & Bosch, 2002). The meaningfulness of the healing event, including an interpretation of its efficacy, is therefore played out in the bodily dialog between patient and healer, and is inevitably structured by the patient-healer relationship.

The means by which we can understand the process of transformation in energetic healing lies not in the polarization of the roles of belief and experience; such a dualism merely artificially splits subjective and objective phenomena, and tells us little about the specifics of how energetic healing is experienced. Rather, healing involves a transformation in the way in which the self orients to the world — its efficacy lies in a change in the phenomenological experience of the person. As Csordas (1997) expresses it: "The recognition of healing is a modulation of orientation in the world, so that one monitors one's symptoms and responds to them by modifying one's activities. This reorientation not only preserves but actually constitutes the healing ... the critical factor is a specific self process, the modulation of somatic attention." (*p.70*).

Conclusions

After close observation of the healing techniques used in this study it is possible to see that the concept of energy is used as a way of mediating and communicating emotional, cognitive and physiological changes in the body-mind state. While it is possible that at some stage it may be technically possible to measure and record subtle energies, at the current level of knowledge, the concept still contributes a good deal to our understanding about how energetic healing may occur. Energy in this context is a signifying and proprioceptive system between healer and healee that is fundamentally phenomenological, embodied and shared. It is perhaps also important to recognize the experiential immediacy of the phenomenon of energy within the healing context; its understanding is not served well by attempts to measure aspects of the experience at the expense of the whole.

4

The Function of Religious Beliefs and Practices: Buffering the Impact of Exposure to Traumatic Events

EVE BINKS

Abstract

This chapter discusses the psychology of religion, with a particular focus on how religious beliefs impact on psychological well-being. Previous research has demonstrated a clear relationship between religious involvement and both physical health and psychological well-being. Religiosity may play a role in the protection from or the reduction of psychological disorders, or stabilizing individual and group identity. Pargament (1997) reasoned that religion and religious involvement may protect psychological and physiological health against the impact of stress and function as a coping mechanism. The author describes a research project which aimed to assess the role of religion as a mechanism for coping with traumatic events, with a specific focus on political violence in Northern Ireland. This country is divided at an individual level by cultural religion and at a societal level by civil religions. This project explored the function of religious beliefs in a society in conflict, focusing on religious beliefs and practices, exposure to traumatic events (as political violence) and psychological well-being (as measured by non-pathological dissociation) among the Catholic and Protestant communities in Northern Ireland as compared to a control group.

Introduction

Although the area of religion has been present in psychology since before the early work of Freud (1927), it is only since the mid 1950's that there has been an empirical approach to the psychology of religion (Hood, Spilka, Hunsberger & Gorsuch, 1996). Researchers such as Beit-Hallahmi and Argyle (1997), Wulff (1997), Smart (1996) and Maltby and Day (2003) have all made attempts at furthering knowledge and understanding of the area.

Although Freud and Freudian psychologists, maintain that people turning to God in search of the meaning of life (and death) is an example of their striving to locate the wisdom of a father-figure to help them cope with misgivings, Freud and his disciples have been unable to provide any detail with regard to the reasons that people frequently do find the answers they are seeking in religion. Freudians provide no detail explaining why these answers, when located, are fulfilling and, for the individuals and communities involved, convincing.

Freud (1923) continued to explore the possible origins of religious belief and suggested that it serves as a defense mechanism, which helps individuals cope with psychological conflict. Freud continued that if individuals did not have religion to utilize as a defense mechanism then there would be an otherwise inevitable development of neuroses. Freud coupled this defense mechanism concept with a fear of death, suggesting that one of the biggest psychological conflicts faced by individuals is that which arises between the survival instinct and the knowledge that death is a certainty.

However, although fear of death would seem a rational, even likely, starting point for many religious individuals, there remains some doubt about the extent to which fear of death is responsible for religious beliefs. A number of studies, particularly in the USA (e.g., Nelson & Cantrell, 1980), indicate that society as a whole communicates very little fear of death for the majority of their lives but instead realize that death is inevitable and, consequently, fear of death, according to Nelson and Cantrell, usually comes only when death is immanent.

However, Gershuny and Thayer (1999) attest that a fear concerning loss of control may occur in individuals who experience trauma and that these individuals, because of their lack or loss of control peritrauma, may be fearful of losing control in future. This fear would not be apparent only at the time of the event, but also at varying degrees after the event and consequently a rationalization of their mortality would be occurring at times other than when death is immanent. As a consequence, for these individuals religion may be an effective defense mechanism for dealing with the fear of loss of control and death.

Although some studies suggest that individuals, on the whole, experience little death anxiety, it is important that this idea is not dismissed completely. A number of studies (e.g., Williams & Cole, 1968; Feifel, 1974) have indicated that individuals do have a significant level of unconscious death anxiety whereby an ego defense mechanism may aid coping.

According to Price and Snow (1998), healthy dissociation may be observed as a "process in which the individual maintains the integrity of the self while transcending the physical reality of the mundane" (*p*.260). In terms of the relationship between dissociation and religion, it has been suggested that religion often provides the triggers for normal, non-pathological dissociative experiences (Dorahy, Unpublished Manuscript). Moreover, Price and Snow (1998) argue that all religious services are characterized by dissociation in some way and that religious dissociation plays an integral part in experiencing faith. Dorahy and Lewis (2001) continue that dissociative states which are often induced by this ritualistic behavior often play an important role in religious celebration as less resistance is made to the religious suggestions which strengthen the beliefs. If it is the case that dissociation is indeed induced by such practice effects, it has been suggested that individuals with "rigid" religious beliefs will experience greater dissociation during their lives than those without these beliefs (Dorahy & Lewis, 2001). Counts (1990) continues that trance-like behaviors which are sometimes witnessed in "high demand" religious movements also act as a cue for an induced dissociative state and in terms of understanding the phenomena of dissociation in a religious setting it is that shift from a normal state to a dissociative state that is often aided by the presence of some "trigger stimuli" (Dorahy, unpublished manuscript).

In his work on dissociation, Schumaker (1992) has concluded that heightened levels of suggestibility are commensurate with dissociative states. Schumaker suggests that this is because, during dissociation, higher order executive functions are not cognitively occurring whereas under non-dissociative circumstances, irrational or inconsistent information is disregarded by these cognitive processes. Therefore information suggested to a non-dissociating individual may be criticized and disregarded whereas the dissociating person may accept these ideas because they are not being subjected to close cognitive scrutiny. Dorahy, Schumaker and Lewis (1997) and Dorahy, Lewis and Schumaker (1998) have supported the theory that the appropriate context (religious worship) coupled with the appropriate stimuli (religious suggestion) results in a dissociative state which operates as a way of strengthening convictions to religious principles (Dorahy, unpublished manuscript).

In terms of dissociation in a religious setting, dissociative cues consist of external stimuli and the psychological state induced by these stimuli which leads to a dissociative state or experience (Dorahy, unpublished manuscript). In addition to this, it is critical to understand that dissociative states in religious settings are induced not only by these external stimuli but also by the presence of a psychological environment which is dissociation accommodating (Dorahy, unpublished manuscript).

If, as Spiegel (1988) suggests, dissociation is responsible for a fragmentation of the self, this could explain Dorahy's (unpublished manuscript) suggestion that group cohesion is aided by dissociation and helps provide individuals with a sense of attachment with others. In terms of dissociation in a religious setting, dissociative states "make it possible to enter more fully into the experience of faith and continue that experience so that faith is nurtured" (Price & Snow, 1998, p. 259).

It has been further suggested that to maintain mental health, a manipulation of reality is necessary in order to make events fit with existing personal and cultural frameworks and further that, in terms of religion, religious beliefs constitute this adaptive manipulation or reality regulation (Schumaker, 1995). Indeed, increased religious attitudes and belief scores are often associated with improved mental health (e.g., Batson & Ventis, 1992; Donahue, 1985; Dorahy, Lewis, Schumaker, Sibiya, Akuamoah-Boateng & Duke, 1998). In addition, Schumaker (1992b) concluded that non-religious people experience significantly more psychological disturbance than their religious counterparts.

The relationship between religion and mental health has been the focus of much research in recent years (e.g., Maltby & Lewis, 1997; Maltby, Lewis & Day, 1999; Levin & Chatters, 1998) with much of the research suggesting a positive correlation between religiosity and psychological well-being. McCullough, Hoyt, Larson, Koenig and Thoresen (2000) have further suggested that there is a relationship between mortality and religiosity, with those individuals who demonstrate little religious involvement being less likely to be alive at the time of a follow-up study than those who demonstrated high levels of religious involvement. That said, researchers such as Batson, Schoenrade, and Ventis (1993) and O'Connor, Cobb and O'Connor (2003) conducted similar research and concluded that there is no such relationship between religious involvement and mortality.

However, as Francis et al. (2004) respond, the research evidence is "more strongly weighted in favor of finding a positive relationship between religiosity and health than in finding either a negative relationship or the absence of a significant relationship" (p. 486). In addition to this, Francis et al. continue that there are over 250 published studies (see Levin & Schiller, 1987) which demonstrate the positive association between religiosity and health, including studies which report religiosity as a protector against cancer (e.g. Berkel & deWaard, 1983) and "all cause mortality (e.g., Comstack & Partridge, 1972; Strawbridge, Cohen, Shema & Kaplan, 1997)" (p. 486).

Although findings in the area are, at best, inconsistent, it is important to understand the reasons for such a correlation, should one exist. Pargament (1997) reasons that religion and religious involvement may protect psychological and physiological health against the impact of stress, indicating that religion may cause a modification of the processes involved in stress appraisal. Thus Pargament suggests that religiosity may be interpreted as a coping process.

In 1987, Rose identified Northern Ireland as one of the most religious countries in the western world and if the suggestions made regarding the links between religion and dissociation are correct (e.g., Price & Snow, 1998; Schumaker, 1995) then there is strong reason to believe that the population of Northern Ireland would dissociate on a greater level than those populations indigenous to other countries. In addition to this, given the social and political unrest by which Northern Ireland has been characterized in recent times, it has often provided a natural environment for assessment of responses to trauma (Cairns & Darby, 1998).

The "Troubles" in Northern Ireland have been estimated to be responsible for in excess of 3,500 deaths and for injuries to over 30,000 people (Cairns, Wilson, Gallagher & Trew, 1995; Wilson & Cairns, 1996). In addition, it has been suggested that approximately 10 percent of the population have had relatives killed as a result of the political violence, while 50 percent know someone who has been killed (Smith, 1987). Wilson and Cairns (1992) indicate that as a result of the strong community ties that exist in Northern Ireland, the psychological effects of the "Troubles" "extend far beyond the immediate relatives of the victims" (p. 247). As a result of this, and the assertion that the violence associated with the "Troubles" has failed to be isolated or predictable, researchers have suggested that the majority of people in Northern Ireland are psychologically affected by the political and societal instability which exists there (Cairns et al., 1995; Wilson & Cairns, 1992; Wilson & Cairns, 1996).

Dorahy et al. (2003) determined that in the Northern Irish population, higher non-pathological dissociation scores were correlated with direct exposure to political violence while age, moral standards and perceived impact of trauma were identified as significant predictors of non-pathological dissociation. In terms of the perceived impact of trauma, Dorahy et al. (2003) suggest that at a non-clinical level, the perception of certain events as traumatic could be an "important cognitive — developmental variable for a dissociative coping or dissociative defense style" (p. 18). However, as Irwin (1998) and Spiegel (1986) point out, this traumatic perception possibly works to predispose the individual to maladaptive dissociative tendencies if accompanying conditions are apparent. However, while Dorahy et al. (2003) acknowledge this suggestion they continue that "adherence to strict standards" may actually serve to reduce susceptibility to dissociation at the non-clinical level (p. 18).

The current research aims to assess the strength of religious beliefs in Northern Ireland and the function of these religious beliefs in the Province.

It is hypothesized that; (i) the Northern Irish population will report higher levels of direct and indirect exposure to traumatic events; (ii) there will be significant associations between religiosity and non-pathological dissociation; (iii) there will be significant associations between specific religious practices and non-pathological dissociation; (iv) there will be significant associations between religious orientations and exposure to traumatic events; and (v) there will be significant associations between specific religious beliefs and practices and exposure to traumatic events.

Methodology

Participants

Participants were 296 opportunity-sampled respondents. Of these, 179 were members of the Northern Irish population. Ages for these respondents ranged from 18–42 years, with a mean age of 21.52 years. Of the 179 members of the Northern Irish population, 55 were male and 124 were female, 124 were Catholic and 48 were Protestant.

177 respondents made up the English control group. Of these, all were born and were permanent residents in England. Ages of these respondents ranged from 17–62 years with a mean age of 26.92 years. Of the 177 members of the English control group, 55 were male and 122 were female.

Materials

Religious orientations were measured using the Credal Assent Scale (King, 1967) and the Age Universal I-E Religious Orientation Scale (Gorsuch and Venable, 1983). The Credal Assent Scale is a measure of religious orthodoxy and the Age Universal I-E Religious Orientation Scale is a measure of Allport and Ross' (1967) intrinsic and extrinsic religious orientations, at a reading level that is appropriate for adolescents as well as adults. The Credal Assent Scale has a Cronbach's Coefficient Alpha of .95 for the current sample while the Intrinsic and Extrinsic subscales have Cronbach's Coefficient Alpha's of .90 and .76 respectively for the current sample. Responses to items on both the Credal Assent Scale and the Age Universal I-E Scale were measured using a 7-point Likert Scale which ranged from 1 (strongly disagree), through 4 (neither agree nor disagree), to 7 (strongly agree).

Psychological well-being was measured by assessing dissociative experiences. These were measured using the Dissociative Experiences Scale (DES)

(Bernstein & Putnam, 1986). The DES is a 28-item self-report measure, which includes items ranging from non-pathological to pathological dissociation. Respondents indicate on a continuum ranging from 0–100 the percentage of the time that certain experiences apply to them. For example: "Some people find that they are sometime able to ignore pain." The factor structure of the DES indicates that there are 4 discrete components; (i) Absorption / derealisation; (ii) Depersonalisation; (iii) Segment amnesia, and (iv) In situ amnesia. The DES has a Cronbach's Coefficient Alpha of .86 for the current sample. For the purposes of the present study, respondents were assessed only on the 12 absorption/derealisation items.

Direct and indirect exposure to traumatic events were measured using questions taken from the Irish Social Mobility Survey (1973), the Social Attitudes Survey (1978), the Social Identity Survey (1995) and the Northern Ireland Referendum and Election Survey (1998) (Hayes & McAllister, 2000) which asked respondents to indicate whether they had, for example, been present when a riot or confrontation took place. For the English control group, questions were subject to minor modifications where necessary in order to assess direct and indirect exposure to traumatic events.

Results

Table 1: Descriptive Statistics to Show the Mean Scores for Religious Orientations of the Northern Irish population and the English Control Group

Group	Intrinsic religiosity	Extrinsic religiosity	Religious orthodoxy
Northern Irish sample	36.38 (10.69) N=171	40.35 (9.32) N=169	36.88 (10.21) N= 166
Northern Irish Catholic sample	36.58 (10.12) N=124	40.87 (8.34) N=124	37.03 (9.92) N=121
Northern Irish Protestant sample	36.91 (12.25) N=45	39.09 (10.87) N=42	37.64 (10.77) N=45
English control group	28.14 (11.97) N=97	36.63 (11.73) N=95	27.30 (11.29) N=127

(Standard deviations are in parentheses)

Descriptive statistics indicate that the Northern Irish population report higher levels of intrinsic religiosity, extrinsic religiosity and religious orthodoxy than the members of the English control group. Additionally, descriptive statistics indicate that the Northern Irish Catholic population exhibit higher levels of extrinsic religiosity, while their Protestant counterparts exhibit higher levels of intrinsic religiosity and religious orthodoxy.

Table 2: Descriptive Statistics to Show Mean
Scores for Direct and Indirect Exposure to Traumatic
Events for Members of the Northern Irish Population
and Members of the English Control Group

Group	N	Direct exposure to traumatic events	Indirect exposure to traumatic events	Overall exposure to traumatic events
Northern Irish sample	172	1.92 (1.18)	3.36 (1.87)	3.38 (2.03)
Northern Irish Catholic sample	121	1.80 (1.22)	3.36 (1.94)	3.12 (1.92)
Northern Irish Protestant sample	45	1.80 (1.21)	2.80 (1.78)	3.62 (2.19)
English control group	175	1.28 (1.16)	2.33 (1.74)	1.11 (.79)

(Standard deviations are in parentheses)

Descriptive statistics indicate that the Northern Irish population have considerably higher levels of exposure to traumatic events than the English control group. Within the Northern Irish population, the Catholic cohort reported higher levels of indirect exposure to trauma, which the Protestant group reported higher overall exposure.

Table 3: Descriptive Statistics to Show Mean
Scores for Levels of Dissociation for Members
of the Northern Irish Population
and the English Control Group

Group	N	Mean Dissociative experiences
Northern Irish sample	171	47.09 (18.77)
Northern Irish Catholic sample	123	47.32 (19.05)
Northern Irish Protestant sample	47	47.76 (18.42)
English control group	177	54.46 (19.40)

(Standard deviations are in parentheses)

Descriptive statistics indicate that the English control group report higher levels of dissociation than their Northern Irish Catholic and Protestant counterparts, with the Northern Irish Protestants reporting higher levels of dissociative experiences than the Northern Irish Catholics in the current study.

Exposure to Traumatic Events

Exposure to traumatic events for the Northern Irish population and the control group were initially analyzed using a Multivariate Analysis of Variance

(MANOVA). This analysis indicated that the differences between the Northern Irish population and control group were significant (Wilks' λ =.693, F =62.01, p<0.001, partial η^2 =.307). Further investigation revealed that there are significant differences between group effects for direct exposure to traumatic events (F (1, 295) =18.50, p<0.001, partial η^2 =.042), indirect exposure to traumatic events (F (1, 295) =24.34, p<0.001, partial η^2 =.055), and overall exposure to traumatic events (F (1, 295) =173.72, p<0.001, partial η^2 =.292).

For direct exposure to traumatic events, there is a significant difference between the English control group (M=1.28, SD=1.16) and the Northern Irish population (M=1.92, SD=1.18) (p<0.001), For indirect exposure to traumatic events, there is a significant difference between the English control group (M=2.33, SD=1.74) and the Northern Irish population (M=3.36, SD=1.87) (p<0.001), For overall exposure to traumatic events, there is a significant difference between the English control group (M=1.11, SD=.79) and the Northern Irish population (M=3.38, SD=2.03) (p<0.001).

MANOVA analysis also indicated that there are significant differences between the English control group, the Northern Irish Catholic population, and the Northern Irish Protestant population (Wilks' λ =.657, F (2, 286) =31.44, p<0.001, partial η^2 =.189) in terms of exposure to traumatic events. Further investigation revealed that there are significant between group effects for direct exposure to traumatic events (F (2, 286) =9.34, p<0.001, partial η^2 =.044), indirect exposure to traumatic events (F (2, 286) =14.02, p<0.001, partial η^2 =.065), and for overall exposure to traumatic events (F (2, 286) =91.10, p<0.001, partial η^2 =.310), with post hoc (Tukey HSD) comparisons indicating that:

(i) For direct exposure to traumatic events, the differences are significant between the English control group (M=1.28, SD=1.16) and the Northern Irish Catholic population (M=1.80, SD=1.22) (p<0.001), and between the English control group (M=1.28, SD=1.16) and the Northern Irish Protestant population (M=1.80, SD=1.21) (p<0.001), but not between the Northern Irish Catholic (M=1.80, SD=1.22) and Protestant (M=1.80, SD=1.21) populations (p>0.05);

(ii) For indirect exposure to traumatic events, there are significant differences between the English control group (M=2.33, SD=1.74) and the Northern Irish Catholic (M=3.36, SD=1.94) populations (p<0.001), but not between the English control group (M=2.36, SD=1.74) and the Northern Irish Protestant population (M=2.80, SD=1.78) (p>0.05) or between the Northern Irish Catholic (M=3.36, SD=1.94) and Protestant (M=2.80, SD=1.78) groups (p>0.05);

(iii) For overall exposure to traumatic events, there are significant differences between the English control group (M=1.11, SD=.79) and the Northern Irish Catholic population (M=3.12, SD=1.92) (p<0.001), and between the English control group (M=1.11, SD=.79) and the Northern Irish Protestant group (M=3.62, SD=2.19) (p<0.001), but not between the Northern Irish Catholic (M=3.12, SD=1.92) and Protestant (M=3.62, SD=2.19) groups (p>0.05).

Dissociation and Religious Orientation

For the Northern Irish population, multiple regression analysis indicated that there were no significant associations between level of dissociation and religious orientation (R^2 =.002, F (3, 144) =.115, p>0.05). The multiple regression model indicated that dissociation was not significantly predicted by the predictor variables of Intrinsic religious orientation (ϐ =.019, p>0.05), Extrinsic religious orientation (ϐ =.027, p>0.05), or religious orthodoxy (ϐ =.016, p>0.05).

For the Northern Irish Catholic population, multiple regression analysis indicated that there were no significant associations between level of dissociation and religious orientation (R^2 =.021, F (3, 121) =1.070, p>0.05). The multiple regression model indicated that dissociation was not significantly predicted by the predictor variables of Intrinsic religious orientation (ϐ =.095, p>0.05), Extrinsic religious orientation (ϐ =.034, p>0.05), or religious orthodoxy (ϐ =.045, p>0.05).

For the Northern Irish Protestant population, multiple regression analysis indicated that there were no significant associations between level of dissociation and religious orientation (R^2 =.034, F (3, 36) =.418, p>0.05). The multiple regression model indicated that dissociation was not significantly predicted by the predictor variables of Intrinsic religious orientation (ϐ =.058, p>0.05), Extrinsic religious orientation (ϐ =.026, p>0.05), or religious orthodoxy (ϐ =-.238, p>0.05).

For the Control sample, multiple regression analysis indicated that there were no significant associations between levels of dissociation and religious orientation (R^2=.010, F (3, 78) =.264, p>0.05). The multiple regression model indicated that dissociation was not significantly predicted by the predictor variables of Intrinsic religious orientation (ϐ =-.020, p>0.05), Extrinsic religious orientation (ϐ =.029, p>0.05), or religious orthodoxy (ϐ =.100, p>0.05).

Dissociation and Specific Religious Beliefs and Practices

In order to assess the effect of specific religious practices on levels of dissociation, further statistical analyses were performed.

For the Northern Irish population, multiple regression analysis indicated that there were significant associations between the level of dissociation and specific religious practices (R^2 =.067, F (4, 157)= 2.81, p<0.05). The multiple regression model indicated that dissociation was significantly predicted by spending time in private thought and prayer ($ɓ$ =.327, $p<0.01$), and by living ones life according to religious beliefs ($ɓ$ =-.324, $p<0.01$).

For the Northern Irish Catholic population, multiple regression analysis indicated that there were significant associations between the level of dissociation and specific religious practices (R^2 =.059, F (4, 120) =2.56, $p<0.05$). The multiple regression model indicated that dissociation was significantly predicted by living ones life according to religious beliefs ($ɓ$ =-.230, $p<0.05$), and by basing ones approach to life on religious beliefs ($ɓ$ =.219, $p<0.05$), but not by spending time in private thought and prayer ($ɓ$ =.188, $p>0.05$), or by preferred frequency of church attendance ($ɓ$ =-.151, $p>0.05$).

For the Northern Irish Protestant population, multiple regression analysis indicated that there were no significant associations between the level of dissociation and specific religious practices (R^2 =.079, F (4, 38) =.81, $p>0.05$). The multiple regression model indicated that dissociation was not significantly predicted by spending time in private thought and prayer ($ɓ$ =.393, $p>0.05$), by living ones life according to religious beliefs ($ɓ$ =-.234, $p>0.05$), by basing ones approach to life on religious beliefs ($ɓ$ =-.215, $p>0.05$), or by preferred frequency of church attendance ($ɓ$ =-.022, $p>0.05$).

Exposure to Traumatic Events
and Religious Orientations

The relationships between exposure to traumatic events and religious orientations were assessed using a Pearson's Product Moment Correlations Coefficient. These analyses concluded that there was a significant positive correlation between indirect exposure to traumatic events and an extrinsic religious orientation for the Northern Irish Catholic population (r =.162, $p<0.05$), and significant negative correlations between indirect exposure to traumatic events and an intrinsic religious orientation (r = -.211, $p<0.05$) and overall exposure to traumatic events and an intrinsic religious orientation (r = -.207, $p<0.05$) for the English control group. All other associations failed to reach significance ($p>0.05$).

Exposure to Traumatic Events
and Specific Religious Practices.

The relationships between direct, indirect, and overall exposure to traumatic events and specific religious practices (spending time in private thought and prayer, living life according to religious beliefs, basing one's whole approach to life on religious beliefs, and preferred frequency of church attendance) were investigated for the Northern Irish population. All associations, for all Northern Irish populations in the current study, failed to reach significance ($p > 0.05$).

For members of the English control group, it was determined that there are significant negative correlations between indirect exposure to traumatic events and time spent in private thought and prayer ($r = -.206$, $p < 0.05$), between overall exposure to traumatic events and time spent in private thought and prayer ($r = -.231$, $p < 0.05$), and between overall exposure to traumatic events and basing one's whole approach to life on religion ($r = -.196$, $p < 0.05$). All other correlations for the English control group failed to reach significance ($p > 0.05$).

Discussion

From analysis of the data it is apparent that partial support may be offered to the hypotheses: (i) the Northern Irish population reported significantly higher levels of direct and indirect exposure to traumatic events than the control group; (ii) there were no significant associations between religiosity and dissociation for any of the current samples; (iii) there were significant associations between specific religious practices and dissociation for members of the Northern Irish Catholic population; (iv) there were significant associations between religious orientations and exposure to traumatic events for members of the Northern Irish Catholic population and members of the English control group; and (v) there were some significant associations between specific religious beliefs and practices and exposure to traumatic events for members of the English control group. Support is offered to these findings from a variety of theories from previous research.

Rose (1987) suggested that Northern Ireland is one of the most religious countries in the western world and current findings would appear to indicate support for this. In addition, Demerath (2000) suggested that Northern Ireland is the European country with the highest levels of religious participation and this would also appear to be supported by the current findings: of the 179 members of the Northern Irish population surveyed, 35 percent indicated that they would prefer to attend church once a week or more, while only 2 percent of the English respondents indicated that this would be their preference. The majority of English participants (49 percent) indicated that they would prefer to attend church "a few times a year or less." This would appear to lend support to Demerath's suggestion that the phenomenon of cultural religion exists in Northern Ireland, whereby both the Catholic and Protestant communities remain entangled in religious legacies which are transferred from generation to generation.

Research presented by Gershuny and Thayer (1999) also appears to have been supported by the current research. They suggest that individuals with experience of traumatic events are more likely to turn to religion as this may help them answer questions related to their mortality and what happens after death. The current findings indicate that members of the Northern Irish population have been exposed, both directly and indirectly, to significantly more traumatic events than their English counterparts and also have higher levels of religious conviction, and therefore it would seem likely that they would have a greater need to answer questions relating to death which have been raised by these traumatic experiences.

Previous research would suggest that exposure to trauma is linked to poorer psychological well-being, for example, the onset and conclusion of the Vietnam War forced researchers and practitioners alike to consider the notion that there could be serious psychopathological consequences from being exposed to trauma. Researchers such as Cardeña and Spiegel (1993) and Candel, Merckelback and Kuijpers (2003) have repeatedly highlighted the links between exposure to traumatic events and poor psychological well-being. The current research, however, appears not to support these theories. Although members of the Northern Irish population reported significantly greater exposure to traumatic events, they also indicated that they experienced significantly fewer psychological intrusions in the form of dissociative experiences. In addition to this, further examination of the data revealed that, for the current sample, there is no significant relationship between exposure to traumatic experiences and dissociation.

However, it may also be the case that these Northern Irish individuals who have greater religious beliefs, are exposed to greater levels of trauma, and appear to have higher levels of psychological well-being than their English counterparts are utilizing religion in a way that differs from the English population. Research by Pargament (1997) suggests that religion and religious involvement may protect the individual against the psychological impact of stress and that religion, therefore, may act as a defense mechanism and coping strategy.

Further research (e.g. Maltby & Lewis, 1997; Maltby, Lewis & Day, 1999; Levin & Chatters, 1998) has assessed the links between mental health and religion and has concluded that there is a positive correlation between religiosity and psychological well-being. In addition, although researchers such as O'Connor, Cobb, and O'Connor (2003) have failed to provide evidence to suggest that religion serves to shield individuals from the impact of stress, the current research would appear to suggest that religion can, in fact, act as a psychological buffer and protect the individual from the harmful psychological effects of exposure to traumatic stressors.

Contrary to this theory, however, is the assertion of Ellis (1980) that "religiousness" is itself a counterpart of psychopathology and involves a degree of irrational thinking and emotional disturbance. By this token, it would appear that the exposure to trauma that is experienced by Northern Irish individuals may, in fact, be responsible for the elevated levels of religious belief. If this is the case, then it would appear that the early assertions of Freud are correct and that religious belief is indeed a defense mechanism which serves to help individuals cope with conflict and fear of death.

In terms of the negative relationship between levels of dissociation and living life according to one's religious beliefs in the Northern Irish sample, it is possible that this finding is mediating the relationship between dissociation and trauma. Although in the current study, no significant relationship was determined between exposure to traumatic events and levels of dissociation in the Northern Irish sample, it is possible that that may be explained by the current finding that a stronger propensity to live life according to one's religious beliefs results in lower dissociative experiences. If living one's life according to one's religious beliefs is indicative of stronger religious convictions and a more intrinsic religious orientation, then it is possible that this acts as a protective buffer against the impact of traumatic events and therefore may result in fewer dissociative experiences. It is suggested, therefore, that future research considers the relationship between these three variables and seeks to determine whether religious practices such as living life according to religious beliefs mediates the relationship between dissociation and trauma.

For the Catholic sample from Northern Ireland, levels of dissociation were significantly predicted by living life according to one's religious beliefs and basing ones approach to life on religion. Again, the relationships between these variables require attention. The association between levels of dissociation and basing ones approach to life on religion was positive though small, indicating that as using religion as the basis for one's life increases, so do levels of dissociation. This finding would seem to indicate some support for Schumaker's (1995) suggestion that religion is one of the behavioral patterns which encompasses a distortion of reality, thus leading to dissociation. Further, this finding would seem to indicate support for the suggestion that "religiousness" is a counterpart of psychopathology and involves a degree of irrational thinking and emotional disturbance (Ellis, 1980) which may, in turn, lead to heightened levels of dissociation.

However, for the Catholic Northern Irish population, the relationship between dissociation and living ones life according to ones religious beliefs is small but negative, therefore inferring that as the tendency of live life according to religious beliefs increases, levels of dissociation decrease. Again, it is possible that the relationship with trauma is crucial here, and that this specific religious practice serves as a protective buffer against traumatic events, and prevents the experience of increased levels of dissociation. It is again suggested that future research should comprehensively examine this relationship between specific religious practices, trauma, and dissociation.

The present findings also indicated that although there was a significant weak positive correlation between extrinsic religious orientation and indirect exposure to traumatic events for members of the Northern Irish Catholic population, for the other groups this was not the case. However, the significant relationship between religion and traumatic events for members of this Catholic population would seem to indicate that this group are increasing their extrinsic religious behavior as their indirect exposure to traumatic events increases.

This would seem to indicate some support for the suggestions made by Feifel (1974), which indicate that religion can act as a mechanism to help individuals cope with life stressors. However, the non-significant relationships that were elicited for the remaining groups may be interpreted as contradicting both Feifel's (1974) suggestion, and Gershuny and Thayer's (1999) suggestion that religion serves to protect the psyche from feeling of loss of control during and after traumatic events. Rather, these non-significant relationships may instead suggest that the current groups are not using religion in this utilitarian way.

It is likely that this lack of relationship between trauma and religious orientations for the Northern Irish groups is related to their attitudes towards religion, where it is suggested that these groups, because they scored highly in terms of religious orientations, are experiencing a "ceiling effect" in terms of their levels of religiosity whereby their levels of religious belief and involvement are already so great that they are unable to increase these further and benefit from the protective effect of religion against traumatic events.

With regard to the English control group, however, there was a significant weak negative correlation between indirect exposure to traumatic events and intrinsic religious orientation, and a weak negative correlation between overall exposure to traumatic events and intrinsic religious orientation. These findings would seem to indicate that, for the control group in the current sample, religion is being utilized as a coping mechanism. This finding would indicate that the members of the control group in the current study appear to have a more utilitarian attitude toward their religion, whereby their attitude appears to be that religion is useful in terms of fulfilling requirements such as gaining comfort and protection in times of sorrow (e.g. Allport & Ross, 1967; Genia, 1996; Genia & Shaw, 1991).

There are a number of factors present in the current study which may affect the generalizibility of the results. Firstly, data from the Northern Irish sample was collected during a ceasefire and this may have had an effect on the responses offered to items on the scale by members of the Northern Irish population. It is possible that if the fear of threat were removed (Gershuny & Thayer, 1999) then individuals would dissociate less frequently than they might if that fear was still present. Secondly, the DES items (Bernstein & Putnam, 1986) used in the current study assessed only the absorptive/derealisation component of dissociation as measured on the continuum as suggested by Ross (1985) and Braun (1986). It is possible that if the taxon of pathological dissociation was also measured the current sample may have elicited greater levels of dissociation. Finally, although respondents were questioned on their exposure to traumatic experiences, they were not questioned on their perception of threat and what, for them, constitutes a traumatic event. It is recommended that future research considers this and attempts to put measures in place to eliminate this ambiguity. However, although there are methodological limitations, it remains the case that there is a paucity of research assessing the function of religious beliefs, particularly in societies in conflict, and this research goes some way to rectifying that and to suggesting some of the functions that religious beliefs may have in these societies.

PART TWO

---

*Exceptional Experiences
and Health*

5

What Meditation Can Do: Mental Health and Exceptional Experiences

STEFAN SCHMIDT

Abstract

This chapter explores the nature of meditation and how meditative practices may impact physical and mental health. For some practitioners (Samādhi practice in Buddhist teachings) meditation refers to the attainment of specific and altered states of consciousness, whilst for others (Vipassanā practice in Buddhist teachings) the focus of meditation is on the observation of the present moment or mindfulness. Outside of the context of Buddhist practice, research on Mindfulness-Based Stress Reduction and Mindfulness-Based Cognitive Therapy have been successfully applied to a range of physical and mental conditions. The author also discusses empirical research on the relationship between meditation and unconventional information transfer (the distant influence of a meditator on the attention of another meditating person) which demonstrates a small but significant overall effect size.

Introduction: Defining Meditation

Meditation and meditation research, after an initial boom in the 70s of the last century, is once again the focus of growing interest. In order to conduct proper research on this topic its subject needs to be defined, which is no easy task. What is understood by the term *meditation* in the West is a large group of different mental techniques which sometimes share few features. How do you find the common denominator between e.g., a "dancing meditation" and a "Zen Sesshin"? Thus it makes more sense to study a specific form of meditation which then can be defined to some extent. Lutz, Slagter,

Dunne & Davidson (2008) compare this situation to using the word "sport" in a generic sense rather than naming and defining the specific sport (e.g., rowing) to be studied.

Interestingly in the Eastern traditions there is no single term for "meditation," but rather a loosely connected array of terms. In the *Śvetāśvatara Upanishads* (after 500 BCE), a set of terms *asana* (sitting), *pratyāhāra* (withdrawal of the senses) and *prānāyāma* (breath restraint), were used. Later Upanishads such as the *Maitri* includes the terms *dhyāna* (roughly, meditation), *dhāranā* (concentration) and *samādhi* (absorption). The later Yoga Sutras uses *dhyāna*, which comes closest to our western notion of *meditation*. Early Buddhism used *bhāvanā* (mental development or contemplation) and *jhāna* (from *dhyāna*; which becomes the stages of absorption). From *dhyāna* comes the Chinese term *ch'an* and Japanese *zen*. In the Tibetan language the term *sgom* is used to describe meditation. A direct translation of *sgom* would be *to familiarize* since meditation here is understood as the task to familiarize with a specific mind state. Alexander Berzin (2009), a scholar in Tibetan Buddhism offers a nice definition of meditation as, "The repeated practice of generating and focusing on a beneficial state of mind in order to build it up as a habit."

Our word "meditation" has a Western origin. It stems from the Latin *meditatio* "to think over," "to consider" and was used in the Medieval era to describe a discourse about a certain subject (see Descartes' famous *Meditationes de prima philosophia*). Seen from this origin "meditation" refers more to a cognitive and rational activity in the sense of structured thinking about a topic. While such an activity is sometimes also practiced in meditation (e.g. in the Tibetan Analytical Meditation) most Eastern meditation approaches discourage cognitive elaboration and reasoning.

There are two suggestions for sets of criteria in order to call a technique "meditation." Cardoso, de Souza, Camano & Leite (2004, *p.* 59) call a procedure meditation if it utilizes (1) a specific technique (clearly defined), involving (2) muscle relaxation somewhere during the process and (3) "logic relaxation:" a necessarily (4) self-induced state, using a (5) "self-focus" skill (coined "anchor").

But of course these criteria are debatable. What about a meditation induction coming from a teacher or a CD? And should meditation necessarily to be linked to muscle relaxation? A Canadian group has written a large HTA-report (health technology assessment) on meditation based interventions (Ospina et al., 2007). In order to include/exclude interventions they defined a set of "demarcation criteria" for meditation in a Delphi-process with experts (Bond et al., 2009). They ended up with three essential criteria: (1) a defined technique, (2) logic relaxation, (3) a self-induced state/mode) and 5 important but not essential criteria, (4) involve a state of psychophysical relaxation somewhere in the process, (5) use a self-focus skill or anchor, (6) involve an altered state/mode of consciousness, mystic experience, enlightenment or suspension of logical thought processes, (7) be in a religious/spiritual/philo-sophical context, (8) involve an experience of mental silence. The limitation for both approaches is that they aim to define meditation based procedures in order to study them as interventions within health research. But this is already a very specific context if one compares it with the original Eastern notion of "to familiarize" or conceptualizes meditation as a spiritual practice in order to reach self-transformation.

Another interesting science based definition was proposed by Shapiro (1982, p. 268). He defines meditation as a family of techniques which have in common a conscious attempt to focus attention in a non-analytical way, and an attempt not to dwell on discursive, ruminating thought."

And I would like to arrive at a minimal description of meditation by starting from this definition.

Minimal Description
of Meditation as a Starting Point

In our view, the core aspect of this definition by Shapiro (1982) is the conscious approach towards attention. The expression *to focus attention* may be too limiting and the term *attention regulation* might be more appropriate (see e.g. Bishop et al., 2004), since not all forms of meditation rely on *focused* attention. While attention regulation is one crucial part of a meditation prac-tice the other necessary ingredient is the *intention* or motivation to perform such a practice. This intention refers not only to the intention to regulate attention in a narrow sense but also to the question *why* somebody is prac-ticing meditation? What is the specific aim of the practice? Where does one want to arrive by practicing a certain technique?

Thus, in order to have a starting point for scientific inquiry we propose a minimal description for *meditation* as a *conscious process of attention regu-lation with a specific intention.*

This description is somewhat similar to a model describing the mecha-nism of mindfulness by Shapiro, Carlson, Astin & Freedman (2006). Here mindfulness is characterized by the three axioms *attention*, *intention* and *atti-tude* which are interacting with each other.

In our minimal description we consider intention as primary over atten-tion. It is the specific intention and motivation which brings people to sit down on the meditation cushion and to perform attention regulation. We also argue that different intentions may result in similar forms of attention regulation but will nevertheless lead to different outcomes from the perspective of the meditator. Somebody may watch her breath in order to get focused and to quiet the mind at the end of a busy day. Another person may also watch her breath but this time in order to arrive empirically at the insight of impermanence of all phenomena and to find ultimate liberation.

This example also points to another important issue. While meditation in its ancient Eastern origin was always practiced as a spiritual discipline in order to promote self-transformation, this is not always the case in the West. Here all kinds of different intentions (spiritual ones and non-spiritual ones) can be found (see Schmidt, 2009 for a detailed discussion). Meditation is popular as a clinical intervention to reduce stress or cope with illness. And many people just practice meditation in order to calm down and/or to connect with themselves in a very demanding society. Shapiro (1992) describes the various intentions to meditate on a continuum ranging from self-regulation (e.g., calming, relaxation, stress reduction) via self-exploration (e.g., studying ones psychological patterns) to self-transformation.

While the *intention* sets the mental state of the practice, the strategy of *regulating and sustaining attention* describes more or less the practical method on how to proceed within a meditation session. There are various dimensions of attention and attention regulation including (1) the focus of attention (e.g., the breath, thoughts, real or visualized objects or none) (2) width of focus (e.g., the tip of the nose vs. the whole body) (3) how to deal with distractions (e.g. to stay with them for a while versus immediately returning to the main focus) or (iv) the effort to sustain attention (high versus low). Each strategy can be described by these underlying dimensions and many of these aspects are also related to the experience of the meditator (e.g., effort to sustain the attention). Two examples of such strategies can be found in Lutz, Slagter, Dunne & Davidson (2008).

Meditation and Mental States: Samādhi and Vipassanā

Meditation practice is often associated with reaching specific and altered mental states. But this does not necessarily need to be so. Again, whether someone is aiming for a specific state which is different from daily consciousness is a matter of intention. A good example to illustrate this can be drawn from traditional Buddhist practices. Here, in most traditions, two main meditation strategies are known, which are often called *Samādhi* and *Vipassanā*. Samādhi stands for a meditation technique with a very narrow and highly selective focus of attention. Here the meditator should only attend to the object of meditation on a moment by moment basis and try not to get distracted. This process of reducing the focus of attention is often referred to as single-pointedness (Wallace, 2006). This procedure is usually practiced in order to calm the mind (quiescence) and if continued to reach deep states of consciousness (Shankman, 2008; Solé-Leris, 1986; Wallace, 2006). So, while Samadhi is clearly aiming for a special and altered mental state, Vipassanā meditation is related to a somewhat different intention. Vipassanā stands for "insight" and is often also translated to "Insight Meditation." Here, the meditator observes the nature of all phenomena coming into his or her mental space, in order to get insights into the true nature of these phenomena. So, in contrast to Samādhi, there is no such thing as distraction in Vipassanā. Rather, the idea is to be aware of every phenomenon which comes into the focus of attention and to observe it without interacting with it (detachment). In order not to get carried away (e.g., by thoughts), usually an anchor (e.g., the breath) is used, where the meditator can return whenever s/he notices that his or her mind was wandering and the detached attention for the content within his or her consciousness was lost. This wide form of attention can be practiced within a certain phenomenal area (e.g., with emotions, thoughts, bodily sensations) or in its most extreme form on all phenomenal realms at once (a technique sometimes called "choiceless awareness"). These two different ways of paying attention within meditation are often also described as *concentrative and as mindfulness meditation* (Dunn, Hartigan & Mikulas, 1999; Kornfield, 1993; Shapiro, 1982; Valentine & Sweet, 1999).

Secularized Meditation Approaches: MBSR

It is the Buddhist practice of mindfulness which is particularly applied in today's Western secularized context. The notion of mindfulness got somewhat diluted by this process (see Schmidt, 2009 for a detailed definition and discussion of this concept). One of the most prominent examples of a secularized context is a medical behavioral intervention program termed Mindfulness-based Stress Reduction (MBSR) by Jon Kabat-Zinn (1990). Kabat-Zinn describes mindfulness "as moment-to-moment, non-judgmental awareness, cultivated by paying attention in a specific way, that is, in the present moment, and as non-reactively and as non-judgmentally and openheartedly as possible" (Kabat-Zinn, 2005, p. 108). MBSR is a structured eight-week group program teaching several types of mindfulness meditation techniques, as well as yoga. Although of ancient Buddhist origin, the program itself is practical, non-religious, and non-esoteric in its orientation. The program was developed at the University of Massachusetts in Worcester, Mass., in 1979 and has been a unique success story ever since.

A regular MBSR course consists of an intake interview, 8 weekly sessions of approximately 2.5 hours, a seven "day of mindfulness" usually taking place between the weeks 5 and 7, a daily homework assignment of approximately 45 minutes and a second personal interview at the end of the course. Participants are provided with CDs containing guided meditations and information leaflets on the course content. During the personal intake interview the motivation of the participant is usually assessed, a rapport with the instructor is established and realistic goals of the intervention are formulated. Each of the eight sessions covers specific exercises and topics within the context of mindfulness practice and training. This includes various types of formal mindfulness practice (e.g., sitting meditation, body-scan, walking meditation), mindful awareness of dynamic yoga postures, and mindfulness during stressful situations and social interactions. Information on the relationship between stress and health and sharing of the experiences of the participants are also relevant parts of this intervention. On the full "day of mindfulness" participants perform their exercises together in silence and also prepare food and practice simple daily life activities with a mindful attitude. The idea is that every activity can be performed with mindful awareness (informal mindfulness) and this transference of the course content into daily life is addressed.

Meta-Analysis of MBSR Effects

Unlike other mindfulness-based intervention, MBSR has no specific indication. Courses can be visited by healthy persons who are interested in stress management as well as patients suffering from chronic diseases. In 2003, we conducted a meta-analysis of all trials assessing the health benefits related to MBSR (Grossman, Niemann, Schmidt & Walach, 2004). In a literature search, we identified all studies applying MBSR as an intervention published before December 2002. We also included unpublished material into the review when an English abstract was available. Overall, 64 empirical reports could be identified. In a next step, we excluded all studies that either did not report on health related outcomes or presented their results in a way that did not allow for a meta-statistical approach (i.e., reported data did not allow for calculating effect sizes). We also included only studies applying validated and standardized scales. Health benefits of MBSR were either operationalized as physical health or mental health. Accordingly, the outcome measures from the included studies were either grouped under mental health (e.g., depression, anxiety, sleep, psychological wellbeing), physical health (e.g., medical symptoms, physical impairment, or physical components of quality of life questionnaires) or excluded from the analysis. We calculated Cohen's d effect sizes by dividing the mean difference by their pooled standard deviation. Two types of mean differences were employed: (1) treatment-control difference (between-group), and (2) post treatment-pretreatment difference (within-group). We included the latter within-group analyses because there were a relatively small number of controlled studies that met criteria, and several rather carefully conducted uncontrolled observational studies that did adhere to criteria. Thus, overall, four separate analyses were computed; two for controlled studies (mental and physical health effects) and two for observational studies, respectively. Effect sizes were first combined within each of the studies and in the next step effect sizes per study were aggregated by a weighted mean (we applied the inverse of the estimated standard deviation of the effect size as a weight see Lipsey & Wilson, 2000). Overall, $k = 20$ studies with $N = 1605$ participants were included in the analyses. The results can be seen in Table 1.

Table 1: Results of the MBSR Meta-Analyses (k, Number of Studies; N, Number of Subjects; d, Mean Effect Size; p-Value, Two-Tailed)

Design	Outcome	k	N	d	p	95 % CI
Controlled studies	mental health	10	771	0.54	<.0001	0.39–0.68
	physical health	5	203	0.53	<.0001	0.23–0.81
Observational studies	mental health	18	894	0.50	<.0001	0.43–0.56
	physical health	9	566	0.42	<.0001	0.34–0.50

Overall, in all our analyses, effect sizes ranged over half a standard deviation ($d = 0.5$). These results confirm that MBSR is a powerful behavioral intervention. The results here are not related to a specific indication since participants in the included studies were either healthy people seeking coping skills for stress or patients suffering from chronic diseases such as chronic pain, fibromyalgia, cancer, coronary artery diseases, depression, anxiety, obesity and binge eating disorder and psychiatric diseases. It can be concluded that an intervention mainly based on learning different meditation techniques can have a positive effect on health. Whether this effect is really due to the regular practice of meditation or due to other aspects of the MBSR program (e.g., social support, regular course, information about stress, etc.) can only be shown by a complex dismantling study assessing the several components of MBSR separately. So far no such study has been conducted.

Mindfulness-based Cognitive Therapy — MBCT

Mindfulness-based Cognitive Therapy (MBCT) is another meditation based intervention quite similar to MBSR. In fact, the program is even based on Kabat-Zinn's MBSR concept. Nevertheless, MBCT shows two unique features for the study of meditation based interventions on mental health. One is that it was designed for a very precise indication, i.e., a program to prevent relapse in patients suffering from depression while they are in remission (Segal, Williams & Teasdale, 2002). The second one is that it is based on a cognitive theory which can explain why mindfulness meditation can make a crucial difference in relapse prevention.

Most patients suffering from a depression disorder experience recurrent depressive episodes with symptom free periods of remission in-between. The likelihood of experiencing another depressive episode increases with every episode a patient has, i.e., the likelihood of having a sixth episode is much higher than the likelihood of having a second episode (Lau, Segal & Williams, 2004). MBCT was designed as a program for patients in remission with the aim to prevent relapse.

The theoretical foundation of MBCT is Teasdale's differential activation hypothesis (Teasdale, 1988). According to Beck's cognitive theory of depression vulnerability to depression is due to dysfunctional attitudes which give rise to automatic thoughts and irrational beliefs which persist even following recovery from a depressive episode. However, several attempts to find elevated levels of dysfunctional attitudes in recovered former depressed patients compared to never depressed controls have failed. Thus, dysfunctional attitudes can explain the maintenance of a depressive episode, but they cannot explain the vulnerability for recurrence of depression among fully recovered patients. The differential activation hypothesis, on the other hand, is based on the observation that recovered depressed individuals react differently to a negative mood challenge than control participants who have never been depressed (Segal, Gemar & Williams, 1999). The formerly depressed patients are more likely to activate negative cognitive patterns acquired in their earlier episode. As a consequence, they tend to interpret the current negative mood as aversive and uncontrollable which then results in automatic thoughts and rumination. Negative thinking patterns are active and maintained during depressive episodes and it is assumed that the duration and intensity of their application within this time determines the accessibility and thus the mood related retrieval during recovery.

Teasdale et al. (1994) suggest to identify and then to stop this escalating process by what they term "meta-cognitive awareness." This refers to a shift in the cognitive set known as "disidentification" or "decentering." Rather than simply *being* their emotions or identifying personally with negative thoughts and feelings, patients *relate* to negative cognitions as mental events in a wider context which can be termed field of awareness ("This is not me, this is just a negative thought which will pass by after some time.") The hypothesis that reduced meta-cognitive awareness is associated with vulnerability to a relapse in depression has been demonstrated empirically in three studies (Teasdale et al., 2002).

This meta-cognitive awareness is strongly related to mindfulness. Mindfulness is the practice of observing one's mental objects without interacting with them and without getting absorbed by them. Thus, such a disidentification can be trained within a meditation practice. The Buddhist conception of mindfulness incorporates the idea that thoughts are just "mental events" which are not real. Rather than ascribing a fixed relationship between thoughts and reality as is usually done in the West (Chambers, Gullone & Allen, 2009), thoughts are considered as events which just arise within consciousness, stay there for a period of time and then vanish again. The application of an Ancient Eastern meditation method within the Western framework of a cognitive theory to explain a mental disorder is an excellent example of a fruitful and successful integration of these rather different systems.

So far, three clinical studies demonstrated effectiveness of MBCT. In a multicenter trial, 145 patients, in remission or in recovery from major depression, were randomized to continue with treatment as usual (TAU) or TAU plus MBCT. For patients with three or more previous episodes of depression, who constituted 77 percent of the sample, relapse rates were 66 percent for the TAU controls, but they were only 37 percent for the patients receiving MBCT in addition, a 44 percent reduction (Teasdale et al., 2000). In a second trial, 75 patients were randomized to either TAU or TAU plus MBCT. MBCT reduced relapse from 78 percent to 36 percent in 55 patients with 3 or more previous episodes (Ma & Teasdale, 2004). In both studies, the smaller groups with a history of two depressive episodes showed no significant difference between intervention and control. The finding that MBCT is more effective in patients suffering from more episodes or a longer history of depression fits the underlying cognitive theory the intervention was built on (Teasdale, Segal & Williams, 1994). Kuyken et al. (2008) ran a equivalence trial with 123 patients with a history of three or more episodes who had been treated with maintenance anti-depressive medication over the past 6 months. Patients were either randomized to the MBCT condition, and encouraged to taper or discontinue the anti-depressive medication or they received treatment as usual. After 15 months, 47 percent of the MBCT patients relapsed compared to 60 percent of the control group ($p=.07$). Furthermore, MBCT was more effective in reducing psychiatric comorbidity and residual depressive symptoms. Patients in the MBCT group also showed a higher quality of life at the end of the follow-up period.

In addition, MBCT was also successfully applied in patients suffering from chronic depression (Eisendrath et al., 2008; Kenny & Williams, 2007) and for patients with suicidal tendencies (Williams, Duggan, Crane & Fennell, 2006).

Meditation and the Study of Anomalies

While there is an obvious link between attending one's own mental state by meditation and health effects, often the question arises whether experiences within meditation are also linked to anomalies like unconventional information transfer or distant effects of certain intentions. These questions have been addressed repeatedly within the field of parapsychology. Here, any unexplained findings and effects are subsumed under the term *psi*. I would first like to give a narrative review of the relevant results in this field and then assess one specific experimental paradigm by presenting the results of a meta-analysis.

The first experimental study on meditation and *psi* was published in 1970 by Gertrude Schmeidler. The design of this study was simple and straightforward. During a class, six students performed a standard ESP test with Zener cards (Irwin, 1999) and then a Swami by the name of Madhavananda came to give a short lecture on meditation and relaxation before they performed a breathing exercise. The ESP test was then repeated and this time students scored significantly ($p = .01$) while the results of the first test were at chance (Schmeidler, 1970).

What has followed up to the present day is a large set of different studies with great variations in their design. Out of these approaches, only one experimental paradigm has evolved which was repeatedly conducted by different researchers. This is the *attention focusing facilitation experiment* (AFFE), first published by Braud, Shafer, McNeill & Guerra in 1995, which will be the subject of a meta-analysis in the next section.

Most of the studies on meditation and *psi* were conducted in the 1970's with a decline in 1980s and almost no publications besides the AFFE one by Braud et al. in the 1990s. In the 2000s meditation research gained a growing popularity within mainstream research for two reasons. One was the increasing body of evidence for the relationship between mindfulness meditation and mental and physical health as described above; the other was the growing interest in imaging studies of experienced meditators within the field of neuroscience (e.g. Brefczynski-Lewis, Lutz, Schaefer, Levinson & Davidson, 2007; Lutz, Brefczynski-Lewis, Johnstone & Davidson, 2008; Lutz, Greischar, Rawlings, Ricard & Davidson, 2004). Here the capacity of meditators to reproduce and maintain reliably certain states of consciousness over time is particularly of interest (Lutz, Dunne & Davidson, 2007). This second move towards meditation research after the 1970s is also reflected in the field of parapsychology with several new studies on meditation and *psi* appearing in the last 5 years.

I would like to begin a narrative review by outlining some designs in parapsychological research involving meditation and will then describe a representative study for each of these designs. The most important distinction is whether meditation is treated as a *state* or a *trait*. In an experiment applying meditation as a state usually the ESP (extra sensory perception) performance during or immediately after a period of meditation is assessed. If, on the other hand, meditation is treated as a trait, then no meditation has to take place during the experiment. Here, either experienced meditators are compared with non-meditators or novices (cross-sectional) or the changes associated with long-term meditation training are assessed over time (longitudinal).

An example of a *state study* can be found in Rao, Dukhan and Rao (1978). They conducted three experiments where they tested meditators immediately before and after a meditation session in an ESP Zener card test. All participants were students of an ashram in Bangalore, South India. The study took place during a period when they had intensive training in meditation. Students were classified as either "juniors" or "seniors" depending on their level of expertise in yoga and meditation and data were analyzed separately for each group. With two groups and three experiments, six comparisons were made. In five out of six comparisons, there was a significant improvement in hit rate from the pre-meditation to the post-meditation test ($p = .001 - .05$). Interestingly five of the six pre-meditation tests showed significant psi-missing effects (where participants score significantly below what would be expected statistically by chance), while four of the six post-tests had significant psi-hitting results. Furthermore they conducted a free-response test with the same participants. Here a sealed target had to be described in a written protocol before and after meditation. Protocols were rated against the targets by independent judges. Again the participants scored significantly better ($p = .05$) following the meditation as compared to before. There was no consistent pattern of the senior students scoring better than the junior students. Similar designs operationalizing meditation as a state were used by Roney-Dougal and Solfvin (2006; 2008) in a precognition task, by Palmer, Khamashta & Israelson (1979) in a Ganzfeld experiment, and by Osis and Bokert (1971), Rao and Puri (1978), and also Nash (1982) in ESP tests.

A typical *trait study* was conducted by Schmidt and Schlitz (1989) where they did a psychokinesis (PK) study on pre-recorded targets. Based on a truly random process, melodic tones of different lengths were mixed with noise of different length and recorded on tape. 568 participants received these tapes with the task of extending the tones and shortening the noise. Overall the experiment showed a significant PK effect of $p = .049$ or $p = .022$ depending on the method of analysis. Participants were asked in a questionnaire "...whether they had at some time practiced meditation" (p. 9). Meditators showed a significant PK effect ($p = .0005$) while non-meditators reached only chance results. The difference between the two groups was also significant ($p = .0007$). Later on, many other studies followed a similar approach when they asked their participants whether they practiced a mental discipline (e.g. meditation, martial arts, Tai Chi, hypnosis, relaxation exercises) and then analyzed the results for these two groups (yes/no) separately. But this approach is of course not specific enough to conclude anything regarding the effects of being a regular meditator on psi performance. Interestingly this procedure was initiated by a comment in Bem & Honorton (1994, p. 13) stating that involvement with meditation or mental disciplines in novices was a significant predictor for success in the autoganzfeld studies. But this is only true when this particular predictor was combined with other predictors (reported personal psi experience, prior psi testing). The classification according to "practicing a mental discipline" alone did not actually yield any significant differences (Honorton, 1997).

A mixture of these two approaches, state and trait studies, can be seen in the experiment by Braud & Hartgrove (1976). They recruited ten experienced meditators practicing Transcendental Meditation (TM) and a matched control group of non-meditators. Participants had to influence a random number generator (PK-test) and to get impressions about a target in a sealed envelope (clairvoyance test) while meditating (meditators) or being at rest (control group). None of the two groups independently obtained significant results in any of the tests. However, meditators scored significantly better ($p = .02$) than non-meditators in the clairvoyance experiment.

Other designs used in research on psi and meditation have operationalized whether the EEG characteristics of a meditation session immediately before an ESP test can be related to the outcome in the ESP test (Stanford & Palmer, 1973); or whether participants trained in a special Tibetan meditation technique for taking-up the suffering and sending-out positive feelings can influence the electrodermal activity of a remote person (Radin et al., 2006).

A narrative review regarding meditation and *psi* up to 1976 can be found in Honorton (1977); Schmeidler (1994) shortly summarizes the research from 1978–1992 and an overview on studies applying meditation in PK-research is available from Braud (1990) and Gissurarson (1992). More recent studies besides the ones already mentioned above are by Kozak et al. (2003), Radin (2008) and Bierman (2008). In Kozak et al. (2003), participants were trained for 30 days in Primordial Sound Meditation before EEG correlations between them were measured. In the study by Radin (2008), trained meditators performed better than non-meditators in a psi-task that requested sustained attention. Dick Bierman conducted an fMRI study on a presentiment effects (see May, Paulinyi & Vassy, 2005) where he also compared trained meditators with non-meditators in a mixed design; meditators were tested twice, once while meditating and once while resting (Bierman, 2008).

Overall, it can be concluded that although meditation was often applied and yielded many significant results in *psi* research it was not as successful as other paradigms which were also based on altered states of consciousness, such as the *Ganzfeld, dream telepathy* studies (Ullman, Krippner & Vaughan, 1989) or *remote viewing* experiments (Utts, 1996). None of the experiments mentioned here were replicated by other researchers, no standard paradigm evolved. Although meditation in many state-based experiments demonstrated *psi*-conducive properties, this effect was not followed up systematically. From the results of the single studies described here, it is difficult to draw a general conclusion, especially given that the claim is controversial. It can be concluded that the topic has yet to be studied systematically. Current and future studies may close this gap and provide deeper insight into the relationship between meditative states or meditation as a trait and *psi* effects.

Meta-Analysis of the Attention Focusing Facilitation Experiment

The *attention focusing facilitation experiment* (AFFE) was first conducted in 1993 by Braud, Shafer, McNeill & Guerra and published in 1995. It was created within Braud's larger program on *direct mental interaction with living systems* (DMILS) studies (Braud & Schlitz, 1989; 1991; Schmidt, 2003; Schmidt, Schneider, Utts & Walach, 2004) in San Antonio, Texas, where many different set-ups were explored. In these experiments, one participant tried to activate or calm another participant from a distance and usually, a physiological parameter was applied as a dependent variable. However, when William Braud and colleagues designed the AFFE study, they were looking for a behavioral measure. Thus, in the attention focusing facilitation experiment, one participant had to focus his or her attention on a candle. Whenever s/he noticed that his or her mind was wandering s/he returned with his or her attention to the candle and pressed a button. Thus, the frequency of button presses within a certain time interval is an indicator of mental distraction from the focus. A second participant was located in a distant and isolated room. No normal means of communication were possible between the two participants. This second person acted as a "remote helper." The helper had a monitor which displayed either one of the two experimental conditions, "Control" or "Help." During "Help" periods, "the helper focused her own attention on a similar object and concurrently maintained an intention for the distant participant to focus well on his or her object and remain free from mental distractions and thus be better equipped to succeed in the attentional task" (Braud, Shafer, McNeill & Guerra, 1995, p. 104). During control periods the helper occupied her mind with other matters and tried not to think about the experiment. Overall, 16 1-minute periods (8 Help and 8 Control) took place in a random and balanced sequence (Schlitz et al., 2003). Sixty participants had, on average, 13.6 button presses during Control and 12.4 during Help periods respectively and the difference was just significant ($p = .049$).

In the description of this experiment, the word meditation was not mentioned. But the task to maintain the attention on one object and to return to it whenever the mind wandered away meets the above mentioned minimal description of meditation. Similarly, Braud et al. conclude in their study:

"If the attention-focusing or concentration exercises of the present study are viewed as protomeditational in nature, then the present findings suggest that one person's meditation process may be directly influenced by the concurrent meditation of another person" (Braud, Shafer, McNeill & Guerra, 1995, p. 114).

The question whether meditators can support each other through their practice has often been raised. Many people experienced with meditation report that it is much easier to maintain a specific way of paying attention in group with other meditators compared to their single practice at home. Such an effect could be described as a *sangha effect*. Sangha is, in the Buddhist tradition, the word for the disciples following the teachings of the Buddha thus, a group of meditators are often termed sangha. Although the experiment described above had a somewhat different aim, its results may also be interpreted as a support for a paranormally mediated *sangha effect*. The specific *intention* of the (helping) meditators here was to support the other meditator in his or her performance. This has some parallel to the so called *metta* meditation practice where the meditator directs feelings of loving kindness towards either him or her self or towards others.

Since this experiment was replicated several times within a very similar design enough, data are available to calculate a meta-analysis on the results (Schmidt, 2008).

Studies were identified by scanning the parapsychological literature since the publication of the first study in 1995 until December 2008. Furthermore we studied reference lists of identified studies and asked investigators involved in this research. Studies were coded and result parameters (N, *t-values*, *p-values*) were extracted. For each study, an effect-size d for the difference between control and experimental condition was calculated by the formula

$$ES(d) = \frac{t}{\sqrt{df}} \text{ with } df = N\text{-}1 \text{ (Rosenthal, 1994, p. 233).}$$

This is a d-type effect size which expresses the difference between experimental and control condition in a metric of standard deviations. For each effect size, an according variance has to be estimated in order to calculate a standard error σ_i for the effect size i. This variance is

estimated by $\hat{\sigma}_i^2 = \frac{1}{N_i}$ and the according σ_i calculates by $\sigma_i = \frac{1}{\sqrt{N_i}}$.

In order to combine studies, they have to be weighted according to the inverse of their variance which is in this case just N. Next it has to be determined whether it is likely that the database forms a homogeneous data set where all single studies are an estimate of the same true effect size. This can be determined by comparing the variance expected to be found as a consequence of the sampling error with the empirical variance found in the dataset. Homogeneity can be determined by the Q-statistic (Laird & Mosteller, 1990). Based on the results of this homogeneity analysis effect sizes were combined by a fixed effect model. Effect sizes are thus integrated according to the formula provided by Shadish and Haddock (1994, p. 265, formula 18–1)

$$\bar{d} = \frac{\sum_{i=1}^{k} w_i d_i}{\sum_{i=1}^{k} w_i}$$

w_i here refers to the weight assigned to each study, therefore $w_i = N_i$.

Altogether 12 studies with more or less the same design were conducted (Brady & Morris, 1997; Braud, Shafer, McNeill & Guerra, 1995; Edge, Suryani & Morris, 2007; Edge, Suryani, Tiliopoulos, Bikker & James, 2008; Edge, Suryani, Tiliopoulos & Morris, 2004; Watt & Baker, 2002; Watt & Brady, 2002; Watt & Ramakers, 2003), four of these studies are not yet published. We also decided to include unpublished literature since the field is relatively small and we had confidence that almost all conducted studies would be identified. Table 2 lists the number of sessions and p-values of these 12 studies. The essential experimental features are the same for all these studies. In every study, the task was operationalized in keeping the attention to a candle for a helpee and a helper. The dependent variable was also the same for all experiments. Helpees had to press a button whenever they noticed that their minds wandered away from the candle. All sessions consisted out of 16 one-minute periods in a randomized sequence of eight control and eight help periods each; only the 2004 and the 2006 study by Hoyt Edge and colleagues applied 8 2-min periods (4 control and 4 help). Furthermore, all investigators applied the same statistics.

Table 2: Attention Focusing Facilitation Experiments, With Year of Publication or Year the Experiment Took Place if Unpublished

	Year	N sessions	p
Braud et al.	1995	60	.05
Brady & Morris	1997	40	.08
Watt & Brady**	2002/1	60	—
Watt & Brady	2002/2	60	.41
Watt & Baker	2002	80	.30
Watt & Ramakers	2003	36	.04
Edge et al.	2001	35	.04
Edge et al.	2002	53	.03
Edge et al.*	2003	40	.66
Edge et al.*	2004	69	.54
Edge et al.*	2005	60	.21
Edge et al.*	2006	43	.27

All p-values are two-tailed and may thus be different from the original report. not published, ** not included in meta-analysis.*

Only $k = 11$ of the 12 studies were eligible, with an overall N of 576 sessions. This was because in one of the two studies published in Watt and Brady (2002) an artifact detected by the original investigators prevented the evaluation of the experiment.

The test of homogeneity yielded $Q = 15.6$ for the eleven attention focus facilitation studies. Q is χ^2 distributed with $df = k-1 = 10$ resulting in $p = .11$. With $\sigma^2 = 0.01$, there remains some variance unexplained by sampling error. But the database is still homogenous enough in order to combine effect sizes by a fixed effect model. Effect sizes were integrated according to the above formula. This resulted in an overall $d = 0.11$ which is significant at $p = .009$ (two-tailed).

Regarding study quality, the sample of 11 studies can be separated into two larger groups (i.e., the Bali studies by Edge et al. and the studies by Watt et al. in Edinburgh) and into two single studies (the one by Braud et al. and the first Edinburgh replication by Brady & Morris). Separate analyses of the two larger subgroups showed more or less the same picture as for the whole sample; none of these subgroups was individually responsible for the overall effect size or the amount unexplained variance. Thus, it can be assumed that study quality is not a significant moderator.

Overall, it could be clearly demonstrated that there is a small but significant overall effect in 11 studies testing AFFE. The small effect size may explain why some of the single studies reached significance and others, not. This is a question of statistical power with small effects needing large samples in order to find significant effects.

In two earlier meta-analyses we combined studies conducted within two experimental paradigms (Schmidt, Schneider, Utts & Walach, 2004). These are *DMILS* studies and *Remote Staring* studies which both used electrodermal activity (EDA) as the dependent variable. These studies were similar in design to the experiments meta-analyzed here and all three designs are testing the effects of a distant intention, operationalized either as helping (attention focus facilitation) gazing (remote staring) or activating and calming (EDA-DMILS). All three meta-analyses yield almost the same effect size as can be seen in Table 3 and Figure 1:

Table 3: Results from Three Meta-Analyses
on Distant Intention Effects, k = Number of Studies,
N = Number of Sessions, d = Mean Effect Size,
p = According p-Value, 95% CI = 95%
Confidence Interval of Mean Effect Size

Experiment	k	N	d	p	95 % CI
DMILS	36	1015	0.106	.001	0.043–0.169
Remote Staring	15	379	0.128	.013	0.027–0.229
AFFE	11	576	0.109	.009	0.027–0.191

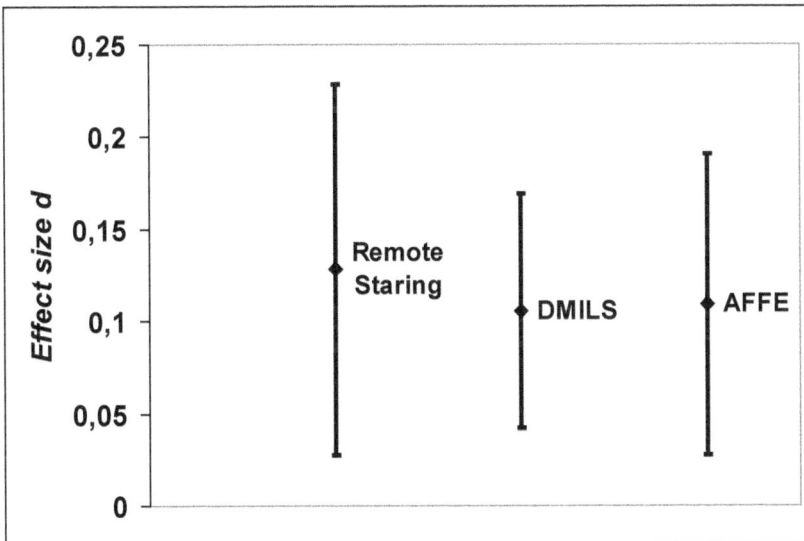

Figure 1. Graphical display of the mean effect sizes d for the three different samples. Error bars indicate the 95 percent confidence interval.

The close similarity of these results can be regarded as mutually independent confirmation of each of the single meta-analyses. Therefore it can be concluded that the three experimental designs are likely to test the same effect. As in two datasets the dependent variable is a physiological one and in the third a behavioral one it can be furthermore assumed that the effect is independent of the measures applied.

Overall it can be concluded from this meta-analysis that there is a small but statistically significant effect of distant intentionality or to put it more specifically of remote support in keeping focused during meditation which cannot be explained in conventional terms.

Acknowledgments

At the time I was writing this manuscript, my work was generously supported by the Samueli Institute, Alexandria, VA, USA. I would like to thank Robert Forman for help in clarifying the different Eastern notions referring to contemplative practices.

6

The Muse in the Machine: Creativity, Anomalous Experiences and Mental Health

NICOLA J. HOLT

Abstract

This chapter examines the nature and correlates of creativity, its relationship with anomalous experiences and how this relationship impacts on mental health. The author explores what is currently known about both creativity and anomalous experiences(AEs), including the problems in defining and measuring these two multidimensional constructs. Several ways in which the relationship between creativity and anomalous experiences are related are presented, including the idea that AEs are implicated in the etiology of creativity. A variety of mechanisms which may underpin this relationship are presented. Finally, the author scrutinizes the relationship between AEs and creativity in terms of its implications for health, given that creativity is often been associated with psychopathology (e.g., biopolar disorder and schizophrenia); positive and meaningful outcomes; the idea of "controllable oddness" and the protective factor model in which the creative expression of an anomalous experience promotes well being. It is concluded that creativity is often associated with healthy anomalous experiences, but there is much scope for future research in this area.

Introduction

It has been postulated that creativity is associated with aspects of both "health" (e.g., resilience, thriving, happiness) and "ill health" (e.g., bipolar disorder, schizophrenia) (Andreasen, 1987; Jamison, 1993; Maslow, 1971; Panells & Claxton, 2008), with both adaptation to consensual reality and imaginal, borderland states of consciousness (Martindale, 1999; Thalbourne, 2000a; Suler, 1980). In this Chapter two theses will be evaluated: (1) that anomalous experiences contribute to creativity, having a functional role; and (2) that anomalous experiences in this context are healthy. I will begin by defining both creativity and anomalous experiences and outlining methodological and interpretative difficulties in this field. I will consider how anomalous experiences might be linked with creativity and will review the evidence for an association between the two, from first-person reports to correlational and experimental research. The putative role of "extraordinary" experiences in creativity is contentious and a critical question is whether or not there is evidence for a direct versus an indirect link between creativity and anomalous experiences, that is, whether or not anomalous experiences play a causal role in the creative process. Subsequently, attention will be given to potential explanatory models for understanding any relationship between creativity and anomalous experiences (neurocognitive, affective and trait models), evaluating their efficacy. Finally, I will reflect upon the implications of this literature for conceptualisations of mental health and wellbeing, asking whether creativity might be a protective factor against ill health, playing a unique role in the processing and interpretation of anomalous experiences.

Definitions

Anomalous experiences (AEs) are those that "touch on areas outside the common-sense reality of our everyday world" (Kohls & Walach, 2006, p. 125), that "deviate from ordinary experience or from the usually accepted explanations of reality" (Cardeña, Lynn & Krippner, 2000, p. 4). AEs involve deviations along dimensions of conscious experience, including cognition, affect, perception, sense of self, awareness of body and attention (Pekala, 1991; Reed, 1988) and include, but are not limited to, lucid dreams (LaBerge & Gackenbach, 2000), hallucinations (Bentall, 1990), mystical experiences (Fontana, 2007), out-of-body experiences (Alvarado, 2000) and subjective paranormal experiences (Targ, Schlitz & Irwin, 2000). Despite the appellation, AEs are relatively common (Glicksohn, 1990; Palmer, 1979). For example, in surveys of the general population, approximately 10 percent report having had at least one, non-drug-induced, vivid hallucinatory experience (Bentall & Slade, 1985), 35 percent, a mystical experience (Greeley, 1975), 10 percent an out-of-body experience (Alvarado, 2000) and 33 to 50 percent, a parapsychological experience such as telepathy (Targ, Schlitz & Irwin, 2000).

A common definition of creativity is the "sequences of thoughts and actions that lead to a novel, adaptive production" (Lubart, 2000–2001, p. 295). This criterion of "adaptive novelty" requires that a creative product demonstrates both (1) the recombination of existing sub-components in an unusual and novel way (Mednick, 1962); and (2) an expression or formulation that is useful, valuable or adaptive.[1] The criterion of adaptivity distinguishes creative thinking from merely original and/or psychopathological thinking (Martindale, 1999). As such, creativity may involve ideation that deviates from the "usual" or "common-place," whilst proffering productive transformation (of ideas, symbols, objects, or of the self). Correspondingly, the creative process is typically (but not always, see Weisberg, 2006) described as biphasic, characterized by a recursive looping between two forms of cognition: convergent, linear, goal-oriented, structured cognition, that is evaluative and leads to one "correct," and thus "useful," solution; versus loose, overinclusive, unstructured, divergent cognition, which is tangential, open-ended and original (Guildford, 1967; Finke, Ward & Smith, 1992). It is this "loose, associative" cognitive style that has been linked with AEs (Martindale, 1977–78).

A Note on Interpretative and Methodological Difficulties

At the outset, it is important to note caveats concerning the literature on creativity and AEs. Difficulties of interpretation arise due to the complex, poly-faceted, multi-dimensional, context-bound nature of the creativity construct and associated inconsistencies in its operational definition and measurement (Feldhusen & Goh, 1995; Plucker & Renzulli, 1999). Creative production emerges from a matrix of interacting factors: cognition (Eysenck, 1993), personality traits (King, Walker & Broylers, 1996) motivation (Amabile, 1996), domain specific skills (e.g., writing or mathematics, Gardner, 1993) and environmental and cultural factors (Zha, Walczyk, Griffith-Ross & Tobacyk, 2006), leading, in fact, to a variety of "creativities" (Sternberg, 2005). Commensurately, creativity has been measured in a plethora of forms, assessing: cognitive styles, such as divergent thinking or remoteness of associations (Torrance, 2000; Mednick & Mednick, 1967); involvement and achievement in specific activities, such as drama or invention (Carson, Peterson, & Higgins, 2005; Hocevar, 1981); personality traits and attitudes associated with creative achievement (Gough, 1979); and peer or expert ratings of a product or a person's creativity (Hocevar, 1981). None of these measures, in isolation, succeeds in adequately identifying or measuring creativity. For example, divergent thinking tests, which require one to think of as many original responses to a stimulus as possible, usually in a limited time frame, do not assess the value of ideas produced; and of course, even being a technically brilliant scientist or artist, is not synonymous with being creative in that domain. Such obfuscation renders the nature of any potential link between creativity and AEs difficult to identify precisely. The literature can appear to be rather piecemeal since different researchers have measured creativity in different ways. Multidimensional creativity measurement is generally recommended but rarely achieved (Feldhusen & Goh, 1995).

Likewise, the construct of AEs is multidimensional. The type of AE measured, for example, hallucinations or depersonalisation, versus positive mystical experiences or lucid dreams, are traditionally of interest to different sub-disciplines of psychology (clinical psychology and humanistic/transpersonal psychology respectively), disciplines which hold different assumptions about the relationships between AEs and mental health. Indeed, the above types of experiences appear to relate differentially to mental health (Hunt, Dougan, Grant & House, 2002), in interaction with other factors, such as meditation practice and evaluation of experiences (Kohls & Walach, 2006; Schofield & Claridge, 2007). Thus, the type of AE that is measured has implications for our understanding of the relationships between AEs, creativity, and well-being.

Further difficulties in the interpretation of any association between AEs and creativity concern the attribution of causal models and mechanisms. In part this is due to an over-reliance on correlational, retrospective self-report data, from which causality is not discernable. Might creativity lead to AEs, AEs to creativity, or might both be different expressions of some third underlying factor? One possibility, concurring with anecdotal reports, is that moments of inspiration arise in an AE, allowing modes of perception and cognition to be experienced that are beyond the culturally endorsed, hence introducing novel associations into the reflective sphere of consciousness (Harman & Rheingold, 1984). This notion has been contested by those who propose that creativity requires only structured cognition, knowledge and trial and error (Boden, 1996; Weisberg, 1989). Another possibility is that the profound nature of AEs leads to a need for expression, their subjective nature being suitable for the arts (O'Reilly, Dunbar & Bentall, 2001). Alternatively, both creativity and a proclivity to have AEs might be underpinned by a common personality trait or organization of the mind, such as openness-to-experience (McCrae, 1987); in which case, AEs themselves may not be required for creative production, although some "milder form" of their expression (e.g., cognitive looseness) might facilitate originality (Eysenck, 1993).

Yet, further considerations concern whether any relationship between creativity and AEs might be linear or curvilinear — there might be an optimal level of anomaly-proneness[2] that is associated with creative functioning (Schuldberg, 2000–2001); whether any proclivity to have AEs only leads to creativity in interaction with particular factors, such as resilience, well-being or intelligence (Barron, 1993; Claridge, 2001); or whether AEs are only associated with particular components of or kinds of creativity (e.g., cognitive looseness or eminent creativity) (Eysenck, 1993; Richards, 2010).

In summary, when evaluating research in this field one must be aware of varying operational definitions of creativity and AEs, reflecting their multidimensional nature, and be cautious when interpreting any data, in particular, of assuming causality. Having thus highlighted some problems hindering attempts to draw conclusions about creativity and AEs from the existing literature, I will now provide a summary of this literature, which consists of anecdotal reports, correlational data, and experimental studies that have attempted to manipulate conscious experience during the creative process.

Is Creativity "Ordinary" or "Extraordinary"? Anecdotal Reports

Oft cited anecdotal reports from famous scientists and artists, such as Henri Poincaré, August Kekulé, Thomas Edison, Samuel Taylor Coleridge and William Blake, reinforce the notion that AEs arise as part of the creative process. These tend to be of different types: hallucinatory-like moments of inspiration; experiences of "the muse"; or intense states of absorption. Examples will be given of each. In the following case a potential solution to a problem unexpectedly arises in what appears to be a hypnagogic state:

> I was sitting, writing at my text-book; but the work did not progress, my thoughts were elsewhere. I turned my chair to the fire and dozed. Again, the atoms were gambolling before my eyes. This time the smaller groups kept modestly in the background. My mental eyes, rendered more acute by repeated visions of the kind, could now distinguish larger structures, of manifold conformation: long rows, sometimes more closely fitted together; all twining and twisting in a snakelike motion. But look! What was that? One of the snakes had seized hold of its own tail, and the form whirled mockingly before my eyes. As if by a flash of lightning I awoke; and this time I spent the rest of the night working out the consequences of the hypothesis [Kekulé, cited by Mavromatis, 1987, p. 203].

Rothenberg (2001, 136) quotes Edvard Munch from his diary in 1891, in which he recorded the hallucinatory impetus for a painting, which was sketched, carefully considered and developed over the next eighteen months into the now famous image of "The Scream":

> I was walking along the road with two of my friends. Then the sun set. The sky suddenly turned into blood, and I felt something akin to a touch of melancholy. I stood still, leaned against the railing, dead tired. Above the blue black fjord sand city hung clouds dripping, rippling blood. My friends went on and again I

stood, frightened with an open wound in my breast. A great scream pierced through nature.

Creative inspiration has been attributed to sensed presences, whether this be divine inspiration, the Greek Muses or automatic writing. Sensed presence is a transient awareness of "another consciousness" in the absence of any corporeal personage (Persinger & Healey, 2002), an "altered state with dissociative presence" (Platt, 2007, p. 38). Experiences of an "anomalous autonomous other" as the source of originality are well-described by Jung's (1967) "visionary creativity," Rowan's (1988) "surrendered creativity" and are exemplified in its most extreme manifestation in Braude's (2000) discussion of the case of Pearl Curran, who attributed her novels to a "channeled" identity, Patience Worth. William Thackery, a "perfectly normal English novelist" explained: "I have been surprised at the observations made by some of my characters. It seems as if an occult power was moving the pen. The personage does or says something, and I ask, how the dickens did he come to think of that?" (Martindale, 1989, p. 215). The poet Theodore Roethke experienced a sensed presence after writing his poem "The Dance" in 1952. The poem was written quickly, in a state of automaticity that followed a long period of "writer's block."

> I felt, I knew, that I had hit it. I walked around, and I wept; and I knelt down — I always do after I've written what I know is a good piece. But at the same time I had, as God is my witness, the actual sense of a Presence — as if Yeats himself were in that room. The experience was in a way terrifying, for it lasted for at least half an hour. That house, I repeat, was charged with a psychic presence: the very walls seemed to shimmer. I wept for joy.... He, they — the poets dead — were with me [Cited by Smith, 2007, p. 114.].

Intense absorption in the act of creative production may constitute an anomalous experience (Csikszentmihalyi, 1992; Holt, 2000). Milner (1950, p. 152) uses the term "creative participation" to describe a loss of self-awareness whilst painting.

The process always seems to be accompanied by a feeling that the ordinary sense of self had temporarily disappeared, there had been a kind of blanking out of ordinary consciousness; even the awareness of blanking out had gone, so that it was only afterwards when I had returned to ordinary consciousness that I remembered that there had been this phase of complete lack of self-consciousness.

"Creative participation" has clear parallels with Csikszentmihalyi's (1992; 1996) construct of "flow," a loss of self-awareness in a state of intense concentration. "People become so involved in what they are doing that the activity becomes spontaneous, almost automatic; they stop being aware of themselves as separate from the actions they are performing" (Csikszentmihalyi, 1992, p. 53). Csikszentmihalyi (1996) observed that the "flow state" was a common component of the creative work of eminent artists and scientists whom he interviewed. Flow occurs when highly developed skills are employed without critical evaluation; as such it is not unique to creative endeavors and arises in a range of activities, such as socializing, athletics and learning in the classroom (Csikszentmihalyi & Larson, 1984; Jackson, 1992; Schweinle & Turner, 2006).

The first-person reports presented above suggest that the creative process involves extreme shifts in awareness: vivid imagery, passivity, affect and an altered sense of self. Perhaps creative persons push themselves into borderland states through discipline and focus, experiencing pseudo-hallucinations and intense imaginative involvement. Perhaps AEs are fecund with original ideation, stimulating scientific innovation or esthetic depiction. However, the reliability of anecdotal reports and the putative role of AEs in creativity have been contested (Baylor, 2001; Sass, 2000–2001). Retrospective reports of the creative process have often been made many years after they are alleged to have occurred and may be contaminated by memory defects or embellished to concur with cultural expectations of a link between "genius" and "inspiration," eccentricity or even "madness" (Becker, 2000–2001).

Weisberg (1989; 2006) is a vociferous advocate of the "ordinary-thinking view" of creativity. Presenting case studies of eminent creatives, Pablo Picasso (his painting of *Guernica*) and Francis Crick (the discovery of DNA), he argues that one can understand the creative processes through trial and error, logical thinking and the use of analogy. Weisberg (2006) attempted to expose the creative cognition employed in artistic creativity through an analysis of Picasso's preliminary sketches for *Guernica*, a non-literal depiction of the horrors of war, based on the bombing of Guernica in the Spanish Civil War. Picasso dated and numbered these sketches, enabling them to be studied in chronological order. Weisberg argues that these show how systematic Picasso was in his development of the image, working out both its overall structure and exploring the portrayal of specific characters within it, before painting it. He proposes that creativity relies upon a gradual modification of existing ideas that requires only "ordinary cognition," hard work and experience — no moments of inspiration or anomalous experiences are necessary. Reports of such are either erroneous or incidental to the creative process itself. Nevertheless, we cannot directly ascertain either cognitive processes or subjective conscious experiences associated with creativity from recorded remnants. Such a conclusion must be based on empirical evidence, to which we shall turn in the following sections.

In summary, while their import and role in the creative process has been disputed, first-person reports of creative scientists and artists describe AEs of various types as playing a vital role in the creative process, including: pseudo-hallucinations, absorbed, expanded states and experiences of an autonomous "other."

Creativity and Anomaly Proneness: Schizotypy, Boundary Thinness and Transliminality

The first strand of relevant research has examined whether anomaly-proneness as a trait is associated with creativity. A number of correlational studies have compared scores on various indices of creativity to personality constructs that measure a proclivity to have AEs: positive schizotypy (Claridge, 1997), boundary thinness (Hartmann, 1991) and transliminality (Thalbourne & Delin, 1994). Scores on these three scales appear to be inter-correlated to a degree that suggests that they are measuring a similar construct ($rs > .40 < .78$, the average correlation being .64) (Farias, Claridge & Lalljee, 2005; Houran, Thalbourne & Hartmann, 2003; Thalbourne, Keogh & Gerke, 2005; Thalbourne & Maltby, 2008). Indeed, Thalbourne and Maltby (2008) reported that all three constructs loaded on a single factor, which accounted for 74.63 percent of the variance. In the paragraphs that follow, I will discuss the evidence for a link between creativity and these traits in turn.

Brod (1997, p. 276) defines schizotypy as "a set of behavioral, affective, and cognitive eccentricities, which in addition to forming some of the under-pinnings for episodes of psychotic illness, also exhibit in the normal population at a non-clinical level." The "unusual experiences" sub-trait of schizotypy assesses a proclivity to have unusual cognitive and perceptual experiences, including auditory hallucinations and pseudo-hallucinations, altered sensations and perceptions of one's own body and the world, hyper-sensitivity to sounds and smells as well as a heightened sensitivity to the external environment, déjà vu, jamais vu and magical beliefs (Mason, Claridge & Williams, 1997). "Unusual experiences" has formed significant positive correlations with measures of creativity in a number of recent studies (Batey & Furnham, 2008 [remote word associations[5]]; Burch, Pavelis, Hemsley, & Corr, 2006 [involvement in visual art]; O'Reilly, Dunbar & Bentall, 2001 [involvement in visual and performance arts]; Nettle, 2006 [involvement in poetry and visual arts]; Rawlings & Locarnini, 2008 [involvement in visual art and music]; Schuldberg, 2000–2001 [creative personality and divergent thinking[6]]; — but not Claridge & Blakey, 2009 [divergent thinking] or Claridge & McDonald, 2009 [divergent thinking]). This research supports the link between AEs and certain types of creativity. Saliently, involvement in the arts has consistently formed significant correlations with unusual experiences, while cognitive measures of creativity have proved to be unreliable predictors.

Thalbourne and Maltby (2008, p. 1618) define transliminality as "a hypersensitivity to psychological material originating in (a) the unconscious, and/or (b) the external environment." Thalbourne (2000b) describes the core correlates of transliminality as general religiosity, frequency of dream interpretation, schizotypal personality, fantasy-proneness, absorption and hyperaesthesia. Transliminality has further formed significant correlations with belief in psi-phenomena, paranormal experiences, daydreaming, introspection, altered consciousness, dream recall, unusual dreams and sensitivity to subliminal cues (Crawley, French & Yesson, 2002; Lange, Thalbourne, Houran & Storm, 2000; Thalbourne & Houran, 2000).

Thalbourne and Delin (1994, p. 23) reasoned that creative individuals should exhibit high transliminality because "their consciousness is characteristically and from time to time presented with thoughts— novel ideas or solutions to problems; connections between elements— that appear not to be the result of direct reasoning." Yet, empirical studies seeking to establish this link have had mixed success. Thalbourne, Bartemucci, Delin, Fox and Nofi (1997) found no significant correlation between transliminality and verbal divergent-thinking (Torrance, 2000). Subsequently, transliminality formed a significant positive correlation with a 9-item creative personality scale devised by Thalbourne himself, but not with the Revised Barron-Welsh Art Scale (1952)[7] (Thalbourne, 2000a). This work provides only weak support for a relationship between creativity and transliminality, with a non-validated measure of creative personality, and not with cognitive or perceptual measures.

The final trait to be considered is Hartmann's (1991) construct of boundary-thinness. Boundary-thinness has been described as a cognitive-style characterized by a fluid and "open" "organization of the mind" (Levin, Gilmartin & Lamontanaro, 1998, p. 25). Thin boundaries are associated with susceptibility to hypnosis and absorption (Barrett, 1989, cited by Hartmann, 1991, p. 106), the Intuition and Feeling sub-scales of the Myers-Briggs Type Indicator (Ehrman, 1993, cited by Hartmann et al., 1998, p. 33), perceiving meaning in randomness (Farias, Claridge & Lalljee, 2005) and access to dream imagery and vivid and unusual dream experiences, such as lucid dreams (Hicks, Bautista & Hicks, 1999; Levin, Gilmartin & Lamontanaro, 1998; Schredl, Kleinferchner & Gell, 1996).

Levin, Galin and Zywiak (1991) hypothesized that thin boundaries would facilitate associational fluency and accessibility to internal fantasy. However, neither a divergent-thinking measure (the Brick Uses Test, Guilford et al., 1957) nor a remoteness-of-associations measure (Mednick & Mednick, 1967) demonstrated significant correlations with boundary-thinness. Again, this corroborates the previous findings that cognitive measures of creativity do not appear to be related to anomaly-proneness.

Holt (2007) extended the battery of creativity measures that had previously been correlated with transliminality and boundary thinness. Anomaly-proneness correlated significantly with both artistic involvement (Griffin & McDermott, 1998) and emotional creativity (intrapersonal and interpersonal problem-solving) (Averill, 1999), but not with problem-solving in science, divergent thinking, remoteness of associations or creative personality (Gough, 1979). Further, professional artists had significantly higher anomaly-proneness scores than both professional scientists and a control group.

Overall, this research is suggestive of a link between non-cognitive and domain-contingent measures of creativity and a proclivity to report AEs. It suggests that only certain types of creativity are associated with anomaly-proneness as a trait: involvement in the arts and emotional creativity. Anomaly-proneness may be linked with creativity that involves paying attention to inner experience, being frequently and intensely concerned with affective and intrapersonal/interpersonal content (Albert & Runco, 1987).

Creativity and Specific Anomalous Experiences: Mystical and Oneiric

Rather than examining scores on a collection of unusual experiences further work has focused on distinct categories of AE, including lucid dreams (Snyder & Gackenbach, 1988), positive mystical experiences (Ayers, Beaton & Hunt, 1999), peak experiences (Taft, 1969), sensed presence (Persinger & Makarac, 1992), subjective paranormal experiences (Holt, Delanoy & Roe, 2004) and synesthesia (Ward et al., 2008). Due to space limitations, I will focus on studies that have examined a number of these concurrently.

An early study by Taft (1969) found significant positive correlations between scores on the Interest in Creative Activities Scale (Zimmerman & Guilford, 1963), covering a wide range of areas such as literature, inventions, art and creativity in everyday life and: *peak experiences* (characterized by a diminished awareness of self and amplified awareness of the external world, accompanied by intense positive emotion); *acceptance of fantasy* (imaginative absorption); and *automatic thought* (engaging in activities without active conscious control). This suggests that creative behavior is associated with AEs that involve a shift in self-awareness, imaginative absorption, dissociation and reduced self-control/rationalization — as exemplified in the first-person reports given earlier. Taft and Gilchrist (1970) extended these findings in a follow-up study, finding significant correlations between creativity (activities and personality) and self-reports of mystical experiences, daydreams and telepathic experiences.

Ayers, Beaton and Hunt (1999) tested the hypothesis that AEs are associated with creativity, controlling for the personality trait of absorption (an individual's openness to self-altering experiences). Might the tendency to enter states of imaginative absorption explain any link between creativity and AEs? A "creative group" (female artists) was compared to a "non-creative" control group that was matched for levels of absorption (female psychology undergraduates). Artists were more likely to report mystical experiences (Hood Mysticism Scale, 1975)and to score highly on a composite measure of what Ayers et al. called "positive altered states" (lucid dreams, archetypal-mythological dreams, mystical experiences and out-of-body experiences). The two groups did not differ on measures of neuroticism, emotional conflict or childhood trauma, suggesting that neither emotional lability nor disturbance were sufficient to explain the AEs of artists. This study leaves us with the question: if neither imaginative absorption nor emotional disturbance account for the association between creativity and AEs, what else might? Ayers et al. conclude that intense creative work in general is associated with a proclivity to have positive AEs. However, it is not clear from this study whether this proclivity applies to creativity in general or artistic involvement in particular.

Further work corroborates the link found by both Ayers et al. (1999) and Taft and Gilchrist (1970) between creativity and mystical experiences (Averill, 1999 [emotional creativity]; Kennedy & Kanthamani, 1995 [rating literary or artistic creativity as a very important aspect of one's life]; Thalbourne & Delin, 1994 [creative personality]). The mystical experience "diverges in fundamental ways from ordinary conscious awareness and leaves a strong impression of having encountered a reality different from the reality of everyday experience" (Wulff, 2000, p. 397). Mystical states of consciousness may involve transcendence (connection with a transcendent "other') accompanied by a sense of the divine, or immanence in some aspect of life, for example, perceiving "inner subjectivity, or life, in all things" (Stace, 1960, p. 131) (Fontana, 2007). However, both types are characterized by a sense of interconnection or unity with something "beyond the self," in addition to positive affect (Stace, 1960) and James's (1902/1985) well-known fundamental qualities: noesis (feelings of perceiving truth, of certitude); ineffability (having transcended rational logic and linguistic constraints); transience (the experience is fleeting) and passivity (reduced cognitive control). As part of the creative process an analogue is perhaps the report of painting accompanied by a loss of self-awareness by Milner (1950), the main commonality between creativity and mystical experiences being described by Brown (2008, p. 365) as a "retreat into the deep subjective."

That creativity is associated with lucid and bizarre dreams has also received additional support (Blagrove & Hartnell, 2000; Domino, 1976). Creativity is linked with both increased awareness of dreams and belief in their importance as a resource for creativity (Sladeczek & Domino, 1985). However, the dreams reported by creative individuals may be qualitatively different from those of less creative peers. Research suggests that the dreams of creatives have more: primary-process content (inconsistencies, symbolism and unusual combinations); archetypal-mythological content; visual imagery; departures from waking reality; dream bizarreness; and reports of lucidity (Blagrove & Hartnell, 2000 [creative personality]; Brodsky, Esquerre & Jackson, 1990–1991 [creative problem-solving task]; Domino, 1976 [composite measure of creative achievement, remote associations and divergent thinking]; Sladeczek & Domino, 1985 [creative artists and scientists]; Snyder & Gackenbach, 1988 [divergent thinking scores, for females only];—but not: Blagrove & Tucker, 1994 [creative personality]; or Wood, Sebba & Domino, 1990 [creative personality, esthetic/figural preference, divergent thinking and remote associations]). These relationships may be explainable by other factors. Firstly, by creatives having higher dream recall (Armitage & Fitch, 1988) (although Blagrove and Hartnell [2000] controlled for this in a study on lucid dreams). Secondly, by having a greater ability to express and record dreams due to verbal intelligence, thus affecting studies that ask participants to keep dream diaries to assess dream bizarreness (Wood, Sebba & Domino, 1990). Thirdly, Domino (1976) suggests that creatives may be more tolerant of unusual Dream content and therefore be more likely to report them. Despite these reservations, it appears, at least, that creative individuals may be more likely to remember and productively utilize "dreaming cognition."

Holt (2007) investigated the relationship between different AEs (measured by the Assessment Schedule for Altered States of Consciousness, van Quekelberghe et al., 1991) and different forms of creativity: emotional creativity, writing and remote word associations, figural divergent thinking, involvement with crafts and visual arts, involvement with music and performance arts, artistic creative personality and scientific creative personality. Controlling for mental health (using Barron's Ego-Strength Scale from the MMPI-2, Schuldberg, 1992) and partialling out the variance shared with other creativity measures, only two types of creativity were significantly associated with AEs. These were emotional creativity (using cognition about affect to solve intrapersonal and interpersonal problems) and artistic creative personality. Emotional creativity was associated with a broad range of AEs: parapsychological experiences (e.g., telepathy and precognition), positive mystical experiences (positive affect, bliss, a sense of unity, loss of self awareness, deep understanding), negative mystical experiences (disintegration of self, fear, horror, feelings of losing one's sanity), vivid and unusual dreams (archetypal dreams, lucid dreams, hypnagogia and paying attention to dreams), dissociation (high levels of concentration and absorption, entering relaxed states in-between waking and sleeping) and hallucinations (perceptual anomalies, e.g., visual and auditory hallucinations and apparitions). However, only having a vivid imagination (strong visualization abilities and daydreaming) and positive mystical experiences, along with scoring *low* on negative mystical experiences, predicted artistic creative personality. These results suggest that there are two pathways between creativity and AEs: (1) affective awareness and creativity — a powerful predictor of AEs in general; and (2) artistic creative personality — a predictor of "positive" AEs only.

From this brief review it appears that reports of AEs do seem to be associated with creativity. However, the precise nature of this relationship is not clear. Although the evidence points most robustly to a link between artistic involvement and AEs, several questions remain unanswered. Is there an underlying cognitive-style or organization of mind that enables both artistic creativity and AEs? Might different types of creativity involve AEs in particular circumstances, as exemplified by the anecdotal reports of AEs amongst scientists? If so, what factors facilitate this? The relationship between AEs and cognitive measures of creativity is inconsistent. However, a significant association might emerge in a meta-analytical review, that considers the role of moderating variables? It is also important to note that while a tendency to report AEs may be related to creativity, the effect sizes are small to moderate, leaving much of the variance in creativity unexplained. Creativity is a componential phenomenon. Other factors play an important role in the creative process such as sedulous preparation, evaluation, practice, motivation and drive.

There are methodological problems with this body of work. A serious problem is that of potential reporting artefacts. Perhaps certain populations (such as artists) are more likely to report or share unusual, potentially taboo experiences; perhaps they pay more attention to intrapersonal experiences and thus are more likely to remember them; or perhaps AEs are likely to be integrated into the worldview of certain populations and are thus reported/remembered. Retrospective reports in general, and those of AEs, have been associated with failures of memory and inaccurate perception: verbal suggestion, post-event misinformation effects, retrospective bias (e.g., misremembering), "imagination inflation" (e.g., in cases of past-life regression through hypnosis) and theory-driven interpretations of past events (e.g. corresponding to a spiritual belief system or to a persona of "eccentric artist"—"misremembering" to avoid cognitive dissonance) (French, 2003). For example, Apelle, Lynn and Newan (2000) emphasize the role of the "cultural prototype" in reports of alien abduction and Barrett, Robin, Pietromonaco and Eyssell (1998) found that while self-reports of emotionality differed according to gender, there was no difference in the actual lived experience of affect according to gender. The previously reported differences, they argue, were based on personal constructs influenced by the cultural stereotype of women being the emotional sex, rather than actual experiences. Such work suggests that we must interpret the correlations between creativity and AEs cautiously — noting only that *reports* of AEs appear to be associated with components of creativity. Further, we still need to investigate whether any relationship between AEs and creativity is direct or indirect — might AEs have a causal role in the creative process?

Direct or Indirect? Do Anomalous Experiences Play a Causal Role in the Creative Process?

It seems clear that there is an association between reporting having had an AE and indices of creativity, especially artistic creativity (Ayers et al., 2007; Burch et al., 2006; Holt, 2007; Kennedy & Kanthamani, 2004; O'Reilly et al., 2001; Nettle, 2006; Rawlings & Locarnini, 2008; Taft, 1969). However, the nature of this predominantly correlational self-report work does not allow us to infer causality. From it we cannot assess whether or not AEs are directly involved in the creative process or are incidental to it. This distinction is important because it enables us to discern whether or not AEs are functional, contributing to creative production and transformation.

The evidence for a direct link is sparse, but several strands of research can be used to inform our opinion on this matter: EEG work on creative problem solving (Martindale, 1999), neurofeedback training to help artists to enter a "flow" or hypnagogic state (Egner & Gruzelier, 2003), incubation studies (Sio & Ormerod, 2009) and research that has attempted to interpolate an altered state of consciousness into the creative process in an experimental setting, through the use of hypnosis (Council, Bromley, Zabelina & Waters, 2007), perceptual isolation (Norlander, Kjellgren & Archer, 2002–2003) or the administration of alcohol or psychoactive drugs (Norlander & Gustafson, 1998; Sessa, 2008). Not all of these studies examine AEs directly, however, they do examine whether shifts in subjective experience that also occur in AEs (e.g. reduced self-awareness) affect creative performance.

Much of this work draws upon and tests the parameters of stage models of the creative process, which have attempted to identify experiential sequences that contribute to creativity. The most commonly cited stage model was expounded by Wallas (1926) and includes four phases: preparation; incubation; illumination; and verification.[9] He posited the following pattern: the creator will immerse themselves in the details of a problem, analyzing and drawing upon knowledge and experience (preparation), until, after a period of struggling and juggling with information they will rest, letting the search for a solution take a low priority in conscious awareness (incubation), until a moment when a potential solution, unexpectedly and vividly, enters awareness (illumination), leading, finally, to the testing of the appropriateness of this potential solution and its practical development or production (verification). Not all subsequent empirical research supported this four-stage model — it has been suggested that the model be extended to include additional stages, such as: "problem finding," the identification of flaws, gaps or inconsistencies (Getzels & Csikszentmihalyi, 1976) (see Lubart, 2000–2001 for a review). Nevertheless, the implication that the creative process involves experiential shifts is clear.

As the name suggests, incubation studies have sought to test the efficacy of the incubation stage of creativity, i.e., whether or not taking a break from a problem enhances its subsequent solution, and if so, what the characteristics of this break optimally are (Dodds, Ward & Smith, 2003). For example, does a particular state of consciousness during this break facilitate a "creative breakthrough"? A recent meta-analysis reported an overall significant incubation effect (Sio & Ormerod, 2009). Completing tasks with high cognitive loads during the incubation period was associated with reduced creativity compared with low cognitive loads or rest, suggesting that the interpolated task is best when it does not demand high levels of attentional resources. The reason for this small incubation effect is, however, not clear, there being support for several models: distraction leading to "set shifting," the forgetting incorrect answers and the restructuring of a problem (Schooler & Melcher, 1995); automatic or unconscious thought (Dijksterhuis & Meurs, 2006); relaxation and reduction of stress/fatigue, perhaps enabling diffuse attention and remote associations (Sio & Ormerod, 2009); or opportunistic assimilation, a chance encounter with a cue (Christensen & Schunn, 2005). In support of the "creativity and AEs" hypothesis, this work at least implies that a shift from focused concentration on a creative problem to a state of reduced cognitive striving facilitates original ideation. Interpolation studies have attempted to manipulate participants' state of consciousness during the incubation stage, or prior to completing a divergent thinking task, through perceptual isolation, the administration of drugs or hypnotic induction.

A number of studies have explored the effects of perceptual isolation upon creative performance (Norlander, Bergman & Archer, 1998; Norlander, Kjellgren & Archer, 2002–2003; Suedfeld, Metcalfe & Bluck, 1987). Suedfeld et al. (1987) conducted a small study with five psychology faculty members. The creativity of new research ideas was compared in two counterbalanced environmental conditions: (1) Restricted Environmental Stimulation Technique (REST); (2) normal office conditions. REST consisted of a 60-minute period in a flotation tank, which is quiet, dark, and enables the participant to float with their face and ventral body surface above water. REST has been associated with deep relaxation and reduced anxiety (Suedfeld, Steel & Wallbaum, 1994). Ratings of the creativity of ideas were significantly higher in the REST condition. Completion of a mood scale indicated that participants felt more positive affect whilst in the flotation tank. Interviews held after each REST session suggested that participants entered what Suedfeld et al. (1987) call a "twilight state," features of which included: (1) alterations in sense of self (loss of self awareness, the self leaving the body or losing sense of space and time); (2) a suspension of critical thinking; and (3) vivid imagery. This supports the thesis that a relaxed, altered state, accompanied by positive affect, might facilitate creativity.

Subsequent studies with larger sample sizes have been conducted by Norlander and colleagues. Norlander, Bergman and Archer (1998) randomly allocated participants to one of three conditions: flotation-REST, control or "dryREST" (lying in a darkened chamber), after which they completed a battery of tests, including those of ideational fluency and originality. Participants in the flotation-REST condition obtained significantly higher originality scores than participants in other conditions. Both REST procedures were associated with relaxation and perceptual isolation, thus why flotation-REST was particularly advantageous to original ideation remained unexplained. Norlander, Kjellgren and Archer (2002–2003) addressed this in a replication study. The original findings were confirmed, creativity scores being higher in the flotation-REST condition. Further, they observed decreased performance on tests of logical thinking after both REST conditions. Self-report data confirmed that although both REST conditions were relaxing, the flotation-REST condition led to altered states of consciousness. Altered states were measured by total scores on a scale entitled Experienced Deviation from Normal State developed by the authors. However, the contents of this scale are not otherwise described. This study appears to support a causal link between AEs and originality, although the experiential components that constituted "altered" were not identified. However, Norlander et al. (2002–2003) did not control for expectation effects associated with different relaxation procedures and also did not measure baseline levels of originality to directly assess whether individuals produced more original ideation after an experience in the flotation tank. Neither can we ascertain whether this effect would be maintained over numerous trials or whether it is an artifact of the relative novelty of the experience.

Further interpolation studies have sought to induce a shift in consciousness through the administration of drugs, in particular alcohol and psychedelic drugs. A complete overview of this research is beyond the scope of this Chapter, thus the reader will be referred to comprehensive reviews (Plucker & Dana, 1999; Norlander, 1999; Sessa, 2008).

In a series of experimental studies, Norlander and Gustafson (1994; 1996; 1997; 1998) tested the impact of alcohol on different stages of the creative process (in comparison with control and placebo conditions). Taken collectively, these studies suggest that a moderate dose of alcohol: impairs the preparation stage, reducing persistency of effort; improves the originality, but not the flexibility, of ideas produced in the incubation/illumination stages; and impairs handicraft ability in the verification stage, where ideas are used in the making of a creative product. Indeed, Roe (1946), in a qualitative study with eminent painters living in New York, found that whilst all of them reported drinking alcohol to relax, they did not use alcohol whilst painting, believing that it had a negative impact on their work. Norlander and Gustafason (1998) suggest that moderate amounts of alcohol may lead to a relaxed state where loose, associative cognition dominates, thus leading to novel ideation.

What then, of psychedelic drugs (lysergic acid diethylamide, mescaline and psilocybin), which might lead to a more extreme shift in consciousness? Psychedelic drugs cause alterations in perception, emotion and expansion of both self and cognitive associations (Sessa, 2008). Work in this area is of course limited due to legal prohibitions. Five studies on psychedelic drugs and creativity were conducted prior to such legislation but these were all small pilot studies, lacking adequate controls, and further, have contradictory results (Krippner, 1972). Nevertheless, Krippner suggests that two studies that worked with creative professionals rather than students were suggestive of a facilitative effect. For example, Harman et al. (1966) selected creative scientists, who were struggling with a problem, to ingest mescaline under positive conditions that suggested creative breakthrough would occur. Scores on creativity tests and judges' ratings of the ideas that were produced as a result of this interpolation led Harman et al. to suggest that psychedelics might facilitate the illumination phase of the creative process. Based on self-reports they identified a number of experiential qualities that might help creativity, such as free association, heightened visual imagery, reduced censorship of thoughts and relaxation. They also noted that the psychedelic state produced hindrances to creativity such as reduced logical thinking, the inability to consciously direct attention, anxiety and a tendency to focus on personal issues. Participants could not judge the effectiveness of their own ideas whilst in the psychedelic state. Overall, this body of work is inconclusive and this area would benefit from modern research with more sophisticated designs (e.g., being double blind and having both control and placebo conditions).

Imaginative thinking has been observed in hypnosis— as confabulation, fantasy, story-telling, the creation of false memories, etc. (Lynn & Sivec, 1992). Might hypnosis facilitate creativity? Unfortunately, the results of research examining the effects of hypnosis on creative performance are mixed and unclear (Shames & Bowers, 1992). Experimental studies with a non-hypnosis control condition have reported a positive effect (for figural divergent thinking only, Gur & Reyher, 1976); partial effects (not for originality of ideas, but for flexibility, fluency and elaboration of figural divergent thinking,[10] Jackson & Gorassini, 1989; and for figural elaboration only, Ashton & McDonald, 1985); and no effect (for verbal divergent thinking, free association to stimulus words and the interpretation of inkblots, Bowers & van der Meulen, 1970). This research is riddled with methodological problems, such as using different creativity measures, and procedural difficulties with using measures when participants are hypnotized, leading to deviations from standard protocol (Shames & Bowers, 1992). Further, whilst hypnosis is thought to modify awareness, leading to a suspension of reality testing and a narrowing or expanding of consciousness, it is not possible to discern from this research what state of consciousness participants were actually in when "being creative."

Only one study has followed up this early work on creativity and hypnosis. Council, Bromley, Zabelina and Waters (2007) attempted to improve ecological validity by assessing improvement in still life drawings (with psychology undergraduates). They also assessed participants' experiential states. Compared to drawings by participants in a control group, who received no hypnotic intervention, drawings in a hypnosis condition were rated by expert judges as being more creative and esthetically pleasing.[11] Participants in the hypnosis condition reported being more relaxed whilst drawing, but, they did not experience more time distortion (which is associated with the flow state and imaginative absorption). Perhaps in future work the experiential qualities of the induced state could be assessed in more detail, using established measures such as Pekala's (1991) Phenomenology of Consciousness Inventory.

Taken as a whole, interpolation studies suggest that relaxed states with low cognitive load increase originality. This appears to come at the cost of reducing performance on tests of logical thinking. This body of work certainly supports the causal hypothesis that shifts in conscious experience are conducive to creativity. Yet, relaxation alone, rather than AEs, may be sufficient; although, altered states (involving alterations in one's sense of self, vivid imagery and reduced cognitive striving) were more fecund with original ideation in the REST studies. More information about the phenomenology of states induced during the interpolation stage is required in order to clarify what experiential factors might improve creative performance. For example, can this be attributed to relaxation, positive affect, bizarre imagery, or a combination of these? The interpolation research is disparate and unsystematic with regards to theory testing. Few studies have directly tested potential underlying processes that might facilitate creativity and it still remains unclear what role factors such as expectancy effects or novelty might play. Most studies have relied upon measures of divergent thinking (with no assessment of how well ideas work in practice) and have not worked with special populations, such as artists. As such, any indication that AEs play a role in creativity can only be weakly inferred.

In the next section, work that has examined neurological correlates of creative performance as indicators of shifts in conscious experience will be considered.

Egner and Gruzelier (2003) assessed artistic *performance* after a period of neurofeedback training. The neurofeedback programme aimed to increase theta over alpha waves and produce a relaxed wakeful state. Frontocentral theta activity has been associated with focused states, meditative concentration and feelings of well-being (Gruzelier, 2009). Working with music students at the Royal College of Music, Egner and Gruzelier found that alpha/theta training significantly improved participants' performances whilst playing music in comparison to a control group who received no neurofeedback training. The ratings of creative performance were made by blind judges (on imagination, communication, rhythmical accuracy and competence). Edge and Lancaster (2004) reported on the musicians' experiences of the training programme and its effect upon their performance — the following is a description by a female pianist:

> During the training sessions I feel extremely relaxed and as though my mind is able to freely glide with my creative ideas bringing a new kind of spontaneity and energy to my thought processes ... this gives me the opportunity to explore other areas of creativity that were previously unavailable to me as I'm free from the physical act of playing the piano whilst mentally being in the state of a performance. It's an extremely satisfying state to be in as it's almost as though I've been introduced to thinking of nothing, which then takes me to a place where creative possibilities seem boundless. (Gruzelier, 2009, p. 104.)

That the expressiveness and technical performance of creatives may be enhanced by alpha/theta EEG-biofeedback has been replicated in a number of subsequent studies, with competitive ballroom dancers (Raymond, Sajid, Parkinson & Gruzelier, 2005), novice singers (Leach, Holmes, Hirst & Gruzelier, *in preparation*, cited by Gruzelier, 2009) and professional singers from the Stuttgart Opera (Kleber, Gruzelier, Bensch & Birbaumer, *in preparation*, cited by Gruzelier, 2009). However, what state of consciousness might this procedure induce? Might it be akin to the hypnagogic state, as Gruzelier (2009) suggests, or to the flow state, as suggested in the quote above, with its emphasis upon automaticity and "being in the state of a performance"? Indeed, the protocol has been criticized for not leading to clear changes in EEG activity post-training, or at least this has not been reported (Vernon, 2005). Vernon (2005) notes that it is not possible to discern whether any putative changes might be due to alpha decreasing, theta increasing, a combination of the two, or both increasing but with a preponderance of theta — or indeed whether there are any long-lasting changes at all. He also criticizes the methodology, noting that the control groups had less contact with the experimenters than the neurofeedback group, which may be a confounding factor.

Neurofeedback has been used in various fields in an attempt to facilitate "optimal performance," particularly in sport, for example, with pre-elite archers (Landers et al., 1991) and as such is not specific to creativity. However, Gruzelier (2009) argues that creative cognition might also be enhanced through alpha/theta neurofeedback training, drawing upon neuropsychological research suggesting that theta facilitates long distance cortical and subcortical connections, which might underpin novel ideation. Boynton (2001) assessed the creative performance of participants before and after alpha/theta neurofeedback and found no enhancement of divergent thinking in comparison to a control group. However, this study had a potential confound in the conditions, where both groups received training that facilitated access to hypnagogia (both groups showed improved creativity). In contrast, Gruzelier (2009) cites a study conducted by himself and colleagues (Thompson, Steffert, Redding & Gruzelier, unpublished) which did find an increase in cognitive creativity after neurofeedback training. Thus, as yet, the effect of alpha/theta training upon creative cognition requires further empirical evidence and validation of the protocol.

An earlier strand of EEG-creativity research focused on alpha levels (Martindale & Hines, 1975; Martindale & Hasenfus, 1978). Martindale's (1999) arousal hypothesis states that creative thinking is enabled by shifts into relaxed states, characterized by low cortical arousal. Martindale (1977–78) suggests that low arousal and loose, undirected cognition are likely to arise in altered states of consciousness, thus explaining anecdotal reports of AEs during the creative process; however, he did not test this directly.

Initial support for this arousal hypothesis came from a study comparing scores on creativity[13] and verbal IQ tests under conditions of low (relaxed environment), medium (pressurized environment) and high (white noise stimulation) arousal. The high arousal condition led to lower creativity scores and the low arousal condition to lower IQ scores, suggesting that states of medium-high arousal diminish creative performance (Martindale & Greenough, 1973). Subsequent studies measured cortical arousal (the inverse incidence of alpha) during tasks analogous to the two-stage model (e.g., illumination and elaboration).

Although creative people (high scorers on divergent-thinking tests) tended to have slightly higher baseline arousal (Martindale, 1977–78), Martindale and Hines (1975) found that they showed reduced cortical arousal while completing a divergent-thinking task, but not when taking an intelligence test. In contrast, the arousal of low creatives was maintained across both tests. Further, while thinking of a story (inspiration), high creatives (as rated by creative writing instructors) had low arousal, but medium-high arousal when writing out the final version (elaboration), whereas, again, low creatives had a steady level of arousal across these stages (Martindale & Hasenfus, 1978). This appeared to indicate that "creatives" shift into defocused states according to task demands. A recent replication of Martindale's work supported the arousal hypothesis (Fink & Neubauer, 2006).[14]

Overall, this collection of experimental research does not enable us to clearly decipher whether or not AEs might lead to creativity. Norlander's work on perceptual isolation comes closest to establishing such a causal link, suggesting that altered, not simply relaxed, states facilitate original ideation. It is difficult to isolate state of consciousness factors from other factors, such as expectation, experimenter contact, novelty, etc. However, the research does suggest that there is scope for further work testing the hypotheses that: (a) absorbed states akin to the flow state enhance performance on skilled tasks through which creative ideas are executed; and (b) that relaxed, perhaps altered, states facilitate remote cognitive associations. The literature suggests that relaxed or altered states are only conducive to creativity at particular stages of the creative process— those which do not require logical thinking. Further, particular AEs and not others might be conducive to creativity, for example, a state akin to "flow" appears to have enhanced creative performance in Gruzelier's research, whilst moderate doses of alcohol impaired performance in Norlander's research. In the future, rigorous research is needed to explore these issues and to build process models of the causal relationship between creativity and AEs, for example, testing whether specific states of consciousness are conducive to creativity, and to particular components and types of creativity.

We are also left with a curious contradiction. While self-report studies suggest that divergent thinking is not, or is at best weakly, associated with AEs, the experimental work suggests that originality on divergent thinking tasks can be improved through relaxation, perceptual isolation and moderate doses of alcohol. Might it be that particular states of consciousness facilitate divergent thinking (i.e., relaxation or daydreams), while more radical departures from everyday conscious experience might be associated with other types of creativity, such as artistic involvement?

Potential Mechanisms: How Might Creativity and Anomalous Experiences Be Linked?

Having established that there is evidence for an association between artistic creativity and AEs, plus some support for the hypothesis that relaxed, and perhaps altered states, play a direct role in the creative process, in this section a review will be made of psychological models that purport to explain such findings. Debate continues about whether any relationship between AEs and creativity might be due to loose cognitive associations, affective lability, valence or intensity, or to personality and motivational variables (Jamison, 1993; Kinney et al., 2001; O'Reilly et al., 2001; Schuldberg, 2000–2001). A review of these models will be made. Although discussed separately, they are not mutually exclusive; for example, a personality trait such as transliminality might be associated with both loose cognitive associations and intense affective states (Thalbourne, 2000).

Neurocognitive Models

The most commonly expounded models to explain links between AEs and creativity are *neurocognitive* (e.g., Eysenck, 1993; Martindale, 1989) and suggest that the making of remote-associations underpins both creativity and anomaly-proneness.

Associative models of creativity focus on the combination of remotely connected elements. Mednick (1962, p. 221) defines creative thinking as "the forming of associative elements into new combinations," constrained by goals and selection criteria, where "the more mutually remote the elements of the new combination, the more creative the process." Creativity, Mednick argued, was enabled by "flat associative hierarchies." A flat associative hierarchy is an organization of mental elements where all potential responses are "weighted" equally, hence, rare responses are as likely to be made to a stimulus as common ones; further, *more* responses are likely to be made (associational fluency). In "steep associative hierarchies," one or two responses are dominant (weighted more heavily). These are usually culturally stereotypical responses. For example, in reaction to the word "foot," a stereotypical response might be "shoe," while more remotely relevant responses may include "stool" or "inch." Mednick suggested that the word-association behavior of a creative individual is less stereotypical. Such a position is still held by those contemporary researchers who argue that all creativity involves the flexible browsing of and connection of remote semantic elements into a cohesive and effective whole (e.g., Gianotti, Mohr, Pizzagalli, Lehmann & Brugger, 2001; Martindale, 1999), and that, as such, loose associative processing might be the cognitive mechanism that underpins the creative process.

Martindale's (1989; 1995; 1999) connectionist model of creativity proposes a mechanism for flat associative hierarchies. Attention is described as the most activated nodes in a neural network. Across and within nodes are represented a wide diversity of facts and associations. When attention is focused, a few nodes are highly activated (a steep associative hierarchy). When attention is defocused activation is more evenly spread out across a greater number of nodes (a flat associative hierarchy). Martindale (1991) proposes that each node receives "information" from other nodes (excitation or inhibition, which facilitates or prevents the activation of other nodes, respectively) and also from the arousal system, so that the total activation of a node follows the following law: (excitatory input — inhibitory input) x arousal. This means that increases in arousal lead to more stereotyped responses (it will amplify the activation of the nodes that have slightly higher overall excitatory activation). In other words, Martindale argues that low arousal is related to defocused attention, flat associative hierarchies and thereby to the making of novel, remote associations/novel ideas. However, Martindale (1977–78) also suggested that very high arousal might lead to flat associative hierarchies too (presumably because if sufficiently high, any overall excitatory input, however low, might be amplified enough to cross the threshold level required to activate the node). Medium arousal, he suggests, is associated with logical, reality-oriented, secondary-process cognition and steep associative hierarchies. Martindale tested the idea that arousal is related to creativity (the results of which were discussed in the previous section and which support his model).[15] The implication of Martindale's work is that creative cognition is enabled by attentional shifts, from relaxed states characterized by low cortical arousal (that enable originality) to focused, active states, characterized by medium-high cortical arousal (that enable preparation and verification). Thus described, creatives are "ambicognitive" (Brod, 1997, p. 286) and might frequently shift into states of low cortical arousal. Low cortical arousal (hypofrontality) is also a correlate of AEs, such as the flow state and mystical experiences (Dietrich, 2003, 2004; Vaitl et al., 2005). Thus, according to this model, creative people may be more likely to have AEs as a function of "ambicognitivity" or lability of cortical arousal.

Eysenck (1993) drew parallels between creative cognition and psychoticism, arguing that both are underpinned by "overinclusive" thinking. Support for his thesis came from research assessing the performance of creative individuals on word-association tasks and object-sorting tasks (e.g. Lovibond, 1954) that assess idiosyncrasies in the categorical assessment of common objects, tests which were developed as indices of psychosis (Dykes & McGhie, 1976; Merton & Fischer, 1999; Rawlings & Toogood, 1999). The notion that a continuum of cognitive looseness underpins both creativity and AEs has also been argued by both Prentky (2000–2001) and Mohr et al. (2001). For example, Prentky (2000–2001) proposed a normally distributed cognitive-style that ranges from "extreme constriction" to "extreme expansion." Creativity requires shifts along this continuum, from wide-attentional, holistic, to focused, detailed processing. However, more extreme deviations lead to unusual experiences—hallucinations and delusions at the constriction end and states of extreme distractibility and defocused attention at the expansion end of the continuum. Support for such a link comes from a study by Tsakanikos and Claridge (2005) who found a significant correlation between verbal fluency (one subcomponent of divergent thinking) and hallucinations. They argued that both are caused by increased spreading of activation within semantic networks. In the case of hallucinations, the over-activation of a lexical unit is thought to lead to an auditory hallucination, whereas, in creativity, activation may lead to a loose associative network, e.g., of lexical units when writing a poem. Experientially, this may be akin to Kekulé's description of ideas arising and combining in a hypnagogic state.

Eysenck (1993) proposed cognitive disinhibition, and more specifically, latent disinhibition, as a mechanism for overinclusive thinking. Latent inhibition has been defined as "the capacity to screen from conscious awareness stimuli previously experienced as irrelevant" (Carson, Peterson & Higgins, 2003, p. 499), an unconscious process that adaptively reduces the load on working memory, selecting relevant stimuli and ignoring irrelevant stimuli (Wuthrich & Bates, 2001). It was hypothesized by Eysenck that reduced latent inhibition would enable unusual, novel or irrelevant information to enter awareness more readily. Indeed, Carson, Peterson and Higgins (2003) observed that high creative achievers had significantly lower latent inhibition scores than low creative achievers. The positive dimension of schizotypy (unusual experiences) has also been associated with latent disinhibition (Gray et al., 2002). Thus, two studies provide support for Eysenck's model, but further replication is required. Claridge (1993) suggested that latent inhibition as a mechanism for creativity is too simplistic and "low level" and too focused on cognitive dysfunction. If "creativity is a cognitive disinhibition syndrome" (Barrantes-Vidal, 2004, p. 60), then high creatives, compared to low creatives should demonstrate further cognitive-disinhibition effects. On the whole, relationships between cognitive inhibition (e.g., negative priming) and divergent-thinking are mixed, providing weak support for this model (e.g., Burch, Hemsley, Pavelis & Corr, 2006; Green & Williams, 1999; Kwiatowski, Oshin & Martindale, 1999; Rawlings, 1985; Wuthrich & Bates, 2001). However, the cognitive inhibition tasks used in these studies don't require creative thinking, and thus, according to Martindale's reasoning, won't require creatives to shift into states associated with cognitive inhibition. More creative research protocols are thus required to test the relationship between originality and cognitive disinhibition.

An alternative explanation for loose cognitive associations is the *right hemisphere preference* model (Prentky, 2000–2001; Weinstein & Graves, 2002). The laterality hypothesis of creativity emerged from work with patients who had had corpus callosotomies (split-brain patients)—these patients showed reduced imaginative capacity (Hoppe, 1994). It was thus hypothesized that the right hemisphere was important for creative ideation. Experimental work has supported a role for the right hemisphere in creativity: presenting words for association to the left visual field (right hemisphere) has resulted in more remote associations (Dimond & Beaumont, 1974); creatives showed better right hemisphere (left ear) localization ability on a dichotic listening task (Weinstein & Graves, 2001); and creatives had more right-hemispheric activity during creativity tasks (Martindale, Hines, Mitchell & Covello, 1984). However, it appears that the activation of *both* hemispheres is important for creative ideation. As such, creativity may be associated with increased hemispheric interaction (Hoppe & Kyle, 1990), particularly in the prefrontal regions (Carlsson, Wendt & Risberg, 2000). Recent brain imaging studies have associated creative cognition with increases in alpha power in the posterior cortex of the right hemisphere with concurrent alpha synchronization in the prefrontal circuits (Fink et al., 2006; Howard-Jones et al., 2006)—supporting both Martindale's arousal model and the laterality hypothesis, where remote associations involve hypofrontality and right hemispheric networks. Reduced hemispheric asymmetry has also been found amongst high schizotypals (Broks, Claridge, Matheson, & Hargreaves, 1984) and has been correlated with AEs such as sensed presence (Persinger & Healey, 2002) and mystical experiences (Beauregard & Paquette, 2006; Fenwick, 2001).

In summary, neurocognitive models of the creative process suggest that originality arises through the contiguity and combination of remote cognitive elements, the likelihood of which is facilitated by defocused states that are underpinned by low cortical arousal, cognitive disinhibition and/or hemispheric laterality. Eysenck (1993) and Prentky (2000–2001) emphasize a continuum of cognitive looseness, with moderate looseness facilitating creativity and extreme looseness facilitating unusual experiences such as hallucinations. For Martindale (1999) creative ideation requires flexible shifting between low and medium-high states of arousal, again, implying an experiential continuum. Shifts in attention, cognition and arousal are key dimensions of phenomenological consciousness that are also implicated in AEs (e.g. Pekala, 1991). It may be that the degree of shift is important in distinguishing between these types of experiences—where small shifts along a continuum lead to original ideation and larger shifts to AEs. If this is the case, neurocognitive models could account for the experimental findings described in the previous sections, where relaxed states appeared to be sufficient for original ideation, but where originality was not consistently associated with anomaly-proneness. Both creative people and anomalous experiments may have in common the ability to have experiences along this proposed continuum, some shifts leading to creative ideation and others to AEs, with no direct link between the two. In this case some other factor is required to explain the significant correlations between artistic creativity and AEs.

In terms of health, neurocognitive models place AEs on a continuum with "everyday" reality-oriented awareness, with no sharp dividing line between the two, with the same mechanisms underpinning them. Martindale's approach is "health" neutral, while Eysenck associates AEs with psychosis. As they stand, neurocognitive models can distinguish neither between different types of AE nor differential health outcomes and thus require the addition of further interacting factors. These may include life stressors and coping skills (Claridge, 2001) and further phenomenological components, such as affective valence and sense of control (Pekala, 1991).

Affective Models

Breadth of attention and arousal are not the only dimensions of consciousness implicated in AEs; further dimensions include imagery, self-awareness and affect (Vaitl et al., 2005). A number of models have propounded the importance of affect to cognition and consciousness (Damasio, 2000; LeDoux, 1989) and several theorists have highlighted the failure to include affect in cognitive models of creativity (Averill, 1999; 2005; Getz & Lubart, 1999; Runco, 1994). Neurocognitive models do not include aspects of overinclusive, primary process cognition that were described by Pine and Holt (1960, p.

370) as being "generally pervaded by intense emotionality—feelings of omnipotence, intense pleasure and/or pain." Likewise, AEs, such the flow state or sensed presence, are often accompanied by intense emotional states— of bliss and fear respectively (Csikszentmihalyi, 1996; Persinger & Healey, 2002). Taft (1969) thus suggested that affective openness might be the common link between creativity and AEs. Persinger and Makarec (1992) speculated whether intense affective states during artistic creative production, such as the writing of a poem with a sense of profound meaning, might trigger a sensed presence.

Affect has been proposed to be involved in creativity in a number of ways: (1) *motivationally*: the expression of emotions through catharsis or purgation (Averill, 2005; Getz & Lubart, 1999); (2) *cognitively*: moods have been shown to affect cognitive processing. States of mild positive affect facilitate divergent thinking, possibly triggering a broad associative network (Isen, 1999; Davis, 2009); (3) *experientially*: emotions may accompany the creative process, the pleasure or excitement of problem-solving, as well as anxiety and frustration (Averill, 2005; Runco, 1994) [this links into 1) as these emotions might provide tension or unusual perspectives that drive the process (Schuldberg, 1994) or positive affect might reinforce creative involvement (Russ, 1999)]; (4) *functionally*: emotions might trigger particular mental content; associations may be made between emotions, images and concepts, as well as between concepts and images alone (Getz & Lubart, 1999; Russ, 1999); (5) *emotional creativity*: Averill (1999) takes this relationship further by arguing that emotions and emotional responses may be products of the creative process in their own right.

Both Russ (1999) and Getz and Lubart (1999) argue that individual differences in affect, such as openness to and tolerance of affect, are likely to impact upon the use of the affective dimension in the creative process. Individuals who are interested in and open to affective states, it is reasoned, will have a more diverse, detailed and complex store of emotional memories or "affect symbols" (Russ, 1999), which are associated with idiosyncratic associative elements. Openness to affect, described by Krystal and Krystal (1994) as the inverse of alexithymia, is, they argue, central to creativity as it makes richer material available for problem-solving. Alexithymia is characterized by an inability to describe emotions and has been related to inhibition of fantasy, creativity and dream recall (Hoppe, 1994). Affective tolerance, Runco (1994) suggests, might increase the ability to handle creative tension (e.g., the disequilibrium of "not knowing') and uncomfortable or negative emotional experiences associated with the creative process. Thus, one would expect individual differences in affect plus tolerance or emotional regulation to moderate the creative process.

Given that affect is an important factor in creative functioning, might individual differences in emotional experience be a common correlate of both AEs and creativity? A range of constructs have in common a tendency towards reflection on emotional experience, a greater awareness of emotions, and in some constructs, the effective regulation of emotions. These are continuum traits and are assumed to be normally distributed in the general population, such as: psychological mindedness (McCallum & Piper, 2000), emotional awareness (Lane, 2000), emotional complexity (Kang & Shaver, 2004), emotional creativity (Averill, 1999) and emotional intelligence (Mayer & Geher, 1996). A small number of studies support the notion that such affective variables are related to creativity. Carlozzi, Bull and Eell (1995) found affective sensitivity — one's ability to detect the affective state of individuals in film-scenes— to predict involvement in creative activities (artistic, scientific and managerial/teaching). Emotional creativity, a construct which includes increased affective awareness (Gohm & Clore, 2002) appears to be associated with divergent thinking, creative personality and involvement in the creative arts (as well as AEs) (Holt, 2007; Ivcevic, Brackett & Mayer, 2007). Further evidence of openness-to-affect being related to creativity has come from tests using anxiety-provoking subliminal stimuli (a threatening face) (Smith & van der Meer, 1994). "Creatives" were less likely to repress or distort subliminal threats. These findings may pertain more to creativity in the arts. In a meta-analysis of creative personality across domains, Feist (1999) found that creative artists were more prone to intense affective experience than creative scientists.

An affective pathway that might link creativity and AEs has been suggested by Dietrich (2004a). Dietrich proposes four "types of creativity," based on different neural circuits. These have either deliberate or spontaneous "processing modes" and process either emotional or cognitive content. The "processing mode" depends upon mental functions associated with activation of the prefrontal cortex (PFC), which enables higher cognitive functions, such as self-reflective consciousness, planning, temporal integration and sustained focused attention, possible because of the sustained buffering of information that is held "on-line" and integrated in working memory. In deliberate processing modes the search for creative insights is instigated from the PFC, and thus, information retrieved conforms to preconceived, structured "search criteria" (akin to Weisberg's [2006] model). In spontaneous modes, information that is represented in working memory is less filtered by top-down processes; it is not driven by the PFC, and leads to more remote or unexpected connections (akin to Martindale's [1999] model). The emotional and cognitive processes, following LeDoux (1989) and Damasio (2000) are described as interacting but separate neural systems: "an emotional brain," which adds "value tags" to information; and a parallel system that enables detailed feature analysis, the representations of which are the blocks of cognitive processes. The emotions play a role in creativity through either the deliberate or spontaneous processing modes. In the deliberate mode the PFC instigates a task-relevant search of affective memory in the emotional structures (the limbic system, amygdala, cingulate cortex and the ventromedial prefrontal cortex). Such processing might occur in psychotherapy, subjective exploration, evocation of an event for creative expression, or in emotional creativity/the solving of personal or social problems. In the spontaneous processing mode, again, the PFC is inhibited, yet information processed in the emotional structures is spontaneously presented in working memory. As these are often "markers for important biological events, they make loud signals," argues Dietrich (p. 9), and have a distinct impression on the phenomenological state — similar to a religious epiphany, with a sense of noesis and meaning. It is this "spontaneous affective" processing mode that might also play a role in AEs such as mystical experiences. Dietrich's affective model helps to explain links between creativity (that involves representations of affect) and AEs (those which involve intense affect). Both may be correlates of emotional awareness, where affective content is more likely to be represented consciously. Lane (2000) reported that individuals scoring high on emotional awareness had increased blood flow in the anterior cingulate cortex when emotions were induced by either watching films or recalling emotional experiences. The anterior cingulate cortex plays a role in conscious experience and helps regulate autonomic, endocrine and motor responses to emotional stimuli. Future work might find that this area is also activated during artistic production.

In summary, emotional as well as cognitive pathways are important to creativity. Affective models of creativity are relatively undeveloped and require further elaboration and empirical exploration. However, individual differences in affective experience, and the activity of affective pathways in the brain, might predict both creativity and AEs. Relevant affective factors include: awareness (forming cognitive representations of affect); intensity; valence; and regulation (coping with and modulating affective experience). The valence of affect is of import when considering creative states of consciousness, as shifts into positive moods facilitate the making of remote associations (Davis, 2009). Relaxed states accompanied by feelings of happiness or contentment (low arousal and positive affect), as reported in the flotation tank studies, might thus be optimal for divergent thinking. A tendency to experience intense emotional states and affective awareness, perhaps underpinned by increased communication along affective pathways, might better explain the correlational findings between artistic and affective creativity and reports of AEs, where intense affective experiences (anomalous and otherwise) might lead to artistic expression (catharsis), or where affective awareness might be a predisposing factor for both AEs and artistic creativity.

Affective variables that are indicative of well-being, such as emotional regulation and positive affect, rather than emotional conflict or lability (Ayers et al., 1999) may be important for creativity that includes AEs. AEs that are permeated by positive emotions are both more likely to lead to remote associations and more likely to be interpreted as being rewarding and life affirming. Emotional regulation, the ability to tolerate and control affective experience, may be a coping resource, giving a sense of control over AEs. Future research could explore the role of affective variables as mediators of the relationship between anomaly-proneness and health.

Personality and Motivational Models: Openness and Drive

The final factors to be considered are trait factors: openness-to-experience and motivation or drive. Let us begin by considering what is known about the "creative personality." Early research on the creative personality led to lists of characteristics that high achievers in the arts and sciences are likely to possess, for example, being more than usually: receptive to new ideas; imaginative; curious; comfortable with ambiguity; attracted to complexity; unconventional; independent of judgment; persistent; driven; and self-confident (e.g., Barron & Harrington, 1981; Gough, 1979). Extrapolating from experimental studies and cognitive models of the creative process, the creative person might be expected to have: a high capacity working memory (Geake, 2005); relevant domain-specific skills and knowledge (Martindale, 1995); and interest in a wide variety of things (Gough, 1979). Such factors, it has been argued, facilitate the synthesis of remote mental elements as well as the recognition of their relevance. Hence, the aphorism by Pasteur (1854, cited by Cropley, 2006, p. 394) that "chance favours only the prepared mind." However, intelligence and learning do not appear to be synonymous with or sufficient for creativity (Feist & Barron, 2002). Martindale (1995, p. 259) thus stresses that creativity has more to do with *how* knowledge is accessed — creative people are those that can "get themselves into primary-process states of defocused attention." Perhaps transliminality (Thalbourne, 2000), as previously discussed, characterizes such an ability as a trait, which may lead to both creativity and AEs. However, this argument begins to get tautologous as transliminality in part is defined by both creativity and a propensity to have AEs. An alternative trait is that of openness-to-experience (Costa & McCrae, 1992).

Creativity is clearly related to the personality trait of openness (Falat, 1998; Feist, 1999; Furnham, 1999; Griffin & McDermott, 1998; King, Walker

& Broylers, 1996; McCrae, 1987). "Open individuals are curious about both inner and outer worlds, and their lives are experientially richer. They are willing to entertain novel ideas and unconventional values, and they experience both positive and negative emotions more keenly than do closed individuals" (Costa & McCrae, 1992, p. 15). Openness-to-experience may facilitate creativity through curiosity, an interest in novel ideas and experiences, enabling a rich network of associations and ideas to be constructed which might enable remote connections (McCrae, 1987). King et al. (1996) found that openness-to-experience predicted creative achievement only amongst participants high in divergent-thinking, and thus argued that openness acts as a catalyst for production, perhaps through excitement about new or bizarre ideas.

Openness-to-experience is also related to traits indicative of a proclivity to have AEs. McCrae (1994) replicated the five-factor model of personality and expanded the "openness" factor to include anomaly-proneness, adding a sub-component that he described as conveying "both the idea of welcoming new input — whether sensory, cognitive, or affective — and the notion of permeability that characterizes the structure and functioning of open minds" (p. 265). An "intrapersonal openness" model would propose that an interest in and heightened awareness of the subjective realm might lead to unusual (and possibly creative) thoughts and experiences. Indeed, Hunt and Chefurka (1976) found that asking participants to introspect in a quiet room for a period of time was sufficient for altered states to be reported. In addition, people who are open-to-experience may be more likely to experiment with behaviors that induce AEs such as meditation or the taking of psychoactive drugs. As such, openness-to-experience might be a third variable that links both creativity and AEs, without AEs necessarily playing a role in the creative process.

Another person-level variable that has importance to our discussion is motivation. In addition to possessing abilities (e.g., divergent thinking and/or domain relevant skills), creativity involves the *disposition to use* these abilities. Drive or intrinsic motivation is an important characteristic of the creative person — i.e., engaging in a task primarily due to one's own interest, for its own sake, rather than external goals or rewards (Amabile, 1996).

O'Reilly, Dunbar and Bentall (2001) reported that a significant correlation between divergent-thinking (TTCT, Torrance, 1974) and AEs was cancelled out when the degree subject of the participants was accounted for (humanities versus creative arts). This led O'Reilly et al. to suggest that AEs encourage individuals to seek their expression in the creative arts, and that the relationship between AEs and creativity is motivational rather than cognitive. Might then, a further third variable be this motivation to express AEs artistically, where the relationship is mediated by domain involvement, the arts enabling idiosyncratic and subjective accounts to be viable creative products?

Thus, trait models suggest that there may be two routes by which creativity and AEs are linked: (1) intrapersonal openness; and (2) motivation to express. The first route is clearly linked with the construct of affective awareness discussed in the previous sub-section. Openness as a trait may be used to explain the correlational findings between artistic and affective creativity and AEs, but is less useful for explaining the experimental work (where relaxed states appear to produce original ideas), as, presumably, trait factors are cancelled out by the random allocation of participants to conditions (although "open" participants may be more likely to take part in such studies). The second factor of motivation reverts the causal direction previously assumed (where a problem arises and an AE assists in its solution), and as such is not useful for explaining the experimental research. Rather, motivation may be a moderating variable in the link between artistic creativity and AEs, where an AE arises spontaneously and through the "Drive to express" becomes the impetus for an artistic product.

Creativity — Healthy or Unhealthy?

In this final section, the relationship between AEs and creativity will be scrutinized in terms of its implications for health. This has been interpreted as indicative of both psychosis and thriving (Csikszentmihalyi, 1996; Eysenck, 1993). I will discuss four models: (1) a medical model, contextualizing anomalous experiences within a disease framework and associating creativity with bipolar disorder and schizophrenia (Jamison, 1993); (2) a "healthy anomalous experiences" model, which suggests that creativity is associated with distinct types of AE that are thought to be inherently positive and meaningful (Ayers et al., 1999); (3) a "controllable oddness" model, which suggests that creative people have a cognitive style that enables them to successfully navigate between anomalous and "ordinary" experience (Barron, 1993); and (4) a "protective factor" model, where creative expression of an AE promotes well-being (Richards, 2010).

The most sustained stream of empirical research related to creativity and AEs has tested the hypothesis that creativity is associated with psychopathology (for comprehensive reviews the reader is referred to: Barrantes-Vidal, 2004; Brod, 1997; Sass & Schuldberg, 2000–2001). Evidence for a link between creativity and mental illness comes from several strands: (1) historiographical studies have diagnosed well-known artistic figures (such as Lord Byron, Sylvia Plath, Vincent van Gogh, Salividor Dali and Virginia Woolf) as having bipolar disorder, schizoaffective disorder or personality disorders (Claridge, Pryor & Watkins, 1998; Jamison, 1993; Murphy, 2009); (2) Studies of living professional and eminent artists have found a higher incidence of psychopathology amongst them in comparison to control groups (Andreasen, 1987; Ludwig, 1992); (3) The relatives and offspring of people with bipolar disorder have been found to be more creative than controls with no such relatives (Richards et al., 1988; Simeonova et al., 2005); (4) Schizophrenics have scored higher than controls on tests of divergent thinking (Keefe & Magaro, 1980); and (5) amongst the general population, creativity has formed significant positive correlations with psychoticism, "a genetic predisposition to develop psychosis under appropriate stress" (Eysenck, 1996, p. 213) (Woody & Claridge, 1977) and schizotypy (Schuldberg, 2000–2001). This body of research situates any link between creativity and AEs within a disease model, arguing that the creative person is exposed to more psychopathology than the average person, including hallucinations and delusions. However, bipolar disorder and schizophrenia can be debilitating and in their worst expressions do not enable creative functioning (Gough, 1993; Richards et al., 1988; Rubinstein, 2008). Thus, many proponents of this stance advocate a "weak" rather than a "strong" link, where a mild, non-clinical, expression of psychopathology is associated with creativity. For a critique of this body of work the reader is referred to Weisberg (2006) who ultimately argues that the similarity between "madness" and creativity is more apparent than real.

An alternative approach questions whether the "odd" experiences that creative people may be prone to are psychopathological at all, suggesting that there is there an over-tendency amongst psychologists to pathologize unusual behavior. Sass (2000–2001) points out that creativity and "insanity" is a modern association — the "ancients" meant by "divine madness" something else — literally a connection with other beings (e.g., the muses) or states of consciousness that were not associated with mental illness. Barron (1993) suggested that high scores on measures of psychosis amongst artists might be due to artists scoring highly on a subset of questions that differ from the typical response set of schizophrenics. Barron (1972, cited in Barron 1993, p. 183) compared the MMPI profiles of artists and patients diagnosed with schizophrenia. Three differences emerged: (1) schizophrenics were apathetic, full of despair and dread; (2) schizophrenics demonstrated confusion, bizarre ideation, delusions of control by others, and an inability to self-regulate mood; (3) artists found joy in life, were not self-pitying, were concerned with practical matters and functioned well physically. Barron argues that the correlational psychometric data suggests that artists are more "schizophrenic" than they really are. Further work corroborates some of his findings, demonstrating links between both happiness and moderate levels of positive affect and creative ideation (Davis, 2009; Pannells & Claxton, 2008). Might artists be prone to different types of AEs than those labeled as schizotypal, schizophrenic or bipolar?

Some AEs, such as mystical experiences, flow, lucid dreams and out-of-body experiences, have been significantly and positively associated with a sense of meaningfulness in life, optimism, well-being and emotional stability (Ayers et al., 1999; Csikszentmihalyi, 1996; Greely, 1975; Hay & Morisy, 1978; Kennedy, Kanthamani, & Palmer, 1994; LaBerge & Gackenbach, 2000; McCreery & Claridge, 2002; Wunthrow, 1978). Research has distinguished between mystical experiences (characterized by unity and integration) and pathological experiences (of dissociation/fragmentation)—where only the latter has been associated with neuroticism, "ego-grasping" (narcissism, low self-esteem and anxiety) and external locus of control, and the prior with absorption (Hunt et al., 2002; Spanos & Moretti, 1988; Kohls & Walach, 2007). This implies that some AEs are inherently healthy while others are indicative of poor functioning.

Is creativity associated with "healthy" rather than "unhealthy" AEs? Correlations reported in earlier sections of this Chapter support this hypothesis, where artistic creativity was associated only with "healthy" AEs: positive mystical experiences, unusual dreams and a vivid imagination; and these experiences could not be attributed to emotional disturbance (Ayers et al., 1999) or poor mental health (Holt, 2007). Support for the converse position, that creativity is not associated with "unhealthy" AEs comes from a study by Wolfradt and Pretz (2001) who investigated the relationship between dissociation (depersonalization experiences [e.g., "I observe myself as a stranger"] and derealization experiences [e.g., "the world around me seems unfamiliar"]) and multiple dimensions of creativity: creative personality (Gough, 1979), involvement with creative hobbies, and scores on a creative story-writing test. Dissociation did not correlate significantly with any of the creativity measurements, but rather, with a rigid, neurotic personality style. The authors used a narrow assessment of dissociative experiences (Edge, 2001) that may be associated with pathological forms. Waller, Putnam and Carlson (1996) distinguish between two distinct types of dissociation: taxonic pathological experiences, such as depersonalization and dissociative amnesia; and non-pathological experiences of dissociation that constitute a continuum related to absorption (Tellegen & Atkinson, 1974). Wolfradt and Pretz's findings suggest that creativity is not associated with "pathological" AEs such as experiences of estrangement from self and world.

However, it can be disputed whether any experiences are inherently healthy or unhealthy. Might well-being depend on other factors, such as good coping skills? Whilst Kohls and Walach (2007) distinguished between psychopathological (e.g., "I clearly hear voices, which scold and make fun of me, without any physical causation") and spiritual (e.g., "Benign light surrounds me") AEs by factor analysis, an important determining factor for well-being was not the reporting of one or other of these types of experience, but how any experience was evaluated — whether or not they were evaluated as having a positive impact one's life [see also chapters 7, 8 and 10 by Simmonds-Moore, Clarke and Belz in the current book].

A third model proposes that the creative personality adaptively integrates "healthy" and "unhealthy" experiences. Barron (1993, p. 183) described creativity as "controllable oddness," where "oddness of thought or feeling, when coupled with an ability to reconsider and reformulate" is a resource for creativity — a balance of conceptual or affective expansion and control and integration (Russ, 2000–2001). Such dual-interactive models include anomaly-proneness/psychoticism, which is moderated by "healthy" variables such as ego-strength (psychological resilience) or high intelligence (Barron, 1968; Carson, Peterson & Higgins, 2003). These "healthy" variables distinguish the creative process from psychopathology (Gough, 1993). Amongst them, Flach (1990) includes: autonomy, setting one's own goals, social poise and a strong sense of responsibility. He presents a "resilience hypothesis" where creativity requires the "successful transit of stress-induced episodes of disorganization and reorganization" (p. 162), helped by flexibility of personality, the ability to tolerate ambiguity and the ability to reintegrate.

Support for this model comes from Fodor (1995) who found that participants with high scores on both psychosis-proneness and ego-strength obtained significantly higher creativity scores (on both remoteness of word associations and expert ratings of solutions to an engineering design problem) than other conditions. A number of studies have shown that while "schizophrenics" and "creatives" both score at a higher level than "normal" groups on measures of novelty (e.g., remote verbal associations), creatives differ in their ability to assess the appropriateness of their responses (Dykes & McGhie, 1976; Merton & Fischer, 1999). Merton and Fischer (1999) found that creatives (writers and actors) and schizophrenics scored higher than controls on an open-ended single-word-association task, however, schizophrenics included more stereotypical responses and were less able to inhibit these when specifically asked to produce word-associations that were uncommon, unlike the other samples. Creatives could better control their response behavior. Thus, Merton and Fischer argue that creativity is not aligned with associational dysfunction, as in schizophrenia, but with flexibility of cognitive-styles.

Analogous findings have emerged from recent work on schizotypy. The unusual experiences factor of schizotypy was discussed earlier in this Chapter, however, attention was not paid to three additional sub-dimensions of schizotypy: cognitive disorganization, which reflects difficulties with attention, concentration and decision-making, alongside a sense of purposelessness, moodiness and social anxiety (Mason, Claridge, & Jackson, 1995); introvertive anhedonia, which is characterized by schizoid solitariness and lack of feeling (Claridge & Beech, 1995). Mason et al. (1995) describe this factor as pervaded by a lack of enjoyment derived from social interaction and physical pleasure, alongside withdrawal from emotional and physical intimacy, independence and solitude; and, "impulsive nonconformity," which includes odd behavior, such as the urge to smash things, and mood lability, leading Claridge and Davis (2003) to suggest that this trait relates to affective forms of psychosis.

These dimensions of schizotypy are typically examined in isolation or as a cumulative score, however, distinct profiles have emerged from cluster analyses (Goulding, 2004, 2005; Holt, Simmonds-Moore & Moore, 2008; Loughland & Williams, 1997): (1) Happy Schizotypes, who score highly on unusual experiences only; (2) Low Schizotypes, who score at a low level on all dimensions of schizotypy; (3) High Schizotypes, who score highly on all three dimensions; and (4) Negative Schizotypes, who score highly on introvertive anhedonia only. These profiles are important because they suggest that there are two types of "anomaly-prone" person, those with and without the potentially debilitating factors of disorganized cognition and flat affect. Happy Schizotypes have been so called as they are prone to AEs, yet, have higher levels of mental health and well-being than High Schizotypes, and in some studies than Low Schizotypes (Claridge, 2001; Goulding, 2004; Jackson, 1997; McCreery & Claridge, 2002). Schofield and Claridge (2007) observed that Happy Schizotypes tended to evaluate AEs as pleasant and High Schizotypes as unpleasant. They attributed this to cognitive disorganization preventing the formation of a reassuring belief system. "Peculiar" beliefs may operate as a buffer against stress (Boden & Berenbaum, 2004) and assist in the interpretation of AEs, thereby preventing distress (Bell, Halligan & Ellis, 2007). In this model, healthy AEs appear to require low levels of introvertive anhedonia and cognitive disorganization (Goulding, 2004) in addition to a socially endorsed meaning structure with which to interpret any AEs (Boden & Berenbaum, 2004; Jackson, 1997). [See also Simmonds-Moore chapter 7, in the current book].

When examining cluster types, Holt, Simmonds-Moore and Moore (2008) found that Happy Schizotypes were more creative than other schizotypal profiles, scoring significantly higher on a composite measure of divergent thinking, emotional creativity, creative behavior and creative personality, as well as scoring higher than High Schizotypes on a measure of well-being (Sense of Coherence, Antonovsky, 1987). This suggests that creative people may have a distinct personality profile that predisposes them to AEs, alongside indicators of mental health, such as well-being and cognitive organization.

A fourth model proposes that artistic involvement directly promotes well-being (Averill, 2005; Richards, 2010). In this model those who are motivated to express their AEs through art (O'Reilly et al., 2001) will find them easier to process and interpret, reducing conflict and negative affect (such as fear) and aiding their integration and assimilation into a coherent belief system. Literature reviews of research in the arts and health movement suggest that artistic involvement can lead to health benefits (mental and physical) (Camic, 2008; Stuckey & Nobel, 2010). Although the mechanisms for this are unclear, it has been proposed that art making leads to meaning making through the construction of narrative; positive affect, the reduction of stress and tension through cathartic release; and feelings of self-mastery and self-esteem (Camic, 2008; Stuckey & Nobel, 2010). As such, art plays a homeostatic function, maintaining emotional balance, and cognitively, the conscious reflection involved in artistic expression may help experiments to integrate, evaluate, accept, identify, develop, explore and deepen beliefs about and understanding of their AEs, encouraging adaptive responses and the positive evaluations that have been associated with health (Kohls & Walach, 2006). A question for future research is how creativity might be used therapeutically to help promote well-being amongst those who are struggling to deal with AEs.

In summary, creativity research gives us particular insights into AEs and health. Not only might AEs play a useful role in the creative process, but creativity may promote healthy AEs through both process and person level factors, by (1) fostering healthy and rewarding AEs that promote relaxation, absorption and positive affect (such as the flow state); (2) the acquisition of personal resources such as cognitive flexibility and resilience, enabling a healthy navigation between AEs and consensual reality; and (3) a drive to express AEs artistically, which may be protective, leading to a positive interpretation of AEs.

Conclusions

The thesis that AEs contribute to creativity is a tenable one, in opposition to the "ordinary cognition" view of creativity advocated by Weisberg (2006). Anomaly-proneness as a trait and the reporting of specific AEs (e.g., positive mystical experiences) appear to be associated with components of creativity, in particular, artistic creativity. Further, there is experimental evidence to suggest that relaxed states are directly implicated in the creative process (facilitating original ideation and performance quality). That at times these relaxed states may also be "anomalous" (with an altered sense of self, vivid imagery and positive affect) is suggested by flotation tank interpolation studies (e.g. Norlander et al., 1998; 2002–2003) and neurofeedback studies (Gruzelier, 2009). However, further research is required to demarcate the experiential features of such states and their import for creative functioning. Indeed, this research requires replication and the honing of experimental protocols in order to eliminate alternative explanations (such as expectation effects, differential treatment across experimental conditions and the role of novelty).

The systematic testing and development of potential explanatory models for a link between AEs and creativity would be fruitful. Currently, models are largely speculative and simplistic, not taking into account the componential and systemic nature of either creativity or conscious experience. The relative import of cognitive, affective and trait factors, nor how they may interact, in explaining a link between creativity and AEs is not clear. Nevertheless, this literature review suggests two routes between creativity and AEs: (1) cognitive (where relaxed and possibly altered states, with hypofrontality and right hemispheric interjections, lead to remote cognitive associations); and (2) affective (an association between artistic creativity and AEs that might be explained by affective or trait models). The nature and direction of this affective link is unknown, whether, for example, having an intense AE motivates some people to express this artistically; artistic expression and AEs are both separate experiences that are indirectly linked by affective awareness (or openness-to-experience); or, affective awareness predisposes one to have intense affective and possibly AEs as part of the creative process; or, indeed, whether such associations are due to reporting artifacts

The outcomes of creativity research have implications for our understanding of AEs and health. Not only do they demonstrate how AEs can be useful and adaptive, potentially contributing to creative ideation, but they also suggest different ways in which AEs might be related to well-being, through (1) "healthy profiles," where cognitive flexibility and resilience enables controllability and the healthy integration of AEs of any type; (2) "art as therapeutic," where catharsis and processing of AEs occurs through artistic expression and reflection; (3) "healthy AEs," where positive affect and a sense of meaning arise through focused, absorbed states in the creative process. These conceptualizations expand the disease model of health as the absence of clinical symptoms, normalizing a broader range of conscious experiences. Indeed, one might even argue that such experiences are essential for a creative and thriving consciousness. Rather than the oft-cited view that creativity is aligned with "madness," creativity might be an indicator of health —facilitating positive evaluations of AEs and positive AEs (e.g., flow states versus depersonalization experiences). Artistic creativity amongst the general population does not appear to be associated with the distressing AEs that characterize psychosis, but with positive, life-affirming experiences, such as positive mystical experiences. There may be something about creativity that is protective against potential risk factors of anomaly-proneness. Further research could profitably examine the import of potential protective factors, for example, emotional regulation, positive affect, coping behaviors, cognitive factors facilitating positive interpretations of AEs, the creative persona or environment that labels oddness as positive in the context of art-making, etc.

Many intriguing questions remain unanswered. For example, are different types of creativity differentially associated with AEs, and if so, why might this be (for example, everyday versus eminent creativity)? Are relationships between creativity and AEs curvilinear —for example, are mild deviations along an "oneiric continuum" associated with relaxed states and original ideas, whereas extreme shifts are associated with intense creative involvement and AEs? Can people be trained to enter specific states of consciousness, thus facilitating creativity? Can creativity training be used in clinical practice to help people integrate and interpret AEs? Are there different routes or pathways between creativity and AEs—cognitive and affective? For the creative researcher and theorist, there is much food for thought.

Notes

1. Adaptive novelty is attributed in different contexts. A distinction has been made between creativity that occurs at an individual level (psychological or "little c" creativity) and that which occurs at a cultural level (historical, eminent, or "big c" creativity) (Boden, 1996). Creativity may also result in an enduring product or in a transient act of performance (such as social problem solving) (Barron, 1968).

2. The term "anomaly-proneness" denotes the idea that some people may be more likely to have AEs than other people, and may do so more regularly. This notion has been supported by research on personality traits that are defined in terms of anomaly-proneness, such as schizotypy, boundary thinness and transliminality. These traits are defined and discussed in a subsequent section of this Chapter.

3. The presence is often "felt," without visual, auditory or tactile sensory determinants, has seemingly close proximity to the percipient and apparent intentionality with respect to the percipient (Nielsen, 2007). Sensed presence occurs in a number of AEs, such as imaginary companions, apparitions of the deceased, old hag syndrome, alien abduction experiences and mediumistic channelling (Persinger & Healey, 2002).

4. The phenomenological qualities of the flow experience are closely related to Maslow's (1971) "peak experience" or the "creative attitude," described as involving detachment from time and space, absorption in the activity of the present moment, deep fascination and concentration, an "innocence of perceiving," loss of ego, receptivity and spontaneity. Further, both the flow state and peak experiences relate conceptually to absorption as a state, which involves "a full commitment of available perceptual, motoric, imaginative and ideational resources to a unified representation of the attentional object" (Tellegen & Atkinson, 1974, p. 274).

5. The Remote Associates Test (Mednick & Mednick, 1967) is a convergent thinking task that assesses the ability to find an association between 30 different sets of three "remote" words. For example, between "wheel," "electric," and "high"-the solution is "chair."

6. Tests of divergent-thinking are open-ended and ask participants to transform cues/ideas. They are scored according to all or some of: originality (the ability to produce a rare idea); flexibility (shifting between different ideas); fluency (the number of ideas produced); and elaboration (the degree of detail in and complexity of the idea). For example, the Alternate Uses Test (Wilson, Christensen, Merrifield & Guilford, 1960) asks for original uses for household objects (e.g. a brick or a coat hanger). Perhaps the most well known tests of divergent-thinking are the figural and verbal forms of the Torrance Tests of Creative Thinking (TTCT) (Torrance, 2000), where, for example, in the repeated figures task one is to draw on nine circles, transforming each one into something else.

7. A measure of esthetic preference (e.g., of asymmetry and complexity) that is a correlate of creative achievement.

8. This emerged from a principal components analysis and consisted of high loadings on self-perceived creativity, the importance of creative practice in one's life, Gough's (1979) creative personality scale (which assesses traits such as imaginativeness, resourcefulness, drive and confidence), involvement in the creative arts and figural expressiveness (based on the figural divergent thinking test).

9. Wallas developed this model through the analysis of introspective reports of eminent creative achievers, such as Poincaré and Helmholtz.

10. Fluency refers to the total number of ideas produced, flexibility to the number of ideas that are different from each other and elaboration refers to the about of detail expressed in an idea.

11. Both conditions encouraged participants to let go of inhibitions and had the same instructions, thus seeking to control for suggestion effects to some degree.

12. Participants are trained to raise theta activity over alpha activity with eyes closed and with the use of acoustic guides-without falling asleep. Alpha usually increases when the eyes are closed, and participants are actually trained to increase alpha over theta (producing the sound of a babbling brook) and then theta over alpha (producing the sound of crashing waves). Theta comes more prominent on the boundary of sleep. Thus, participants are trained to stay awake in a state that usually leads to sleep and to maintain wakefulness, and are assessed according to their ability increase the theta/alpha ratio over time (Egner, Strawson & Gruzelier, 2002).

13. Across this series of studies, Martindale assessed creativity with the Remote Associates Test (Mednick & Mednick, 1967) and the Alternate Uses Test of divergent-thinking (Wilson, Christensen, Merrifield & Guilford, 1960).

14. As he found that creatives are worse than low creatives at alpha enhancement biofeedback tasks Martindale refutes the suggestion that the shifts in arousal he observed are due to conscious control (Martindale & Armstrong, 1974; Martindale & Hines, 1975). He suggests (1977-78) that the arousal of creatives might be more labile in general and that creative people enter relaxed states spontaneously. This was subsequently supported in a study where creativity scores correlated positively with spontaneous fluctuations in galvanic skin-response (Martindale, Anderson, Moore & West, 1996).

15. See Kasof (1997) for a review of studies where creative performance diminishes with presumed increase of arousal due to e.g. time pressure, noise or the presence of others.

16. Ranked with low to high creativity (1-4) according to interviewer ratings of artistic and literary creative activities.

7

Exploring Ways of Manipulating Anomalous Experiences for Mental Health and Transcendence

CHRISTINE SIMMONDS-MOORE

Abstract

This chapter discusses anomaly proneness as a trait and a state of consciousness. *Positive schizotypy* is presented as an anomaly-prone trait personality dimension. Scoring high is neutral in terms of mental health but interacts with other factors to affect mental health. The factors which may be implicated in the pathologization of anomalous experiences are explored. The author proposes that it is possible to encourage more anomalous experiences via the use of methods to access sleep related states of consciousness. However, it is noted that this should be undertaken responsibly and in a healthy manner, by considering a series of moderating factors which include methods to increase control over (automatic) experiences, methods to organize and assimilate experiences, the use of mental imagery, the use of rituals, having a meaningful context for experiences, having a useful application for experiences and being able to share experiences in a social context.

Introduction

Anomalous experiences have the potential to lead to transcendence and personal growth; however, they can also be intrusive and frightening and associated with clinical problems (see Hunt, 1995; Neppe, 1988; Parker, 1975; see also chapters by Clarke and Belz in this volume). Given that anomalous experiences are not uncommon within the general population (e.g., Gallup & Newport, 1991), and the continuing popularity of "psychic development" programs, it is important to develop greater understanding about the differences between healthy and less healthy experiences and the moderating factors associated with both. By so doing, it may be possible to cultivate healthy anomalous experiences and enable unwanted experiences to be attenuated or switched off. The chapter takes an interactionist approach to anomalous experiences and health, and explores how trait personality variables associated with anomaly proneness (mainly positive schizotypy) may interact with a variety of factors[1] to lead to healthy or less healthy experiences.

Interactionism refers to the idea that "personality" is better understood as a complex interaction between internal personality traits (how one is "wired"), the demands of a given situation and other moderating factors (for example, gender, mood, state of consciousness, hormones and cognitive style, etc.). This concept can easily be applied to academic research that addresses experiences that are unusual or anomalous (such as subjective paranormal experiences, out of body experiences, experiencing a sense of presence, etc.). The idea that variables function interactively (like a recipe) in relation to a particular behavioral or experiential outcome is not a new one. Despite this, much research on anomalous experiences has explored how personality traits relate to an outcome variable (e.g., paranormal belief or experience) in a linear [correlational] manner. In fact, traits associated with anomaly proneness might be better considered in tandem with how people score on *other* traits, their cognitive styles as well as considering within-person variance; how traits interact with a variety of factors to result in different behavioral outcomes. A more comprehensive understanding of anomaly-proneness will encompass considerations of trait-state-other interactions, and in this context, how anomalous experiences might become modified or controlled.

This chapter will explore "anomaly proneness" as both "trait" and "state" variables that reflect a [relatively] loosened cognitive-perceptual system. I will argue that methods to loosen the system might be employed to encourage more anomalies, whilst methods to tighten the system might be employed to reduce anomalies, or gain control over experiencing them. This will be considered alongside moderating factors that allow for healthy experiences. This chapter will begin by introducing the concept of anomaly-proneness, describe what this means in terms of personality and as a state of consciousness. It will proceed to discuss ways of encouraging and experiencing healthy forms of anomalous experience and "switching off" experiences that are unpleasant.

Anomaly Proneness

What is Anomaly-Proneness?

For the purposes of this chapter, *anomaly-proneness* will be defined as the propensity to experience a range of "anomalous" experiences—experiences that are uncommon or unusual, and include paranormal experiences, mystical experiences, religious experiences and transpersonal experiences. Being anomaly-prone also incorporates the tendency to hold beliefs in a range of unusual phenomena.

Anomalous perception/cognition can be broken down into three forms and considered hierarchically in terms of the cognitive-perceptual system (Berenbaum, Kerns & Raghavan, 2000). Anomalous sensory perceptions refer to auditory, visual, tactile, olfactory, gustatory, kinesthetic, pain and equilibrium phenomena. Anomalous experiences are a wider concept than perceptions, but may encompass and include them as their building blocks (e.g., experiencing a "ghost" potentially consists of the anomalous sensations of hairs standing on the back of the neck, a sensed presence, feeling cold, etc.). Belief refers to the cognitive information an individual holds regarding the existence of any particular paranormal or unusual phenomenon (e.g., belief in ghosts) (Berenbaum et al., 2000). It is possible for a given individual to hold beliefs without having experiences, and vice versa, however, it is clear that experiences and beliefs are related, and beliefs may often develop as a consequence of personal experience (e.g., Blackmore, 1984).[3] As such, when considering how it might be possible to manipulate anomalies, a hierarchical perspective should be taken into account.

What Is Positive Schizotypy?

Several authors have recently argued that trait anomaly-proneness may be synonymous with the personality dimension *positive schizotypy* or psychosis proneness (see Simmonds, 2003). Research consistently supports positive schizotypy as an anomaly-prone personality, with the variable correlating with experiencing out of body experiences (McCreery, 1997; McCreery & Claridge, 2002), spiritual experiences (e.g., Jackson, 1997), mystical experiences (Thalbourne, 2000) transpersonal experiences (Bradbury, Stirling, Cavill & Parker, 2009), traditional and less traditional (i.e., New Age) religious experiences (Day & Peters, 1999; Maltby, Garner, Lewis & Day, 2000; Smith, Riley & Peters, 2009) and subjective paranormal experiences (e.g., Simmonds-Moore, 2009a). Interestingly, Bradbury et al's (2009) work also found that the tendency toward experiencing anomalous phenomena moderately correlated with the tendency to experience transpersonal phenomena. Those who score higher on positive schizotypy also tend to have more beliefs in anomalous and paranormal phenomena (e.g., Simmonds, 2003). Some research has also demonstrated better performance at an ESP task among those scoring higher on scales measuring positive schizotypy (e.g., Holt & Simmonds-Moore, 2008; Lawrence, & Woodley, 1998; Parker, 2000), although others have not found such a relationship (Simmonds, 2003; Simmonds & Fox, 2004).

The traits which underpin positive schizotypy are considered by many (e.g., Gruzelier, 1996) to be analogous to, but diluted forms of the positive symptoms of schizophrenia. These include magical or religious beliefs; altered sensations and perceptions of one's own body and the world; hypersensitivity to sounds and smells and a generally heightened perceptual sensitivity; increased likelihood of reporting déjà vu and jamais vu and an increased tendency to hear voices. It has been argued that scoring on this variable is distributed on a continuum within the general population, which results in psychosis only among very high scorers and in combination with other factors (see later discussion on healthy versus less healthy positive schizotypy, see also Claridge, 1997).To date, there is much empirical support for the continuity model (see Johns & van Os, 2001) which normalizes psychotic experiences, and suggests that "psychotic" experiences are experienced in a watered down form (as anomalous experiences) among many members of the non-psychiatric population.

A greater understanding of the biases underpinning positive schizotypy/anomaly proneness may provide insights for controlling anomalous experiences. The schizotypy construct is multidimensional, and comprises three dimensions in addition to positive schizotypy (negative, disorganized/paranoid and impulsive aspects, see Claridge, 1997). Although positive schizotypy is the strongest and most consistent factor in factor analyses (Mason, Claridge & Williams, 1997), scoring on the other dimensions may impact on healthy versus less healthy anomalous experiences, which will be revisited later in this chapter.

The Nature of the Anomaly-Prone System — *Introducing* Boundary Thinness

This section will explore the biases underpinning anomalous experiences. The biology and cognition of anomaly-proneness might be understood by adopting the metaphor "boundary thinness" (after Hartmann, 1991). This term is adopted from Hartmann's construct of psychometric boundary thinness (e.g., Hartmann, 1991), whereby thinner boundaries reflect a relative *connectedness* of psychological processes and thicker boundaries reflect a relative *separateness* of psychological processes (Hartmann, Rosen & Rand, 1998). Boundary thinness is employed as an umbrella term for a neural and cognitive system that exhibits increased *connectivity* (functional and anatomical) in terms of neural structures, cognition and consciousness. It will be employed here to describe trait measures which correlate strongly and positively with one another (e.g., Thalbourne & Maltby, 2008; Simmonds-Moore, 2009–2010) and display increased boundary thinness. These include *Hartmann's Boundary Thinness* (e.g., 1991), *Transliminality*, or the tendency for information to "cross thresholds into or out of consciousness" (Thalbourne & Houran, 2000, p. 861), *temporal lobe lability*, or the extent to which temporal lobe structures are connected with the rest of the brain (e.g., Persinger & Makarec, 1987), and Positive Schizotypy. The term can also be employed to describe boundary thinness as a state of consciousness (see Simmonds-Moore, 2010).

A Hierarchy of Boundaries/Anomaly Proneness

I have previously argued that *boundaries* might be considered hierarchically (Simmonds-Moore, 2010), beginning with neurochemistry of boundaries (e.g., dopamine and serotonin), moving up to biological connections (increased neural connections and decreased inhibitory processes), more complex structures, cognitive processes and conscious experiences. These reflect lateral connectivity (more connectivity between cortical hemispheres; effectively a greater influence of the right hemisphere on the usually dominant left hemisphere), hierarchical connectivity (connectivity between the cortical areas of the brain and the sub-cortical structures of the brain; effectively more influence of sub cortical processes on the usually dominant left cortex of the brain), cognitive-perceptual connectivity (as synesthesia and the tendency to make associations, find a signal, and find meaning amid randomness) information processing boundaries (as attentional widening — more information that is usually outside of conscious awareness is available in awareness) and interpersonal boundaries (as a tendency to get very close to other people/experience empathy) (Simmonds-Moore, 2010). I have also argued that different types of "boundary thinness" might result in different types of anomaly, and it would be useful to ascertain *which* contribute to *which* types of experiences.

Biases Underpinning Anomaly Proneness

In general, the positive schizotypal nervous system may be characterized as exhibiting an increased level of neural and cognitive connectivity (or boundary thinness). For example, McCreery and Claridge (1996) described it as an "open nervous system [...] where excitatory mechanisms are high and inhibitory processes low" (McCreery & Claridge, 1996b, p. 756). In addition to other biases, this general bias of may underpin anomalous sensations, experiences and cognitions (Berenbaum et al. 2000).

Anomalous Sensations and Experiences. A range of biases associated with positive schizotypy result in the increased tendency to *experience* anomalous or unusual phenomena. These include a labile nervous system, which renders the person more reactive to environmental stimuli (or "hyperaesthesia," Thalbourne, 1998) and to internal (particularly emotional) stimuli (e.g., Farias, Claridge, & Lalljee, 2005); anomalies of the experience of the body (e.g., Arzy, Mohr, Michel, & Blanke, 2007); increased vividness of mental imagery (Oertel, Rotarska-Jagiela, van de Ven, Haenschel., Grube, Stangier, Maurer, & Linden, 2009); better dream recall (Watson, 2003); increased autonoetic awareness, or "a greater feeling of mental time travel and reliving/"preliving" imagined events" (Winfield & Kamboj, 2010); an increased likelihood of entering altered states of consciousness (such as the hypnagogic state) when wide awake (*c.f.* McCreery, 1997) and more daytime hypnagogic experiences (Jones, Fernyhough, & Meads, 2009[4]; Parra, & Espinoza Paul, 2009) and more nocturnal sleep anomalies (Koffel, & Watson, 2009).

Anomalous Cognitions. Reduced inhibition also results in cognitive outcomes. For example, attention is less focused (e.g., Claridge & Beech, 1995; Claridge, Clark & Beech, 1992; Hofer, Della Casa & Feldon, 1999), and information that is usually maintained at a lower level of consciousness (automatic and preconscious processing) may interject into conscious awareness, and potentially be experienced as "anomalous" (e.g., Bullen, Hemsley & Dixon, 1987).[5]

Positive schizotypes are more likely to blur the boundaries between reality and imagination, e.g., to perceive their mental imagery to derive from an external source (e.g., Bentall, 2000). They are also prone to experience false memories (e.g., Dehon, Bastin, & Larøi, 2008[6]). This may also be underpinned by the increased influence of temporal lobe structures on the cortex as the hippocampus does not distinguish between imagery from a mundane perception, a wish, thought, fantasy or dream (Persinger, 1996). The tendency may also derive from vivid imagery, dream recall and the greater tendency to relive past experiences or prelive imagined events.

A reduction in the dominance of the left hemisphere among those scoring higher on positive schizotypy results in a general bias toward using the right hemisphere. This is the case particularly for language (e.g., Leonhard & Brugger, 1998; Mohr, Krummenacher, Landis, Sandor, Fathi, & Brugger, 2005), but also for face processing (Leonards & Mohr, 2009) and general attention (Brugger, & Graves, 1996). The bias has been suggested to underpin both creative and paranormal thought (e.g., Brugger, Gamma, Muri, & Schafer, 1993) via an increased tendency to make "loose" cognitive associations (e.g., Gianotti et al., 2001) and find meaning or see significance (Brugger, Regard, Landis, Cook, Krebs & Niederberger, 1993), which is also known as apophenia (e.g., see Fyfe, Williams, Mason & Pickup, 2008). The latter tendency may also reflect the increased influence of temporal lobe structures (in particular, the amygdala[7]) on conscious awareness (see Skirda & Persinger, 1993).

The Role of Both Perceptual and Cognitive Biases in Trait Anomaly Proneness. The co-existence of biases leading to anomalous sensations, experiences and cognitions in positive schizotypy may provide a key insight into understanding *how* people experience anomalies and develop beliefs (e.g., see Schofield & Claridge, 2007). Sumich et al. (2008), for example, explored both experiential and cognitive aspects of positive schizotypy and found that there were different neural processes underpinning each.[8.] The existence of two factors within positive schizotypy is not always tapped by using independent psychometric measures, and many incorporate both tendencies within a single scale.[9]

Previous research has indicated that the simultaneous expression of two "modes" of thinking (intuitive and logical) may be implicated in anomalous experiences, beliefs and perceived ability — and is associated with positive schizotypy (Wolfradt, Oubaid, Straube, Bischoff & Mischo, 1999; Genovese, 2005). Wolfradt et al. suggested that the combination of the two modes results from the brain's attempted psychological regulation of two very different types of thought. This might reflect the assimilation of experiences and cognitions derived from various sources (e.g., associational processing associated with the right hemisphere, information from the unconscious mind,[10] and logical thinking/interpretation associated with the input of the left hemisphere) and that anomaly-proneness may be associated with the ability to entertain two different ways of approaching the world simultaneously.[11] This may well relate to the *both/and* type of thinking that is characteristic of transpersonal and spiritual experiences (e.g., Clarke, 2005) that may lead to insights outside of the normal (rational) way of seeing and experiencing the world (e.g., Liester, 1996).

It has also been suggested that the co-existence of two modes of thinking may relate to Maher's explanation of the development of delusions in schizophrenia — with belief serving as an explanation for anomalous perceptions to the self (e.g., see Berenbaum, Kerns, & Raghavan, 2000). Bell, Halligan and Ellis (2007) found evidence that anomalous perceptual experience is not necessary for the presence of delusions, thus challenging this as an etiology of unusual beliefs. Although, possessing a traditional belief framework was found to be particularly important for organizing anomalous experiences among the non-clinical population (Schofield & Claridge, 2007). Experiencing and believing actually probably reflect both *top down* and *bottom up* influences, which should be taken into account when considering how to manipulate the occurrence of anomalous experiences.

Healthy and Less Healthy
Forms of Trait Anomaly-Proneness

There are clear overlaps between (trait) anomaly proneness and psychopathology (e.g., Bradbury, Stirling, Cavill & Parker, 2009; Nettle, 2006). However, the relationship between anomalous experiences and psychopathology is far from straightforward (e.g., Berenbaum et al., 2000). Indeed, anomaly proneness is also associated with good mental health (e.g., Goulding, 2004, 2005; Goulding & Ödéhn, 2009; Holt, Simmonds-Moore & Moore, 2008), subjective meaning in life (e.g., Kennedy, Kanthamani & Palmer, 1994) and other adaptive traits, including creativity (e.g., Holt et al., 2008 and this book), spirituality (Jackson, 1997) and religiosity (e.g., Day & Peters, 1999; Maltby, Garner, Lewis & Day, 2000).

The overlap between positive schizotypy and mental health is approached differently in the literature. Some researchers (e.g., the Chapman group, see Claridge & Beech, 1995) consider that *any* presence of "schizotypal traits" are indicative of psychopathology. This reflects the *quasi*-dimensional or deficit view of schizotypy that anomalous experiences are examples of watered down psychopathology. On the other hand, the alternative, and perhaps more convincing perspective (e.g., see Rawlings, Williams, Haslam, & Claridge, 2008) is the fully dimensional or personality view (e.g., see Claridge, 1997) whereby being anomaly-prone is understood to be neutral in its relationship with mental health, but interacts with other factors[12] in terms of health or illness. This approach considers anomaly-proneness as a personality dimension, which is normally distributed in the general population. Implicit with this view is the idea that the traits associated with positive schizotypy are useful at a watered down level, and that there are some scorers who are psychologically healthy.

The adaptive high scorer has previously been labelled as the *happy* or *benign* schizotype — a person who exhibits adaptive traits and is happy in spite, or *because* of their subjective anomalous experiences (e.g., Jackson, 1997; McCreery & Claridge, 2002). In support of this, McCreery & Claridge (2002) found that out-of-body experiences were associated with healthy positive schizotypy. In addition, Nettle and Clegg (2006) found that positive schizotypy statistically predicted creativity, which is associated with evolutionary advantages (mating success) (Nettle & Clegg, 2006). Religion/religious experiences are also associated with evolutionary benefits (see Sanderson, 2008) and may well be associated with good mental health (Bradbury et al., 2009; Levin, 2005). It seems, therefore, that (some) anomalous and paranormal experiences do indeed have adaptive value.

Recent work (mostly from a cluster analytic perspective) supports the existence of two types of profile of higher scorers on positive schizotypy/

anomaly-proneness (e.g., Holt, Simmonds-Moore & Moore, 2008; Goulding, 2004, 2005; Loughland & Williams, 1997; Williams, 1994[13]). These clusters differ in terms of how one scores on the *other* aspects of schizotypy. Negative schizotypy is comprised of a lack of enjoyment from social and other activities (social anhedonia), alongside a dislike of emotional and physical intimacy (physical anhedonia) (Mason et al., 1995).Cognitive disorganization traits relate to problems in attention, concentration and decision-making alongside subjective feelings of purposelessness, moodiness and social anxiety (Mason et al., 1995). The variable also includes aversiveness and paranoid ideation (Claridge & Beech, 1995). Finally, impulsive nonconformity traits reflect disinhibited and impulsive characteristics, violent, self-abusive and reckless behaviors, or more moderately, a preference for a free living and non-conforming lifestyle (Mason et al., 1995). Research employing cluster analysis has found that one cluster — "healthy schizotypy" includes people who score high on positive aspects of schizotypy and low on all other aspects of schizotypy. A second cluster — "high schizotypy" — includes those who score high on positive aspects of schizotypy, *in addition to* scoring high on cognitive disorganization, introvertive anhedonia, and possibly also impulsive nonconformity — see Holt et al., 2008 and Chapter 6, by Holt, this volume).[14]

Both positive schizotypy groups have enhanced levels of paranormal beliefs and creativity (see Holt, Simmonds-Moore & Moore, 2008[15]). However, healthy schizotypy is associated with good mental health, whilst high schizotypy is associated with poorer mental health (see Holt et al., 2008; Goulding, 2004, 2005). An example of this type of personality was described by Nettle (2006), who noticed that creative individuals who practiced poetry and art were characterized by scoring high on positive aspects of schizotypy but with a *lack* of negative symptoms (no anhedonia and avolition). Similar patterns were observed by McCreery and Claridge (2002) for those prone to experiencing out-of-body experiences. Negative traits and cognitive disorganization traits may therefore be implicated in the *pathologization* of anomaly-proneness. The pathologizing influence of negative traits has also been noted in the real world. For example, Chapman, Chapman, Kwapil, Eckblad and Zinser (1994), found that although Magical Ideation was related to psychotic breakdown, this was more likely if one had negative in addition to positive traits of schizotypy.

Recent work (Goulding & Ödéhn, 2009) indicates that the relationship between anomaly proneness and mental health is complex, and potentially *curvilinear* — with low *and* high scorers both reporting good mental health, whilst those with average to slightly elevated scores having poorer mental health. These authors suggest that this may be impacted by cognitive disorganization among those with slightly elevated anomaly proneness. The role of cognitive disorganization is implicated in how pleasant one *appraises* ones' anomalous experiences and whether one is psychologically healthy or less healthy (Schofield & Claridge, 2007). Specifically, these authors found that those who were cognitively organized demonstrated a positive relationship between positive schizotypy and pleasant paranormal experiences. On the contrary, those who were cognitively disorganized demonstrated no relationship between positive schizotypy and pleasantness of paranormal experiences, but a relationship existed between negative schizotypy and the tendency to find paranormal experiences distressing. Bell, Halligan and Ellis (2007) also found that the *acceptance* of anomalous experiences served to protect against stress (cited in Bradbury et al., 2009). Specifically, they found that having similar levels of anomalous experiences and "delusional ideation" seemed to be protective against distress, while having more anomalous experiences than delusional ideation related to psychological distress. Brett, Peters, Johns, Valmaggia, and McGuire (2007) also found that the appraisal of anomalous experiences was important in mental health outcomes. This implies a healthy role for a certain degree of paranormal beliefs in *accommodating* experiences (see also chapter 8 by Clarke in this book).

The existence of a healthy and less healthy form of anomaly proneness may explain some of the mixed findings in the literature in terms of the relationship between anomalous cognitions and perceptions and mental health (see Auton, Pope & Seeger, 2001 for a review). Consideration of the impact of these other dimensions of schizotypy will be considered alongside other moderating factors when considering how to encourage healthy anomalous experiences among members of the general population.

Pathologizers of Trait Anomaly Proneness

As noted in the previous section, the possession of anomaly-prone traits seem to be pathologized by the simultaneous expression of a higher level of *other* traits; namely those relating to negative schizotypy and those relating to cognitive disorganization. A higher expression of impulsive traits may also have a pathologizing impact (e.g., Holt, Simmonds-Moore, & Moore, 2008). Recent research (e.g., see Goulding & Ödéhn, 2009) indicates that disorganization may well have the greatest impact on psychopathology among members of the general population. This section will briefly explore the possible *reasons* why these traits have a negative impact on mental health.

Negative Schizotypy

The pathologizing influence of negative schizotypy traits may derive from a lack of social contact resulting from anhedonia. However, problems may also derive from physical anhedonia, which may relate to the emotional appraisal of anomalous experiences. Applegate, El-Deredy & Bentall (2009) found that the ability to *savor* positive events is indeed impaired in negative schizotypy. They propose that *savoring* is associated with recalling information about past positive events and seeking to repeat them. In terms of anomalous experiences, then, negative traits may minimize the memory for positive outcomes of anomalous experiences. Other research supports the idea that the emotional response to anomalous experiences is pivotal in whether one is healthy or less healthy (Brett et al., 2007). This may implicate savoring as something to focus on in helping people to experience more pleasant anomalies. Negative schizotypy is associated with poorer performance on a range of cognitive tasks (see Barrantes-Vidal, Fañanás, Rosa, Caparrós, Riba, & Obiols, 2003). This is particularly the case for working memory (Matheson & Langdon, 2008) and as such, memory aides could enable greater memory for positive anomalous experiences.

Scoring high on this variable is also associated with problems in logic (associated with reduced theory of mind ability[16]) relating to other peoples' emotions and reasoning about one's own experiences, which could lead to delusions (Young & Mason, 2007). This supports anomaly-prone traits as neutral, but implies that *cognitions* about anomalous experiences (and their source?) are important in terms of mental health. Cognitions about anomalous experiences could potentially be targeted in increasing healthy experiences.

Cognitive Disorganization

Cognitive disorganization may influence anomaly proneness in several ways. Schofield and Claridge (2007) have proposed that being more organized could serve to moderate anomalies by constructing a *framework* for experiences (Schofield & Claridge, 2007).With a belief framework, anomalous experiences may be better assimilated. This is also supported by Bell et al.'s (2007) work, whereby having similar levels of anomalous experiences and beliefs seemed to protect against distress, while having more anomalous experience than belief was associated with distress—implying that having too many anomalous experiences may be associated with pathology. Other research supports the protective role of a framework, for example, those who are anomaly prone (i.e., scoring high on schizotypy) and also members of a new age group seem to be more healthy (Peters, Day, McKenna, & Orbach, 1999, Smith, Riley & Peters, 2009).

Disorganization is also associated with problems in inhibiting information "at an early pre-attentive stage of processing but not at a later early attentive stage" (Evans, Gray & Snowden, 2007, p. 159). Attentional problems may reflect a propensity to distraction due to reduced ability to inhibit information or stimuli that are not relevant. This might lead to a sense of feeling overwhelmed and not "in control" of one's anomalous experiences. Interestingly, although "schizotypy" is often associated with attentional problems, Braunstein-Bercovitz (2000) found that the attentional problems were associated with trait anxiety (and negative aspects of schizotypy) rather than positive schizotypy *per se*. With this in mind, anxiety reduction (increasing relaxation) may also have an impact on the inhibition of irrelevant information — experiencing anomalous phenomena in a more controlled way.

Impulsivity

To date, little work has explored how impulsive traits impact upon the pathologization of anomalous experiences. Recent work (Holt, Simmonds-Moore & Moore, 2008) has indicated that impulsiveness scoring *is* different between healthy and high schizotypy groups. For the high schizotypy group impulsiveness was high, while for the healthy schizotypy group it was average. Impulsiveness may have a negative impact on anomalous experiences when it manifests to a high degree, particularly in conjunction with negative traits and cognitive disorganization. Impulsivity is also associated with increased distractibility (see Stanford, Mathias, Dougherty, Lake, Anderson, & Patton, 2009 for a review), which may add to the subjective sense of intrusiveness of anomalies which already exists in the absence of cognitive organization.

Insights from the Hallucination Literature

The observations about less healthy schizotypy may dovetail with insights from the hallucination literature, where several authors have considered the differences between healthy and less healthy hallucinations. For example, Honig, Romme, Ensink, Escher, Pennings and Devries (1998) observed that the *form* of auditory hallucinations is no different between patients and non-patients. However, pathological hallucinations are unpredictable, uncontrollable, persistent and intrusive (Al Issa, 1995) and are appraised as uncontrollable and dangerous (Morrison et al., 2000). Honig et al. (1998) summarize the main differences between healthy and less healthy forms of experience in terms of their content, emotional quality and locus of control. Negative and pathological experiences of hearing voices were also more often associated with a history of trauma and abuse. Healthy hallucinations on the other hand were generally perceived to be under the control of the experiment, more positive, and people were not alarmed or upset by experiences. Sometimes healthy voices were actually positively integrated into the lives of the experiencers (Honig et al., 1998, see also chapter 8 by Clarke and chapter 10 by Belz, this book).

Summary of the Reasons Behind
the Pathologization of Anomalous Experiences

This discussion lends some insights into the reasons behind the pathologization of otherwise neutral anomaly-prone traits. In conclusion to trait approaches to anomalous experiences; healthy experiences may be summarized as (1) Experiencing pleasant rather than unpleasant anomalous phenomena (as such, one might focus on increasing the savoring of an experience); (2) Anomalous experiences are integrated into the rest of the cognitive-perceptual system, potentially by a belief framework as too many experiences that fall outside of such a framework may seem overwhelming, or other ways of experience management; (3) Anomalous experiences are not experienced as automatic/intrusive (as such one should focus on developing the means to control what seems to be out of control); (4) On consideration of the social issues experienced by those with negative schizotypal traits, anomalous experiences might also be more healthy when socially contextualized/supported. These observations will be revisited later, when we consider how to switch on anomalous experiences in a healthy manner. The following section will consider ways of manipulating anomalous experiences and go on to consider how to do so healthily.

The Manipulation of Boundary Thinness

It was noted earlier that schizotypes have an anomalous arousal system and are wired to experience alterations in consciousness (*cf.* McCreery, 1997). Anomaly proneness might therefore also be conceptualized as a *state* (see Simmonds-Moore & Holt, 2007; Zanes, Ross, Hatfield, Houtler, & Whitman, 1998). A "trait-state" approach would argue that those who score higher on psychometric measures of positive schizotypy have more natural *access* to "boundary thin" states which encourage a range of anomalous experiences. However, anomalous experiences are also possible in anyone who accesses one of these states of consciousness. If we can manipulate state boundary thinness, this may allow for the manipulation of anomalous experiences. However, given the complex relationship between psychopathology and anomaly proneness, one should think about (a) how to manipulate anomalous experiences but also (b) how to manipulate them in a healthy manner. Insights from the previous discussion on pathologizers of trait anomaly-proneness will therefore be incorporated into this discussion.

Switching Experiences On

Several factors may moderate boundary thinness and therefore anomaly-proneness. Persinger noted that meditation, hypoglycaemia (prolonged fasting), hypoxia, fatigue, alterations in vascular flow associated with drugs and the biochemical effects caused by personal crises (i.e., stress) all impact on temporal lobe lability (see Persinger & Makarec, 1987; Persinger, 1989). As noted earlier, this correlates highly with schizotypy (e.g., Simmonds-Moore, 2009–2010). Thalbourne, Crawley & Houran add that boundary thinness may be mediated by intense emotional states and driven by activation of the limbic system, which, via connectivity with the sensory cortex can produce anomalous phenomena (see Thalbourne, Crawley & Houran, 2003). However, not all of these would be advisable for *healthy* boundary manipulation.

Simmonds-Moore has argued previously (e.g., 2010) that sleep and other altered states (e.g., the ganzfeld and meditation) may function to moderate psychological boundaries and interact with pre-existing trait boundary thinness (see Simmonds-Moore & Holt, 2007). Those who score high on psychometric positive schizotypy might experience more naturally occurring sleep states during wakefulness and waking (or semi-waking) states during sleep due to anomalies in the usual boundaries between wakefulness and sleep. This biological tendency may lead to a range of nocturnal and diurnal anomalous experiences (see Koffel & Watson, 2009).

A "sleep state" might be defined as a state that is analogous to that *usually* associated with falling sleep or nocturnal sleep cycles. McCreery (e.g., 1997) has cogently argued that the best candidate for a sleep related correlate of anomalous phenomena interjecting into wakefulness is the hypnagogic state. Hypnagogic thinking exhibits many aspects of boundary thinness, and is more commonly experienced by those who are anomaly-prone (e.g., Jakes & Hemsley, 1987; Parra & Espinoza Paul, 2009)

It is a paradoxical state of consciousness, reflecting more influence of the right hemisphere, more influence of sub cortical processes on the cortex, more synesthetic thinking and more associational thinking that is characteristic of right hemispheric processing (see Mavromatis, 1987). It is also associated with a range of anomalous experiences (see Sherwood, 2000).

One might therefore apply this knowledge when considering how to encourage such a state among members of the general public. Although hypnagogia is (by nature) associated with falling asleep (see Mavromatis, 1987), it is not always fixed to physiological sleep onset (see Wackermann, Pütz,

Büchi, Strauch, & Lehmann, 2002). In fact, hypnagogic experiences can occur during relaxed wakefulness in the daytime (Foulkes & Fleisher, 1975; Gurstelle & de Oliveira, 2004). As such, these experiences might be encouraged during the daytime by simply lying down, closing the eyes and relaxing.

It has been suggested that anomalous phenomena may be associated with processes associated with sleep *interjecting* into waking consciousness (see McCreery, 1997; Simmonds-Moore & Connell, in preparation). McCreery suggests that this may be due to *over-arousal* (as stress) as well as *under arousal (as extreme tiredness)*. If anomalous experiences interject into consciousness as a sleep response, they might be experienced more if one is sleep or dream deprived. There is support for increased hypnagogic hallucinations among those who experience poorer nocturnal sleep (Naitoh, Kales, Kollar, Smith, & Jacobson, 1969). In addition, those with shorter sleep (Soper, Kelly & Von Bergen,1997) and poorer sleep quality (Simmonds-Moore & Connell) report more daytime hallucinations. In terms of anomalous experiences, poorer sleep quality (but not sleep length) weakly predicted anomalous experiences (Simmonds-Moore 2009–2010). This implies that more anomalous experiences may result from reducing nocturnal sleep, which may not be a healthy practice in the long term.

More healthily, such states might be encouraged via employment of methods for relaxation during the daytime; e.g., the ganzfeld and various meditative techniques. The ganzfeld results in a state that has been described as "hypnagoid"[17] (Wackermann, Pütz, Büchi, Strauch, & Lehmann, 2002); it appears to encourages a range of anomalous experiences (e.g., McCreery & Claridge, 1996a),[18] and is a method that was designed to encourage a "psi-conducive" state among members of the public (e.g., see Palmer, 2003 and Storm, Tressoldi & Di Risio, 2010, for a good review).

Although there are many forms of "meditation" (see Schmidt, this volume) the resulting state(s) may encourage "boundary thinness" in a number of domains; greater inter-hemispheric synchrony (or lateral connectivity) (Travis & Arenander, 2006), more efficient processing of information that is outside of the normal range of attention (e.g., Sudarsham Kriya yoga meditation, see Srinivasan & Baijal, 2007), more influence of sub cortical processes on the cortex (e.g., Woodfolk, 1975 cited in Yardi, 2001) and more synesthesia (Walsh, 2005).

Hemi sync[19] technology (see Atwater, 2004) might also be used to thin boundaries and access anomaly proneness. This technology has been associated with increased synchronization between hemispheres and greater influence of sub cortical processes on conscious awareness. Other research implies that meditative states of consciousness may also allow for a *more efficient* unity of consciousness (see Hebert, Lehmann, Tan, Travis and Arenander, 2005). With this in mind, it is of note that meditation and hemi sync have both been related to anomalous experiences, including extrasensory perception (see Atwater, 2004, Palmer, Khamashta & Israelson, 1979; Rao & Rao, 1982 and Schmidt, chapter 5, this book).

Summary: Methods to Encourage Anomalous Experiences. In summary, by adopting a state-trait approach to anomaly proneness, it may be possible to encourage anomalous experiences by employing methods which increase the amount of daytime opportunities for hypnagogic thought and other mild altered states of consciousness (e.g., using the ganzfeld technique, meditation techniques, and technologies such as Hemi-Sync).

Manipulating Healthy *Anomaly Proneness*

If people are engaging in procedures to encourage "thinner" boundaries, it is important to do this responsibly. Thinning boundaries may well lead to more anomalous experiences, but this may lead to *both* healthy and less healthy anomalous experiences. Given that there are *two* types of trait anomaly proneness, moderating factors should be included which allow for healthy rather than less healthy anomalous experiences. In the following discussion, we will apply what we know about healthy trait anomaly proneness to anomalous experiences in general.

A Combination of Thin and Thick Boundaries

In his book on personality and psychological boundaries, Hartmann (1991) observed that healthy individuals exhibit *both* thick and thin boundaries and score somewhere in the middle on his psychometric scale. As such, if one has *very* thin boundaries, this might be equivalent to an *open unfiltered nervous system*, which could lead to anomalous experiences which are subjectively experienced as overwhelming, in the absence of moderating factors.

A metaphor (which maps back to the subjective experience of intrusiveness of anomalous experiences) is of opening up a flood-gate, in the absence of "valves" which might otherwise control the flow of the experiential information reaching conscious awareness. In the absence of effective inhibitory processes such as selective attention, sensory experiences might overload the system and feel frightening. A healthy anomaly-prone personality, on the other hand, can cope well with anomalous experiences due to the existence of moderating factors (or the co-existence of thin and thick boundaries), which effectively serve as valves which enable experiences to be experienced healthily.

A mixture of thin and thick boundaries reflects both a proneness toward anomalous experiences, in addition to rational thinking and *controlled* cognition. A healthy anomaly-prone personality, therefore, might often but *not consistently*, experience anomalous phenomena, as they are (1) able to control these experiences and (2) a*pply* these experiences. In support of this, Zanes et al. (1998) found that inconsistency in scoring on a schizotypy scale related to creativity (a socially acceptable application) whilst consistency in scoring related more to psychopathology (Zanes et al., 1998). This supports the idea that anomaly proneness may be better understood as a state. Those who are anomaly prone are more likely to enter such states, but healthy anomalous experiences are associated with the ability to access and leave anomalous states *at will* and apply them.

Healthy anomalous experiences would therefore be associated with those with high cognitive flexibility who are applying or contextualizing their experiences. This might include those who are creative, those who are spiritual healers or those who work as mediums (among others).[20] Initial insights from a series of interviews carried out by the author with people working as psychic/spiritual healers indicate that many used to have an open-system (some indicating that they had indeed felt overwhelmed by their anomalous experiences), but thicker boundaries and an ability to *dip into* anomalous experiences had developed over time.[21] Examples given included the use of psychological "filters" for unwanted and desired anomalies, e.g., visualizing a physical boundary around the self (e.g., a golden light) which would serve to protect the sense of self and enable a filter to be activated to experiences of a "psi" origin only.

Increasing the Sense of Control
Over Automatic Experiences

This section will consider which methods might enable people to dip into anomalous experiences at will. Brod (1997) previously suggested that intelligence may allow for "more flexible psychological resources" and enable psychological protection for those who are anomaly prone (Brod, 1997, p. 282). However, research findings are mixed on whether there are IQ differences between healthy schizotypes and high schizotypes (Barrantes-Vidal, Fañanás, Rosa, Caparrós, Riba, &. Obiols, 2003; Holt, Simmonds-Moore & Moore, 2008[22]). With this in mind, other factors could also be implicated.

Given that cognitive disorganization appears to be the main pathologizer of anomalous experiences, and is associated with attentional anomalies, being able to have control over attention allocation may be important. Recent work (Moore & Malinowski, 2009) explored the impact of mindfulness on atten-

tional functions and cognitive flexibility. Mindfulness is defined as "the awareness that emerges through paying attention on purpose, in the present
moment, and non-judgmentally to the unfolding of experience moment by
moment" (Kabat-Zinn, 2003, cited in Moore & Malinowski 2009, p. 177, see
also chapter 5 by Schmidt, this book). They compared meditators with non-
meditators on a series of attentional task (including the stroop task and the
d2 test of attention which assesses participants' ability to suppress interfering
information). They were interested in how mindfulness might impact on cognitive flexibility, or "the ability to interrupt or deautomatize automated
responses, that is to respond non-habitually" and found differences between
the groups. Being able to stop or intervene in automatic processing may
be particularly relevant for anomaly-prone people who are less psychologically healthy (potentially because of higher levels of cognitive disorganization).

Unfortunately, we cannot change the biases of society re anomalous experiences. For example, Al Issha (1995, and others, e.g., Bentall, 2003; Liester,
1996) note that the West actually *pathologizes* the hallucination, thus, supply-
ing a socially derived fear of the anomalous (hallucination = pathology).
Gaining more control may also allow for a re-appraisal of anomalous experiences as pleasant (i.e., increase savoring) and for experiences to become
more organized in a relaxed and positive way.

Attention allocation could *naturally* be associated with better working
memory abilities among happy schizotypes, which may not be directly tapped
by IQ measures. Alternatively, those who are happy schizotypes could have
developed better attention allocation, e.g., via meditation and other practices.

Spiritual/Religious/Meaningful Context or Framework

As suggested by the earlier discussion on pathologizers of anomalous
experiences, having a [spiritual] context or application for experiences may
play a key role in healthy anomalous experiences. Interestingly, the development of Psychic/spiritual healers was often intertwined with some form of
spiritual development (often in new age practices). Psychic/spiritual healers
scored significantly higher on psychometric measure for "spirituality" (Spiritual Transcendence) than a group of non-healers (Palmer, Simmonds-Moore,
& Baumann, 2006). Interestingly, in Palmer et al.'s (2006) work, boundary
thinness scores did not differ between a group of healers and non-healers.
However, boundary scores correlated positively with spirituality for the healer
group but not for the control group; indicating that boundary thinness was
cultivated or *applied to a particular context (spirituality)* in the case of the
healers. This may result from formal training in a New Age practice, but the

key may be that there is some kind of framework applied to the experience (after Schofield & Claridge, 2007).

It may be that many practices inherent within traditional organized religions are bound to the encouragement of healthy versus less healthy experience. New age religions may also foster healthy practices (see Farias et al., 2005; Day & Peters, 1999; Smith, Riley & Peters, 2009).

Liester (1996) suggested that healthy voice hearing is associated with the ego being transcended, which is common to many spiritual traditions and supports a role for (formal) spiritual or transpersonal development (see Daniels, 2005). In addition, he notes that healthy experiences arise in a state of "receptive awareness and inner silence" which sounds like a meditative or prayer state. Spiritual aspects of anomalous experiences may constitute a healthy form of anomalous experience (see Bradbury et al., 2009). Prior research indicates that spiritual beliefs are associated with several positive mental health measures (see Moreira-Almeida, Neto & Koenig, 2006 for a review). This may relate to having an organized framework for ones experiences (see Schofield & Claridge, 2007) or that *finding meaning* may well be important for healthy experiences (see Kennedy, Kanthamani & Palmer, 1994).

Interpretation and meaning-seeking may be important in healthy anomalous experiences. For example, Liester (1996) gave several examples from history (including experiences of Carl Jung) whereby inner voices were transcribed and attended to, and found to contain insightful messages. This practice may relate to traditional dream interpretation, which may bestow psychological benefits to a given individual (Siegal, 2010). Interestingly, some spiritual/new age workshops encourage people to look at their own mental imagery, do drawings and facilitate interpretation of personal symbols and metaphors. Creativity is the acceptable face of anomaly-proneness (e.g., Mohr & Leonard, 2005). This may serve as another application for meaningful anomalous experiences. This kind of approach is supported by apparently positive results for a range of arts based therapies for psychological and psychiatric problems (see Burton, 2009).

Inducing "Controlled" Anomalous Experiences

Another means to manipulate *healthy* anomalous experience might be to *imagine* oneself experiencing such anomalies. The use of imagination has been demonstrated to be useful in other areas where one "practices" certain motor activities, (including singing — see Kleber, Birbaumer, Veit, Trevorrow, &. Lotze, 2009). Anomalous experiences may be difficult or too complex to imagine, as such, anomalous experiences might also be induced in a *controlled* manner in the laboratory, e.g., via use of technologies to stimulate anomalous experience, that may be switched on and off at will, e.g., Hemi-Sync (Atwater, 2004) or applying weak magnetic pulses to the temporal lobes of the brain (see Persinger, Tiller, & Koren, 2000). The experiment would therefore have an anomalous experience in a controlled manner, and learn that nothing bad happens as a consequence of experiencing them (like systemic desensitization). Interestingly, at The Monroe Institute, facilitators are trained to help people to process their unusual experiences arising from the use of Hemi-Sync tapes. This may increase the acceptability of anomalous experiences, which may otherwise seem to be frightening and outside of personal control. As savoring is important in increasing healthy experiences, one might also focus on increasing the perceived pleasantness of anomalous experiences. This could be achieved via diary keeping, and asking experiments to try to find positive meaning in experiences in addition to observation of the actual impact of an anomalous experience. E.g., if one moved out of the body, did he or she come back? This relates to methods employed in Cognitive Behavioral Therapy, that try to teach people what the real [emotional] impact of a particular experience is. This may also help to increase memories for positive anomalous experiences (see also chapter 9 by Clarke, this book).

Social Support

As social isolation is a key component of negative schizotypy — one of the trait factors implicated in pathologizing anomalous experiences social support may be a key moderating factor in healthy versus less healthy experiences (for one clinical perspective, see Clarke, this volume, who discusses her work with those suffering from psychosis and what is real and what is not workshops). As such, the approaches described in the preceding section should be best placed in a social context; among other people who are also experiencing anomalies, and shared (e.g., in paranormal experience groups. For example, there are online and face to face groups that may already be doing this (see Simmonds-Moore, this volume). For example, the Rhine Research Center in Durham, North Carolina, runs a "PEG" (or Paranormal Experiences Group) where members of the public can come and share their paranormal experiences in a value free environment. The group might also help people to realize if they are experiencing mental problems, particularly if those with clinical training are also available for support or referral.

Summary of Methods to Induce
Healthy Anomalous Experiences

In summary, healthy anomalous experiences are associated with being able to access anomaly prone states at will rather than experience them consistently, this may be applied via the use of methods to increase cognitive control and flexibility in accessing experiences (e.g., through the use of imagery and meditation) experiences that are applied (e.g., creativity, those working as mediums, healers, some psychics and shamans who access altered states to attain information that is then used for the benefit of the community they work in)experiences that are interpreted as meaningful and pleasant (e.g., within a particular framework/interpretation). It was also suggested that people might practice having anomalous experiences in a controlled manner — e.g., by use of methods such as hemi-sync or brain stimulation, in combination with facilitators who might help people to integrate experiences. Finally, it is clear from the earlier discussion that social support factors are also important for healthy anomalous experiences.

Eliminating or Attenuating Anomalous Experiences

It was noted earlier that some people consult research centers and universities who conduct research on paranormal and anomalous phenomena to ask about how to stop their unwanted or overwhelming anomalous experiences. This section will present several methods which may help to eliminate or attenuate unwanted anomalous experiences. Following on from the idea that anomaly proneness is a state and trait variable, sleep experiences may be targeted to reduce the number of anomalous experiences among some people. Other methods will also be introduced which could enable a reduction in anomalous experiences.

Improving or Replacing Nocturnal Sleep

Methods to improve nocturnal sleep quality or replace lost sleep, may help to increase boundary thickness, and by so doing reduce the number of unwanted anomalous experiences. Nocturnal sleep quality (or sleep length) may be improved by using self-hypnosis or other relaxation/good sleep suggestion techniques. Daytime napping or some forms of meditation might also be employed with the purpose of *replacing* lost or disturbed nocturnal sleep during the daytime. This is theoretically supported by Horne's (e.g., 1988; 2000) arguments that humans only *need* four hours of "core" sleep during the night. The rest (mostly REM sleep) is considered by Horne to be *optional*, and potentially replaceable with relaxed wakefulness. From this perspective, it should not matter *when* one gets their quota of relaxed wakefulness. As such, (some) boundaries might well also be thickened by meditative practice or taking naps in the daytime. With this in mind, it is of interest that certain spiritual traditions encourage the reduction of nocturnal sleep patterns whilst increasing the amount of daytime meditation (e.g., Ram Dass, 1971) which may serve to increase anomalies, but attain more control over them (via meditation).

However, it may be that sleep is disturbed due to factors *outside* of the control of the experiment — either in their external environment (a noisy neighbor, or a new baby) or internally (those who are anomaly prone are more wired to experience alterations in the normal state of consciousness, which include interjections of wakefulness into sleep as well as vice versa). It may well be that sleep is disturbed *because of* one's anomalous experiences (*c.f.* Simmonds-Moore, 2009–2010; Koffel & Watson, 2009) and therefore we might be dealing with a complex etiology regarding personality and anomalous phenomena. If this is the case, and one is wired to be nocturnally and diurnally anomaly-prone, other ways "switching off" experiences should be considered.

Learning to Ignore Irrelevant Stimuli

The focus of this chapter is on the non-clinical population — those people who will, in all likelihood *not* present with a breakdown, but who may well still benefit from assistance in managing, ignoring or switching off their anomalies. Various approaches were considered earlier under the section discussing the manipulation of healthy anomalous experiences. One key suggestion was in the use of meditation for enabling greater control of anomalous experiences which may otherwise be experienced as intrusive. It was noted earlier (*c.f.* Moore & Malinowski, 2009) that mindfulness meditation may allow for increased cognitive flexibility and control over otherwise automatic (anomalous) experiences and that this may be applied to anomalous experiences. Meditation may also be applied to selectively filter out what is not needed in a given moment (effectively *switching off* the irrelevant stimulus). For example, Liester (1996) described the healthy cultivation of the inner voice experience as refocusing attention away from distracting stimuli (e.g., the normal buzz of sensory experience and thinking). This seems very similar to some aspects of meditative or prayer practice, in particular, mindfulness, and "distracting stimuli" could include unwanted anomalous perceptions or experiences.

Bentall (1990) has noted that in the presence of a lot of environmental stimulation, hallucinations decrease when attention is occupied with reading, writing and rate of presentation, and when stimuli are meaningful rather than random. *Occupying* the attentional window with other linguistic information may assist in the control of auditory hallucinations. In certain forms of meditation, one becomes absorbed in the repetition of a meaningful mantra (which would be equivalent to linguistic information) or sub vocalizing or vocalizing a prayer.[23] Although one might display caution in recommending one particular spiritual pathway over another, it may be that some forms of meditation and prayer may help to prevent or reduce some invasive anomalous experiences.

Rituals, Imagery and Metaphors

The idea of using imagery or metaphorical boundaries may also be important for switching experiences off. Indeed, in the healing study described earlier, healers often reported rituals employing the use of synesthetic metaphors which enabled a visual-kinesthetic switch into and out of an anomaly-prone state (these included chanting, using the breath, and other idiosyncratic methods). Effectively, during a certain set time period, anomalous experiences may be invited or encouraged, but after that time period they would be unwelcome. This is clearly seen in Blackmore's (Blackmore & Hart-Davis, 1995) advice on using the Ouija board. Although Blackmore is skeptical about the veridicality of paranormal experiences arising from Ouija board use, she recognizes the need to formally say "good bye" to the Ouija board, so that there are no negative post event experiences. She suggests that people should respect the Ouija board experiences, and clearly switch off the context for any ensuing anomalous experiences. This author's observations of mediums and healers also corroborates this advice, in a different way, by the deployment of a psychological procedure for *entering* a psi state, and a psychological procedure for *ending* that psi state. Problems associated with anomalous experiences generally reflect the sense that something unwanted is invading the consciousness, and that one has no control over that experience. Psychic development courses (and anyone exploring states that might lead to anomalous experiences) should take these observations on board, and consider the role of ritual for switching off as well as switching on anomalies.

Summary of Methods to Eliminate or Attenuate Anomalous Experiences

In summary, anomalous experiences might be switched off by reducing the amount of diurnal sleep interjections by increasing sleep quality or supplementing lost sleep with daytime relaxation/naps or meditation. Some forms of meditation and prayer may help to ignore irrelevant or distracting information. Finally, rituals and imagery may be useful in terms of delineating when anomalous experiences are welcome and not welcome.

Conclusions

This chapter has presented an interactionist approach to anomaly-proneness with a view to gaining insights about how one might encourage anomalous experiences for health and transcendence or eliminate or attenuate them if they are unwanted. The chapter focused on strategies for use among members of the non-psychiatric population who are interested in learning how to *control* their anomalous experiences.

The discussion focused on positive schizotypy as an anomaly prone personality trait and hypnagogic thinking as an anomaly-prone state of consciousness. Factors which pathologize the otherwise neutral anomaly proneness were considered and suggestions were made with regard to the encouragement of healthier anomalous experiences.

It was argued that boundary thinness is a good metaphor for understanding anomaly proneness. However, the idea that being boundary thin leads to anomalous experiences and boundary thickness leads to less anomalous experiences should be supplemented by consideration of factors associated with healthy anomalies. It seems that those who are able to control their access to boundary thin states, or ignore irrelevant experiences associated with being boundary thin may be equivalent to healthy and adaptive individuals (the happy schizotype). As such, manipulation of boundary thinness should be undertaken alongside other strategies which enable this ability. It was argued that meditation, the use of rituals, symbols and metaphors, the application of the products of an anomaly-prone personality (mediumship, creative writing, etc.) and a social context for sharing ones experiences are all of potential benefit for experiencing anomalous phenomena in a healthy manner.

There is a need for academics who are working with anomalous experiences, and anyone interacting with members of the public who experience such anomalies, to be clinically responsible, even if one has not undertaken clinical training themselves. Parapsychologists and those involved in the psychic development world have a responsibility to understand personality and clinical perspectives on anomalous experiences.

Notes

1. These include states of consciousness, cognition (particularly attention), imagination and cognitive strategies, a meaningful context and useful application of the contents or products of anomalous experiences.
2. See Funder (2009) for a recent discussion of interactionism.
3. The etiology of paranormal beliefs is complicated, and may involve social factors, childhood experiences, cognitive style, etc. Readers are referred to Irwin's (2009) excellent monograph on

the topic of paranormal beliefs, in particular, chapter 8 where he presents a theoretical integration of a model for the development of beliefs in "scientifically unaccepted phenomena."

4. These authors employed the Transliminality variable, which incorporates schizotypy.

5. However, recent work by Holt et al. (2008) implies that attentional boundaries are not implicated in anomalous beliefs.

6. However, recent research (Dagnall & Parker, 2009) found that high scorers on positive schizotypy did not have more false memories.

7. This is associated with attaching significance or meaning to ones experiences and memories.

8. Unusual experiences may reflect altered sensory/early attention (N100) mechanisms while paranormal ideation relates to alterations in contextual updating processes.

9. However, both aspects are explored by the Chapman group, who formulated one questionnaire-the Magical Ideation scale -to measure magical thinking (Eckblad & Chapman, 1983),and a second questionnaire; the Perceptual Aberration scale (Chapman, Chapman, & Raulin, 1978)-to measure unusual experiences.

10. This information may or may not include genuine "psi" information.

11. Irwin and Young (2001) did not find the combination pattern in their later study, and note that Wolfradt et al. failed to find it in a replication of their 1999 study. In fact, Irwin and Young found that paranormal beliefs were more related to an intuitive (and not rational) thinking style. However, there was a trend toward a relationship between a combination of rational and intuitive thinking and "New Age beliefs."

12. Brod (1997), for example, has suggested that intelligence might be one protective factor.

13. For the most part, cluster analyses have omitted impulsive nonconformity. They have also resulted-generally-in a 3 cluster solution reflecting happy schizotypy-high scoring on positive but low on other aspects; low schizotypy who score low on all aspects of schizotypy and a third group high schizotypy reflecting higher scores on cognitive disorganization, introvertive anhedonia and higher than average scores on positive schizotypy.

14. Goulding and Ödéhn's (2009) recent study found a slightly different cluster solution in random sample study with Swedish nationals. Their work indicated the following cluster groupings; low schizotypy, positive schizotypy, cognitive disorganization and negative schizotypy.

15. However, healthy schizotypes have exceptionally high creativity. Readers are referred to the chapter on creativity by Nicola Holt in this volume.

16. Reduced theory of mind ability is implicated in many of the symptoms of full blown schizophrenia (e.g., see Frith & Corcoran, 1996).

17. This corresponds to some hypnagogic thinking alongside some aspects more characteristic of waking thought.

18. For example, McCreery and Claridge found that this encouraged the OBE, detachment experiences, increased imagery, hallucinatory experiences and so on, but particularly among those who scored high on positive schizotypy.

19. Hemi sync is a technology developed by the Monroe institute in Virginia, USA and is designed to synchronize functioning of the two hemispheres of the brain.

20. This statement is neutral as to the veridicality of the claims of healers and mediums.

21. This was undertaken as part of Palmer, Simmonds-Moore & Baumann's 2006 work on intentionality and hemolysis of red blood cells. The series of interviews are currently being transcribed and formally analyzed and the results will be described in a future publication.

22. Holt, Simmonds-Moore & Moore (2008) found no differences between their clusters on IQ, while Barrantes-Vidal et al. (2003) found a significant difference, with less healthy positive schizotypes having a lower IQ.

23. However, it is not clear that this kind of approach would help hallucinatory experiences which could potentiate from a more genuine psi source.

8

Transformative and/or Destructive: Exceptional Experiences from the Clinical Perspective

ISABEL CLARKE

Abstract

This chapter explores the overlaps between spiritual and transcendent experiences and madness (in particular, psychosis) drawing on recent theory and research and the author's observations as a clinician. The author begins by discussing semantic issues pertaining to exceptional experiences. She goes on to describe research which has explored the similarities and differences between psychosis and spirituality, and notes how the concept of schizotypy as a continuum of openness or vulnerability to anomalous experiences has helped to normalize exceptional experiences. The author proposes the "transliminal" (after Thalbourne) as a value free term to describe experiences which occur when a person steps beyond the bounds of their individuality, where anomalies are accessible, and where experiences can be mythological or "archetypal" in nature. Transliminal experiences are then discussed via grounding in an empirically based model of human information processing, *Interacting Cognitive Subsystems*. A de-stigmatizing approach to therapy for psychosis, based on this model is then presented. The transformative potential of transliminal experiences is discussed, alongside the importance of a supportive context for this potential to be realized. The recently formed *Spiritual Crisis Network* is introduced as an attempt to create such a context.

Introduction: Words

I want to start with the form of words, "exceptional human experience." Finding a way to talk about this subject has engaged me for a long time. Quibbling about definition and choice of words can seem a dry, academic exercise. On this topic, I would argue, it is anything but. In human terms, the choice of words can make the difference between hope and despair; between self acceptance and self (and other) rejection. In extreme but not necessarily rare, cases, it can mean the choice between life and death.

So why is language so sensitive here? A word about the trouble with words. Words are all we have got to communicate precise meaning to one another, to investigate and pin down, to attempt to get to the heart of the matter. Words do discriminate between things, experiences and ideas, but they have a complementary function to carry associations. They are already laden with meaning and association before we pick them up to use in our argument in order to convey our chosen meaning. These hidden meanings can subtly influence the discussion, perhaps subverting the original intention. This is because words both distinguish and associate — accurately reflecting the two central faculties of human intelligence. This point will be returned to later in the chapter, in elucidating the distinction between exceptional and ordinary human experience, and the source of this distinction comes from in information processing terms.

So, why is it that language is so peculiarly slippery and treacherous in this area of discourse? There could be a number of reasons. The fact that we are attempting to be clear about things that are on or over the edge of normal, rational, comprehension is one. Another is the emotional and supernatural charge associated with the subject, a charge that seems to hover around that edge between the knowable and the un-knowable. High emotion arises from intense personal meaning. The way in which someone's exceptional experience is defined is crucial for their own and other people's judgment of that individual's worth as a person. To be considered to be undergoing a spiritual emergency on the route to higher states of consciousness has vastly different personal implications from being diagnosed with schizophrenia. Research quoted later proves that exactly the same sort of experience can receive either label. This raises the possibility that mental health services, such as the one I work in, are doing unjustifiable damage to people's self-image and standing in the world, undermining their mental well-being in the process. And yet, there is such a thing as madness. This has been recognized by every society through the ages. We need these words to disentangle concepts, but we need to be alert to their limitations.

A strong emotional reaction is inevitable and justified where a person's self and societal reputation is on the line, as can be the case where exceptional experiences are concerned. The supernatural, numinous glow that hangs around experience and conceptualization at that edge or horizon of knowing that this collection of essays is bravely exploring, is harder to pin down. This is another powerful factor impeding definition. We have here strayed into the territory of the sacred — where it is death for the uninitiated to venture — or the territory of dreams—fascinating but easily dismissed. This is territory where meanings and value systems shimmer between opposites: ultimate truth or illusion/delusion; psychotic or mystical experience.

To return to the current descriptor, "exceptional experience"; in the context, I take it that it is meant to cover what might variously be described as paranormal, spiritual/mystical or psychotic experience, depending on the context and intentions of the speaker. It has the advantage of not entirely pre-judging whether the experiencer has been endowed with special powers or is deserving of psychiatric diagnosis. However, it does tend towards the first. Exceptional does not have to mean superior, but carries that flavor. It aligns naturally with Maslow's descriptor, "peak experience" (Maslow 1964) which suggests the positive. Another important way to get a handle on a word is to look at its opposite. This can often tell us as much about the meaning the concept insinuates into the discussion as the word itself. In the case of exceptional, the opposite that suggests itself is "ordinary." This I see as helpful. "Ordinary" simultaneously conveys rational solidity and boredom, which creates a nice balance.

Earlier Definitions and Recent Research

A brief survey of other attempts to cover this conceptualization will precede the attempt to make psychological sense of such experience. When I first grappled with this subject in my paper "Psychosis and Spirituality: finding a language" in the late 1990s (Clarke, 2000), the dichotomy seemed everywhere quite stark. Most people were exercised with a distinction between psychotic and spiritual/mystical experience that they considered to be quite fixed, but sometimes difficult to discern (e.g., Wilber, 1980 and the "pre-trans fallacy). Grof's notion of *spiritual emergency* (Grof & Grof, 1991), which followed on naturally from Laing's of psychotic breakdown as potentially a process of breakthrough (Laing, 1965), certainly represented a softening of this dichotomy. However, both Grof and Laing held ultimately that there was on the one hand a transformative process that involved elements of dissolution, and, on the other, psychotic illness.

I was unhappy with this dichotomy as my own introduction to this field was through offering cognitive therapy to individuals who had been under a psychiatric rehabilitation service for years, and whose experiences had invited the diagnosis of chronic schizophrenia, and yet described to me initial experiences that matched well with the accounts of the great mystics I was acquainted with from my earlier study of medieval history. Further, the scientist in me balked at it. What evidence, apart from the way the person's life turned out, would determine the distinction? Why should a disastrous subsequent course of life invalidate the experience itself? If there was an irreducible difference from the start, as the likes of Wilber would assert, how did they know?

I am delighted to say that things have moved on considerably in the intervening 10 years in the direction of softening those hard-line distinctions. Research evidence has been crucial here, and has proved a powerful corrective to unfounded assertion. When I was putting together my edited book on psychosis and spirituality (Clarke, 2001), Mike Jackson and Emmanuelle Peters' research provided a crucial foundation. Emmanuelle Peters gave the same questionnaires, designed to measure psychotic symptoms, to diagnosed people in hospital and to people involved in new religious movements (Peters et al., 1999). She found substantial overlap in types of experience and beliefs — the only difference being in degree of preoccupation and distress. Mike Jackson undertook an extensive quantitative and qualitative study comparing a sample of people reporting spiritual experiences from the general population and another diagnosed sample, with the same result (Jackson, 1997). His qualitative study illustrates clearly how there is a broad area of overlap where the two groups are indistinguishable (Jackson, 2001). In terms of impact on someone's life and in determining how the experiences are construed both by the individual and society, however, there is a vast gulf between considering that you have been through a challenging spiritual upheaval and that you "have" schizophrenia.

In the intervening years this research has been continued and taken further by Jackson and collaborators, and the concept of "schizotypy," a continuum of openness to unusual experience, which featured in Gordon Claridge's chapter of the 2001 book (Claridge, 2001), has been brought into the Cognitive Behavior Therapy (CBT) for psychosis literature (e.g. Holmes & Steele, 2004). I myself have found this concept to be a powerful way of normalizing such experiences for the people in mental health hospital with whom I work, and enabling them to see this openness as both a gift and a vulnerability rather than simply a despised "illness" (Freemantle & Clarke, 2008, Phillips et al., in submission).

Another milestone along the route of this normalization is an impressive and thorough research project, principally carried out by Caroline Brett, at the Institute of Psychiatry, under the supervision of Emmanuelle Peters (Brett et al., 2007). This was a further, particularly thorough, comparison between an undiagnosed sample, collected from various New Age, spiritualist etc. sources and a diagnosed group. This research demonstrated the factors that might mediate the difference between anomalous experiences that lead to clinical "caseness" (with associated stigma) as opposed to those that are managed without need for mental health care. By using the terminology "anomalous experiences" as opposed to "symptoms" they have already found a way of normalizing a wide area of exceptional experience. In this, they are following in the foot-steps of the "hearing voices" tradition (Romme & Escher, 1989), but casting the net wider than auditory hallucinations.

The factors that discriminate between contact with services and no contact that Brett et al. found were: greater controllability, a more positive emotional response (but not entailing lower arousal), less avoidance and immersion (by which they mean tendency to act in response to the experience) and a more normalizing way of making sense of the experiences. The undiagnosed sample were more likely to make internal, psychological attributions for their anomalous experiences, but where they did make externalising attributions, these were more likely to be attributions to supernatural forces as opposed to attributions to the action of other people (as in paranoid attribution).

Brett and collaborators have developed a sensitive and comprehensive measure of anomalous experiences, the Appraisals of Anomalous Experiences Interview (AANEX). These results are in accordance with the findings of Richard Warner (2003) that more traditional societies show better outcomes than Western medicine in terms of relapse and chronicity with psychotic presentations.

Introducing the Transliminal

The very words we use when talking about this area of human experience will prejudice the argument, and that there are profound issues at stake here to do with how human beings see themselves in relation to their social group, whether in the elevated position of a spiritual voyager or the lowly place assigned to those diagnosed with mental health problems. Behind this distinction lies another, even thornier, issue — that of the meaningfulness or otherwise of transcendent reality. Spiritual experience acquires its caché from the notion that the experiencer is in touch with "realms" beyond the ordinary; in communion with gods or goddesses, perhaps? or with "higher" states of consciousness. Religions whose founders transmit teachings from this beyond to their followers, generally claim "truth" (though in the light of the two ways of knowing argument to be introduced below, this concept becomes elusive). Immediately we find ourselves in a territory of loaded and radically indefinable, scientifically dubious, words. These words might be challenging to science, but the very persistence of the concepts suggests that they describe something enduring in human experience. That is an experience of connection beyond the self and beyond the precisely knowable, with something higher, greater, deeper — an experience which is probably best captured by the word "transcendence."

Of course, transcendence is controversial. The "How do they know?" question is only too relevant here. Just because a lot of people believe it does not mean that it is "true." On the other hand, there are regularities in human experience that persist in the face of such scepticism. Belief in a connection, a relationship, with that which is greater and beyond is one example of such persistence. Belief in transfer of information and experience in scientifically inexplicable ways (i.e., the paranormal) is another. In what follows, I will attempt to offer a framework for understanding both of these in the light of what we do know about cognitive psychology; about the way in which the human brain is wired up.

Psychology has already grappled with this area. Jung was the pioneer here with the concept of the "collective unconscious." It is the special province of transpersonal psychology and psychotherapy. These theories have mapped the territory, the characteristics to be expected of that other state. Entering this territory entails stepping beyond the bounds of the individual, so into a place of boundlessness. Jung has alerted us to the mythological, "archetypal" nature of experience here (e.g., Jung 1964). In seeking to explore the concept, I adopt Thalbourne's term, "the transliminal" from Claridge (1997). I prefer this term because the direction "across" (trans) is value free, and the idea of a threshold (limen) conveys the sense of stepping into what feels like another world, but which is merely a hairsbreadth away from "this one." (See Clarke 2008, p. 50)

Interacting Cognitive Subsystems

In order to make sense of how it might be possible for someone to pass from the "ordinary," individually grounded "world" into another one where the boundaries between people dissolve, where the individual is open to influence from outside, and where experience is "extraordinary," I am going to appeal to the cognitive theory known as Interacting Cognitive Subsystems (Teasdale & Barnard, 1993, Teasdale, 1999). This presents a model of human cognitive organization based on a couple of decades of experimentation into the way memory operates, bottlenecks in information processing, etc. This body of empirically grounded knowledge suggests that the human mind is modular and works by different subsystems passing information from one to another and copying it in the process. In this way, each subsystem has its own memory. Different systems operate with different coding; verbal, visual, auditory, for instance. There are higher-order systems that translate these codings, and integrate the information.

The crucial feature of this model is that there is not one but two meaning-making systems at the apex. The verbally coded propositional subsystem gives us the analytically sophisticated individual that our culture has perhaps mistaken for the whole. However, the wealth of sensory information from the outside world, integrated with the body and its arousal system, is gathered together by the implicational subsystem, which looks after our relatedness, both with others and with ourselves. The implicational subsystem is on the lookout for information about threat and value in relation to the self — we are, after all, social primates, and where we stand at any one time in the social hierarchy is crucial for our well-being, if not, normally, for our survival, (see Gilbert 1992, for an exposition of this line of argument). We experience "where we stand" in the form of our current emotion, be it happy contentment, vague apprehension or seething anger.

We are unaware of this gap between our two main subsystems because they work seamlessly together most of the time, passing information between them, so that we can simultaneously take the emotional temperature and make an accurate estimate in any situation. It is the propositional subsystem that deals in the precise meanings of words, whereas the implicational is on the look out for associations and significance. This gives us the roots of that trouble with words discussed at the beginning of the paper. The apparently seamless communication between the two higher order subsystems starts to break down in states of very high and very low arousal. To be human is to know what it is like to be "*in a flap*,"[1] and unable to think clearly — because the body has switched to action mode in response to perceived threat, and fine-grained thought goes out of the window. In our dreams, and on falling asleep, we enter another dimension where logic is totally absent. The application of certain spiritual disciplines, or certain substances, can effect this decoupling between the two subsystems in waking life, so affording a different quality of experience where the sense of individuality becomes distorted or merged into the whole. In the extreme circumstances where extended periods are spent in this state, exceptional experiences become the norm and the transliminal has been accessed.

Relationship and the Implicational Subsystem

The implicational subsystem; the older part of our make-up, that we share with our non-human ancestors, regulates our relatedness. I further suggest that the human being does not work properly as a lone individual, but only as part of a web of connection, and that this is built deeply into our make-up. The way in which the nature and quality of our earliest relationships are written into our selfhood has been well explored by a number of schools of psychotherapy, and in particular delineated by attachment theory (Ainsworth et al., 1978). Studies in group process (Dalal, 1998), and the therapeutic concept of transference illustrate the subtle blending of people in relationship. I suggest that this extends to non-human creatures as pet owners and shamanic practitioners, among others, are aware. The idea that we carry within us templates of relationship, "object relations" in Kleinian terms, or "Reciprocal Roles according to Cognitive Analytic Therapy" (Ryle, 1995) recurs in the therapeutic canon. Perhaps these are more than templates. Maybe they constitute the fabric of our being.

This web of connection starts with the most significant relationships, but extends outwards, upwards, downwards and beyond; to other humans on the planet; to our ancestors and those who will come after us; to the non-human creatures and the earth, and to the ultimate — God, Goddess, great spirit — however designated. In the midst of this infinitely extended web, the human being performs a more-or-less successful balancing act. When the two subsystems are working together, we feel grounded in the "ordinary" world. When we enter more into our relational, implicational, potential, we start to step over the threshold. Here we can encounter that intimate connection with the stars and beyond. It is my guess, and it can only be a guess, that it is the encounter with this cosmic vastness, achieved when the human being steps beyond the threshold of their individuality, that gives these sorts of experience their flavor of numinosity and huge significance.

To look at it from the other way around, it could be the propositional subsystem which closes off this openness to relationship, by filtering our perceptions down to the precisely manageable. It is also possible that it is this very openness that makes possible psychic phenomena such as telepathy and precognition, where communication happens in ways that violate ordinary boundaries, including the boundary of time. Other frequently attested experiences that defy conventional scientific theory such as intimations of past lives and possession could be explained by the possibility of transfer of psychic contents when in this "relational" state of mind.

Many of the puzzling experiences related by people diagnosed with psychosis can be understood in terms of such openness and loosening of boundaries. The most obvious one is the boundary between inner and outer experience, leading to thoughts being experienced as voices. Many such experiences can be explained by the intrusion of past trauma into present consciousness (Steele, Fowler & Holmes, 2005), but others cannot. The old ideas of possession and being taken over by alien influences cannot, I suggest, be dismissed out of hand, and the idea that a part of our being is essentially relational gives at least a framework for understanding this disturbing notion.

Clinical Applications

The ICS model offers a way of making sense of psychosis that is complementary to the conventional CBT for psychosis approach. CBT for psychosis has made a powerful argument for normalization through the continuity of thinking processes (see Garety et al., 2001 for a recent review of the field). Taken to extremes, this can appear to ignore the different quality of experience in psychosis, though works such as Gumley & Schwannauer's (2006) book on preventing relapse do acknowledge the importance of the nature of the experience (e.g., p. 23). ICS provides a possible basis for understanding this different quality. Barnard (2003) has extended the model to account for psychosis, identifying desynchrony between the two central meaning making systems as an explanation for anomalous experience. This makes sense, as the individual relies on the propositional subsystem for precise meanings, and where this part of the cognitive apparatus is temporarily unavailable, the implicational can hold sway with its powerful sense of meaning and significance but lack of distinctions.

This is further in line with other authorities who link disruption in information processing to the psychotic experience. Frith (1992) suggests an explanation at the neuro-psychological level in the form of a self-monitoring deficit that leads both to a breakdown in willed intention, and anomalous conscious experiences such as heightened perception, thought broadcast and synchronicities. Gray, Hemsley and others (e.g., Gray et al., 1991) also link the characteristic difficulties observed in psychosis/schizophrenia to possible underlying neurological difficulties. Problems such as perceptual disturbances and disruption of activity can be ascribed to "disturbance in the moment-by-moment integration of stored regularities with current sensory input," Hemsley (1998, p. 116). Fowler (2000) has identified confusion between inner and outer origin of stimuli as a way of understanding the confusion between voices and inner speech among other phenomena. All of these explanations contain an element of the disruption of the part of the mind that gives stimuli their current context, which would fit well with the idea of desynchrony between the propositional and implicational subsystems.

This links with the earlier argument that this dissolution of context and boundaries, combined with a heightened sense of meaning, can produce a sense of oneness and participation in the whole which can be exhilarating in the short term (as in a spiritual or drug induced experience), but frightening and persecutory in the longer term. Despite constituting the ultimate experience of connection, this state condemns to isolation and loneliness if prolonged, as propositional input is vital to maintain ordinary human relations. The loss of boundaries can be seen as the source of psychotic experiences such as the instability of the sense of self and openness of the mind to intrusion from outside (through the television for instance). Such a perspective both provides a normalizing explanation for someone's unnerving experiences, and a rationale for mindfulness as a treatment. Mindfulness for psychotic symptoms is being pioneered by Chadwick (see Chadwick, 2006 for details of the approach, and Chadwick, Newman-Taylor & Abba, 2005, for the latest research on this).

The link between psychotic experience and the dominance of the implicational subsystem opens the way to applying the skills for managing emotion developed by Dialectical Behavior Therapy (DBT), (Linehan, 1993) to psychosis (Freemantle & Clarke, 2008). DBT makes the distinction between "Emotion Mind" and "Reasonable Mind" which maps naturally onto the two central subsystems of ICS, with the connection between them, facilitated by mindfulness, corresponding to "Wise Mind." The focus of DBT is on the regulation of emotion, and at first sight, there appears to be a considerable gulf between overwhelming emotion and the more dissociated states characteristic of much psychosis. However, there has been recent advance in the sophistication of our understanding of the relationship between emotion and psychosis. Research such as Morrison's on the overlap between anxiety disorders and intrusive thoughts and psychotic symptoms (Morrison 1998;2001) point to a close relationship. My own clinical experience of the monitoring forms completed by participants in the voices and symptom groups I have run over many years demonstrate that vulnerability to these phenomena is correlated with states of high and of low arousal. These are precisely the times when the propositional subsystem is most sidelined, and therefore the implicational is to a greater or lesser extent in charge — as is the case at times of overwhelming emotion.

Therapeutic Approach

Viewing psychosis in this way provides a number of useful openings for therapy, in the form of the new normalization of the psychotic quality of experience, collaboratively exploring the two types of experience (shared and idiosyncratic); using mindfulness and other skills to navigate between them, and in understanding and working with emotion and the self in psychosis.

It also facilitates motivational work where the attractions of the psychotic reality for the individual lead to risk and continued hospitalization.

Negotiating a language that is acceptable to the individual, rather than imposing an external language is also crucial. The individual who is adamant that they do not have schizophrenia can often identify times of "confusion" or even "weird thinking," to give clinical examples. Simple, grounding, mindfulness is taught as the skill that can anchor them in the present, view internal experiences such as voices or convinced ideas dispassionately, and enable them to discern whether they are in the shared or the individual sphere of experience. Drawing out the characteristics of the non shared reality, such as a sense of super-specialness of the self, or of the supernatural, is further useful in normalizing bizarre experiences and putting them into perspective. I have published a case illustrating this elsewhere (Clarke, 2002)

I make the point about the connection between high schizotypy, creativity and vulnerability to psychosis when I run groups in the hospital where I work designed to help people cope with the symptoms of psychosis. The group is called the "What Is Real and What Is Not" group.

The purpose of the group is threefold. Firstly, it is to help people to recognize that there are two distinct ways of experiencing. There are distinct advantages to knowing which you are in at any one time. This can be the basis for developing the ability to move from one to another at will. The second aim is to introduce and discuss methods of managing the threshold between the two ways of experiencing: methods such as arousal management and mindfulness. The third aim is to establish the idea that these sorts of experience are normal and associate them with valued areas such as creativity. As the stigma associated with a diagnosis like schizophrenia can be considerably more disabling than the condition itself, this boost to morale is possibly the most important part of the program. As in all groups, there is the added bonus of people being able to share experiences, note their similarity, and so recognize that they are not alone.

This program has had notable success in engaging previously disaffected individuals. As a result, we were able to evaluate it with the help of a small grant from the national Care Service Improvement Program (CSIP) (Phillips et al. in submission), and an extension of the program for local community mental health teams, and the assertive outreach team is being developed, in collaboration with service user graduates of the group.

Transformative Potential

The destructive and disruptive potential of getting lost in the transliminal is clear from the preceding section on psychosis. The transformative element is the other side of the coin. Grof's (Grof 1988; Grof & Grof, 1991) ideas about transliminal encounters, spontaneous or induced (by LSD in his earlier work, and later using Holotropic Breathwork) as a process of growth towards higher states of human consciousness have already been cited. Such a viewpoint fits in with a well-established tradition in Buddhist literature. In the Christian contemplative tradition, such experiences are seen as encounters that can strengthen the connection with the divine and so confirm the devotee in resolve to pursue a Christian life. Both traditions, in common with Grof, recognize that such encounters can be negative as well as positive (see Chapters 6 and 7 in Clarke 2008, for more on this). Religious and spiritual traditions characteristically counsel adherents against becoming attached to transliminal experience for its own sake, rather seeing it as a path to spiritual growth and effective action in the world.

Mike Jackson (Jackson 1997;2001) has a more prosaic way of making sense of this, that I find eminently convincing. He argues that it is at the point of impasse, when life appears to have led the individual up a blind alley, that accessing the transliminal can reveal a new vista. He characterizes this as "problem solving." In terms of ICS, the problem solving potential of the usual loop between the propositional and implicational subsystems is exhausted, and the wider resources of the implicational, which as we have seen, can extend beyond the individual, need to be accessed. The danger is that there are no guarantees or boundaries in this area, hence the potential for not returning smoothly to ordinary, synchronized, reality.

The suggestion is that the return will, in any case, not be to exactly the same place. The encounter with the transliminal has the potential to be truly transformative. It certainly dents faith in straightforward, propositional, either/or, logic and opens the way to the mind expanding, both/and, logic of the transliminal (see Bomford, 1999 for a discussion of these different logics). It can lead to the integration of aspects of the person that had become split off, usually by the dissociative process triggered by emotional pain. This is the link between trauma and openness to transliminal experience. Exposure to a sense of greater unity can be liberating and expanding both of consciousness and of compassion. On the other hand, as we have seen, it can go either way. The re-awakened wounds from the past can intrude into the present and take over, destroying that balance that we depend on to navigate human life.

Moreover, the encounter with a wider whole can seduce; the sense of individual self, dependent on that interchange between implicational and propositional, is temporarily unavailable. This can lead either to a loss of a sense of self, deeply disturbing in itself, or to a sense of the supreme importance of the self, a sense of specialness and mission. The problem arises when this is assumed to have valence in the "shared" world. Except in the case of acknowledged gurus and founders of new religions, other people tend to dis-agree. Such problems are most likely to arise when the individual is not strong or well-grounded enough to take the transliminal encounter in their stride (lack of ego strength). The quality of holding and containment from those around them is also crucial to the successful negotiation of the threshold. Brett's research illustrates the importance of such containment, and indeed the medieval monastics and others who have reported on their mystical expe-riences will have relied on the nurturing context of their institutions. In our society such contexts are harder to find.

Where the person fails to find their way back, or where, having returned from their transliminal journey, they fail to adapt to the ordinary world, the result can be as described above in the clinical section. The "unshared reality" may engulf them and impede full participation in the shared world, and so have to be masked by powerful neuroleptic medication, which in its turn prejudices motivation and functioning (Arias-Carrion, & Peoppel, 2007). Alternatively, or as well, as human beings with choice, they may not wish to return. This is the "motivational" problem described above. Particularly where their experiences have attracted a depressing diagnosis, joining the rest of society and relinquishing the specialness offered by their experience is not an enticing prospect. Failing to take prescribed medication or using street drugs can facilitate a more permanent retreat into the transliminal. Grof & Grof (1991, Chapter 5.) explore the link between spiritual crisis and addictions Even where the mental health services are not implicated, the response to such experiences can be diminishing rather than expanding, where the indi-vidual seeks to cling onto them, rather than taking their expanded empathy and horizons into action in the shared world. The culminating stage of per-sonal development, effective action in the world is omitted and the individual is locked into a sterile backwater of new age indulgence.

For this reason, we conclude our group program by discussing the issue of the personal meaning of the transliminal encounter for the individual, and how they might take it forward in the "shared" reality. People are invited to reflect (without necessarily sharing) on what opened them up or made them vulnerable to such experiences, and on what it might mean for them in the context of their lives. In line with the subtly manipulative orientation of moti-vational interviewing (Miller & Rollnick, 1991), we are always encouraging participants to accept the challenge of making their way in the shared world, while never devaluing their experiences where these are valued, or the depth that these can add to the individual. In this we are offering a different message from that of the medical context within which we operate, but one that is often more palatable and life enhancing — and at the same time more chal-lenging.

That challenge of operating between "two worlds" is, I would suggest, inherent in the human condition. Those who encounter exceptional experiences through travel in the transliminal merely experience this in a sharper form than most. As more has been vouchsafed to them, perhaps more is expected of them. Not all can rise to the challenge and complete the journey, either because they are not strong enough, or the will fails them, or, more importantly, because our secular society fails to provide a sufficient, nurturing context to enable them to weather safely the spell of disintegration that so often precedes the re-integration. Shortage of such containment was the impetus behind the development of the Spiritual Crisis Network in the United Kingdom (www.SpiritualCrisisNetwork.org.uk) This organization is in its infancy, but hopes to foster a network of people prepared to offer hope and some support to those in crisis in their locality. Currently it offers a well used website and has a few local groups.

Notes

1. This is a British term meaning, "having nervous energy or anxiety about something."

9

Counseling at the IGPP
— An Overview

EBERHARD BAUER AND MARTINA BELZ

Abstract

This chapter describes the history and development of the counseling service for those experiencing distressing exceptional experiences (ExE) which currently exists at the Institut für Grenzgebiete der Psychologie und Psychohygiene (IGPP) in Freiburg, Germany. The work of the IGPP has included the development of a documentation system (the DOKU), and the allocation of exceptional experiences into a spectrum of basic experiential patterns. The authors describe the IGPP counseling team, the socio-demographics of those seeking help, the efficacy of the counseling service in terms of the expectations of clients and the extent to which distress is alleviated as a result of the program. The majority of people with ExE who are seeking advice feel distressed by their exceptional experiences in addition to experiencing other personal and social problems. As such, the authors argue that counseling should include the consideration of the phenomena themselves, the explanatory models (with a particular focus on the client's interpretation of the phenomena) and the characteristics of the particular person presenting as a client (for example, whether they have experienced traumatic life events), in order to be effective.

History and Development
of Counseling at the IGPP

Five years after the end of the Second World War, in 1950, Professor Hans Bender (1907–1991), the pioneer of German post-war parapsychology, inaugurated the Freiburg "Institut für Grenzgebiete der Psychologie und Psychohygiene" (or IGPP, for short) with a programmatic lecture on "Occultism as a Problem for Mental Hygiene" (Bender, 1950). Bender observed:

Various social beliefs and attitudes are based on genuine or spurious occult experiences. In times of crises, people are readier to turn to occultisms. Many are searching for a hold by contacting individuals who allegedly possess occult abilities, such as clairvoyants, fortune-tellers, astrologers, psychographologists, etc. While some are hoping for information about the whereabouts of missing relatives, others are driven by failures and frustrations in dealing with the occult [...] Mental hygiene here is confronted with a major challenge: viz., education; the imparting of knowledge on the ways the extraordinary may appear; the design of a structured conceptual scheme that is comprehensible to the man in the street and that allows him to put a name to what otherwise would disturb him. As is well known, demons are caught through invocation [Bender, 1950, p. 35].

This quote from Bender's inaugural lecture makes it quite clear that, right from its foundation, information, counseling and education concerning genuine or alleged "occult," "magical," "supernatural" and "paranormal" (or psi) phenomena have been central tasks of the IGPP. The IGPP's legacy in terms of mental hygiene also encompasses related areas such as spiritism, divinatory practices including unaccredited "unorthodox" counseling techniques (such as astrology), or aspects of so-called "alternative medicine," e.g., "mental healing." Bender also described this kind of approach to the "occult"—critical education and counseling—as a "positive critique of superstition." He used this phrase to express his conviction that it was far better to adequately investigate those opinions, practices and attitudes, which, as "folk beliefs," are widespread among the general population and which appear to deviate from the "official" scientific mainstream, than to base discrediting verdicts of "deception" or even "delusion" on rationalistic prejudice.

Therefore, "mental hygiene," as stipulated in the 4th bylaw of the Institute, comprises, "the application of medical, psychological and parapsychological findings regarding diagnostics, counseling, intervention and prevention in connection with those scientific questions and psychosocial problems that derive from, or are related to, anomalous and/or paranormal phenomena. This includes the following activities:

1. the development of specific counseling concepts as well as the establishment of a counseling network and an outpatient care unit for those individuals who are distressed by anomalous and/or paranormal experiences;
2. specific counseling services, intervention measures and the provision of therapeutic offerings;
3. the evaluation of applied techniques according to scientific standard;
4. the production and publication of scientific knowledge regarding the investigation of anomalous and/or paranormal phenomena, domestic and abroad;

5. critiques of scientifically unfounded views and activities relating to anomalous and/or paranormal phenomena, especially protection against the misguidance and exploitation of, and possible damage to, individuals and the public at large based on the improper application or the pretence of such phenomena;
6. public education with the assistance of the mass media.

   Support for the new generation of scientists through intensifying interdisciplinary research in the field of anomalous phenomena, as well as through improved care for the general population in terms of mental hygiene."

   Ever since its foundation, the IGPP has crucially relied on private funding sources, and for many years it operated with a very limited budget and manpower.

Establishment of a Special Research
and Outpatient Project, 1996–2001

Development and Implementation of a Documentation System. In 1996, substantial new funding became available from a private foundation. In collaboration with the Institute of Psychology of Freiburg University, the IGPP launched a special research project focusing on "Counseling and Help for People Claiming Exceptional Experiences." Between 1998 and 2001, the project was directed by clinical psychologist and psychotherapist Dr. Martina Belz-Merk (for details, see Belz, 2009a, 2009b). The project's goal was the development, implementation and evaluation of a special counseling and treatment system for individuals who felt distressed or burdened by exceptional experiences (ExE). In accordance with current regulations and standards for basic documentation in psychotherapy, the research group developed a special documentation system ("DOKU") to systematically record socio-demographic, anamnestic and phenomenon-specific data. Aided by this documentary system, it became possible to make continuous and systematic records, and to provide statistical evaluation of the IGPP counseling cases for the first time. In an on-going process of data collection and evaluation, the DOKU System was repeatedly modified and optimized. To date, there is a carefully-documented database of IGPP counseling cases (N=1615) that can be used for various research strategies. Over the years, the results have revealed relatively consistent patterns in terms of socio-demographics, clinically significant variables and the range of phenomena that contribute to ExE (Bauer et al., 2010).

Counseling and Care Activities at the IGPP

Current Counseling Structure at the IGPP

The core members of the IGPP counseling team are all trained and certified psychotherapists; they meet on a weekly basis to discuss incoming cases. Actual cases are presented, whenever possible, with the aid of tape and video recordings. Psychotherapeutic treatment can then be offered for clients (see Bauer et al., 2010).

Selected clients also can be investigated psychophysiologically, behaviorally and diagnostically in close collaboration with the IGPP's "Clinical and Physiological Psychology" department (Ambach, 2010).

Twice a year, the IGPP counseling team offers special educational seminars on ExE counseling predominantly for psychotherapists and counselors. One of these seminars usually focuses on conceptual and theoretical issues (e.g., phenomenological structures of ExE; models to describe and understand ExE; relations between ExE, biography and mental processes; issues of differential diagnosis of ExE versus symptoms of psychopathology). The second seminar concentrates on practical issues of counseling work including various intervention strategies (for details, see Belz, 2009a, 2009b).

Networking

In Germany, professional counseling services that deal with or even specialize in ExE are rare. In addition to the counseling services at the IGPP, there is also the Parapsychological Counseling Office which is also located in Freiburg. The Parapsychologial Counseling Office was established in 1989, and since that time has been directed by Walter von Lucadou. The Parapsychologial Counseling Office is officially supported by the Scientific Society for the Advancement of Parapsychology (WGFP; see Zahradnik, 2007). The only other counseling service specifically designated for ExE outside of these two institutions, is provided by the "Sekten-Info Essen e.V.," which was funded by the IGPP for several years.

Since many of those who seek counseling and advice need both outpatient and inpatient psychological, psychotherapeutic or psychiatric care, the national structures for counseling and therapy with respect to ExE are permanently screened. Currently, the IGPP counseling service maintains contacts with outpatient departments of psychiatric university hospitals, psychotherapists, clinics and self-help groups that are familiar with or interested in the topic of ExE.

In addition, the IGPP counseling team continuously offers lectures, seminars and advanced training courses for mental-health professionals (especially for psychiatrists, psychotherapists and clinical psychologists) in order to introduce topics relating to ExE counseling and to improve future relationships with the clinical community.

Numbers of Counseling Cases

From 2006 to 2007 (quite similar to previous periods), inquiries from about 500 individuals from all over Germany were received and registered at the IGPP's Counseling and Information Department. Approximately 60 percent of all initial contacts for counseling were conducted by phone. Taken together, these 500 inquiries required some 2,200 counseling contacts; 48 percent of all contacts were realized by phone, 35 percent by e-mail, 15 percent by letter, and 2 percent face to face at the IGPP, or the homes of the clients. In addition, several hundred requests for information (by e-mail, telephone and letters) from journalists, students, scientists and others interested in parapsychological research and phenomena were received in the given period.

Socio-Demographic Description
of the IGPP Clientele

When the DOKU system was applied over a period of several years, a rather stable picture of the basic socio-demographic characteristics of our clientele emerged (for details see Table 1; for a discussion see also Bauer et al., 2010; Belz, 2009b; Belz-Merk & Fach, 2005).

Almost 64 percent of the clients were women, and the average age of clients was 42.6 years old. About a quarter of the clients identified as having a non-denominational religion. Roughly one third had obtained high-school diplomas (Abitur/Matura), approximately 8 percent had graduated from a technical school, and approximately one quarter held university degrees.

These data reveal a conspicuous trend toward social isolation amongst those who have sought help from the IGPP. For example, nearly two thirds of the clients were single, divorced or widowed and almost 46 percent lived alone. In addition, at the moment of initial contact, about 40 percent were unemployed, unable to work or retired.

Two thirds of the clients reported social conflicts (divorces, financial difficulties, etc.), and just as many reported psychological problems (proneness to fear, depression, etc.). More than one third described physical symptoms and diseases. In addition, more than half of the clients felt distressed and burdened by their general living conditions, outside of their ExE.

Table 1: Socio-Demographic and Mental Health Information of IGPP Clientele

Variable		Valid %	Numbers
Sex (N=1615)	Male	36.3	586
	Female	63.7	1029
Age	12-17	0.8	9
(N= 1177)	18-24	8.2	96
	25-34	23.3	274
	35-44	27.3	321
	45-54	18.9	223
	55-64	13.1	154
	>74	2.6	31
Denomination	Catholic	37.9	251
(N=662)	Protestant	29.9	198
	Non-denominational	26.6	176
	Other denominations	5.6	37
Education	Primary School	20.6	362
(N=762)	Secondary School	44.8	60
	High school diploma	34.3	156
	Other graduation	0.4	191
			11
			3
Occupation	Still in school or training	5.3	27
(N=515)	Part-time work	6.2	32
	Full time work	23.3	120
	Self employed	13.2	68
	Unemployed	19.0	98
	Permanently unable to work	8.5	44
	Retired	11.8	61
	Housewife	5.4	28
	Others	4.3	22
Marital status	Single	37.2	419
(N=1127)	Married	36.8	415
	Divorced	19.3	217
	Widowed	6.7	76
Living situation/	With spouse or partner	38.1	410
domestic circumstances	Solitary person	45.9	494
(N=1077)	With parents	8.1	87
	Flat-sharing community	3.5	38
	Others	4.5	35
Factors of distress	Physically distressed (N=1643)	40.4	433
	Mentally distressed (N=1651)	39.5	649
	Social impacts (N=1644)	50.6	832
Psychiatric/psycho-	Earlier psychotherapy (N=830)	41.8	347
therapeutic treatment	Earlier psychiatric treatment (N=835)	34.3	286
Symptoms of mental problems (N=1078)	Not suggestive of mental disorder	48.7	525
	Presumed mental disorder symptoms	51.3	553

Before contacting the IGPP, about 40 percent of the clients had undergone earlier psychotherapeutic or psychiatric treatment. About 25 percent received psychotherapeutic treatment whilst they were in touch with the IGPP. About 50 percent reported symptoms that the counselors characterized as psychological impairments.

Requests, Quality and Effectiveness of ExE-Counseling

Research concerning the efficacy and effectiveness of interventions for people with disturbing and irritating ExE is in its early stages. There are several reasons for this. Firstly, the psychosocial and clinical field did not see the relevance and necessity of delivering special treatment for people with ExE. In addition, people reporting ExE were often pathologized or just not taken seriously. This has made the development of appropriate counseling and therapy approaches difficult, to say nothing about their effectiveness and evaluation. What makes things even more complicated is the fact that people with ExE often do not show a clear problem or relevant suffering which can be easily measured. Similar problems are known from the area of self-experience where it is notoriously difficult to undertake outcome research.

When first contacting the IGPP a relevant number of the advice-seeking individuals considers their ExE not primarily as a psychological but as a "paranormal" issue which are not so much connected with themselves and real world problems but with ghosts, black magic, voodoo, witchcraft and otherworldly problems. As a result, there is only limited motivation to fill out any psychological questionnaires before the counseling process that could be used as pre-measures. Nevertheless, people looking for help and advice because of their ExE do often express a significant level of distress. As such, it is possible to evaluate levels of distress retrospectively at the end of the counseling process, or some time afterwards.

In 2000 a questionnaire based systematic evaluation of the counseling service of the IGPP was conducted for the first time (Kühn, 2001). Clients were asked how satisfied they were with the counseling; if and to what extent their expectations towards counseling were met; if there were any changes after counseling; how these changes were evaluated and to what they attributed these changes.

The sample consisted of all IGPP clients that had turned to the IGPP for counseling between 1996 and 2000. As many of the clients preferred to stay anonymous or did not have a valid address at the time the study was conducted, the questionnaire could only be sent to N=415 former clients. 46 percent (N=191) of them returned the questionnaire but only 185 clients could actually be included in the study.

Requests and Expectations of Clients with ExE

From the moment the clients realized they were in need of an ExE-specific information and counseling service until they found out about such counseling possibilities and contacted the IGPP, 40 percent said it took them more than five years to be successful. Only 25 percent found a counseling service within the first half year after they had looked for one.

Nearly 60 percent of the clients had some concern with regard to approaching the counseling service of the IGPP. The dominant worry was the fear of not being taken seriously by the counselor, not being understood or considered to be mentally ill due to the reported ExE.

A range of requests brought these help-seeking individuals to approach the IGPP. A high percentage (33 percent) of the clients wanted an evaluation of their reported ExE or "abilities" and a diagnostic check-up of their mental health. Twenty-seven percent expected the IGPP to help them get connected with a self-help group or other people with ExE. Twenty percent wanted some kind of clarification of their ExE (explanation, information), help and support or some specific training with the development of their "paranormal abilities" (17.8 percent). Nearly 12 percent wanted advice on how to activate their resources in dealing with ExE and stress in general. 9.2 percent asked for support with coping with the consequences of their ExE

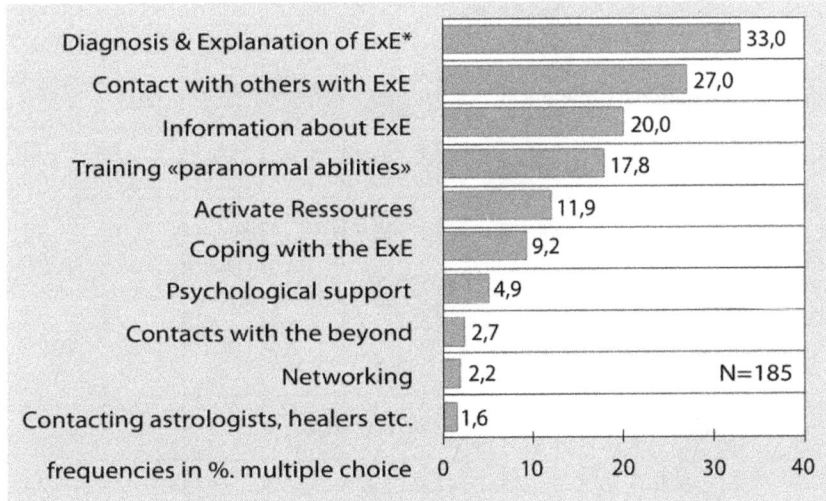

Figure 1. Requests of Clients with ExE

Many of the expectations that clients had about the counselors were met. These included diagnosis and explanation of ExE, information about ExE, activation of resources, coping with ExE, psychological support and networking. However, other expectations about the counselors were not met. These included providing contact with other individuals who had exceptional experiences, with astrologers, healers, etc., or training paranormal abilities.

The four most important goals of any psychosocial counseling (Grawe, 2004) are clarification, coping, activating resources and relief. Clarification and activating resources are the most important ones for the clients. In this context, clarification means that implicit meanings of ExE have to become explicit and made available for reflection within the context of life history and situation. By activating resources we mean building up action alternatives in order to be better able to deal with ExE.

Level of Distress at First Contact and Follow Up

Please see Figure 2 for a summary of levels of distress reported by IGPP clients. In terms of the ExE, the level of distress at first contact was relatively high (average of 2.69 on a scale between 0=no and 4=high). Two-thirds of the clients said that their level of distress resulting from the ExE was rather high or very high. Only 18.4 percent said that they were only a little distressed, or not distressed at all. Quite a few of the clients also named family and private problems, psychological and physical problems in addition or as a separate problem to the ExE. A significant correlation was found between stressful ExE and reported psychological problems.

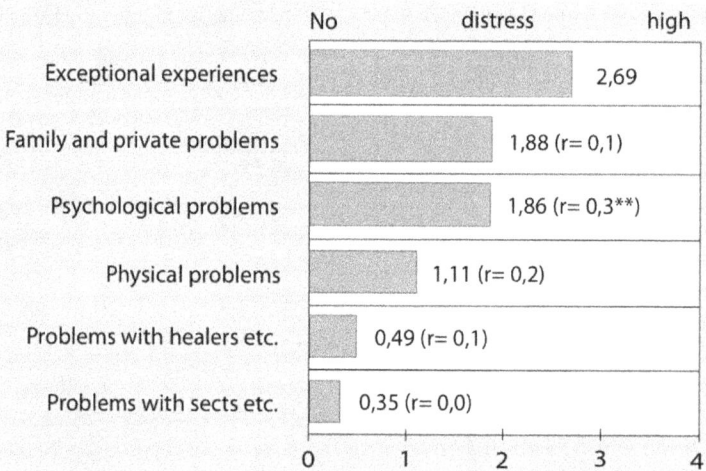

Figure 2. Degree of distress of IGPP-clients at first contact (N=185)

The ExE-specific counseling approach did appear to affect the outcome for the clients in the real world as the reported changes at follow-up (between one and five years after counseling) were quite positive for the clients. For example, clients felt much less distressed by their ExE compared to the time when they first contacted the counseling unit, they reported that they were much better able to deal with their ExE and the problems connected to the ExE had also improved.

Evaluation of the Counseling Process and Outcome

In order to assess the quality of the counseling process, the clients were asked what they had expected from the counselor during the process of counseling (e.g., *"How much did you expect the counselor to....?"*) and immediately following that question, they were asked to judge what the counselor had actually done during the counseling process (e.g., *"How much did the counselor ....?"*). The quality judgment was operationalized by the difference between the subjective judgment of the clients and their initial expectation.

The evaluation of the counseling effects from the view of the clients was undertaken by a two-step approach. At first, clients were asked for perceived change with respect to different dimensions (e.g., *"Compared to the time directly before the contact with the counseling team by now I can understand my ExE better or worse"*). The questions were oriented toward the counseling goals and could be assessed by the clients on a seven point scale.

In a second step, the clients were asked if the aforementioned changes were connected to the IGPP-counseling per se (e.g. , *"If anything has changed in this area to which degree is this connected to the contact with our Institute?"*). This was assessed on a five point Likert scale with a range between "very much" and "not at all."

Altogether, the results are very encouraging with regard to satisfaction and changes resulting from the counseling. At the same time, it is clear the counseling approach should be clinically oriented. As shown above, the level of distress is remarkable not only because of the ExE but also because of problems in many other areas of social and personal life.

On average, the changes were quite positive across all clients. Meaningful changes were reported in terms of activating resources (the client has better abilities to deal with their ExE); clarification (the client can understand their ExE better); connection to situation and history of life (the client can see connections between ExE and life more clearly); relief (the client feels less distressed) and counseling in own area (following the IGPP counseling, it is now easier for the client to find counseling in their own area).

Interestingly, those changes that were attributed to the counseling were significantly more positive than the ones that were not attributed to counseling.

A second study was undertaken in July 2007 within the framework of quality management and concomitant research of the IGPP (see Bauer et al., 2010). In this study, a revised and expanded version of the 2000 questionnaire was sent to all clients with available addresses who had approached the IGPP between 2000 and 2007. Clients were asked about their experiences with the information and counseling provided by the IGPP, their prior expectations, and to what extent these expectations were fulfilled. The questionnaire was supplemented with a short but still multidimensional and change-sensitive outcome measure composed of several short versions of currently widely used measures in German-speaking outpatient centers and mental health hospitals (those are the Symptom-Checklist, SCL-90-R; the Inventory of Emotional Distress, EMI; the Inventory of Interpersonal Problems, IIP; and the Questionnaire of Incongruence, INK) (Lutz, Tholen, Schürch & Berking, 2006). In addition, the PAGE questionnaire of the phenomenology of exceptional experiences, developed at the IGPP (Lehmann, 2008), was administered to see if different phenomenological groups of ExE are associated with different outcomes.

A total of 963 questionnaires were mailed, out of which 287 were returned as undeliverable. Two hundred and thirty-three questionnaires were filled in and returned, which gives a response rate of 35 percent. The analysis of the questionnaire data is based on 231 questionnaires with sufficient data (Schupp-Ihle, 2010).With regard to age, sex, marital status, denomination and occupation, the two post-counseling questionnaire samples are representative of the data from the entire counseling clientele of the IGPP.

Clients who took part in the post-counseling survey also form a representative sample with regard to their allocation in terms of the spectrum of basic experiential patterns. There are four basic experiential patterns, which reflect anomalies in the self-model (internal phenomena), anomalies in the world model (external phenomena), anomalies in the connection between self and world models (coincidence phenomena) and anomalies in the separation of self and world models (dissociation) (see Belz, 2009a and Belz's chapter 10 in this book). Only clients from the Internal Presence category are slightly under-represented in this sample, which among other reasons could be due to the fact that members of this group prefer to remain anonymous more often than others.

The evaluation of the clinical tests found that clients who, based on their ExE phenomenology, were allocated to the Mediumism category (see Belz's chapter in the current volume) show increased values on the SCL "fearfulness" sub-scale. Clients in the Poltergeist and Internal Presence categories showed above-average values on the IIP "introvert/shy" sub-scale. Clients in the ESP category demonstrated increased values on the IIP "caring" sub-scale. The total INK incongruence value was raised for clients in the Internal Presence category.

Consequences for Counseling

The results of these studies show that the majority of people with ExE who look for help and advice feel distressed not only by their ExE but also because of manifold problems in their personal and social life. This supports the argument of using a clinical orientation for counseling in this field. The most important request of the clients is to get feedback concerning the phenomena, clarify the experience in the context of the life situation and history of the client and to activate resources and learn coping strategies when dealing with these problems. This requires two basic skills: profound knowledge of the various phenomena as well as skills that are learned via clinical training (diagnostic and intervention). Beyond that, there is a need for scientifically developed models that are able to explain the phenomena and help affected people to find meaning within their ExE. Figure 3 shows how all three factors have to be taken into consideration when counseling people with ExE; the phenomena, the models and the special characteristics of people reporting ExE. Only then we will be able to do justice to the field and arrive at an innovative approach. If we miss just one of them, people will have a hard time accepting our approach, we might be too pragmatic and thus dismiss a scientific explanation or we might be in danger of overseeing the necessity of helping people to tackle real world problems.

In terms of including these perspectives during intervention, the first step in counseling and therapy with individuals reporting ExE is to try to get a good picture of the person, his or her explanatory model, and the experience based on the phenomena. This information is summarized in an individual case conceptualization with the relevant descriptive and prescriptive information. More details about the process of coming to an individual case conceptualization can be found Belz's chapter 10 in this book. The central goals and strategies for intervention have been described in detail elsewhere (Belz, 2009b), but a short overview is given here in order to provide help in understanding the basic ideas of counseling at the IGPP.

Based on an individual case conceptualization and a counseling strategy that takes into account the aforementioned factors, several counseling goals and tasks integrate the empirical knowledge to be administered when working with ExE clients. Firstly, the counselor should help to integrate the ExE into

Phenomena	Acknowledge their central role (phenomena are not disturbing factors but contain meaning!) and explore perceptions before interpretations (clarify the possibility of an altered state of consciousness during ExE).
Explanatory Model	Take on a constructivist attitude (there are many truths and all are based on our view of the world and the self), consider possible functional value and meaning of the explanation for client
Person	Explore possible individual characteristics (perception, information processing, emotion regulation and overlap with symptoms of disorder) and biography (especially traumatic life events, "insecure" attachment style).
Relationship	Develop individually tailored motive oriented counseling or therapy relationship while paying special attention to self-worth, control, attachment.

Figure 3. How the central factors of phenomenon, model and person characteristics should be considered in treatment planning.

the self-concept and support sense and meaning-making processes. Secondly, he or she should help to see the etiological and functional relations between ExE, actual life situation and history of life (for example, traumatic life events). Thirdly, the counselor should help to improve the client's self-control and support their search for healthy and functional ways of fulfilling their basic needs (especially in terms of balanced intimacy/autonomy and self-worth). Finally, the counselor should support flexible patterns of thinking and help to tackle old fixed and dysfunctional explanatory models (making sure that this is done in a responsible manner, i.e., the counselor should not cut the branch a client is sitting on unless an alternative ladder is given to help him or her to climb down the tree).

10

Clinical Psychology
for People with Exceptional
Experiences in Practice

MARTINA BELZ

Abstract

This chapter explores the relationship between the study of exceptional experiences (ExE) and clinical psychology. Reports of ExE are often considered as misperceptions of normal and naturally explainable events, as non-existent, or as signs of a mental disorder, often in combination with an unscientific and esoteric world view. As a consequence, people reporting ExE are either referred to a psychiatrist for medication or considered to be strange characters. In fact, ExE are reported by many members of the general population, only some of whom will experience psychological problems. The author discusses the necessity for clinical practitioners to differentiate between a mental disorder and ExE, given that mental health problems and ExE can be intertwined. The author discusses healthy and less healthy ExEs, the overlaps between ExE and clinical disorders and where clinical psychological knowledge can be applied to distressing ExE. Approaches for counseling and psychotherapy are presented which ensure that health care professionals can be effective and efficient when working with those who report ExE.

Introduction

Although the fields of parapsychology and clinical psychology are usually thought of as completely different disciplines, they actually have a lot in common. Both deal with exceptional experiences (ExE); experiences, which — from the point of view of those affected by these experiences — are incompatible with their personal and environmental explanations of reality

223

as far as the quality, process and origin of the experiences are concerned. It therefore seems natural to employ both perspectives to better understand these experiences and apply knowledge from both fields to help people who are affected by them in an unsettling, problematic, troubling or threatening way. However, the reality of such a fusion is yet to be realized. The issue is mainly being treated as the "enlightened or delusional"—issue (Johnson & Friedman, 2008). Although many in the clinical parapsychology field warn against the pathologization of ExE, and others even consider them to be signs of an individuals' spiritual development and growth, there is a profound lack of interest and ignorance within the main stream arenas of clinical psychology and psychotherapy when it comes to the issue of ExE. Within the clinical sciences ExE are mainly considered as misperceptions of normal and naturally explainable events, as non-existent, or as signs of a mental disorder so that beyond psychiatric treatment, they do not deserve further attention or thorough research.

Seeing ExE as signs or symptoms of a mental disorder is to some extent understandable because in the current categorical systems of diagnosis; the fourth edition of the *American Psychiatric Association's Diagnostic and Statistical Manual (DSM IV-TR*, 2000), and the tenth edition of the World Health Organization's International Classification of Diseases (ICD-10, 1992), we find several criteria of mental disorders which are also known to be typical perceptions and experiences reported by individuals during ExE. This is particularly the case for disorders of the schizophrenic spectrum and schizotypal disorder, which include symptoms such as unusual visual, auditory or kinesthetic perceptions or so-called strange beliefs, which are not compatible with cultural norms such as hearing voices when no one is present, seeing a deceased person and feeling his presence, etc. Yet the mere fact that an overlap exists between several mental disorders and ExE does not justify their conceptualization as markers of psychopathology.

In 1994, the new diagnostic category "Religious or Spiritual Problem" (Code V62.89) was accepted for the *Diagnostic and Statistical Manual— Fourth Edition (DSM IV*, 1994). This made it possible to see different forms of distress associated with spiritual and religious practices and experiences as a clinical problems that should also be in the focus of attention of mental health professionals. Since this time, the new category has received much research and attention worldwide, and will also be integrated in the forthcoming DSM V. Even though this development can be seen as remarkable progress, this category only marginally includes ExE which are traditionally considered as paranormal experiences such as poltergeist phenomena, extrasensory perceptions like precognition, telepathy and clairvoyance as well as apparitions, unusual dreams, experiences with occultism or experiences with alternative healers which are not associated with religious or spiritual practices or experiences. If these ExE were very rare one could take the position that no diagnostic and health care system is perfect and that we cannot develop approaches for every rare specialty encountered in clinical work. However, on the contrary, ExE are far from being rare. Several representative studies and surveys (Bauer & Schetsche, 2003) suggest that the commonality of ExE calls for a better understanding and an appropriate professional way of dealing with the experiences and affected people. This is particularly the case if the experiences cannot be integrated in the world view and view of the self, and are therefore unsettling, problematic, troubling or threatening.

Differentiating between a mental disorder and ExE can be difficult and sometimes almost impossible, especially if we take into account the strong impact that culture has in making a diagnosis. Only if we can accomplish this we will be able to avoid unjustified pathologization of ExE and identifying psychological disorders which need adequate treatment in addition to the interplay between the two. This will help to increase the competence of mental health professionals in their sensitivity towards individuals who present with problems and issues related to ExE.

Definition and Phenomenology of Exceptional Experiences?

The term "ExE" serves as an umbrella term for subjective paranormal experiences like poltergeist phenomena, precognition, telepathy, clairvoyance etc. It also includes experiences triggered by practices focusing on changing one's state of consciousness, such as hyperventilation, hypnosis and meditation or phenomena or experiences, which emerge in the context of occultism, Spiritism or alternative-esoteric practices. Some other terms that are used to describe the special quality of the experiences are extraordinary, unusual, anomalistic, parapsychic, transpersonal, magic, supernatural, supersensory, spiritual, mystical or transcendental experiences, etc. As such, ExE can be defined as experiences, which —from the point of view of those affected by these experiences— are incompatible with their personal and environmental explanations of reality as far as the quality, process and origin of these experiences are concerned.

In order to be able to build ideas and concepts about ExE on solid empirical ground, in 1998, a documentary system for advice seeking individuals with ExE was developed at the counseling department of the "Institut für Grenzgebiete der Psychologie und Psychohygiene e.V." in Freiburg, Germany (IGPP) (Belz-Merk, 2002). Since then, the instrument has been revised and tested several times and introduced in the counseling department. The documentary system allows a very differentiated phenomenological categorization of the reported ExE including their frequency, the onset and duration of the ExE, as well as different contextual factors such as the state of consciousness, the external circumstances under which the ExE occurred as well as the subjective beliefs and theories of the clients. Inter-rater relability has been tested several times with sufficiently good results and a Kappa-coefficient of κ=0.6.

To date, 1615 cases of people with ExE who turned to the IGPP for help and advice between the years 1996–2007, can be documented with this instrument with sufficient quality. Based on these empirical data, the reported phenomena associated with ExE can be divided into two main groups (Belz-Merk, 2000; Belz & Fach, 2005; Fach, 2006); those associated with *External phenomena* (localized in the outer physical world) and those associated with *Internal Phenomena* (localized in the inner mental world).

These phenomenological groups can be organized according to Metzinger's theory of mental representations (Fach, 2007). Metzinger (1993, 2003) postulates that the human being creates a mental *reality model* as "internal description" of parts of reality. This reality model consists of two fundamental components, the *self-model* and the *world model* (for more details see Belz & Fach, in press).

Based on the aforementioned components of the reality model, exceptional phenomena can be reduced to four basic possibilities of anomalies in the reality model (see Figure 1). Some exceptional phenomena are concerned with *internal* versus *external* phenomena, with the former relating to anomalies in the self-model and the latter relating to anomalies that occur in the world model including the body model. Other phenomena may occur that concern the relationship between the self and the world model.

During psychophysical dissociation, a separation of the normally integrated components of the self and the body model occur. When coincidence phenomena occur, unusual links between representations in the self and/or world model arise. On closer inspection, these four categories of ExE form two complementary pairs. One of them concerns the *localization* ("inside versus outside") of the phenomena in the fundamental components of the reality model. The other concerns the *relation* between these components, i.e., the self and the world model with respect to the elements which are portrayed in them ("separated versus related").

When analyzed by means of a principle component analysis, the documented phenomena can be combined into meaningful patterns that describe a well-known phenomenology (Belz & Fach, in press). See Table 1 for the factors and their frequencies.

**Psychophysical
Dissociation**
Separation of usually entangled elements of
the self- and body model

**Internal
Phenomena**
Anomalies in the self model

**External
Phenomena**
Anomalies in the world model
(including the body model)

Coincidence Phenomena
Entanglement of usually separated
elements of the self- and/or world model

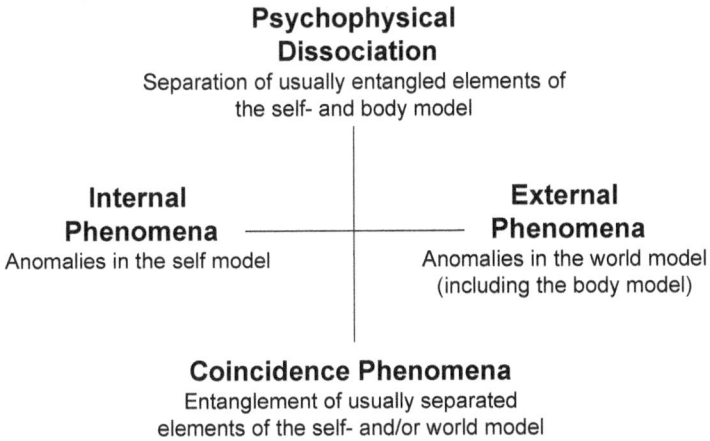

Figure 1. Fundamental categories of exceptional phenomena

*Table 1: The Factors Corresponding to Different
Types of ExE and Their Frequencies*

Factor	Frequency
Poltergeist and apparitions	53%
Extrasensory perception	41%
Internal presence and influence	38%
External presence and nightmare	15%
Meaningful coincidence	10%
Automatism and mediumism	7%

The three factors corresponding to poltergeist (1), internal (3) and automatism (6) represent specific phenomena from the internal, the external spectrum and the spectrum of psychophysical dissociation. Factor 4 combines anomalies of the dissociative and the external area. Factors 2 and 5 differentiate between mere external coincidence phenomena and those in which internal experiences correspond to external elements. Figure 2 shows a heuristic allocation of the six patterns with regard to their proximity to the four basic phenomenological categories—external, internal, dissociative and coincidence phenomena.

Even though the ExE patterns are based on a phenomenological documentation system that was especially developed to record descriptions of ExE (Belz & Fach, 2005), the described phenomenological patterns already contain evaluative aspects. This shows the difficulty in ascribing purely phenomenological descriptions and indicates the importance of the (sub-)cultural and

Psychophysical Dissociation

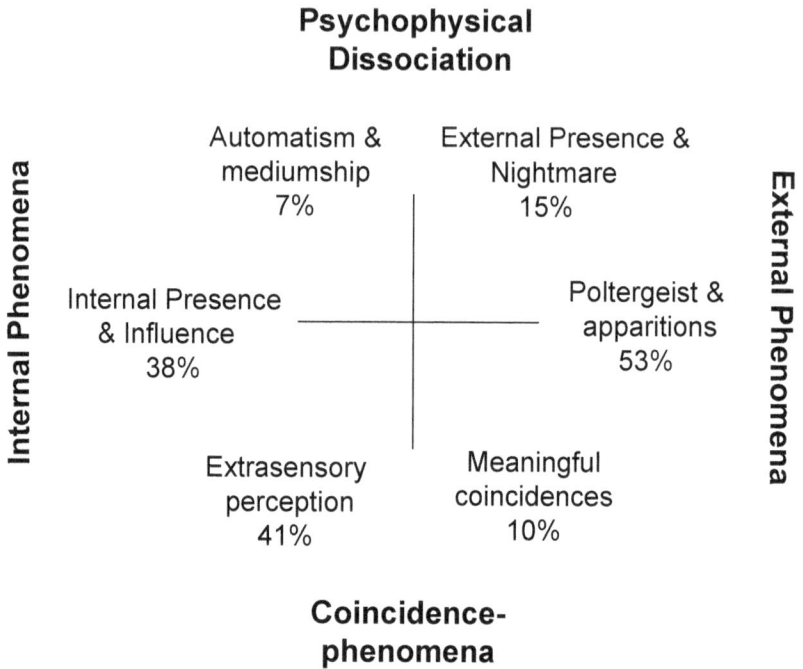

Automatism & mediumship 7%	External Presence & Nightmare 15%
Internal Presence & Influence 38%	Poltergeist & apparitions 53%
Extrasensory perception 41%	Meaningful coincidences 10%

Internal Phenomena

External Phenomena

Coincidence-phenomena

Figure 2. Exceptional Experiences Patterns

psychological framework within which the phenomena are perceived and processed.

ExE and Mental Health

Psychological diagnosis faces unique challenges when trying to differentiate nonpsychopathological ExE from those that might evidence psychopathology. The *DSM-IV-TR* "Religious or Spiritual Problem," v-code (V62.89), currently allows for a non-pathologizing conceptualization of symptoms that meet the criteria for psychotic spectrum disorders (APA, 2000) but offers no guidelines for determining when someone has a "religious or spiritual problem" or is simply psychotic.

When we compare different perceptions that are reported during ExE with the criteria for the diagnosis of a mental disorder we therefore find a large overlap which impedes a clear distinction between the two (see Table 2).

Table 2: Overlap Between Perceptions Related to ExEs and Symptoms of Mental Disorders According to DSM IV and/or ICD-10

Phenomena associated with ExE	Schizophrenia	Schizotypy	Organic Psychosis	Delusion	Hallucination	Dissociative Disorder	Somatoform Disorder	Paranoia	Bipolar Disorder	Post traumatic stress disorder	Borderline Disorder
External Phenomena											
Optical phenomena apparitions	x		x		x		x				x
Acoustic phenomena mimicry noise	x	x	x		x						x
Tactile phenomena temperature changes	x				x				x		
Olfactory phenomena	x				x						
Feeling of a presence atmosphere	x										
Kinetic phenomena (de-)materializations											
Physical changes stigmata	x						x				
Audio-/photo-/object-anomalies											
Reference to events in the personal domain	x	x			x			x			
Reference to events of a general kind	x	x			x			x			
Internal Phenomena											
Visual phenomena pictures/imageries					x	x				x	x
Auditory phenomena hearing voices		x			x	x				x	x
Somatic phenomena body sensations	x	x			x		x			x	
Unusual emotions/moods	x										x
Body paralysis											
Out-of-body						x				x	x
Automatism/ mediumism channeling					x						
Unusual thoughts thought insertion	x	x	x		x			x	x		x
Sudden knowing	x	x	x					x			x

The greatest overlap can be found between ExE and symptoms of schizotypal disorder, disorders of the schizophrenic spectrum and disorders occurring as a consequence of trauma.

It therefore seems desirable to specify clear distinctions between "healthy" and "unhealthy" groupings of different extraordinary perceptions and phenomena.

A representative survey in Germany in 2000 showed that between 50 and 70 percent of the general population believe in the existence of paranormal phenomena and report at least one personal subjective paranormal experience in life (Bauer & Schetsche, 2003). As far as we know from current epidemiological data about mental health (Jacobi, Hoyer & Wittchen, 2004), the one month prevalence of psychological disorders in Germany is 31 percent and lifetime prevalence is 43 percent. Similar results for ExE and psychopathology can be found for other western countries as well. These numbers suggest that there will be some overlap between the large percentage of individuals who have some kind of psychological disorder and the two thirds of the population who report personal ExE and believe in their existence.

Criteria to Differentiate Between ExE and A Mental Disorder

Psychiatric diagnoses based on the criteria of DSM or ICD can affect peoples' lives in many respects. For example, they influence their relationship with other people and institutions and they determine their eligibility for appropriate treatments. Therefore, it is imperative for professionals working in the mental health system to keep in mind that DSM and ICD diagnoses are powerful instruments, and that the reliability and validity of many their categories are unverified. However, professionals are and will be confronted with affected people and as such have to be able to recognize the symptoms of a mental disorder and/or the typical characteristics of an ExE before they make a decision about the best possible intervention. There is a growing amount of research which indicates that there is no clear boundary between mental health and mental illness and that psychotic experiences are just the extreme expression of traits that are widely expressed in the normal population (Claridge, 1985; 1994). A number of studies have been conducted on the epidemiological spread of auditory hallucinations. They are often used as a crucial indicator for psychosis in clinical practice but are at the same time frequent in clinical and nonclinical groups and arise often during ExE. This literature will be reviewed in the following section.

Studies Exploring Hallucinations
in Clinical and Non-Clinical Groups

The following studies offer some interesting numbers regarding this issue:

- Reports about ExE from clinical groups are more bizarre, more detailed and disturbing than those of non-clinical groups (Bentall, 2000; Jackson, 1997).
- Individuals diagnosed psychotic, as opposed to healthy individuals are not able to recognize the strangeness of their ExE (Targ, Schlitz & Irwin, 2000).
- Individuals who score high on paranormal belief scales (i.e., have a paranormal belief system) and give an account of their own subjective ExE report significantly more traumatic experiences (Irwin, 1992, 1993; Perkins & Allen, 2006) than the normal population.
- Tien (1991) reports that 10–15 percent of the normal population in the United States have had some kind of hallucinatory experience in their lives. Similar prevalences have been reported in France (16 percent) (Verdoux et al., 1998) and New Zealand (13 percent) (Poulton et al., 2000) whereas only about 1 percent of the population is actually diagnosed schizophrenic.
- Hearing voices is a typical sign of grief processes (Schuchter & Zisook, 1993) and 82 percent report experiencing dialogues with the deceased (Grimby, 1998).
- 71 percent of a student population report verbal hallucinations in a questionnaire (Posey & Losch, 1983) and 37 percent indicated that they heard their thoughts aloud at least once a month, (Barett & Etheridge, 1992).
- Hallucinations that occur while falling asleep (hypnagogic) or waking up (hypnopompic) are considered to be within the range of normal experience. In the Barett & Etheridge study 26 percent reported hallucinations in the process of falling asleep, 15 percent while waking up.
- A study of the NIMH "Epidemiologic Catchment Area Programme" ECA conducted between 1980 and 1984 (with N = 18,500 the first time and again with N=15,300), 13 percent of healthy individuals reported hallucinations, of which 4.3 percent were auditory.
- An association between childhood trauma and auditory as well as visual hallucinations has consistently been reported, both in individuals who appear otherwise healthy and in clinical subjects (Morrison & Peterson, 2003; Shevlin, Dorahy & Adamson, 2007; Andrew, Gray & Snowden, 2008).
- Romme and Escher (1989) report that the actual onset of hearing voices is for 70 percent after a traumatic experience. Clinical groups report that their auditory hallucinations are uncontrollable whereas nonclinical groups have

the feeling that they can control them (Honig, Romme, Ensik, Escher, Pennings & Devires, 1998).

• Peters et al. (1999) showed that scoring high on delusional measures is not necessarily indicative of pathology.

• High scores on schizotypy are connected to a paranormal belief system but not necessarily to mental health problems, neuroticism, depression, somatic complaints and social isolation (Goulding, 2004).

• Schizotypal traits are compatible with both well-being and impaired functioning Goulding (2004).

• Elevated levels of neutral schizotypal traits are associated with all forms of ExE. These traits only clustered with indices of pathogenic ExE within groups of participants who also endorsed items consistent with maladaptive learning experiences (Allen, 2008).

• When schizotypal traits are combined with stressors they are likely to produce more pathogenic varieties of ExE that are qualitatively different than the ExE observed in other schizotypal individuals (Claridge, 1997).

• Allen (2008) differentiated three high schizotypy groups, with one characterized by unambiguously growth-enhancing ExE (i.e., mystical experience), another characterized by unambiguously pathogenic ExE (i.e., dissociation and cognitive distortion), and a third characterized by an ambivalent mixture of ExE (i.e., mystical experience and cognitive distortion). Within these three high schizotypy groups only those with either perceived conflicts in parental bonding and/or self-schema instability demonstrated signs of pathogenic anomalous experience .

• Goretzki (2007) found a high correlation of .7 between a Spiritual Emergencies (SE) Scale and an Experience of Psychotic Symptoms Scale, and argues that it is open to interpretation whether psychosis is nothing more than SE or whether SE is nothing more than psychosis.

• Content, form and processing of ExE differed between a psychotic group and a group with benign ExE (Jackson (2001). In terms of content; the psychotic experiences group reported more idiosyncratic, bizarre and alienating content, expressed themes of grandiosity and a sense of infallibility, they experienced a malignant, idiosyncratic entity and lost their sense of control. In terms of the form; the psychotic group reported much more chaotic critical auditory hallucinations. The delusions/revelations were bizarre, incorrigible beliefs with the absence of insight. In terms of the processing; the psychotic group displayed more self-centeredness and their experiences seriously impaired their daily functioning. Individuals from both groups believed that their experiences directly addressed their most pressing psychological needs at the time and there were similar phenomenological themes present in both groups.

- Hunt (2000) and Garety, Kuipers, Fowler, Freeman & Bebbington (2001) suggested that poor parental experiences and self-schema instability may predispose individuals to having more conflicted forms of ExE.
- Individuals with a Paranomal Belief System, "magic thinking" and "perceptual distortions" also show good results in artistic abilities and creativity (Goulding, 2004, see also chapter 6 by Holt in the current book).
- A subgroup of individuals with high scores on a Paranormal Belief Scale and with ExE has a high sense of coherence connected with low neuroticism which is an indicator of mental health (Goulding, 2004).
- Healthy individuals who experience unusual phenomena (e.g., so-called hallucinations and delusions) associated with profound spiritual experiences tend to interpret them as positive and purposeful (Jackson & Fulford, 1997).
- Individuals with a spiritual background evaluate ExE much more positively than a clinical group and have better mental health (Kohls, 2004).

This summary of studies could be extended almost ad nauseum with similar results. So, the evidence concerning the relationship and overlap between symptoms of a mental disorder as listed in the current *DSM* or *ICD* and ExE is evident, yet inconsistent and ambiguous. To make it even more complicated, we have to acknowledge that symptoms such as delusions and hallucinations are also prevalent in healthy subjects.

In either case, individuals with a paranormal belief system and a personal ExE cannot be categorized as mentally disordered in principle, although this may well be true for some of them. Even if for a substantial part of perceptions during ExE and different paranormal beliefs there is an overlap with several symptoms and diagnoses of mental disorders, for a well-grounded decision it is necessary to see the whole person in terms of her psychological functioning and ability to manage everyday life. As there is evidence that the risk of experiencing psychotic symptoms as well as having ExE is influenced by stressful biographical and environmental factors, such as insecure attachment relations and exposure to sexual and other kinds of trauma (Irwin, 1992, 1993; Fonagy, 2003; Perkins & Allen, 2006; Belz, 2009), it seems adequate to use an approach that deals with the perceptions and experiences people report in a phenomenological way first, then connect the experiences to biography and life situation before deciding how to categorize them. Therefore, if we have to decide whether the reported and observed phenomena resemble the symptoms of a mental disorder or if they can be better understood as the expression of an ExE we should take into consideration that a mental disorder is always seen as disturbance in the functioning of the individual (Saß, Wittchen & Zaudig, 2003). It is therefore a necessary condition that the phenomena and symptoms cause suffering and impairment in a clinically relevant way in the interpersonal and working context. Emotion, cognitions and aspects of self harm or being a risk to others, as well as the suffering and distress of the individual are all relevant.

Findings of a search in the literature for criteria that might differentiate between healthy and unhealthy ExE suggest that it is not the experience itself that is an indicator for mental health or psychopathology. For example, Bentall (2004) argued that hearing voices, hallucinations and other symptoms of "severe" mental illness are just exaggerations of quirks experienced by us all.

Therefore, it is of particular importance to see how the affected individuals and the personal and professional surrounding, as well as the cultural background evaluate these experiences. This evaluation determines if these experiences can be integrated in an adaptive way into the psychological functioning of the experients. Symptoms, phenomena and experiences that are evaluated negatively or considered irritating and disruptive by the individual and his or her social and cultural environment have a higher probability of being categorized as signs of a mental disorder than positively evaluated ExE.

Even if we come to a valid diagnostic description of the experience, we don't know what that means for the further development of the individual's functioning. There is a need to consider to what extent ExE and a given mental disorder are based on the same processes and to what extent the individual possesses the skills to integrate these experiences. Relevant skills could include metacognitive, information processing, and emotion regulation abilities (Belz & Berger, 2008, Bentall, 2000).

The idea that a clear-cut taxonomy of healthy or unhealthy ExE can be constructed seems at this point neither realistic nor adequate. In order to do justice to the complexity of ExE, as well as mental health problems, we need an approach that is able to consider the individual and his psychological functioning without reinventing the wheel every time.

Individual Case Conceptualization and Plan Analysis

As there is evidence that the risk of experiencing psychotic symptoms, as well as having ExE, is influenced by stressful biographical and environmental factors such as insecure attachment relations and exposure to sexual and other kinds of trauma (Irwin, 1992, 1993; Fonagy, 2003; Perkins & Allen, 2006; Belz, 2009) it seems adequate to use an approach that deals with the perceptions and experiences people report in a phenomenological way first, then connect the experiences to the biography and life situation and general needs and individual motives before deciding how to evaluate and categorize them in a single case. Flexible case conceptualizations of individuals reporting ExE allow an individual understanding of the psychological functioning, and its use as a basis for therapy planning and for making prognoses regarding their further development.

Plan Analysis (Caspar, 1995; 2007) is a well developed method for case conceptualization and therapy planning in research and practice based on the perspective of instrumental functioning. If used in psychotherapy, interventions show better outcomes, much better process and fewer drop outs (Grawe, Caspar & Ambühl, 1990). The use of the term "Plan" deviates from the use of plan in everyday language and is therefore capitalized. Plans are not necessarily conscious and there is no rationality assumed, but there must be an objective or subjective advantage for an instrumental behavior to survive and become typical for a person. Plans are not seen as a reality in the patient's mind, but as a construct ascribed by an observer. By definition, a Plan includes a goal/purpose/motive and at least minimal means to accomplish the goals/purpose/motive. The means serve a purpose, that is in the end the fulfillment of the most important human needs like attachment, orientation/control, self-esteem and avoidance of pain versus seeking pleasure and that purpose brings about and guides the means (Grawe, 2004). If these Plans are threatened or blocked, negative emotions come up. Under unfavorable or difficult circumstances people develop maladaptive strategies or strategies with unwanted side-effects in order to realize their Plans. The fundamental question that Plan Analysis aims to answer, *"For what purpose does a person behave in a particular way?"* Plan Analysis reduces complexity by focusing on an instrumental perspective of functioning and allows for the development of a comprehensive overview of an individuals' problem(s), his behavior and experiences. Plan Analysis includes interpersonal and intrapsychic aspects.

An individual's instrumental strategies are represented in drawn Plan structures, a visual aid used in practice and research to get an overview of the patient's functioning. This therefore serves as a basis for developing case conceptualizations. The explicit case conceptualization explains, evaluates and uses the information from the Plan structure, puts it into a wider context, uses it to develop ideas for counseling and therapeutic goals and strategies, and tells us how to individually tailor the therapeutic relationship. In such an analysis, problems as well as strengths and resources can be analyzed together which is especially important when we deal with ExE as they may contain pathogenic as well as salutogenetic components.

The special qualities of Plan Analysis allow for application in both practice and research and the transfer of information between the two. To illustrate the characteristics of a Plan structure, an example will be presented which describes a real case, with some elements changed in order to protect the patient's identity (see Figure 3). Figure 3 may look rather complicated at a first glance. The accompanying text should help to walk the reader through the figure and understand it. The structure itself is a compromise between a complexity that is normally needed for a case conceptualization in research as well as in clinical practice and the readability of the structure.

The client presented here is a fifty year old woman, living alone with no permanent job. Relevant life events in the last few years include a divorce, the loss of her job, and the death of her father who was a very dominant person who was always ready to solve her problems. Following the end of her marriage to a rather well-to-do and dominant husband, she did not find a new and satisfying job and life situation. In addition, her children developed several problems that they continue to struggle with; her son is a drug-addict and her daughter has a severe eating disorder. In order to cope with this sum of life events and in an attempt to regain happiness and wealth, the client contacted a so-called magician. She felt that being hit by so many difficulties could not be explained naturally but must have some paranormal origin which could only be helped by counter-magic. Over the course of several years, she paid the magician more than one million Euros and by so doing, lost all the money she received after the divorce. Although she kept paying more and

Case example "Magic and Millions"

Figure 3. Case example of a Plan Structure

more money, she did not find the desired help and support she was seeking. Instead, she has financial problems and feels threatened by the magician because she stopped meeting his demands for further money. In addition, she has also a list of physical problems for which she has contacted a medium, who told her that all her symptoms are just a sign of spiritual growth. For the client, explaining her life situation and symptoms as a mixture of black magic and spiritual growth provides the advantage of not being responsible for these problems, but instead being the victim of external negative influences and fate. This helps to regain some control in life and to regulate her self-esteem, as this way she has an explanation for all that has happened to her. However, this explanation of "how it came all about" helps only temporarily. The day to day living conditions do not really change as a result. In this situation, the idea of defining her psychophysiological symptoms as signs of spiritual growth gives her a sense that she might possess special abilities which could help her to find a job as a medium. However, as her real life problems pile up, the inconsistencies in this explanatory model increased and stimulated her to come to our counseling service for advice. Here she hoped to find help for the old problems as well as new perspectives and maybe find a more benign substitute for the magician and the medium which would be in line with her learned dependent role in relationships.

Now we can consider which guiding Plan the behavior "reporting life experiences as paranormally caused" might serve. A hypothesis could be "show you are the victim"— going further up in the Plan structure the guiding Plan of the Plan "externalize problems" could be "control your life (at least by giving a conclusive explanation and prove that you understand what is happening)." As can be seen, a subordinated Plan like "show you are the victim" always represents the means by which a particular goal, for example, "externalize problems" is reached.

Usually Sub-plans or behaviors are consciously or unconsciously constructed in such a way that they serve or are in line with several guiding Plans simultaneously, a principle that is called "multiple determination." For example, the Plan "show you are the victim" could be expressed alongside "externalize problems" to serve the Plan "avoid feelings of guilt and shame" which comes up whenever she talks about her "failure" as mother and wife and all the money she wasted in giving it to the magician after her marriage without being able to build a new life.

Clinically, it is often crucial to understand not only the most obvious but all important determining Plans. For important Plans, there are usually several Sub-plans or behaviors that can be used interchangeably or in a complementary manner by the patient. Clinically, it is important to ask about alternative meanings of a given Plan: the use of behaviors that associated with negative side effects "says that black magic caused all her problems" or "explains severe life-events paranormally" can often be understood as resulting from a lack of more useful and adaptive alternatives.

If needed, we can break behaviors further down, e.g., excessive engagement in paranormal thoughts about how could all this happen may have been instigated by opening a letter from the magician, reading it, thinking about it, etc. Step by step, a structure is developed which includes all important interpersonal and intrapsychic strategies of a person, from their behavior up to their general needs.

In recent years, Plan Analysis has been used in several studies for people reporting ExE (Tölle, 2003; Spitz, 2005, Belz & Berger 2008). The first study (Tölle, 2003) explored whether it is possible to identify typical Plans of individuals with ExE; i.e., Plans that are common for many individuals who have sought help for their ExE. The second study (Spitz, 2005) explored whether there are any peculiarities in the emotion regulation of people with ExE. The third study (Belz & Berger, 2008) used sequential Plan Analyses to undertake a detailed analysis about which strategies are used by people with ExE who seek help and advice when difficult topics are addressed and how they deal with their upcoming emotions. All three studies are based on data from individuals who called on the counseling service of the Institut für Grenzgebiete der Psychologie und Psychohygiene e.V. in Freiburg, Germany (IGPP) primarily reporting internal and coincidence phenomena as well as psychophysical dissociative phenomena. Help-seeking individuals with external phenomena are generally underrepresented in these studies, and it may be possible that these might be described by another prototypical structure. The limits of these prototypical Plans lie in the fact that they consider only those who seek help and advice because of their ExE. It might very well be that there are many who have unproblematic ExE and which are not characterized by the identified prototypical Plans.

Independent of the pattern of ExE and the prevalence of symptoms of a mental disorder, ExE are integrated into the psychological functioning of an individual such that that they serve certain purposes (see Table 3).

The prototypical Plans found for individuals with ExE can be a helpful basis from which to develop a case conceptualization for every single individual seeking help and advice as a result of their ExE. They also help the therapist to understand the role of the ExE within the overall psychological functioning of a person. Prototypical Plans can allow for the observation of inconsistencies between motivational goals and the degree to which they can be realized, and whether the strategies employed to reach these goals are likely to have severe side-effects (e.g., externalization, avoiding difficult emotions, using ExE as a surrogate for "real world" experiences).

Table 3: Plans and Corresponding
Counseling and Therapeutic Tasks

Coping strategy	Subplans
1. Externalize problems/make misery bearable	reject responsibility for life-events and failure show you are the victim explain life events "paranormally" (e.g., black magic, telepathic influences)
2. Keep your life controllable and understandable	reject information which is incompatible with your belief system /or your worldview explain chaos in real life problems with coherent anomalistic theory prove that your ExE are real and you are a healthy person
4. Look for sense in life/create meaning	explain difficult life events/irritating ExE in a meaningful way explain your ExE as part of spiritual development find a new perspective in life
5. Avoid difficult emotions/reduce tension	avoid inconsistencies in your perception show that you successfully coped with difficult life events switch to positive emotions as coping strategy if difficult topics arise

These coping strategies might initially reduce tensions but in the long run, they produce even more inconsistencies and tensions within a persons' psychological functioning. If at that point in life, individuals with ExE see a health professional in order to get support it seems crucial that the treatment and support they get is based on a profound understanding of the phenomena, the person and the persons' belief system. Following from that, for every Plan we can define specific counseling and therapeutic tasks which are summarized in Table 4.

Even though these tasks are derived from empirically based prototypical Plan Analyses, we do not know to what extent these interventions are helpful and effective. Empirical evidence comes from an evaluative study undertaken at the Counseling unit of the IGPP in Freiburg in 2000 (Kühn, 2001) and a later replication analyzed by Schupp-Ihle (2010). These results indicate that offering counseling at an early stage of distress and irritation concerning ExE could have a preventive effect.

Bechdolf, Ruhrmann, Wagner, Kuhn, Janssen, Bottlender, Weineke, Schulze-Lutter, Maier & Klosterkotter (2005) have also argued for early inter-

Table 4. Plans and Corresponding Counseling and Therapeutic Tasks

Plan of Client	Task of Counselor/Therapist
Externalize problems/ make misery bearable	Validate the clients search for explanation and tell him that it is understandable and even evident to consider external causes for the ExE but also necessary to understand why they happen now and why to him/her. Encourage him/her to explore alternative explanatory models in a nonthreatening way
Show you are exceptional	Validate underlying motive for recognition and acknowledgement. Tell client that ExE are not necessarily a consequence of special abilities but may occur in special situations and might bear a special message
Look for meaning in life	Validate wish to understand ExE and offer help in trying to create meaning of ExE together with client in context of life Not "What do you want from life?" but "What do you think is it that life wants from you at this point?"
Keep your life controllable and understandable	Tell client that ExE are normal experiences which are widely distributed in the general population and not necessarily a sign of abnormality/psychopathology. Teach client to differentiate between perception and explanation Be a model for flexibility and openness in worldview to enable patient to stand inconsistencies and discrepancies
Avoid difficult emotions	Teach emotion regulation. Use small easy to digest steps when it comes to stressful emotions and tell client that you ask for ok when working with emotions and using deepening interventions. If indication: Help to integrate traumatic life events

vention programs that target subclinical ExE. While there is undoubtedly good rationale for such interventions in some instances, as long as we know so little about diagnosis and treatment in the field of ExE, we should use a thorough case conceptualization for every single case, integrate our few empirical findings and add our empirically supported knowledge from other areas of clinical psychology and psychotherapy research as a starting point.

Conclusions

The mental health field has been growing more sensitive to religion and spirituality as important factors in health and well-being since it was integrated into the DSM IV. This has also instigated more and more research in the field. What we need now is a comparable development for people with a broader range of ExE, that are not necessarily associated with religion and spirituality. However, at this point the empirical findings in the field of mental distress and ExE are still scarce. What we do know is that there is a significant overlap between ExE and different mental disorders. Looking at the issue merely from a phenomenological perspective does not allow us to say much about the pathological or nonpathological nature of the person and the experience. What is even more difficult is providing any further prognosis about the expected process and answering questions like: "Will the individual be able to integrate the experience?," "Is the experience indicative of the beginning of a psychotic process or is it just a crisis situation with a positive potential?," "Which are relevant risk factors for a problematic processes which are protective factors?," "Which kind of support — if any — does the individual need for a positive process?," "Which factors determine an effective outcome?," etc.

All of the above questions need thorough research and the field for which this should and could be a genuine task is clinical psychology and psychotherapy. There we find the necessary research tools, methodology, models and theories that will help us to test hypotheses and models that have been developed in the field of ExE. If our approach is independent of therapeutic orientations and ideological or epistemiological presumptions but based on empirical findings, it will allow us to take an integrative stance, go beyond the enlightened versus delusional polarity and stimulate the development of new models and theories. This can provide useful guidance in giving help and advice for people struggling with ExE and will hopefully stimulate communication between clinical psychology and parapsychology for the benefit of both.

Clinical Parapsychology in the United Kingdom

IAN TIERNEY

Abstract

This chapter discusses the overlaps between clinical psychology and parapsychology in the United Kingdom, given that some people who contact parapsychology research units with distressing anomalous experiences may be experiencing a first episode of psychosis. Before raising some relevant questions of practice, the implications of using the shorthand term "clinical parapsychology" rather than more neutral, and less provocative, terms— such as "counseling anomalous experience" is discussed. The author then discusses how counseling of individuals who are distressed by their AEs might best be undertaken, and by whom. The advantages and disadvantages of several perspectives are explored, including whether it may help to enroll the experiment as a "scientist," encouraging close observation and recording of the AE. The latter approach has been employed at The Koestler Parapsychology Unit (KPU) for many years and has definite practical and theoretical implications which have been discussed by, among others, Walter von Lucadou. Von Lucadou's "Model of Pragmatic Information" is described, and a large European study; the Europsi study introduced, which seeks to further understand experiences of the recurrent spontaneous psychokinesis type.

Introduction

This chapter examines the situation in the United Kingdom in relation to counseling exceptional/extraordinary/ anomalous experience, the status of the term "clinical parapsychology," and the work that is required to possibly justify its use.

In a project called the "Europsi Study" which began in October 2009, over 60 university academics and officers of societies for psychical research throughout Europe have agreed to participate in an experimental test of Walter von Lucadou's Model of Pragmatic Information (Lucadou & Zahradnik, 2004), which is being undertaken by the author and Caroline Watt. Those individuals who have kindly agreed to participate will do so by encouraging members of the public who contact them describing anomalous experience of the recurrent spontaneous psychokinesis (RSPK) "type," and who can use the internet, to access the "Europsi" website.

In the process of contacting people throughout Europe with an academic interest in anomalous human experience, it has emerged that more than a third of such individuals live in the United Kingdom. This disproportion is, in the main, attributable to the efforts of the late Professor Robert Morris to promote the study of anomalous experience as a legitimate academic discipline in the United Kingdom, and indeed world-wide, directly as academic teacher/supervisor or indirectly in other ways. The author worked with Bob Morris as one of three volunteer clinical advisors to the Koestler Parapsychology Unit (KPU) from its inception in 1985 until Bob's death in 2004. This developed an interest established by attending John Beloff's Parapsychology Seminars at the University of Edinburgh in the 10 years prior to the establishment of the KPU.

From 1985 onward, the KPU was contacted by increasing numbers of people who described being distressed by their anomalous experiences (Tierney, 1993). In addition to varying levels of distress, which was and is the criterion for referral to a clinical advisor, for the most part they were asking for help or at least an explanation for their experience. Unfortunately, because the clinical advisors were fitting referrals into spare time after addressing already overfilled waiting lists in their "day jobs," the various therapeutic approaches employed, the recording of information, and the outcome data obtained were unsystematic and of limited subsequent value. However, an analysis of some of the available data, collected between 1992–2005, was undertaken (Tierney, Coelho & Lamont, 2007) along with a survey of the attitudes and practices of some of the other units in the United Kingdom with an interest in anomalous experience (Coelho, Tierney & Lamont, 2008). These studies were prompted by the realization that there is an increasing body of evidence (see, McGorry, Nordentoft, & Simonsen, 2005) that early identification and treatment of psychoses is associated with beneficial outcomes, and that an unknown proportion of contacts to the KPU were by individuals whose anomalous experience, reviewed in the context of other information they gave, suggested they were in the early stages of a psychotic illness and had not revealed their state to anyone else in a position to give clinical advice. This seemed to place an onus on academic units who professed publicly (via the press or internet) an interest in anomalous experience to have a policy towards the contacts of this type that their interest might attract.

Tierney *et al.* (2007) found that roughly 50 percent of the assessed contacts (N = 120) by distressed individuals to the KPU gave descriptions of their experience (other than their anomalous experience) which suggested some clinically relevant condition. This did not necessarily preclude the co-existence of psi-relevant experience. Some 6 percent of this group described behavior which suggested (1) they were experiencing a psychotic state for the first time, and (2) that this contact with the KPU was their first request for help or advice.

The other 50 percent comprised the "worried well" who had experienced a range of unusual experiences which they felt might be relevant to parapsychology. It is important to note that in all cases the experiments spontaneously reported their various degrees of distress, from unpleasant surprise, through various degrees of disconcertion, to being extremely afraid, and that the contacts were unsolicited, apart from the fact that a web site and press reports indicated that the KPU was involved in parapsychological research. People who were simply curious or intrigued by their experience, or whose only interest was in having their experience "validated" in some sense, were not referred to the clinical advisors. It can be argued that this judgment itself may have excluded a range of individuals who were in the very early stages of illness from potentially beneficial clinical contact. However, given the very limited resources and the fact that the unit was receiving well over a hundred contacts of all types each year, it was necessarily to draw a line somewhere.

Attitudes and Practice in UK Units

In a survey of staff in five of the eight units extant in the United Kingdom in 2005 which both professed an interest in anomalous experience, and who agreed to participate, Coelho *et al.* (2008) found considerable unease among members of staff about contact with distressed members of the public. The detail of the various responses is available in the journal article (Coelho et al., 2008). However, three categories of response are illustrative of the situation: the responses of staff to contacts about distressing anomalous experiences in each of the five units, each units' concerns about responding to contacts of this type, and the resources and information units felt were required to improve their response. These results must be viewed in the context that, with the exception of the KPU, none of the units had formal links with clinical advisors.

The responses of all of the units with the exception of the KPU varied

Table 1. Types of Current Responses or Actions Taken by the 5 Units to Contacts About Distressing Experiences

No action: associated with uncertainty regarding appropriateness of response.	2/5
No action: associated with ratio of effort involved in responding and effectiveness of response.	2/5
No action: associated with concerns regarding ethical, insurance and legal issues involved in such contacts.	1/5
One-off exploration of non-paranormal explanation for experience(s).	3/5
One-off exploration of psychological state associated with experience(s).	2/5
Prolonged interaction with contacting individual.	3/5

both within the staff of each unit and between units (see Table 1). For two of the units, the preferred response to most contacts was "no action" (for more than one reason), but with exceptions. However, the criteria for undertaking interaction when it did occur were unclear or inconsistent.

The concerns of those working in the research units (Table 2) were, for the most part, understandable although the third concern one was more related to doubts about which type of mental health advisor would subsequently take full clinical responsibility for advice, leaving the unit free of responsibility.

The units' responses about resources they lacked to deal with contacts of this kind (see Table 3) were insightful and appropriate.

Tierney *et al.* (2007) have made the clinical and organizational case for more formal contacts between units of this kind and interested clinicians. In addition to helping individuals in the United Kingdom, the benefits to the National Health Service are likely to be a reduction in treatment costs due to both early intervention (where appropriate) and a reduction in "non-compliance with treatment" where individuals with a diagnosed and treated condition look for an alternative explanation for their anomalous experience.

These survey results highlight the lack of formal links between units (in 2009, four years after the survey was undertaken, the number of units had grown from 8 to 14) and clinical advisors which in turn raises the issue of information available to such interested clinicians about the subject. Until very recently, there has been a dearth of informed advice readily available to trainee and established clinical practitioners about what constitutes anomalous experience. The book *Varieties of Anomalous Experience* (Cardeña, Lynn & Krippner, 2000) is a very welcome source for practitioners to begin distinguishing possibly psi-relevant experience from — "what looks like it, but isn't!" — meaning the alternative neuro-psychological, psychological, and anthropological interpretations (Morris, 1986). Furthermore, the work of Martina Belz and others (Belz, 2008a,b, Belz & Fach, *in press*, Belz and Bauer and Belz, chapter 7, this book) connected with the systematic collection of

Table 2. Units' Concerns About
Responding to Contacts of This Type

Danger of unqualified intervention with vulnerable adults.	4/5
Concerns regarding the responsibility to respond ("duty of care") to unsolicited contacts.	3/5
Concerns regarding ethical/legal/professional liability after referral to an appropriate advisor (e.g., mental health advisor).	2/5

Table 3. Resources/Information Needed
to Improve Response to Contacts

Response protocol or guidelines for distressed telephone contacts.	4/5
Ethical, insurance and legal guidelines for responses given to distressed contacts.	4/5
Advice from or "referral" to mental health advisor(s).	3/5
Pre-prepared educational/informational packages for contacting individuals.	4/5

case data at the Institut für Grenzgebiete der Psychologie und Psychohygiene e.V (IGPP) in Freiburg, Germany from the mid 1990s onward is by far the most comprehensive collection and analysis of such cases available.

Another helpful type of information, which is missing at present, is via the "case-conference' approach. These are held in environments where anonymity and confidentiality are maintained, and where the experient's report can be examined in detail (West, 1993). Unlike the IGPP there is nowhere in the United Kingdom where discussions of this type take place. For several years starting in the mid 1990s, clinical meetings were held monthly in the KPU involving Bob Morris, the author (who is a clinical psychologist) and two psychiatrists Drs James McHarg and Thomas Field, to whom cases were also referred by the KPU. In addition, at that time, Canon Michael Perry regularly convened an ecumenical meeting of priests, ministers, and other religious at Durham Cathedral, along with invited speakers with relevant specialist knowledge (psychiatrists and psychologists), to discuss specific cases of anomalous experience encountered during their pastoral duties (Perry, 1987). This was an additional useful source of informed discussion about these experiences, and the positive and negative aspects of the various pastoral and clinical approaches which were being employed. I know of no such meetings now taking place in the United Kingdom.

Clinical Parapsychology

This term has developed as a short-hand term subsuming topics related to the counseling of individuals distressed by their anomalous experience. The term first appears in Montague Ullman's 1977 paper on "Psychopathology and Psi Phenomena," but was not used in general discussions about this topic prior to the 38th PA conference, in Durham, N.C., where it was the title of a panel discussion (Solfvin,1995). It was notably absent in the first conference on this subject, organized by the Parapsychological Foundation in London in 1989 (Coly & McMahon, 1993), or in earlier discussions on this topic (Alberti, 1974; Hastings 1983). More recently, it has occurred as a suggested teaching topic (Klimo,1998), as a conference topic at the 1st International Expert-Meeting on Clinical Parapsychology, Naarden in 2007 (although the title of the book that is emerging, very slowly, from that conference uses a different term) where Tierney (*in press*) raised concerns about its use and suggested alternatives, and , most recently by Martina Belz (2009) as the title for her paper at the Utrecht II conference, in which she also discussed the *pros* and *cons* of the phrase. In its favor "clinical parapsychology' can be viewed as a useful term which distinguishes a body of knowledge, distinct from the rest of abnormal psychology, which advocates psychotherapy (of various types) for distress caused by phenomena which, *in someone's judgment*, are not only exceptional/extraordinary/anomalistic, but in particular, within the purview of parapsychology. It is possible that the distinction between the terms "exceptional/extraordinary" and "anomalous" experience is more than trivial. Arguably "exceptional/extraordinary" have the connotation of "outside mundane/ expected" experience while "anomalous" points to the "unexplained" nature of the same. Frequent experience of psychokinesis or verified precognition would render the experience no longer extraordinary or exceptional but it is likely to remain anomalous. In their discussion of the terms *anomalous*, *anomalies*, and *anomalistic*, Cardeña, Lynn and Krippner (2000, p. 3–5) give four interpretations of these terms (see Table 4), ranging from statistically uncommon experiences, through experiences that involve altered states of consciousness or statistically rare beliefs, to "unexplainable events" (i.e., a demonstrable occurrence) rather than experiences (i.e., a psychological event that may or may not be associated with a demonstrable consensual occurrence)."

It is arguable that the first three interpretations indicate experiences which fall within the province of "established" psychology, both experimental and clinical. Discussions of hallucinations, delusions, rare beliefs, mystical experiences and other claims of parapsychological experience with absolutely no corroborating evidence, while important clinically and germane to an understanding of the varieties of human experience (Harary, 1993) may not warrant a separate term; whereas the last of the interpretations given by Cardeña *et al.* (2000) is the distinguishing one that might justify its use. Clearly there is a simple element of choice by therapists in deciding which interpretation of anomalous experience they choose to counsel, but arguably less so when the experience falls within the last interpretation.

Table 4. Defining "Anomalous Experience":
Cardeña, Lynn & Krippner, 2000

Uncommon experience or one that is believed to deviate from the usually accepted explanations of reality.	Focus on the experience, not the consensual validity, external nature or "unusual people'; this was the definition used in Varieties of Anomalous Experience.
Altered state of consciousness	Out-of-body and near death experiences, but not synesthesia, hypnosis or meditation.
Non-abnormal, belief based	e.g., Alien abduction
Unexplain(able)ed	Externally validated phenomena (e.g., ESP or RSPK). A demonstrable, consensual, occurrence which contradict the usually accepted explanations of reality.

Set against this is both the expectation of outcome implicit in the term "clinical parapsychology," and the implication that experients of anomalous experience are suffering mental or behavioral disorders. Terms for professions or practices which start with "clinical' followed by an "...ology," normally imply treatment of pathological conditions using evidence-based interventions which have been subjected to well-designed outcome trials. For instance, when we use the term "clinical psychology" we imply the use of evidence-based psychological knowledge in the structured treatment of individuals with mental and behavioral disorders, based on random, controlled, or other forms, of structured trials. It is the case that in disciplines of this type, before such trials can take place, there is a stage of data collection and analysis which leads to testable models and hypotheses. It has been suggested (Tierney, *in press*) that the counseling of people distressed by their anomalous experiences is in this preliminary stage. At this time there are few outcome results of clinical trials in the counseling of anomalous experience, and none where the experience is of the exclusively external type. In this volume and elsewhere (Belz, 2008 a, b, Belz & Fach, *in press*) Belz has presented a useful typology or classification of experiences which contrasts *external vs internal* phenomena within the experient's *self and/or world* model. It can be argued that the distinction between external and internal phenomena is that *in principle* an incident of external phenomena may be witnessed/experienced by an observer whereas *in principle* it is not possible for another person to witness/experience an incident of internal phenomena.

The analyses of the IGPP data are presented within this framework. Belz has described some of the characteristics of these experiences which may distinguish them from the reports of individuals with a clearly diagnosed mental disorder. Among these are: (a) reports about anomalous experience from clinical groups tend to be more bizarre, more detailed and disturbed; (b) clinical groups tend to report that their auditory hallucinations are uncontrollable whereas nonclinical groups have the feeling that they can control them; (c) individuals diagnosed psychotic are less able to recognize the strangeness of their anomalous experience compared to healthy individuals.

What may be required now is an extension of the IGPP work, collecting a great deal more data on each "type" of anomalous experience, and in particular, those which by reason of evidence appear most relevant to parapsychology. After the analyses and interpretations of detailed information of this type are available, then the next stage, the controlled assessment of various treatment modalities based on hypotheses or models of the processes involved, can be undertaken with confidence. At present, an alternative phrase such as "counseling anomalous experience" (providing it is clear what type of experience is meant) may be preferable to "clinical parapsychology."

Confounding Clinical and Parapsychological Aims

Some of the results of the Coelho *et al.* (2008) survey were attributable to the potential conflicts between parapsychological and clinical aims. The clinician's aim is usually interpreted as facilitating the individual's understanding of, or at least their accommodation to, the anomalous experience, both in their own terms and in the light of other behaviors or symptoms they are exhibiting. The clinician's concern is less, if at all, with the validity of the experience in the eyes of others. The aim is to ameliorate distress, if not immediately, then in the medium/long term using the therapeutic method(s) that the therapist chooses. By contrast, most professed academic parapsychologists and many academics are interested in understanding the nature of anomalous events, particularly when the experience has significant external characteristics which sets it at odds with the consensus world model of causation (Belz, 2008). Kramer (1993) noted in the context of a discussion of the practice at the Parapsychologisch Adviesburo in Holland in the late '80s that:

> Do not expect that counseling clients with psi experiences brings in new cases for collections of spontaneous cases. In counseling you have to concentrate on and be aware of other aspects of the client's story than when you are looking for evidence of spontaneous psi phenomena. In theory, of course, it is possible to do both but in practice it does not work that way....

It is possible that the aim of doing both *within the same case* is not achievable, even in theory. The various processes used within the scientific method to evaluate phenomena of any kind involve considerable time, repetition, intrusion and controls, which are inappropriate in most therapies which are client-centered either individually or in groups. Tierney (*in press*) has described in detail the effects (potentially negative, but fortuitously positive in the case described) of confusing clinical and parapsychological aims when counseling an individual who demonstrated the anomalous experience (in that case psychokinesis, PK) which was causing distress.

The Therapist's Attitude to Psi: Therapeutic Approaches to Anomalous Experience

Implicit within the above discussion of clinical and parapsychological aims is the necessity for a judgment by both the experiment and the therapist about the relevance of psi to the experience in question, which in turn depends on the world model of each. For instance, in one of the earliest detailed description of counseling of this type Hastings (1983) described seven steps (Table 5) in working with someone who has had a disturbing psychic experience.

While steps 1, 2, 3, and 7 may be part of standard non-directive counseling, steps 4, 5, and 6 impose the therapist's knowledge and belief to a marked degree. To point out the obvious, such an approach, which can be described as a "normalization" one, depends on the therapist's judgment about what is normal, or at least possible.

Depending on the client's self and world model (Belz, 2008) it is possible that effective counseling of anomalous experience of the purely internal type can be undertaken without what Kramer (*ibid.*) described as "profound knowledge of the achievements of parapsychological research," although the interpretation of the phenomena may be different (over the years there have been a number of contacts to the KPU from clinicians reporting what they believe are the inexplicable experiences of their patients). Kramer viewed this knowledge as a necessary, though secondary, requirement to experience and knowledge of psychotherapy when undertaking counseling of this type. However, when the anomalous experience involves external phenomena the interpretations and attitudes of therapists will depend on conclusions they have come to about the status of such experiences. Cases where the anomalous experience is of the external type (where circumstances do not support reasonable alternative physical or psychological explanations) and causes distress, are rare. In the author's experience over 35 years and several hundred contacts certainly less than 5 percent and possibly as low as 2 percent of contacts have been of this type. With one exception, involving (verified) precognition of particularly distressing accidents and consequent feelings of guilt about causation (being responsible), these have involved PK or RSPK.

Table 5. Suggested Stages in Counseling
Psychic Experience; Hastings, 1983

1 Ask the person to describe the experience or events.
2 Listen fully and carefully, without judging.
3 Reassure the person that the experience is not "crazy" or "insane" (if this is appropriate).
4 Identify or label the type of event.
5 Give information about what is known about this type of event.
6 Where possible, develop reality tests to discover if the event is genuine or if there are non-psychic alternative explanations.
7 Address the psychological reactions that result from the experience.

Various forms of therapeutic intervention with distressed individuals experiencing anomalous events have been published. These include: broadly psychodynamic (Ullman, 1977), "normalization" (Hastings, 1983), family therapy (Snoyman, 1985), system theory, and Rogerian client-centered therapies (Kramer 1993), humanistic group therapy (Montanelli & Parra, 2004), case specific formulations (Belz, 2008, Lucadou & Posner, 1997), and a cognitive behavior therapy approach which encouraged recording and the evaluation of thoughts/attitudes to the experience (Coelho, Tierney & Lamont, 2008). Belz (2008a) has described the constraints which influence the clinical approach used in counseling anomalous experiments with a wide range of unusual experience, as well suggesting some of the core elements of useful intervention. However, as stated earlier, there is limited information on outcome measures from the various therapies, and in particular the effect of the variable just discussed, the therapist attitude/beliefs about psi (Tierney, 2007). With the exception of the humanistic group therapy approach, most reported counselling is conducted on a one-to-one basis, either face to face or by telephone. In such situations and given the circumstances it is inevitable that at some point the client will ask the therapist for their view on the prevalence, "validity," and personal experience of these experiences. While it is possible to avoid such discussions by redirection, this can be deleterious to the quality of trust in the interaction.

In the humanistic group therapy approach Parra and his colleagues have remarked that

> to operate effectively with a group, the therapist must trust the abilities of the group members to help one another grow in positive directions. Unless this is the case, the therapist may feel pressure to exert more control over the group process than is helpful. When this occurs, it works against the therapeutic potential of the group, since the latter operates most effectively when members are free to help one another and determine their own direction for growth [Montanelli &Parra, 2004, p. 24].

The therapist's opinions about psi intrude to a minimal degree in this approach. This is one of the few studies where outcome measures are employed to evaluate the effectiveness of therapy.

The approach developed in the KPU encouraged the experiment both to record the various incidents of the experience as well as wider aspects of their life. They were encouraged to take an empirical view of events, testing the experience where they could, examining the alternative explanations to psi, and evaluating the outcome in the light of this process. In the small number of evidentially external cases mentioned earlier the consequence of this type of intervention appeared to be a rapid, if not immediate, cessation of the phenomena. While this could be viewed as useful in terms of helping to reduce the distress it tended to raise as many issues as it solved (for an example of this, see Tierney, in press). The obvious skeptical position, that there was no substance to these anomalous experiences that could bear the light of systematic recording, was only tempered by two elements, the author's personal experience of witnessing these anomalous events and the similar observations made by Lucadou and his colleagues in RSPK cases treated at the WGFP Parapsychological Counseling Office in Freiburg (Lucadou & Zahradnik, 2004).

These latter observations, among other information, have led Lucadou over many years to develop a Model of Pragmatic Information (MPI) which is specifically relevant to anomalous experience of the RSPK type. In a number of papers, including the most recent formulation, the MPI/Weak Quantum Theory Model (Lucadou, Römer & Walach, 2007. For an overview of this topic see Radin, 2006) a number of testable hypotheses have been proposed. The "Europsi Study," referred to in the introduction to this chapter, is an attempt to formally test this model, while at the same time collecting case material.

The Europsi Study

One prediction of the MPI is that observers can control the RSPK activity by their observation or documentation. This is because the effect-size of the phenomena is limited by the quality of their documentation (Lucadou & Zahradnik, *ibid*). In later formulations this is further described in terms of entanglement correlations which develop when global and local observables are "complimentary" or incompatible (Lucadou, Romer & Walach, *ibid*). The Europsi Study assesses the outcome, in terms of changes to frequency and form of the anomalous experience (in two groups of experiments collected from across Europe whose anomalous experience is of RSPK type) when the experiment's data for half the group is treated in a significantly different ("increased entanglement") manner from the similar data of the remaining half.

While this is not a clinical study, it has developed from clinical observations and may have relevance in the future to counseling anomalous experience of this type. In addition, if the case collection process is maintained after the conclusion of the anticipated two year study duration, and there are very limited financial consequences if this is done, then this will contribute to what the author has suggested is a prerequisite for the development of a body of knowledge, distinct but related to other forms of psychotherapy, which might merit the title of "clinical parapsychology" or, as has been suggested, "counseling anomalous experience of specific types."

Bibliography

Abbot, N. C. (2000). Healing as a therapy for human disease: A systematic review. *Journal of Alternative and Complementary Medicine, 6,* 159–169.

Achterberg, J. (1985). *Imagery in healing: Shamanism and modern medicine.* London: Shambhala Publications.

Aftanas, L. I., & Golocheikine, S. A. (2002). Non-linear dynamic complexity of the human EEG during meditation. *Neuroscience Letters, 330,* 143–146.

Aftanas, L. I., Lotova, N. V., Koshkarov, V. I., Makhnev, V. P., Mordvintsev Y. N., & Popov, S. A. (1998). Non-linear dynamic complexity of the human EEG during evoked emotions. *International Journal of Psychophysiology, 28,* 63–76.

Ainsworth, M. D., Blehar, M., Waters, E., & Wall, S. (1978). *Patterns of attachment.* Hillsdale, NJ: Erlbaum.

Al Issha, I. (1995). The illusion of reality or the reality of illusion: Hallucinations and culture. *British Journal of Psychiatry, 166,* 368–373.

Albert, R., & Runco, M. (1987). The possible different personality dispositions of scientists and nonscientists. In D. Jackson & J. Rushton (Eds.), *Scientific excellence: Origins and assessment* (pp. 67–97). London: Sage Publications.

Alberti, G. (1974). Psychopathology and parapsychology: Some possible contacts. In A. Angoff & B. Shapin (Eds.), *Parapsychology and the sciences.* New York: Parapsychology Foundation.

Allen, M. (2008). *Beyond the happy schizotype: Opportunities for personal transformation in putatively pathogenic schizotypal experiences.* Unpublished dissertation: Miami University.

Allport, G. W., & Ross, J. M. (1967). Personal religious orientation and prejudice. *Journal of Personality and Social Psychology, 5,* 432–443.

Alvarado, C. (2000). Out-of-body experiences. In E. Cardeña, S. Lynn, & S. Krippner (Eds.), *Varieties of anomalous experience: Examining the scientific evidence* (pp. 183–218). Washington, DC: American Psychological Association.

Alvarado, C., & Zingrone, N. (2003). Exploring the factors related to the after-effects of out ofbody experiences. *Journal of the Society for Psychical Research, 67,* 161–183.

Amabile, T. (1996). *Creativity in context: Update to "The social psychology of creativity."* Boulder, CO: Westview Press.

Ambach, W. (2010). Experimental investigations of subjects with extraordinary experiences. In D. Vaitl (Hrsg.), *Tätigkeitsbericht — Biennial Report 2008–2009* (pp. 57–58). Freiburg: Institut für Grenzgebiete der Psychologie und Psychohygiene e.V.

Andreasen, N. (1987). Creativity and mental illness: Prevalence rates in writers and their first-degree relatives. *American Journal of Psychiatry, 144,* 1288–1292.

Andrew, E. M., Gray, N. S., & Snowden, R. J. (2008). The relationship between trauma and beliefs about hearing voices: A study of psychiatric and non-psychiatric voice hearers. *Psychological Medicine, 4,* 1–9.

Antonovsky, A. (1987). *Unravelling the mystery of health.* San Francisco: Jossey-Bass.

Appelle, S., Lynn, S., Newman, L. (2000). Alien abduction experiences. In E. Cardeña, S. Lynn, & S. Krippner (Eds.), *Varieties of anomalous experience: Examining the scientific evidence* (pp. 253–282). Washington, DC: American Psychological Association.

Applegate, E., Wl-Deredy, W., & Bentall, R. P. (2009). Reward responsiveness in psychosis-prone groups: Hypomania and negative schizotypy. *Personality and Individual Differences, 47*, 452–456.

Arias-Carrion, O., & Peoppel, E. (2007). Dopamine, learning and reward seeking behavior. *Acta Neurologicae Experimentalis, 67*, 481–488.

Armitage, R., & Fitch, R. (1988). Cognitive style differences among high and low frequency dream recallers. *Sleep Research, 17*, 107.

Arns, M., de Ridder, S., Strehl, U., Breteler, M., & Coenen, A. (2009). Effects of neurofeedback treatment on ADHD: The effect on inattention, impulsivity and hyperactivity: a meta-analysis. *Clinical Encephalography and Neuroscience, 40*, 180–189.

Arzy, S., Mohr, C., Michel, C.M, & Blanke, O. (2007). Duration and not strength of activation in temporo-parietal cortex positively correlates with schizotypy. *NeuroImage, 35*, 326–333.

Ashby, F. G., Valentin, V. V., & Turken, A. U. (2002). The effects of positive affect and arousal on working memory and executive attention: Neurobiology and computational models. In: S. Moore and M. Oaksford (Eds), *Emotional cognition: From brain to behaviour* (pp. 245–287). Amsterdam: John Benjamins.

Ashton, M., & McDonald, R. (1985). Effects of hypnosis on verbal and non-verbal creativity. *International Journal of Clinical and Experimental Hypnosis, 33*, 15–26.

Atkinson, R. P., & Crawford, H. C. (1992). Individual differences in afterimage persistence: Relationships to hypnotic responsiveness and visuospatial skills. *American Journal of Psychology, 105*, 527–539.

Atwater, F. H. (2004). The Hemi-Sync process. Retrieved on 29th February, 2008 from http://www.monroeinstitute.com/PBWedi tor/upload/File/the_hemisync_process_20 04.pdf.

Auton, H. R., Pope, J., & Seeger, G. (2001). It isn't that strange: Paranormal belief and personality traits. *Social Behavior and Personality, 31*, 711–720.

Averill, J. (1999). Individual differences in emotional creativity: Structure and correlates. *Journal of Personality, 67*, 331–371.

Averill, J. (2005). Emotions as mediators and as products of creative activity. In J. Kaufman & J. Baer (Eds.), *Creativity across domains: Faces of the muse* (pp. 225–243). Mahwah, NJ: Erlbaum.

Ayers, L., Beaton, S., & Hunt, H. (1999). The significance of transpersonal experiences, emotional conflict, and cognitive abilities in creativity. *Empirical Studies of the Arts, 17*, 73–82.

Baldwin, A. L., & Schwartz, G. E. (2006). Personal interaction with a Reiki practitioner decreases noise-induced microvascular damage in an animal model. *Journal of Alternative and Complementary Medicine, 12*, 15–22.

Barbosa, P. C. R., Giglio, J. S., & Dalgalarrondo, P. (2005). Altered states of consciousness and short-term psychological after-affects induced by the first time ritual use of ayahuasca in an urban context in Brazil. *Journal of Psychoactive Drugs, 37*, 93–201.

Bardos, P., Degenne, D., Lebranchu, Y., Biziere, K., & Renoux, G. (1981). Neocortical lateralisation of NK activity in mice. *Scandinavian Journal of Immunology, 13*, 609–611.

Barnard, P. (2003). Asynchrony, implicational meaning and the experience of self in schizophrenia. In, T. Kircher & A. David (Eds.), *The self in neuroscience and psychiatry* (pp. 121–146). Cambridge: Cambridge University Press.

Barrantes-Vidal, N., Fañanás, L., Rosa, A., Caparrós, B., Riba, M. D., &. Obiols, J. E. (2003). Neurocognitive, behavioral and neurodevelopmental correlates of schizotypy clusters in adolescents from the general population. *Schizophrenia Research, 61*, 293–302.

Barrantes-Vidal, N. (2004). Creativity and madness revisited from current psychological perspectives. *Journal of Consciousness Studies, 11*, 58–78.

Barrett, T. R., & Etheridge, J. B. (1992). Verbal hallucinations in normals: I. People who hear voices. *Applied Cognitive Psychology, 6*, 379–387.

Barrett, L., Robin, L., Pietromonaco, P., & Eyssell, K. (1998). Are women the "more emotional" sex? Evidence from emotional experiences in social context. *Cognition and Emotion, 12*, 555–578.

Barron, F. (1968). *Creativity and personal freedom*. Princeton: D. Van Nostrand.

Barron, F. (1993). Controllable oddness as a resource in creativity. *Psychological Inquiry, 4*, 182–184.

Barron, F., & Harrington, D. (1981). Creativity, intelligence and personality. *Annual Review of Psychology, 32,* 439–476.

Batey, M., & Furnham, A. (2008). The relationship between measures of creativity and schizotypy. *Personality and Individual Differences, 45,* 816–821.

Batson, C. D., Schoenrade, P., & Ventis, L. (1993). *Religion and the individual.* Oxford: Oxford University Press.

Batty, M. J., Hawken, M. B., Bonnington, S., Tang, B-K, Gruzelier, J. H. (2006). Relaxation strategies and enhancement of hypnotic susceptibility: EEG neurofeedback, progressive muscle relaxation and self-hypnosis. *Brain Research Bulletin, 71,* 83–90.

Bauer, E., Belz, M., Fach, W., Fangmeier, R., Schupp-Ihle, C., & Wiedemer, A. (2010). Counseling and information. In D. Vaitl (Ed.), *Tätigkeitsbericht — Biennial Report 2008–2009* (pp. 69–73). Freiburg: Institut für Grenzgebiete der Psychologie und Psychohygiene e.V.

Bauer, E., & Schetsche, M. (2003). (Hrsg). *Alltägliche wunder. Erfahrungen mit dem übersinnlichen — wissenschaftliche befunde.* Würzburg: Ergon.

Baumann, S. B., Joines, W. T., Kim, J., & Zile, J. M. (2005). Energy emissions from an exceptional subject. In *Proceedings of Presented Papers: The Parapsychological Association 48th Annual Convention,* 219–223.

Baylor, G. (2001). What do we really know about Mendeleev's dream of the periodic table? A note on dreams of scientific problem solving. *Dreaming, 11,* 89–92.

Beauregard, M., & Paquette, V. (2006). Neural correlates of a mystical experience in Carmelite nuns. *Neuroscience Letters, 405,* 186–190.

Bechdolf, A., Ruhrmann, S., Wagner, M., Kühn, K. U., Janssen, B., Bottlender, R., Wieneke, A., Schulze-Lutter, F., Maier, W., & Klosterkötter. (2005). Interventions in the initial prodromal states of psychosis in Germany: Concept and recruitment. *British Journal of Psychiatry, 187,* 45–48.

Becker, G. (2000–2001). The association of creativity and psychopathology: Its cultural-historical origins. *Creativity Research Journal, 13,* 45–68.

Beit-Hallahmi, B., & Argyle, M. (1997). *The psychology of religious behavior, belief, and experience.* London: Routledge.

Bell, V., Halligan, P. W., & Ellis, H. D. (2007). The psychosis continuum and the Cardiff Anomalous Perceptions Scale (CAPS): Are there mulitiple factors underlying anomalous experience? *European Psychiatry, 22,* s28.05.

Belz, M. (2008). *Ausergewohnliche erfahrungen: Fortschritte der psychoterapie.* Göttingen: Hogrefe.

Belz, M. (2009a). Clinical parapsychology: Today's implications, tomorrow's applications. In C. A. Roe, W. Kramer & L. Coly (Eds.), *Proceedings of an International Conference Utrecht II: Charting the future of parapsychology* (pp. 326–362). New York: Parapsychology Foundation.

Belz, M. (2009b). *Ausergewöhnliche erfahrungen.* (Fortschritte der Psychotherapie, Band 35). Göttingen: Hogrefe.

Belz, M., & Berger, T. (2008). Psychisches wohlbefinden, Außergewöhnliche erfahrungen und emotionsregulation. *Zeitschrift für Anomalistik, 8,* 118–134.

Belz-Merk, M., & Fach, W. (2005). Beratung und hilfe für menschen mit aussergewöhnlichen erfahrungen. *Psychotherapie, Psychosomatik, Medizinische Psychologie, 55,* 256–265.

Belz, M., & Fach, W. (in press). Reflections on counseling and therapy for individuals reporting exceptional experiences. In Kramer, W. H., Bauer, E., & Hövelmann, G. H. (Eds.), *Clinical aspects of parapsychology.* Utrecht: Stichting Het Johan Borgman Fond

Belz-Merk, M. (2000). Counseling and therapy for people who claim exceptional experiences. *Journal of Parapsychology, 64,* 238–239.

Belz-Merk, M. (2002). *Beratung und hilfe für menschen mit außergewöhnlichen* Erfahrungen. Unveröffentlichter Abschlussbericht: Albert-Ludwigs-Universität Freiburg.

Bem, D. J., & Honorton, C. (1994). Does psi exist? Replicable evidence for an anomalous process of information transfer. *Psychological Bulletin, 115,* 4–18.

Bender, H. (1950). Der okkultismus als problem der psychohygiene. *Neue Wissenschaft, 1,* 34–42.

Bennett, B. M., Laidlaw, T. M., Dwivedi, P., Naito, A., & Gruzelier, J. H. (2006). A qualitative study of the experience of self-hypnosis or Johrei in metastatic breast cancer using interpretative phenomenological analysis. *Contemporary Hypnosis, 23*, 127–140.

Benor, D. J. (2002). Energy medicine for the internist. *Medical Clinics of North America, 86*, 105–125.

Bentall, R. (1990). The illusion of reality: A review and integration of psychological research on hallucinations. *Psychological Bulletin, 107*, 82–95.

Bentall, R. P. (2000). Hallucinatory experiences. In E. Cardeña, S. J. Lynn & S. Krippner (Eds.), *Varieties of anomalous experience: Examining the scientific evidence* (pp. 85–120). Washington, DC: American Psychological Association.

Bentall, R. (2003). *Madness explained: Psychosis and human nature.* London: Penguin books.

Bentall, R. P. (2004). *Madness explained.* London: Penguin Books.

Bentall, R., & Slade, P. (1985). Reality testing and auditory hallucinations: A signal-detection analysis. *British Journal of Clinical Psychology, 24*, 159–169.

Berenbaum, H., Kerns, J., & Raghavan, C. (2000). Anomalous experiences, peculiarity, and psychopathology. In E. Cardeña, S. J. Lynn & S. Krippner (Eds.), *Varieties of anomalous experience: Examining the scientific evidence* (pp. 25–46). Washington DC: American Psychological Association.

Bernstein, E., & Putnam, F. (1986). Development, reliability and validity of a dissociation scale. *Journal of Nervous and Mental Disease, 174*, 727–735.

Bernstein, P., & Allix, S. (2009). *Manuel clinique des expériences extraordinaires.* Paris: InterEditions.

Berzin, A. (2009). The Berzin Archives. Glossary English Terms. http://www.berzinarc hives.com/web/en/about/glossary/glos sary.html#xM (last accessed 03/04/2010).

Betancur, C., Neveu, P. J., Vitiello, S., & Le Moal, M. (1991). Natural killer cell activity is associated with brain asymmetry in male mice. *Brain, Behavior and Immunity, 5*, 162–169.

Bierman, D. J. (2008). FMRI and photo emission study of presentment: the role of "coherence" in retrocausal processes. (Abstract). *Poster presented at Bial Foundation 7th Symposium Behind and Beyond the Brain, Porto, Portugal, March 26–29 2008.*

Bishop, S. R., Lau, M., Shapiro, S., Carlson, L. E., Anderson, N. D., Carmody, J., Segal, Z. V., Abbey, S., Speca, M., Velting, D., & Devins, G. (2004). Mindfulness: A proposed operational definition. *Clinical Psychology: Science and Practice, 11*, 230–241.

Blackmore, S. J. (1984). A postal survey of OBEs and other experiences. *Journal of the Society for Psychical Research, 52*, 225–44.

Blackmore, S. (1986). Out of body experiences in schizophrenia: A questionnaire survey. *Journal of Nervous and Mental Disease, 174*, 615–619.

Blackmore, S. J., & Hart-Davis, A. (1995). *Test your psychic powers.* London: Thorsons.

Blagrove, M., & Hartnell, S. (2000). Lucid dreaming: associations with internal locus of control, need for cognition and creativity. *Personality and Individual Differences, 28*, 41–47.

Blagrove, M., & Tucker, M. (1994). Individual differences in locus of control and the reporting of lucid dreaming. *Personality and Individual Differences, 16*, 981–984.

Blanke, O., & Arzy, S. (2005). The out-of-body experience: Disturbed self-processing at the temporo-parietal junction. *The Neuroscientist, 11*, 16–24.

Bockmeuhl, K. (1990). *Listening to the God who speaks.* Colorado Springs: Helmers and Howard.

Boden, M. (1996). What is creativity? In M. Boden (Ed.), *Dimensions of creativity* (pp. 75–117). Cambridge, MA: MIT Press.

Boden, M., & Berenbaum, H. (2004). The potentially adaptive features of peculiar beliefs. *Personality and Individual Differences, 37*, 707–719.

Bomford, R. (1999).*The symmetry of God.* London: Free Association Books.

Bond, K., Ospina, M. B., Hooton, N., Bialy, L., Dryden, D. M., Buscemi, N., Shannahoff-Khalsa, D., Dusek, J., & Carlson, L. E. (2009). Defining a complex intervention: The development of demarcation criteria for "meditation." *Psychology of Religion and Spirituality, 1*, 129–137.

Bowden, D., Goddard, L., & Gruzelier, J. H. (2010a). A randomised controlled single-blind trial of the effects of Reiki and positive imagery on well-being and salivary cortisol. *Brain Research Bulletin, 81*, 66–72.

Bowden, D., Goddard, L., & Gruzelier, J. H. (2010b). A randomised controlled single-blind trial of the efficacy of Reiki at benefitting mood and well-being. Submitted for publication.

Bowden, D., Goddard, L., & Gruzelier, J. H. (2010c). A double-blind randomised controlled trial of the effects of Reiki on the germination of gamma-irradiated canary seeds. Submitted for publication.

Bowers, S., & van der Meulen, K. (1970). Effect of hypnotic susceptibility on creativity test performance. *Journal of Personality and Social Psychology, 14*, 247–256.

Boynton, T. (2001). Applied research using alpha/theta training for enhancing creativity and well-being. *Journal of Neurotherapy, 5*, 5–18.

Brady, C., & Morris, R. L. (1997). Attention focusing facilitated through remote mental interaction: A replication and exploration of parameters. *The Parapsychological Association 40th Annual Convention. Proceedings of Presented Papers* (pp. 73–91). Durham, NC: The Parapsychological Association.

Bradbury, D. A., Stirling, J., Cavill, J., & Parker, A. (2009). Psychosis-like experiences in the general population: An exploratory factor analysis. *Personality and Individual Differences, 46*, 729–734.

Braid, J. (1846/1970). The power of the mind over the body. In M. M.Tintero, *Foundations of hypnosis: From Mesmer to Freud*. Springfield, IL: Thomas.

Braud, W. G. (1990). Meditation and psychokinesis. *Parapsychology Review, 21*, 9–11.

Braud, W. G., & Hartgrove, J. (1976). Clairvoyance and psychokinesis in trascendental meditators and matched control subjects: A preliminary study. *European Journal of Parapsychology, 1*, 6–16.

Braud, W. G., & Schlitz, M. J. (1989). A methodology for objective study of transpersonal imagery. *Journal of Scientific Exploration, 3*, 43–63.

Braud, W. G., & Schlitz, M. J. (1991). Conscious interactions with remote biological systems: Anomalous intentionality effects. *Subtle Energies, 2*, 1–46.

Braud, W. G., Shafer, D., McNeill, K., & Guerra, V. (1995). Attention focusing facilitated through remote mental interaction. *Journal of the American Society for Psychical Research, 89*, 103–115.

Braude, S. (2000). Dissociation and latent abilities: The strange case of Patience Worth. *Journal of Trauma and Dissociation, 1*, 13–48.

Braude, S. E. (2002). The problem of superpsi. In F. Steinkamp (Ed.), *Parapsychology, philosophy and the mind: Essays honoring John Beloff* (pp. 91–111). Jefferson, NC: McFarland

Braun, B. G. (1986). Issues in the psychotherapy of multiple personality disorder. In B. G. Braun (Ed.), *Treatment of multiple personality disorder* (pp. 1–28). Washington, DC: American Psychiatric Press.

Braunstein-Bercovitz (2000). Is the attentional dysfunction in schizotypy related to anxiety? *Schizophrenia Research, 46*, 255–267

Breen, R., Devine, P., & Robinson, G. (Eds.). (1995). *Social attitudes in Northern Ireland: The fourth report (1994–1995)*. Belfast: Appletree Press.

Brefczynski-Lewis, J. A., Lutz, A., Schaefer, H. S., Levinson, D. B., & Davidson, R. J. (2007). Neural correlates of attentional expertise in long-term meditation practicioners. *Proceedings of the National Academy of Science, 104*, 11483–11488.

Brett, C. M. C., Peters, E. P., Johns, L. C., Tabraham, P., Valmaggia, L. R., & Mcguire, P. K. (2007). Appraisals of Anomalous Experiences Interview (AANEX): A multidimensional measure of psychological responses to anomalies associated with psychosis. *The British Journal of Psychiatry, 191*, 23–30.

Brod, J. H. (1997). Creativity and schizotypy. In G. Claridge (Ed.), *Schizotypy: Implications for illness and health* (pp. 274–298). New York: Oxford University Press.

Brodsky, S., Esquerre, J., & Jackson, R. (1990–91). Dream consciousness in problem solving. *Imagination, Cognition and Personality, 10*, 353–360.

Broks, P., Claridge, G., Matheson, J., & Hargreaves, J. (1984). Schizotypy and hemispheric function: IV story comprehension under binaural and monoaural listening conditions. *Personality and Individual Differences, 5*, 649–656.

Brown, J. (2008). The inward path: Mysticism and creativity. *Creativity Research Journal, 20*, 365–375.

Brugger, P., Gamma, A., Muri, R., & Schafer,

M. (1993). Functional hemispheric asymmetry and belief in ESP: Towards a "neuropsychology of belief." *Perceptual and Motor Skills*, 77, 1299–1308.

Brugger, P., & Graves, R. E. (1997). Right hemispatial inattention and magical ideation. *European Archives of Psychiatry and Clinical Neuroscience*, 247, 55–57.

Brugger, P., Regard, M., Landis, T., Cook, N., Krebs, D., & Niederberger, J. (1993). "Meaningful" patterns in visual noise, effects of lateral stimulation and the observer's belief in ESP. *Psychopathology*, 26, 261–265.

Bullen, J. G., Hemsley, D. R., & Dixon, N. F. (1987). Inhibition, unusual perceptual experiences and psychoticism. *Personality and Individual Differences*, 8, 687–691.

Burch, G., Pavelis, C., Hemsley, D., & Corr, P. (2006). Schizotypy and creativity in visual artists. *British Journal of Psychology*, 97, 177–190.

Burton, A. (2009). Bringing arts-based therapies in from the scientific cold. *The Lancet Neurology*, 8, 784–785.

Buysse, D. J., Reynolds, C. F., III, Monk, T. H., Berman, S. R., & Kupfer, D. J. (1989). The Pittsburgh Sleep Quality Index: A new instrument for psychiatric practice and research. *Psychiatry Research*, 28, 193–213.

Cairns, E., & Wilson, R. (1989). Mental health aspects of political violence in Northern Ireland. *International Journal of Mental Health*, 18, 38–56.

Cairns, E., Wilson, R. Gallagher, T., & Trew, K. (1995). Psychology's contribution to understanding conflict in Northern Ireland. *Peace and Conflict: Journal of Peace Psychology*, 1 (2), 131–148.

Callahan, R. (2001). The impact of Thought Field Therapy on heart rate variability. *Journal of Clinical Psychology*, 57 (10), 1153–1170.

Callahan, R., & Trubo, R. (2002). *Tapping the healer within*. New York: McGraw-Hill.

Callaway, J. C. (1988). A proposed mechanism for the visions of dream sleep. *Medical Hypotheses*, 26, 119–24.

Callaway J. (1995). Pharmahuasca and contemporary ethnopharmacology. *Curare*, 18, 395–398.

Camic, P. (2008). Playing in the mud: Health psychology, the arts and creative approaches to health care. *Journal of Health Psychology*, 13, 287–298.

Candel, I., Merckelback, H., & Kuijpers, M. (2003). Dissociative experiences are related to communications in emotional memory. *Behaviour Research and Therapy*, 41, 719–725.

Canter, M. B., Bennet, B. E., Jones, S. E., & Nagy, T. E. (1994). *Ethics for psychologists: A commentary on the APA Ethics Code*. Washington, D. C.: American Psychological Association.

Cardeña, E., Lynn, S., & Krippner, S. (2000). Anomalous experiences in perspective. In E. Cardeña, S. Lynn, & S. Krippner (Eds.), *Varieties of anomalous experience: Examining the scientific evidence* (pp. 3–21). Washington, DC: American Psychological Association.

Cardeña, E., & Spiegel, D. (1993). Dissociative reactions to the San Francisco Bay area earthquake of 1989. *American Journal of Psychiatry*, 150, 474–478.

Cardoso, R., de Souza, E., Camano, L., & Leite, J. R. (2004). Meditation in health: An operational definition. *Brain Research Protocols*, 14, 58–60.

Carlozzi, A., Bull, K., Eell, G., & Hurlburt, J. (1995). Empathy as related to creativity, dogmatism, and expressiveness. *Journal of Psychology*, 129, 365–372.

Carlsson, I., Wendt, P., & Risberg, J. (2000). On the neurobiology of creativity: Differences in frontal activity between highly and low creative subjects. *Neuropsychologia*, 38, 873–855.

Carney, O., Ross, E., Bunker, C., Ikkos, G., & Mindel, A. (1994). A prospective study of the psychological impact on patients with a first episode of genital herpes. *Genitourinary Medicine*, 70, 40–45.

Carson, S., Peterson, J., & Higgins, D. (2005). Reliability, validity and factor structure of the Creative Achievement Questionnaire. *Creativity Research Journal*, 17, 37–50.

Caspar, F. (1995). Plan analysis. Toward optimizing psychotherapy. Seattle: Hogrefe-Huber.

Caspar, F. (2007). *Beziehungen und probleme verstehen. Eine einführung in die psychotherapeutische plananalyse*. Bern: Huber.

Caspar, F. (2007). Plan analysis. In T. Eells (Hrsg.), Handbook of psychotherapeutic case formulations (2d ed.) (pp. 251–289). New York: Guilford.

Catalan, J., & Burgess, A. (1995). *Psychological*

medicine of HIV infection. Oxford: Oxford Medical Publications.

Chadwick, P. D. J. (2006). *Person-based cognitive therapy for distressing psychosis*. Chichester: John Wiley & Sons.

Chadwick, P. D. J., Newman-Taylor, K., & Abba, N. (2005). Mindfulness groups for people with distressing psychosis. *Behavioral and Cognitive Psychotherapy, 33*, 351–360.

Chambers, R., Gullone, E., & Allen, N. B. (2009). Mindful emotion regulation: An integrative review. *Clinical Psychology Review, 29*, 560–572.

Chapman, L. J., Chapman, J. P., Kwapil, T. R., Eckblad, M., & Zinser, M. (1994). Putatively psychosis-prone subjects 10 years later. *Journal of Abnormal Psychology, 103*, 171–183.

Chapman, L. J., Chapman, J. P., & Raulin, M. L. (1978). Body-image aberration and social anhedonia. *Journal of Abnormal Psychology, 87*, 399–407.

Christensen, B., & Schunn, C. (2005). Spontaneous access and analogical incubation effects. *Creativity Research Journal, 17*, 207–220.

Cikurel, K., & Gruzelier, J. (1990). The effect of an active-alert hypnotic induction on lateral asymmetry in haptic processing. *British Journal of Experimental and Clinical Hypnosis, 7*, 17–25.

Claridge, G.S.(1985). *Origins of Mental Illness*. Oxford: Basil Blackwell.

Claridge, G.S (1993). When is psychoticism psychoticism? And how does it really relate to creativity? *Psychological Bulletin, 4*, 184–188.

Claridge, G.S (Ed.). (1997). *Schizotypy: Implications for illness and health*. Oxford: Oxford University Press.

Claridge, G.S. (1998). Creativity and madness. In A. Steptoe (Ed.), *Genius and the mind: Studies of creativity and temperament* (pp. 227–250). Oxford: Oxford University Press.

Claridge, G.S.(2001). Spiritual experience: Healthy psychoticism? In I. Clarke (Ed.), *Psychosis and spirituality: Exploring the new frontier* (pp. 90–106). Philadelphia, PA: Whurr Publishers.

Claridge, G.S., & Beech, T. (1995). Fully and quasi-dimensional constructions of schizotypy. In A. Raine, T. Lencz, & S. A. Med-

nick (Eds.), *Schizotypal personality* (pp. 192–216). Cambridge: Cambridge University Press.

Claridge, G.S., & Blakey, S. (2009). Schizotypy and affective temperament: Relationships with divergent thinking and creativity styles. *Personality and Individual Differences, 46*, 820–826.

Claridge, G. S., Clark, K. H., & Beech, A. R. (1992). Lateralization of the "negative priming" effect: Relationships with schizotypy and with gender. *British Journal of Psychology, 83*, 13–23.

Claridge, G.S, & Davis, C. (2003). *Personality and psychological disorders*. London: Arnold.

Claridge, G.S, & McDonald, A. (2009). An investigation into the relationships between convergent and divergent thinking, schizotypy and autistic traits. *Personality and Individual Differences, 46*, 794, 799.

Claridge, G.S., Pryor, R., & Watkins, G. (1998). *Sounds from the bell jar: Ten psychotic authors*. Cambridge, MA: Malor Books.

Clarke, C. (Ed.). (2005). *Ways of knowing: Science and mysticism today*. Charlottesville, VA: Imprint Academic.

Clarke, I. (2000). Psychosis and spirituality: Finding a language. *Changes, 18*, 208–214.

Clarke, I. (Ed.). (2001). *Psychosis and spirituality: Exploring the new frontier*. London: Whurr.

Clarke, I. (2002). Case experience from a rehabilitation service. In D. Kingdon, & D. Turkington (Eds.), *The case study guide to cognitive behavior therapy of psychosis*. Chichester: John Wiley and Sons.

Clarke, I. (2008). *Madness, mystery and the survival of God*. Winchester: O Books.

Cloninger, C. R., Svrakic, D. M., & Przybeck, T. R. (1993). A psychobiological model of temperament and character. *Archives of General Psychiatry, 50*, 975–990.

Coelho, C., Tierney, I., & Lamont, P. (2008). Contacts by distressed individuals to UK parapsychology and anomalous experience academic research units—A retrospective survey looking to the future. *European Journal of Parapsychology, 23.1*, 31–59.

Cohen, S., Kamarck, T., & Mermelstein, R. (1983). A global measure of perceived stress. *Journal of Health and Social Behavior, 24*, 385–96.

Cole, S. W., Kemeny, M. E., Fahey, J. L., Zack, J. A., & Naliboff, B. D. (2003). Psychological risk factors for HIV pathogenesis: Mediation by the autonomic nervous system. *Biological Psychiatry, 54*, 1444–1456.

Colquhoun, D. (2007). *DC's improbable science.* Available online at: http://www.dcscience.net/[Accessed 4 February 2010]

Coly, L., & McMahon, J. D. S. (Eds.). (1993). *Psi and clinical practice.* New York, NY: Parapsychology Foundation.

Cortoos, A., DeValck, E., Arns, M., Breteler, M. H., & Cluydts, R. (2009). An exploratory study on the effects of tele-neurofeedback and tele-biofeedback on objective and subjective sleep in patients with primary insomnia. *Journal of Applied Psychophysiology and Biofeedback, 30*, 1–10.

Costa, P. T., Jr., & McCrae, R. R. (1992). *NEO PI-R professional manual.* Odessa, FL: Psychological Assessment Resources Inc.

Costa, P., & McCrae, R. (1992). *Professional manual: Revised NEO personality inventory (NEO PI-R) and NEO five-factor inventory (FFI).* Odessa, FL: Psychological Assessment Resources, Inc.

Council, J., Bromley, K., Zabelina, D., & Waters, C. (2007). Hypnotic enhancement of creative drawing. *International Journal of Clinical Experimental Hypnosis, 55*, 467–85.

Crawford, H. J. (1989). Cognitive and physiological flexibility: Multiple pathways to hypnotic responsiveness. In V. Ghorghui, P. Netter, H. Eysenck, & R. Rosenthal (Eds.), *Suggestion and suggestibility: Theory and research* (pp. 155–168). Berlin: Springer-Verlag.

Crawford, H. J. (1994). Brain dynamics and hypnosis: Attentional and disattentional processes. *International Journal of Clinical and Experimental Hypnosis, 102*, 204–232.

Crawford, H. J., & Allen, S. N. (1983). Enhanced visual memory during hypnosis as mediated by hypnotic responsiveness and cognitive strategies. *Journal of Experimental Psychology: General, 112*, 662–685.

Crawford, H. J., & Gruzelier, J. (1992). A midstream view of the neuropsychophysiology of hypnosis: Recent research and future directions. In W. Fromm & M. Nash (Eds.), *Hypnosis: Research Developments and Perspectives*, 3d ed. (pp. 227–266). New York: Guildford Press.

Crawley, S., French, C., & Yesson, S. (2002). Evidence for transliminality from a subliminal card-guessing task. *Perception, 31*, 887–892.

Cropley, A. (2006). In praise of convergent thinking. *Creativity Research Journal, 18*, 391–404.

Csikszentmihalyi, M. (1992). *Flow: The psychology of happiness.* London: Ryder.

Csikszentmihalyi, M. (1996). *Creativity: Flow and the psychology of discovery and invention.* New York: HarperCollins.

Csikszentmihalyi, M., & Larson, R. (1984). *Being adolescent: Conflict and growth in the teenage years.* New York: Basic Books.

Csordas, T. J. (1988). Elements of charismatic persuasion and healing. *Medical Anthropology Quarterly, 2* (2), 121–142.

Csordas, T. J. (1993). Somatic modes of attention. *Cultural Anthropology, 8* (2), 135–156.

Csordas, T. J. (1997). *The sacred self. A cultural phenomenology of charismatic healing.* Berkeley: University of California Press.

Csordas, T. J. (2008). Intersubjectivity and intercorporeality. *Subjectivity, 22*, 110–121.

Curran, P. S., & Miller, P. W. (2001). Psychiatric implications of chronic civilian strife or war: Northern Ireland. *Advances in Psychiatric Treatment, 7*, 73–80.

Dagnall, N., & Parker, A. (2009). Schizotypy and false memory. *Journal of Behavior Therapy and Experimental Psychiatry, 40*, 179–188.

Dalal, F. (1998). *Taking the group seriously: Towards a post-Foulkesian group analytic theory.* London: Jessica Kinglsey.

Damasio, A. (2000). *The feeling of what happens: Body, emotion and the making of consciousness.* London: Vintage.

Daniels, M. (2005). *Shadow, spirit, self: Essays in transpersonal psychology.* Charlottesville, VA: Imprint Academic.

Darbellay, G. A. (1999). An estimator for the mutual information based on a criterion for independence. *Computational Statistics and Data Analysis, 32*, 1–17.

Davis, M. (2009). Understanding the relationship between mood and creativity: A meta-analysis. *Organizational Behavior and Human Decision Processes, 108*, 25–38.

Davie, G. (1994). *Religion in Britain since 1945.* London: Blackwell.

Day, S., & Peters, E. (1999). The incidence of schizotypy in new religious movements. *Personality and Individual Differences, 27*, 55–67.

De Alverga, A. P. (2000). *Forest of visions: Ayahuasca, Amazonian spirituality, and the Santo Daime tradition* (S. Larsen, Ed., R. Workman, Trans.). Rochester, VT: Part Street Press.

De Graaf, T. K., & Houtkooper, J. (2004). Anticipatory awareness of emotionally charged targets by individuals with histories of emotional trauma. *Journal of Parapsychology, 68*, 93–127.

de la Fuente-Fernandez, R., Ruth, T. J., Sossi, V., Schulzer, V., Calne, D. B., & Stoessl, A. J. (2001). Expectation and dopamine release: Mechanism of the placebo effect in parkinson's disease. *Science, 293*, 1164–1166.

de Wolf, F., Spijkerman, I., Schellekens, P., Langendam, M., Kuiken, C., Bakker, M., Roos, M., Coutinho, R., Miedema, F., & Goudsmit, J. (1997). AIDS prognosis based on HIV-1 RNA, CD4+ T-cell count and function: Markers with reciprocal predictive value over time after seroconversion. *Aids, 11*, 1799–1806.

DeYoung, C. G, Peterson, J. B., & Higgins, D. M. (2005). Sources of openness/intellect: Cognitive and neuropsychological correlates of the fifth factor of personality. *Journal of Personality, 73*, 825–858.

Deere, J. (1993). *Surprised by the power of the spirit.* Grand Rapids, MI: Zondervan.

Deere, J. (1996). *Surprised by the voice of God.* Grand rapids, MI: Zondervan.

Dehon, H., Bastin, C., & Larøi, F. (2008). The influence of delusional ideation and dissociative experiences on the resistance to false memories in normal healthy subjects. *Personality and Individual Differences, 45*, 62–67.

Demerath, N. J., III. (2000). Changes, troubles, and the rise of 'cultural religion' in European Christendom, *Social Compass, 49.*

Dennis, M., & Philippus, M. J. (1965). Hypnotic and non-hypnotic suggestion and skin response in atopic patients. *American Journal of Clinical Hypnosis, 7*, 342–345.

Devereux, P. (2008). *The long trip: A prehistory of psychedelia* (2nd ed.). Brisbane: Daily Grail Publishing.

Di Padova, F., Pozzi, C., Tondre, M. J., & Tritapepe, R. (1991). Selective and early increase of IL-1 inhibitors, IL-6 and cortisol after elective surgery. *Clinical and Experimental Immunology, 85*, 137–42.

Diagnostic and statistical manual of mental disorders DSM-IV. (1994). Washington, DC: American Psychiatric Association.

Diagnostic and statistical manual of mental disorders DSM-IV-TR. (2000). Washington, DC: American Psychiatric Association.

Dick-Read, G. (1959). *Childbirth without fear.* New York: Harper.

Dietrich, A. (2003). Functional neuroanatomy of altered states of consciousness: The transient hypofrontality hypothesis. *Consciousness and Cognition, 12*, 231–256.

Dietrich, A. (2004a). The cognitive neuroscience of creativity. *Psychonomic Bulletin and Review, 11*, 1011–1026.

Dietrich, A. (2004b). Neurocognitive mechanisms underlying the experience of flow. *Consciousness and Cognition, 13*, 746–761.

Dijksterhuis, A., & Meurs, T. (2006). Where creativity resides: The generative power of unconscious thought. *Consciousness and Cognition, 15*, 135–146.

Dimond, S., & Beaumont, J. (1974). *Hemisphere function in the human brain.* London: Elek Science.

Dobkin de Rios, M. (1972). *Visionary vine: Hallucinogenic healing in the Peruvian Amazon.* Prospect Heights, IL: Waveland Press.

Dobkin de Rios, M. (1990). *Hallucinogens: Cross-cultural perspectives.* Bridport, UK: Prism.

Dobkin de Rios, M., & Rumrill, R. (2008). *A hallucinogenic tea, laced with controversy: Ayahuasca in the Amazon and the United States.* Westport, CT: Praeger.

Doblin, R. (1991). Pahnke's Good Friday experiment: A long-term follow-up and methodological critique. *Journal of Transpersonal Psychology, 23*, 1–28.

Dodds, R., Ward. T., & Smith, S. (2003). Review of experimental literature on incubation in problem solving and creativity. In M. A. Runco (Ed.), *Creativity research handbook*, vol. 3. Cresskill, NJ: Hampton Press.

Domino, G. (1976). Primary process thinking in dream reports as related to creative achievement. *Journal of Counselling and Clinical Psychology, 44*, 929–932.

Dopp, J. M., Miller, G. E., Myers, H. F., & Fahey, J. L. (2000). Increased natural killer-cell mobilization and cytotoxicity during marital conflict. *Brain, Behavior and Immunity, 14*, 10–26.

Dorahy, M. J., & Lewis, C. A. (1998). Trauma induced dissociation and the psychological effects of the "Troubles" in Northern Ireland: An overview and integration. *Irish Journal of Psychology, 19,* 332–344.

Dronfield, J. (1996). The vision thing: Diagnosis of endogenous derivation in abstract arts. *Current Anthropology, 37,* 373–391.

Dunn, B. R., Hartigan, J. A., & Mikulas, W. L. (1999). Concentration and mindfulness meditations: Unique forms of consciousness? *Applied Psychophysiology & Biofeedback, 24,* 147–165.

Dunne, B. J., & Jahn, R. G. (2003). Information and uncertainty in remote perception research. *Journal of Scientific Exploration, 17,* 207–41.

Dykes, M., & McGhie, A. (1976). A comparative study of attentional strategies of schizophrenic and highly creative normal subjects. *British Journal of Psychiatry, 128,* 506.

Eckblad, M., & Chapman, L. J. (1983). Magical ideation as an indicator of schizotypy. *Journal of Consulting and Clinical Psychology, 51,* 215–225.

Edelman, S., Craig, A., & Kidman, A. D. (2000). Can psychotherapy increase the survival time of cancer patients? *Journal of Psychosomatic Research, 49,* 149–156.

Edge, L. (2001). The spectrum of dissociation: From pathology to self-realisation. *The Journal of Transpersonal Psychology, 33,* 53–63.

Edge, J., & Lancaster, L. (2004). Enhancing musical performance through neurofeedback: Playing the tune of life. *Transpersonal Review, 8,* 23–35.

Edge, H., Suryani, L. K., & Morris, R. L. (2007). *Pursuing psi in a non-EuroAmerican culture: Behavioral DMILS in Bali.* Bial Grant 127/02. (Unpublished).

Edge, H., Suryani, L. K., Tiliopoulos, N., Bikker, A., & James, R. (2008). *Comparing conscious and physiological measurements in a cognitive DMILS study in Bali.* Bial Grant 116–04. (Unpublished).

Edge, H., Suryani, L. K., Tiliopoulos, N., & Morris, R. (2004). Two cognitive DMILS studies in Bali. *Journal of Parapsychology, 68,* 289–321.

Edwards, A. G., Hailey, S., & Maxwell, M. (2004). Review: Existing evidence does not support a survival benefit for women with metastatic breast cancer who participate in group psychological interventions compared with usual care. *Cochrane Database Systematic Reviews,* cd004253.

Edwards, S. E. (2008). Breath psychology: Fundamentals and applications. *Psychology and Developing Societies, 20,* 131–164.

Egner, T., & Gruzelier , J. (2003). Ecological validity of neurofeedback: Modulation of slow wave EEG enhances musical performance. *Neuroreport: For Rapid Communication of Neuroscience Research, 14, 1221–1224.*

Egner, T., & Gruzelier, J. H. (2001). Learned self-regulation of EEG frequency components affects attention and event-related brain potentials in humans. *NeuroReport, 12,* 411–415.

Egner, T., & Gruzelier, J. H. (2004). EEG biofeedback of low beta band components: Frequency-specific effects on variables of attention and event-related brain potentials. *Clinical Neurophysiology, 115,* 131–139.

Egner, T., Jamieson, G., & Gruzelier, J. H. (2005). Hypnosis decouples cognitive control from conflict monitoring processes of the frontal lobe. *NeuroImage, 27,* 969–978.

Egner, T., Strawson, E., & Gruzelier, J. H. (2002). EEG signature and phenomenology of alpha/theta neurofeedback training versus mock feedback. *Applied Psychophysiology and Biofeedback, 27,* 261–270.

Eisendrath, S. J., Delucchi, K., Bitner, R., Fenimore, P., Smit, M., & McLane, M. (2008). Mindfulness-based cognitive therapy for treatment-resistant depression: A pilot study. *Psychotherapy and Psychosomatics, 77,* 319–320.

Elbert, T., Ray, W. J., Kowalik, Z., Skinner, J. E., Graf, E., & Birbaumer, N. (1994). Chaos and physiology: Deterministic chaos in excitable cell assemblies. *Physiological Reviews, 74,* 1–47.

Eliade, M. (1972). *Shamanism: Archaic techniques of ecstasy.* Princeton, NJ: Princeton University Press. (Originally published in French in 1951).

Elliot, R., & Shapiro, D. A. (1988). Brief structured recall: A more efficient method for studying significant therapy events. *British Journal of Medical Psychology, 61,* 141–153.

Ellis, A. (1980). Psychotherapy and atheistic values: A response to A. E. Bergin's "Psychotherapy and religious values." *Journal of Consulting and Clinical Psychology, 48,* 635–639.

Ernst, E. (2007). Commentary on Bishop: The fascination of complementary and alternative medicine (CAM). *Journal of Health Psychology*, 12, 868–870.

Ernst, E., & White, A. (2000). The BBC survey of complementary medicine use in the UK. *Complementary Therapies in Medicine*, 8, 32–36.

Evans, F. J. (1991). Hypnotizability: Individual differences in dissociation and the flexible control of psychological processes. In: S. J. Lynn & J. W. Rhue (Eds.), *Theories of Hypnosis* (pp. 144–168). London: Guildford Press.

Evans, L. H., Gray, N. S., & Snowden, R. J. (2007). Reduced P50 suppression is associated with the cognitive disorganization dimension of schizotypy. *Schizophrenia Research*, 97, 152–162.

Evans, F. J., & Graham, C. (1980). Subjective random number generation and attention deployment during acquisition and over learning of a motor skill. *Bulletin of the Psychonomic Society*, 15, 391–394.

Evans, P., Hucklebridge, F., & Clow, A. (2000). *Mind, immunity and health: The science of psychoneuroimmunology.* London: Free Associations Books.

Eysenck, H. (1993). Creativity and personality: Suggestions for a theory. *Psychological Inquiry*, 4, 147–178.

Eysenck, H. (1996). The measurement of creativity. In M. Boden (Ed.), *Dimensions of creativity* (pp. 199–242). Cambridge, MA: MIT Press.

Fach, W. (2006). Formenkreise aussergewöhnlicher erfahrungen. In D. Vaitl (Hrsg.), *Tätigkeitsbericht 2004–2005*, 50–51. Freiburg: Institut für Grenzgebiete der Psychologie und Psychohygiene e.V.

Fach, W. (2007).*A psychophysical approach to extraordinary experiences.* Paper presented at the 1st International Expert-Meeting on Clinical Parapsychology, The Netherlands, May 31–June 3, 2007.

Feifel, H. (1974). Religious conviction and fear of death among the healthy and the terminally ill. *Journal for the Scientific Study of Religion*, 13, 353–360.

Finlay, L. (2005). Reflexive embodied empathy: A phenomenology of participant-researcher intersubjectivity, *Methods Issue: The Humanistic Psychologist*, 33, 4, 271–292.

Fonagy, P. (2003). The development of psychopathology from infancy to adulthood: The mysterious unfolding of disturbance in time. *Infant Mental Health Journal*, 24, 212–239.

Fontana, D. (2003). *Psychology, religion, and spirituality.* Oxford: Blackwell Publishing.

Fowler, D. G. (2000). Psychological formulation of early psychosis: A cognitive model. In M. Birchwood, D. Fowler & C. Jackson (Eds.), *Early intervention in psychosis: A guide to concepts, evidence and interventions.* Chichester: John Wiley and Sons.

Fox, P. A., Henderson, P. C., Barton, S. E., Champion, A. J., Rollin, M. S. H., Catalan, J., McCormack, S. M. G., & Gruzelier, J. H. (1999). Immunological markers of frequently recurrent genital herpes simplex virus and their response to hypnotherapy: a pilot study. *International Journal of STD & AIDS*, 10, 730–734.

Freemantle, B., & Clarke, I. (2008). Making sense of psychosis in crisis. In I. Clarke, & H. Wilson (Eds.), *Cognitive behavior therapy for acute inpatient mental health units: Working with clients, staff and the milieu.* London: Routledge.

Freud, S. (1907). *Obsessive actions and religious experience.* London: Hogarth Press (in Vols. 4–5 of the Collected Works).

Freud, S. (1923). *The Ego and the id.* London: Hogarth Press (in Vol. 19 of the Collected Works).

Freud, S. (1927). *Future of an illusion.* London: Hogarth Press (in Vol. 21 of the Collected Works).

Freud, S. (1930). *Civilisation and its discontents.* London: Hogarth Press (in Vol. 21 of the Collected Works).

Frith, C. D. (1992). *The cognitive neuropsychology of schizophrenia.* Hove: LEA.

Fröhlich, H. (1978). Coherent electric vibrations in biological systems and the cancer problem. *IEEE Transaction on Microwave Theory and Techniques MTT*, 26, 613–617.

Fry, L., Mason, A. A., & Pearson, R. S. B. (1964). Effect of hypnosis on allergic skin responses in asthma and hay-fever. *British Medical Journal*, 1, 1145–1148.

Furnham, A., & Steele, H. (1993). Measuring locus of control: A critique of general, children's, health and work-related locus of control questionnaires. *British Journal of Psychology* 84, 443–480.

Gaens, T., Sagaert, S., & Vandermeulen, D. (1991). Non-rigid registration using mutual information. In T. M. Cover & J. A. Thomas, *Elements of information theory*. New York: John Wiley & Sons.

Gallese, V., & Lakoff, G. (2005). The brain's concepts: The role of the sensory-motor system in conceptual knowledge. *Cognitive Neuropsychology*, *22*, 3–4, 455–47.

Gallese, V. (2006). Mirror neurons and intentional attunement: commentary on Olds. *Journal of the American Psychoanalytic Association*, *54*, 47–57.

Gardner, H. (1993). *Creating minds: An anatomy of creativity seen through the lives of Freud, Einstein, Picasso, Stravinsky, Eliot, Graham and Gandhi*. New York: Basic-Books.

Garety, P. A., Kuipers, E., Fowler, D., Freeman, D., & Bebbington, P. E. (2001). A cognitive model of the positive symptoms of psychosis. *Psychological Medicine*, *31*, 189–195.

Garza, G. (2007). Varieties of phenomenological research at the university of dallas: An emerging typology. *Qualitative Research in Psychology*, *4*, 313–342.

Geake, J. (2005). Neural correlates of intelligence as revealed by fMRI of fluid analogies. *Neuroimage*, *26*, 555–564.

Genovese, J. E. C. (2005). Paranormal beliefs, schizotypy, and thinking styles among teachers and future teachers. *Personality and Individual Differences*, *39*, 93–102.

George, L. K., Larsons, D. B., Koenig, H. G., & McCullough, M. E. (2000). Spirituality and health: What we know, what we need to know? *Journal of Social and Clinical Psychology*, *19*, 102–116.

Gershuny, B. S., & Thayer, J. F. (1999). Relations among psychological trauma, dissociative phenomena and trauma-related distress: A review and integration. *Clinical Psychology Review*, *19*, 631–657.

Geschwind, N., & Behan, P. (1984). Laterality, hormones and immunity. In N. Geschwind & N. Galaburda (Eds). *Cerebral dominance*. Cambridge, MA: Harvard University Press.

Geschwind, N., & Galaburda, A. M. (1985). Cerebral lateralisation: Biological mechanisms, associations and pathology: I. A hypothesis and a program for research. *Archives of Neurology*, *42*, 428–459.

Getz, I., & Lubart, T. (1999). The emotional resonance model of creativity: Theoretical and practical extensions. In S. Russ (Ed.), *Affect, creative experience and psychological adjustment* (pp. 41–56). Philadelphia, PA: Brunner/Mazel.

Getzels, J., & Csikszentmihalyi, M. (1976). *The creative vision: A longitudinal study of problem finding in art*. New York: John Wiley & Sons.

Gianotti, L., Mohr, C., Pizzagalli, D., Lehmann, D., & Brugger, P. (2001). Associative processing and paranormal belief. *Psychiatry and Cognitive Neurosciences*, *55*, 595–603.

Gilbert, P. (1992). *Depression: The evolution of powerlessness*. New York: Guildford Press.

Giles, M., & Cairns, E. (1989). Colour naming of violence related words in Northern Ireland. *British Journal of Clinical Psychology*, *28*, 87–88.

Gill Taylor, A., Goehler, L. E., Galper, D. I., Innes, K. E., & Bourguignon, C. (2010). Top-down and bottom-up mechanisms in mind-body medicine: Development of an integrative framework for psychophysiological research. *Explore: The Journal of Science and Healing*, *6*, 29–41.

Gissurarson, L. R. (1992). Methods of enhancing PK task performance. In: S. Krippner (Ed.), *Advances in parapsychological research 5* (pp. 89–125). Jefferson, NC: McFarland.

Glicksohn, J. (1990). Belief in the paranormal and subjective paranormal experience. *Personality and Individual Differences*, *11*, 675–683.

Glisky, M. L., Tataryn, D. J., Tobias, B. A., Kihlstrom, J. F., & McConkey, K. M. (1991). Absorption, openness to experience, and hypnotizability. *Journal of Personality and Social Psychology*, *60*, 263–272.

Gohm, C., & Clore, G. (2002). Four latent traits of emotional experience and their involvement in well-being, coping, and attributional style. *Cognition and Emotion*, *16*, 495–518.

Goldmeier, D., & Johnson. A. (1982). Does psychiatric illness affect the recurrence rate of genital herpes? *British Journal of Venereal Disease*, *58*, 40–43.

Goretzki, M. (2007). *The differentiation of psychosis and spiritual emergency*. Unpublished Dissertation: University of Adelaide.

Gorsuch, R. L., & Venable, G. D. (1983). Development of an "Age Universal" I-E Scale. *Journal for the Scientific Study of Religion, 22,* 181–187.

Gough, H. (1979). A creative personality scale for the adjective check list. *Journal of Personality and Social Psychology, 37,* 1398–1405.

Gough, H. (1993). The assessment piece of the creativity pie. *Psychological Inquiry, 4,* 196–200.

Gould, S. J. (1991). The self-manipulation of my pervasive, perceived vital energy through product use: An introspective-praxis perspective. *Journal of Consumer Research, 18,* 194–207.

Goulding, A. (2004). *Mental health aspects of paranormal and psi related experiences.* Unpublished Dissertation: Göteborg University.

Goulding, A. (2004). Schizotypy models in relation to subjective health and paranormal beliefs and experiences. *Personality and Individual Differences, 37,* 157–167.

Goulding, A. (2005). Healthy schizotypy in a population of paranormal believers and experients. *Personality and Individual Differences, 38,* 1069–1083.

Goulding, A., & Ödéhn, N. (2009). Schizotypy and mental health in the general population: A pilot study. *Personality and Mental Health, 3,* 193–202.

Grawe, K. (2004). *Psychological therapy.* Seattle: Hogrefe.

Grawe, K., Caspar, F., & Ambühl, H. R. (1990). Differentielle psychotherapieforschung: Vier therapieformen im vergleich: Die berner therapievergleichsstudie. *Zeitschrift für Klinische Psychologie, 19,* 294–376.

Gray, J. A., Feldon, J., Rawlins, J. N. P., Hemsley, D. R., & Smith, A. D. (1991). The neuropsychology of schizophrenia. *Behavioral and Brain Sciences, 14,* 1–20.

Gray, N., Fernandez, M., Williams, J., Ruddle, R., & Snowden, R. (2002). Which schizotypal dimensions abolish latent inhibition. *British Journal of Clinical Psychology, 41,* 271–284.Greely, A. (1975). *The sociology of the paranormal: A reconnaissance.* Beverly Hills, CA: Sage Publications.

Green, M., & Williams, L. (1999). Schizotypy and creativity as effects of reduced cognitive inhibition. *Personality and Individual Differences, 27,* 262–276.

Green, E., & Green, A. (1977). *Beyond biofeedback.* New York: Delta.

Green, J., & Kocsis, A. (1997). Psychological factors in recurrent genital herpes. *Genitourinary Medicine, 73,* 253–258.

Greer, S. (1983). Cancer and the mind. *British Journal of Psychiatry, 143,* 535.

Gregerson, M., Roberts, I., & Amiri, M. (1996). Absorption and imagery locate immune responses in the body. *Biofeedback and Self Regulation, 21,* 149–165.

Greyson, B. (1977). Telepathy in mental illness: Deluge or delusion? *Journal of Nervous and Mental Disease, 165* (3), 184–200.

Griffin, M., & McDermott, D. (1998). Exploring a tripartite relationship between rebelliousness, openness to experience and creativity. *Social Behavior and Personality, 26,* 347–356.

Griffiths, R. R., Richards, W. A., McCann, U., & Jesse, R. (2006). Psilocybin can occasion mystical-type experiences having substantial, sustained personal meaning and spiritual significance. *Psychopharmacology, 187,* 268–283.

Griffiths, R. R., Richards, W. A., Johnson, H. W., McCann, U., & Jesse, R. (2008). Mystical-type experiences occasioned by psilocybin mediate the attribution of personal meaning and spiritual significance 14 months later. *Psychopharmacology, 22,* 621–632.

Grimby, A. (1993). Bereavement among elderly people: Grief reactions, post-bereavement hallucinations and quality of life. *Acta Psychiatrica Scandinavia, 87,* 72–80.

Grinspoon, L., & Bakalar, J. B. (1998). *Psychedelic drugs reconsidered* (2nd ed.). New York: The Lindesmith Centre.

Grof, C., & Grof, S. (1991). *The stormy search for the self.* London: Mandala.

Grof, S. (1988). *The adventure of self-discovery.* Albany, NY: State University of New York Press.

Grof, S. (2001). *LSD psychotherapy* (3rd ed.). Sarasota, FL: Multidisciplinary Association for Psychedelic Studies.

Grof, S. (2009). *LSD: Doorway to the numinous.* Rochester, VT: Park Street Press.

Grossman, P., Niemann, L., Schmidt, S., & Walach, H. (2004). Mindfulness-based stress reduction and health benefits: A meta-analysis. *Journal of Psychosomatic Research, 57,* 35–43.

Gruzelier, J. H. (1984). Hemispheric imbalances in schizophrenia. *International Journal of Psychophysiology, 1,* 227–240.

Gruzelier, J. H. (1989). Lateralisation and central mechanisms in clinical psychophysiology. In G. Turpin (Ed.), *Handbook of clinical psychophysiology* (pp. 135–174). Chichester: John Wiley & Sons.

Gruzelier, J. H. (1996). The factorial structure of schizotypy: I. Affinities and contrasts with syndromes of schizophrenia. *Schizophrenia Bulletin, 22,* 611–620.

Gruzelier, J. (1998). A working model of the neurophysiology of hypnosis: A review of evidence. *Contemporary Hypnosis, 15,* 5–23.

Gruzelier, J. (1999). Functional neuro-psychophysiological asymmetry in schizophrenia: A review and reorientation. *Schizophrenia Bulletin, 25,* 91–120.

Gruzelier, J. H. (2000a). Unwanted effects of hypnosis: A review of the evidence and its implications. *Contemporary Hypnosis, 17,* 163–193.

Gruzelier, J. H. (2000b). Redefining hypnosis: Theory, methods and integration. *Contemporary Hypnosis, 17,* 51–70.

Gruzelier, J. H. (2002a). A Janusian perspective on the nature, development and structure of schizophrenia and schizotypy. *Schizophrenia Research, 54,* 95–103.

Gruzelier, J. H. (2002b). A review of the impact of hypnosis, relaxation, guided imagery and individual differences on aspects of immunity and health. *Stress, 5,* 147–163.

Gruzelier, J. H. (2002c). The role of psychological intervention in modulating aspects of immune function in relation to health and well being. *International Review of Neurobiology, 52,* 383–417.

Gruzelier, J. H. (2003). Theory, methods and new directions in the psychophysiology of the schizophrenic process and schizotypy. *International Journal of Psychophysiology, 48,* 221–245.

Gruzelier, J. H. (2006). Frontal functions, connectivity and neural efficiency underpinning hypnosis and hypnotic susceptibility. *Contemporary Hypnosis, 23,* 15–32.

Gruzelier, J. H. (2009). A theory of alpha/theta neurofeedback, creative performance enhancement, long distance functional connectivity and psychological integration. *Cognitive Processing, 10,* 101–110.

Gruzelier, J. (2009). A theory of alpha/theta neurofeedback, creative performance enhancement, long distance functional connectivity and psychological integration. *Cognitive Processes, 10 (Suppl 1),* pp. S101–S109.

Gruzelier, J. H., Brow, T. D., Perry, A., Rhonder, J., & Thomas, M. (1984). Hypnotic susceptibility: A lateral predisposition and altered cerebral asymmetry under hypnosis. *International Journal of Psychophysiology, 2,* 131–139.

Gruzelier, J. H., & Brow, D. (1985). Psychophysiological evidence for a state theory of hypnosis and susceptibility. *Journal of Psychosomatic Research, 29,* 287–302.

Gruzelier, J. H., & Warren, K. (1993). Neuropsychological evidence of left frontal inhibition with hypnosis. *Psychological Medicine, 23,* 93–101.

Gruzelier, J., & Doig, A. (1996). The factorial structure of schizotypy: II. Patterns of cognitive asymmetry, arousal, handedness and gender. *Schizophrenia Bulletin, 22,* 621–634.

Gruzelier, J., Burgess, A., Baldeweg, T., Ricchdio, M., Hawkins, D., Stygall, J., Catt, S., Irving, G., & Catalan, J. (1996). Prospective associations between lateralised brain function and immune status in HIV infection: Analysis of EEG, cognition and mood over 30 months. *International Journal of Psychophysiology, 23,* 215–224.

Gruzelier, J., Clow, A., Evans, P., Lazar, I., & Walker, L. (1998). Mind-body influences on immunity: lateralised control, stress, individual difference predictors and prophylaxis. *Annals of New York Academy of Sciences, 851,* 487–494.

Gruzelier, J., Wilson, L., Liddiard, D., Peters E., & Pusavat, L. (1999a). Cognitive asymmetry patterns in schizophrenia: Active and Withdrawn syndromes and sex differences as moderators. *Schizophrenia Bulletin, 25 (2),* 349–362.

Gruzelier, J., Richardson, A., & Wilson, L. (1999b). Cognitive asymmetry patterns in schizophrenia: Retest reliability and syndrome-related modifiability with recovery. *International Journal of Psychophysiology, 34,* 323–332.

Gruzelier, J., Smith, F., Nagy, A., & Henderson, D. (2001a). Cellular and humoral immunity, mood and exam stress: The influences of self hypnosis and personality predictors. *International Journal of Psychophysiology, 42,* 55–71.

Gruzelier, J. H., Levy, J., Williams, J. D., & Henderson, D. (2001b). Effect of self hypnosis with specific versus nonspecific imagery: Immune function, mood, health and exam stress. *Contemporary Hypnosis 18*, 97–110.

Gruzelier, J. H., Gray, M., & Horn, P. (2002a). The involvement of frontally modulated attention in hypnosis and hypnotic susceptibility: Cortical evoked potential evidence. *Contemporary Hypnosis, 19*, 179–189.

Gruzelier, J. H., Champion, A., Fox, P., Rollin, M., McCormack, S., Catalan, P., Barton, S., & Henderson, D. (2002b). Individual differences in personality, immunology and mood in patients undergoing self-hypnosis training for the successful treatment of a chronic viral illness, HSV-2. *Contemporary Hypnosis, 19*, 149–166.

Gruzelier, J., De Pascalis, V., Jamieson, G., Laidlaw, T., Naito, A., Bennett, B., & Dwivedi, P. (2004). Relations between hypnotisability and psychopathology revisited. *Contemporary Hypnosis, 21*, 169–170.

Gruzelier, J. H., Egner, T., & Vernon, D. (2006). Validating the efficacy of neurofeedback for optimising performance. In C. Neuper , W. Klimesch, Event-related dynamics of brain oscillations. *Progress in Brain Research, 159*, 421–431.

Gruzelier, J. H., Inoue, A., Steed, A., Smart, R., & Steffert, T. (2010). Acting performance and the experiential flow enhancement with sensory-motor rhythm neurofeedback using an ecologically valid immersive virtual reality and training screen scenario. *Neuroscience Letters*, accepted.

Guilford, J. (1967). *The nature of human intelligence*. New York: McGraw-Hill.

Gumley, A., & Schwannauer, M. (2006). *Staying well after psychosis: A cognitive interpersonal approach to recovery and relapse prevention*. Chichester UK: Wiley.

Gur, R., & Reyher, G. (1976). Enhancement of creativity via free-imagery and hypnosis. *American Journal of Clinical Hypnosis, 18*, 237–249.

Gurstelle, E. B., & de Oliveira, J. L. (2004). Daytime parahypnagogia: A state of consciousness that occurs when we almost fall asleep. *Medical Hypotheses, 62*, 166–168.

Gustafson, R., & Norlander, T. (1994). Effects of alcohol on persistent effort and deduc-

tive thinking during the preparation phase of the creative process. *Journal of Creative Behavior, 28*, 124–132.

Haddock, G., Slade, P. D., Bentall, R. P., Reid, D., & Faragher, E. B. (1998). A Comparison of the long-term effectiveness of distraction and focusing in the treatment of auditory hallucinations. *British Journal of Medical Psychology, 71*, 339–349.

Handelman, D. (1967). The development of a Washo shaman. *Ethnology, 6*, 444–464.

Hanslmayer, S., Sauseng, P., Doppelmayr, M., Schabus, M., & Klimesch, W. (2006). Increasing individual upper alpha by neurofeedback improves cognitive performance in human subjects. *Applied Psychophysiology and Biofeedback, 30* 1–10.

Harary, K. (1993). Clinical approaches to reported psi experiences: The research implications. In L. Coly & J. D. S. McMahon (Eds.), *Psi and clinical practice*. New York: Parapsychological Foundation.

Hardy, Sir A. (1979). *The spiritual nature of man*. Oxford: Oxford University Press.

Harman, W., & Rheingold, H. (1984). *Higher creativity: Liberating the unconscious for breakthrough insights*. New York: G. P. Putnam's Sons.

Harman, W., McKim, R., Mogar, R., Fadiman, J., & Stolaroff, M. (1966). Psychedelic agents in creative problem solving: A pilot study. *Psychological Reports, 19*, 211–227.

Harner, M. (1980). *The way of the shaman* (3rd ed.). San Francisco: HarperSanFrancisco.

Hartmann, E. (1991). *Boundaries in the mind: A new psychology of personality*. New York: Basic Books.

Hartmann, E., Rosen, R., & Rand, W. (1998). Personality and dreaming: Boundary structure and dream content. *Dreaming, 8*, 31–39.

Hartmann, E., Harrison, R., & Zborowski, M. (2001). Boundaries in the mind: Past research and future directions. *North American Journal of Psychology, 3*, 347–368.

Hastings, A. (1983). A counseling approach to parapsychological experience. *The Journal of Transpersonal Psychology, 15*, 143–167.

Hay, D., & Morisy, A. (1978). Reports of ecstatic, paranormal, or religious experiences in Great Britain and the United States: A comparison of trends. *Journal for the Scientific Study of Religion, 17*, 255–268.

Hayes, B., & McAllister, I. (2000). Sowing dragon's teeth: Support for political violence and paramilitarism in Northern Ireland. *The UK Political Studies Association Meeting, London,* April 10–13, 2000.

Hebert, R., Lehmann, D., Tan, G., Travis, F., & Arenander, A. (2005). Enhanced EEG alpha time-domain phase synchrony during transcendental meditation: Implications for cortical integration theory. *Signal Processing, 85,* 2213–2232.

Heidegger, M. (1962). *Being and time.* (Trans. by John Macquarrie and Edward Robinson). New York: Harper & Row. (Original, 1927).

Heller-Roazen, D. (2007). *The inner touch: Archaeology of a sensation.* Brooklyn: Zone Books.

Hemsley, D. R. (1998). The disruption of the "sense of self" in schizophrenia: Potential links with disturbances of information processing. *British Journal of Medical Psychology, 71,* 115–124.

Hicks, R., Bautista, J., & Hicks, G. (1999). Boundaries and level of experience with six types of dreams. *Perceptual and Motor Skills, 89,* 760–762.

Hilgard, E. R. (1965). *Hypnotic Susceptibility.* New York: Harcourt, Brace and World.

Hilgard, E. R. (1986). *Divided Consciousness; Multiple controls in human thought and action.* Expanded edition. New York: Wiley.

Hill, G., Clarke, I., & Wilson, H. (2008). The "making friends with yourself" and the "what is real and what is not" groups. In: Clarke, I. and Wilson, H. (Eds.), *Cognitive behavior therapy for acute inpatient mental health units: Working with clients, staff and the milieu* (pp. 161–173). Hove, UK: Routledge.

Ho, M. W. (2008). *The rainbow and the worm: The physics of organisms.* Hackensack, NJ: World Scientific Publishing Company.

Hoad, T. F. (1993). *The oxford dictionary of English etymology.* Oxford: Oxford University Press.

Hocevar, D. (1981). Measurement of creativity: Review and critique. *Journal of Personality Assessment, 45,* 450–464.

Hofer, I., Della Casa, V., & Feldon, J. (1999). The interaction between schizotypy and latent inhibition: Modulation by experimental parameters. *Personality and Individual Differences, 26,* 1075–1088.

Holden, J. M., Vanpelt-Tess, P., & Warren, S. (1999). Spiritual emergency: An introduction and case example. *Counseling and Values, 43,* 163–177.

Holmes, E. A., & Steel, C. (2004). Schizotypy as a vulnerability factor for traumatic intrusions: An analogue investigation. *Journal of Nervous and Mental Disease, 192,* 28–34.

Holt, N. (2000). *Art: A phenomenological exploration of the creative process.* Unpublished Masters thesis, Liverpool John Moores University.

Holt, N. (2007). *Creativity, states of consciousness and anomalous cognition: The role of epistemological flexibility in the creative process.* Unpublished Doctoral thesis, University of Northampton.

Holt, N., Delanoy, D., & Roe, C. (2004). Creativity, subjective paranormal experiences and altered states of consciousness. In *Proceedings of the Parapsychological Association 47th Annual Convention.* New York: Parapsychological Association, 433–436.

Holt, N., Simmonds-Moore, C., & Moore, S. (2008). Benign schizotypy: Investigating differences between clusters of schizotypy on paranormal belief, creativity, intelligence and mental health. In *Proceedings of Presented Papers: The Parapsychological Association 51st Annual Convention.* New York: Parapsychological Association, 82–96.

Holt, N., & Simmonds-Moore, C. (2008). *Creativity, schizotypy, paranormal experiences and mental health: Developing a new cognitive-parapsychological paradigm for the assessment of psi-performance in the laboratory.* Unpublished Final report of research findings (for the Bial foundation).

Honig, A., Romme, M. A. J., Ensink, B. J., Escher, S. D. M. A. C., Pennings, M. H. A., & Devries, M. W. (1998). Auditory hallucinations: A comparison between patients and non patients. *The Journal of Nervous and Mental Disease, 186,* 646–651.

Honorton, C. (1977). Psi and internal attention states. In: B. Wolman (Ed.), *Handbook of Parapsychology* (pp. 435–472). New York: Van Nostrand Reinhold.

Honorton, C., & Ferrari, D. C. (1989). Future telling: A meta-analysis of forced choice precognition experiments, 1935–1987. *Journal of Parapsychology, 53,* 281–308.

Honorton, C. (1997). The Ganzfeld novice: Four predictors of initial ESP perfomance. *Journal of Parapsychology, 61,* 143–158.

Hood, R. W., Spilka, B., Hunsberger, B., & Gorsuch, R. (1996). *The psychology of religion: An empirical approach.* London: Guilford Press.

Hoppe, K., & Kyle, N. (1990). Dual brain, creativity, and health. *Creativity Research Journal, 3,* 150–157.

Hoppe, K. (1994). Affect, hemispheric specialization and creativity. In M. Shaw & M. Runco (Eds.), *Creativity and affect* (pp. 213–224). Norwood, NJ: Ablex Publishing Corporation.

Horne, J. (1988). *Why we sleep: The functions of sleep in humans and other mammals.* New York: Oxford University Press.

Horne, J. (2000). REM sleep — By default? *Neuroscience and Biobehavioral Reviews, 24,* 777–797.

Houran, J., Thalbourne, M., & Hartmann, E. (2003). Comparison of two alternative measures of the boundary concept. *Psychological Reports, 96,* 311–323.

Howard-Jones, A., Blakemore, S., Samuel, E., Summers, I., & Claxton, G. (2005). Semantic divergence and creative story generation: An fMRI investigation. *Cognitive Brain Research, 25,* 240–250.

Hunt, H., & Chefurka, C. (1976). A test of the psychedelic model of consciousness. *Archives of General Psychiatry, 33,* 867–896.

Hunt, H. T. (1995). *On the nature of consciousness. Cognitive, phenomenological, and transpersonal perspectives.* New Haven: Yale University Press.

Hunt, H. T. (2000). Experiences of radical personal transformation in mysticism, religious conversion, and psychosis: A review of the varieties, processes, and consequences of the numinous. *The Journal of Mind and Behavior, 21,* 353–397.

Hunt, H., Dougan, S., Grant, K., & House, M. (2002). Growth enhancing versus dissociative states of consciousness: A questionnaire study. *Journal of Humanstic Psychology, 42,* 90–106.

Humphrey, N. (2002). *Great expectations: The evolutionary psychology of faith-healing and the placebo effect.* Retrieved 8th December 2010 from http://cogprints.org/1078/1/placebopaper3.htm.

Husserl, E. (1931). *Ideas: General introduction to pure phenomenology.* (Trans. W. R. Boyce Gibson). London: George Allen & Unwin. (Original 1913).

Hutchinson, G. T., Patock-Peckham, J. A., Cheong, J. W., & Nagoshi, C. T. (1998). Personality predictors of religious orientation among Protestant, Catholic, and nonreligious college students. *Personality and Individual Differences, 24,* 145–151.

Hyman, R. (1995). Evaluation of the program on anomalous mental phenomena. *Journal of Parapsychology, 59,* 321–51.

Irwin, H. J. (1992). Origins and functions of paranormal belief: The role of childhood trauma and interpersonal control. *Journal of the American Society for Psychical Research, 86,* 199- 208.

Irwin, H. J. (1993). Belief in the paranormal: A review of the empirical literature. *Journal of the American Society for Psychical Research, 87* (1), 1–39.

Irwin, H. J. (1999). *An introduction to parapsychology* (3d. ed.). Jefferson, NC: McFarland.

Jackson, L., & Gorassini, D. (1989). Artifact in the hypnosis-creativity relationship. *Journal of General Psychology, 116,* 333–44.

Jackson, M. (1997). Benign schizotypy? The case of spiritual experience. In G. Claridge (Ed.), *Schizotypy: Implications for illness and health* (pp. 227–250). Oxford: Oxford University Press.

Jackson, M. (2001). Psychotic and spiritual experience: A case study comparison. In I. Clarke (Ed.), *Psychosis and spirituality: exploring the new frontier.* London: Whurr.

Jackson, M., & Fulford, K. (1997). Spiritual experience and psychopathology. *Philosophy, Psychiatry and Psychology, 1,* 41–65.

Jackson, S. (1992). Athletes in flow: A qualitative investigation of flow states in elite figure skaters. *Journal of Applied Sport Psychology, 4,* 161–180.

Jacobi, F., Hoyer, J., & Wittchen, H.-U. (2004). Seelische gesundheit in Ost und West: Analysen auf der grundlage des bundesgesundheitssurveys. *Zeitschrift für Klinische Psychologie und Psychotherapie, 33,* 251–260.

James, W. (1958). *The varieties of religious experience.* New York: New American Library of World Literature.

James, W. (1902/1985). *The varieties of religious experience.* New York: Penguin Books.

Jamison, K. (1993). *Touched with fire: Manic-depressive illness and the artistic temperament.* New York: Simon & Schuster.

Jamieson, G., & Gruzelier, J. H. (2001). Hypnotic susceptibility is positively related to a subset of schizotypy items. *Contemporary Hypnosis, 18,* 32–37.

Jeong, J., Gore, C., & Peterson, B. S. (2001). Mutual information analysis of the EEG in patients with Alzheimer's disease. *Clinical Neurophysiology, 112,* 827–835 .

Jerome, L., Mojeiko, V., & Doblin, R. (2009). The psychedelic research renaissance: A review of recent psychedelic psychotherapy research. In S. Grof, *LSD: Doorway to the numinous* (pp. 243–259). Rochesta, VT: Park Street Press.

Jessop, D. (1998). Evidence for mind-body connection increases. *The Lancet, 351,* 1185.

Johnson, C. V., & Friedman, H. L. (2008). Enlightened or delusional? Differentiating religious, spiritual, and transpersonal experiences from psychopathology. *Journal of Humanistic Psychology, 48,* 505–527.

Johnson, J. A. (2000). *Chinese medical Qigong therapy: A comprehensive clinical guide.* Pacific Grove, CA: International Institute of Medical Qigong.

Johnston, J., & Barcan, R. (2006). Subtle transformations: Imagining the body in alternative health practices. *International Journal of Cultural Studies, 9,* 25–44.

Jonas, W. B., & Crawford, C. (2002). *Healing, intention and energy medicine.* Philadelphia: Churchill Livingstone.

Joyce, K. (2005). Appealing images: Magnetic resonance imaging and the production of authoritative knowledge. *Social Studies of Science, 35* (3), 437–462.

Jung, C. (1967). *The spirit of man in art and literature.* London: Routledge & Kegan Paul.

Kabat-Zinn, J. (1990). *Full catastrophe living: Using the wisdom of your body and mind to face stress, pain, and illness.* New York: Bantam Dell.

Kabat-Zinn, J. (2005). *Coming to our senses: Healing ourselves and the world though mindfulness.* New York: Hyperion.

Kaiser, J, Barker, R., Haenschel, C., Baldeweg, T., & Gruzelier, J. (1997). Hypnosis and event-related potential correlates of error processing in a stroop-type paradigm: A test of the frontal hypothesis. *International Journal of Psychophysiology, 27,* 215–222.

Kallio, S., Revonsuo, A., Hamalainen, H., Markela, J., & Gruzelier, J. (2000). Changes in anterior attentional functions and word fluency associated with hypnosis. *International Journal of Clinical and Experimental Hypnosis, 49,* 95–108.

Kang, D. H., Davidson, R., Coe, C., Wheeler, R. E., Tomarken, A. J., & Ershler, W. B. (1991). Frontal brain asymmetry and immune function. *Behavioral Neuroscience, 105,* 860–869.

Kaptchuk, T. J., Friedlander, E., Kelley, J. M., Sanchez, M. N., Kokkotou, E., Singer, J. P., Kowalczykowski, M., Miller, F. G., Kirsch, I., & Lembo, A. J. (2010). Placebos without deception: A randomized controlled trial in irritable bowel syndrome. *PLoS ONE, 5* (12), 1–7, *www.plosone.org.*

Karlin, R. A. (1979). Hypnotizability and attention. *Journal of Abnormal Psychology, 88,* 92–95.

Keizer, A. W., Verschoor, M., Verment, R. S., & Hommel, B. (2010). The effect of gamma enhancing neurofeedback on the control of feature bindings and intelligence measures. *International Journal of Psychophysiology, 75,* 25–32.

Kekulé, A. (1890). Benzolfest: Rede. *Berichte der Deutschen Chemischen Gesellschaft, 23,* 1302–11.

Kennedy, J. E., Kanthamani, H., & Palmer, J. (1994). Psychic and spiritual experiences, health, well being and meaning in life. *Journal of Parapsychology, 58,* 353–383.

Kenny, M., & Williams, J. M. G. (2007). Treatment resistant depressed patients show a great response to Mindfulness-based Cognitive Therapy. *Behavior Research and Therapy, 45,* 617–625.

Kensinger, K. M. (1973). *Banisteriopsis* usage among the Peruvian Cashinahua. In M. J. Harner (Ed.), *Hallucinogens and shamanism* (pp. 9–14). New York: Oxford University Press.

Kent, J. (2005). The case against DMT elves. In C. Pickover (Ed.), *Sex, drugs, Einstein, and elves* (pp. 102–105). Petaluma, CA: Smart Publications.

King, M. (1967). Dimensions of religiosity in "Measuring the Religious Variable." *Journal for the Scientific Study of Religion, 6,* 173–190.

Kinsbourne, M. (1982). Hemispheric specialisation and the growth of human understanding. *American Psychologist, 37,* 411.

Kirsch, I., & Council, J. R. (1992). Situational and personality correlates of hypnotic responsiveness. In E. Fromm and M. Nash (Eds.), *Contemporary hypnosis research* (pp. 267–291). New York: Guildford Press.

Kleber, B. Birbaumer, N. Veit, R. Trevorrow, T., & Lotze, M. (2007). Overt and imagined singing of an Italian Aria. *NeuroImage, 36*, 889–900.

Klimo, J. (1998). Clinical parapsychology and the nature of reality. In the *Annual Proceedings of the United States Psychotronics Association* (pp. 110–115), http://www.jonklimo.com/Papers/clinpara-USPA.pdf.

Koenig, H. G., Hays, J. C., Larson, D. B., George, L. K., Cohen, H. J., McCullough, M., Meador, K. G., & Blazer, D. G. (1999). Does religious attendance prolong survival? A six-year follow-up study of 3,968 older adults. *Journal of Gerontology, 54A*, M370–7.

Koestler, A. (1964).*The act of creation*. London: Arkana.

Koffel, E., & Watson, D. (2009). Unusual sleep experiences, dissociation, and schizotypy: Evidence for a common domain. *Clinical Psychology Review, 29, 548–559.*

Kohls, N. B. (2004). *Außergewöhnliche erfahrungen — blinder fleck der psychologie?* Münster: LIT Verlag.

Kornfield, J. (1993). The seven factors of enlightment. In: R. Walsh & F. Vaughan (Eds.), *Paths beyond ego: The transpersonal vision* (pp. 56–59). Los Angeles: J.P. Tarcher/ Perigee.

Kosslyn, S. M., Thompson, W. L., & Constantini-Ferrando, M. F. (2000). Hypnotic visual illusion alters brain color processing. *American Journal of Psychiatry, 45*, 327–33.

Kozak, L., Johnson, L. C., Richards, T., King, H., Standish, L. J., Schlitz, M. J., Simon, D., & Chopra, D. (2003). *EEG evidence of correlated neural signals between physically and sensory isolated subjects who have undergone Primordial Sound Meditation (PSM) training.* (Unpublished).

Kramer, W. H. (1993. Recent Experiences with psi counseling in Holland. In L. Coly & J. D. S. McMahon (Eds.), *Psi and clinical practice.* New York: Parapsychological Foundation.

Krippner, S., & Welch, P. (1992). *Spiritual dimensions of healing.* New York: Irvington.

Krippner, S. (1995). A model of dreaming derived from the Mapuche tradition in Chile. In R. I. Heinze (Ed.), *Proceedings of the 12th International Conference on the Study of Shamanism and Alternate Modes of Healing.* Berkeley, CA: Independent Scholars of Asia, 97–106.

Krippner, S. (2000). The epistemology and technologies of shamanic states of consciousness. *Journal of Consciousness Studies, 7*, 93–118.

Krippner, S. (2009). *Anyone who dreams partakes in shamanism.* Paper presented as a keynote address at the Annual Convention of the International Association for the Study of Dreams, Chicago, IL, June 26–28, 2009.

Krippner, S., & Luke, D. (2009). Psychedelics and species connectedness. *Bulletin of the Multidisciplinary Association for Psychedelic Studies, 19*, 12–15.

Kühn, S. (2001). *Entwicklung eines erhebungsinstruments zur evaluation psychologischer beratung aus sicht der klienten.* Unveröffentlichte Diplomarbeit: Albert-Ludwigs-Universität Freiburg.

Kumar, V. K., Marcano, G., & Pekala, R. J. (1996). Behavioral and subjective scoring of the Harvard Group Scale of hypnotic susceptibility: Further data and an extension. *American Journal of Clinical Hypnosis, 38*, 191–9.

Kuyken, W., Byford, S., Taylor, R. S., Watkins, E., Holden, E., White, K., Barrett, B., Byng, R., Evans, A., Mullan, E., & Teasdale, J. D. (2008). Mindfulness-based cognitive therapy to prevent relapse in recurrent depression. *Journal of Consulting and Clinical Psychology, 76*, 966–978.

Kwekkeboom, K, Huseby-Moore, K., & Ward, S. (1998). Imaging ability and effective use of guided imagery. *Research in Nursing and Health, 21*, 189–198.

LaBerge, S., & Gackenbach, S. (2000). Lucid dreaming. In E. Cardeña, S. Lynn, & S. Krippner (Eds.), *The varieties of anomalous experience* (pp. 151–182). Washington DC: American Psychological Association.

Laidlaw, T. M. (1994). Hypnosis and breathing training in the treatment of anxiety: Three cases. *Australian Journal of Clinical and Experimental Hypnosis, 22*, 137–145.

Laidlaw, T. M. (1999). The interrupt distraction procedure: A brief hypnotic intervention for belief change and diminishing distress. *American Journal of Clinical Hypnosis, 42,* 22–34.

Laidlaw, T. M., Naito, A., Dwivedi, P., Enzor, N., Brincat, C. E., & Gruzelier, J. H. (2003). Mood changes after self-hypnosis and Johrei prior to exams. *Contemporary Hypnosis, 20,* 25–40.

Laidlaw, T. M., Bennett, B. M., Dwivedi, P., Naito, A., & Gruzelier, J. (2005). Quality of life and mood changes in metastatic breast cancer after training in self-hypnosis or Johrei: A short report. *Contemporary Hypnosis, 22,* 84–93.

Laidlaw, T. M., Kerstein, R., Bennett, B. M., Naito, A., Henderson, D. C., Dwivedi, P., & Gruzelier, J. H. (2004). Hypnotisability and immunological response to psychological intervention in HIV. *Contemporary Hypnosis, 21,* 126–135.

Laing, R. D. (1965). *The divided self.* Harmondsworth: Penguin Books.

Laird, N. M., & Mosteller, F. (1990). Some statistical methods for combining experimental results. *International Journal of Technology Assessment in Health Care, 6,* 5–30.

Lakoff, G., & Johnson, M. (1999). *Philosophy in the flesh: The embodied mind and its challenge to Western thought.* New York, NY: Basic Books.

Landers, D., Petruzzello, S., Malazar, W., Crews, D., Kubitz, K., Gannon, T., & Han, M. (1991). The influence of electrocortical biofeedback on performance in pre-elite archers. *Medicine and Science in Sports and Exercise, 23,* 123–129.

Lane, R. (2000). Levels of emotional awareness: Neurological, psychological, and social perspectives. In R. Bar-On and J. Parker (Eds.), *The handbook of emotional intelligence: theory, development, assessment and application at home, school and in the workplace* (pp. 171–191). San Francisco: Jossey-Bass.

Lange, R., Thalbourne, M., Houran, J., & Storm, L. (2000). The revised transliminality scale: Reliability and validity data from a rasch top-down purification procedure. *Consciousness and Cognition, 9,* 591–617.

Lawrence, T. R., & Woodley, P. (1998). Schizotypy as a predictor of success in a free response ESP task. In *Abstracts from the 22nd International Conference of the Society for Psychical Research,* 14.

Lau, M. A., Segal, Z. V., & Williams, J. M. G. (2004). Teasdale's differential activation hypothesis: Implications for mechanisms of depressive relapse and suicidal behavior. *Behavior Research and Therapy, 42,* 1001–1017.

Leder, D. (2005). "Spooky actions at a distance": Physics, psi and distant healing. *The Journal of Alternative and Complementary Medicine, 11,* 923–930.

LeDoux, J. (1989). Cognitive-emotional interactions in the brain. *Cognition and Emotion, 3,* 267–289.

Lehmann, V. (2008). *Entwicklung eines fragebogens zur erfassung der phänomenologie aussergewöhnlicher erfahrungen (PAGE).* Unveröffentlichte Diplomarbeit: Albert-Ludwigs-Universität Freiburg.

Leister, M. B. (1996). Inner voices: Distinguishing transcendent and pathological characteristics. *The Journal of Transpersonal Psychology, 28,* 1–30.

Leonhard, D., & Brugger, P. (1998). Creative, paranormal and delusional thought: A consequence of right hemisphere semantic activation. *Neuropsychiatry, 4,* 177–183.

Leonards, U., & Mohr, C. (2009). Schizotypal personality traits influence idiosyncratic initiation of saccadic face exploration. *Vision Research, 49,* 2404–2413.

Levin, J. (2005). The transcendent experience: Conceptual, theoretical, and epidemiologic perspectives. *Explore, 1,* 89–101.

Levin, J. S., & Chatters, L. M. (1998). Religion, health, and psychological well-being in older adults: Findings from three national surveys. *Aging Health, 10,* 504.

Levin, R., Galin, J., & Zywiak, B. (1991). Nightmares, boundaries, and creativity. *Dreaming, 1,* 63–74.

Levin, R., Gilmartin, L., & Lamontanaro, L. (1998). Cognitive style and perception: The relationship of boundary thinness to visual-spatial processing in dreaming and waking thought. *Imagination, Cognition and Personality, 18,* 25–41.

Levin, J., & Mead, L. (2008). Bioenergy healing: A theoretical model and case series. *EXPLORE: The Journal of Science and Healing, 4,* 201–209.

Levy, S. M., Herberman, R. B., Simons, A., Whiteside, T., Lee, J., McDonald, R., & Beadle, M. (1989). Persistently low natural killer cell activity in normal adults: immunological, hormonal and mood correlates. *Natural Immunity and Cell Growth Regulation, 8,* 173–186.

Lewis-Williams, J. D., & Dowson, T. A. (1988). The signs of all times: Entoptic phenomena in Upper Paleolithic art. *Current Anthropology, 29,* 201–245.

Lillienfield, S. O., Fowler, K. A., Lohr J. M., & Lynn, S. J. (2005). Pseudoscience, nonscience and nonsense in clinical psychology: Dangers and remedies. In R. H. Wright and N. A. Cummings (Eds.), *Destructive trends in mental health: The well-intentioned path to harm.* (pp. 187–218). London: Routledge.

Lindsay, J. (1987). Laterality shift in homosexual men. *Neuropsychologia, 25,* 965–969.

Linehan, M. (1993). *Cognitive behavioral treatment of borderline personality disorder.* New York: Guildford Press.

Lipsey, M. W., & Wilson, D. B. (2000). *Practical meta-analysis.* Thousand Oaks, CA: Sage.

Loughland, C. M., & Williams, L. M. (1997). A cluster analytic study of schizotypal trait dimensions. *Personality and Individual Differences, 23,* 877–883.

Lubart, T. (2000–2001). Models of the creative process: Past, present and future. *Creativity Research Journal, 3 & 4,* 295–308.

Lucadou, W. V., & Poser, M. (1997). *Geister sind auch nur menschen* [Ghosts are just humans]. Freiburg: Herder.

Lucadou, W., Römer, H., & Walach, H. (2007). Synchronistic phenomena as entanglement correlations in generalized quantum theory. *Journal of Consciousness Studies, 14,* 50–74.

Lucadou,W. V., & Zahradnik, F. (2004). Predictions of the model of pragmatic information about RSPK. In S. Schmidt (Ed.), *Proceedings of Presented Papers of the Parapsychological Association 47th Annual Convention,* Vienna University August 5–8, 2004, 99–112.

Ludwig, A. (1992). Creative achievement and psychopathology: Comparison among professions. *American Journal of Psychotherapy, 46,* 330–355.

Luke, D. (2008a). *Death, and the God of a thousand eyes.* Paper presented at the Day of the Dead Festival, The Horse Hospital, Bloomsbury, London, November 1, 2008.

Luke, D. (2008b). Disembodied eyes revisited: An investigation into the ontology of entheogenic entity encounters. *Entheogen Review: The Journal of Unauthorized Research on Visionary Plants and Drugs, 17,* 1–9, 38–40.

Luke, D. P. (2008c). Inner paths to outer space: Journeys to alien worlds through psychedelics and other spiritual technologies by Rick Strassman et al. [book review]. *Journal of Scientific Exploration, 22,* 564–569.

Luke, D. P. (2008d). Psychedelic substances and paranormal phenomena: A review of the research. *Journal of Parapsychology, 72,* 77–107.

Luke, D. P. (2009). *Telepathine (ayahuasca) and psychic ability: Field research in South America.* Paper presented at the British Psychological Society, 13th Transpersonal Section Annual Conference, Scarborough, September 18–20.

Luke, D. P. (2010). Rock art or Rorschach: Is there more to entoptics than meets the eye? *Time & Mind: Journal of Archaeology, Consciousness and Culture, 3,* 9–28.

Luke, D., & Friedman, H. (2009). The neurochemistry of psi reports and associated experiences. In S. Krippner and H. Friedman (Eds.), *Mysterious minds: The neurobiology of psychics, mediums, and other extraordinary people* (pp. 163–185). Santa Barbara, CA: Praeger.

Luke, D. P., & Kittenis, M. (2005). A preliminary survey of paranormal experiences with psychoactive drugs. *Journal of Parapsychology, 69,* 305–27.

Lukoff, D. (1998). From spiritual emergency to spiritual problem: The transpersonal roots of the new DSM-IV category. *Journal of Humanistic Psychology, 38,* 21–50.

Luna, L. E. (1984). The concept of plants as teachers among four mestizo shamans of Iquitos, Northeastern Peru. *Journal of Ethnopharmacology, 11,* 135–156.

Luna, L. E. (2008). The varieties of ayahuasca experience. In R. Strassman, S. Wojtowicz, L. E. Luna & E. Frecska, *Inner paths to outer space: Journeys to alien worlds through psychedelics and other spiritual technologies* (pp. 120–142). Rochester, VT: Park Street Press.

Luna, L. E., & White, S. F. (Eds.), (2000). *Ayahuasca reader: Encounters with the Amazon's sacred vine.* Santa Fe, NM: Synergetic Press.

Lutz, A., Brefczynski-Lewis, J., Johnstone, T., & Davidson, R. J. (2008). Regulation of the neural circuitry of emotion by compassion meditation: Effects of meditative expertise. *PLos ONE, 3*, e1897. Found online at http:// www.ncbi.nlm.nih.gov/pmc/articles/PMC 2267490/?tool=pubmed.

Lutz, A., Dunne, J. D., & Davidson, R. J. (2007). Meditation and the neuroscience of consciousness: An introduction. In: P. Zelazo, M. Moscovitch & E. Thompson (Eds.), *Cambridge handbook of consciousness* (pp. 499–554). Cambridge: Cambridge University Press.

Lutz, A., Greischar, L. L., Rawlings, N. B., Ricard, M., & Davidson, R. J. (2004). Long-term meditators self-induce high-amplitude gamma synchrony during mental practice. *PNAS, 101*, 16369–16373.

Lutz, A., Slagter, H. A., Dunne, J. D., & Davidson, R. J. (2008). Attention regulation and monitoring in meditation. *Trends in Cognitive Science, 12*, 163–169.

Lutz, W., Tholen, S. Schürch, E., & Berking, M. (2006). Die entwicklung, validierung und reliabilität von kurzformen gängiger psychometrischer instrumente zur evaluation des therapeutischen fortschritts in psychotherapie und psychiatrie. *Diagnostica, 52*, Heft 1, 11–25.

Lutzenberger, W., Preissl, H., & Pulvermüller, F. (1995). Fractal dimension of electroencephalographic time series and underlying brain processes. *Biological Cybernetics, 73*, 477–482.

Lycke, E., Norrby, R., & Roos, B-E. (1974). A serological study on mentally ill patients with particular reference to the prevalence of herpes virus infections. *British Journal of Psychiatry, 124*, 273–9.

Lynn, S. J., & Rhue, J. W. (1986). The fantasy-prone person: Hypnosis, developmental antecedents, and psychopathology. *American Psychologist, 43*, 35–44.

Lynn, S. J., & Rhue, J. W. (1991). An integrative model of hypnosis. In S. J. Lynn and J. W. Rhue (Eds.), *Theories of hypnosis* (pp. 397–438). London: Guildford Press.

Lynn, S. J., & Sivec, H. (1992). The hypnotisable subject as a creative problem-solving agent. In E. Fromm & M. Nash (Eds.), *Contemporary hypnosis research* (pp. 292–333). New York: Guildford Press.

Ma, S. H., & Teasdale, J. D. (2004). Mindful-ness-based cognitive therapy for depression: Replication and exploration of differential relapse prevention effects. *Journal of Consulting and Clinical Psychology, 72*, 31–40.

MacDonald, A. W., Cohen, J. D., Stenger, V. A., & Carter, C. S. (2000). Dissociating the role of the dorsolateral prefrontal and anterior cingulated cortex in cognitive control. *Science, 288*, 1835–1838.

MacDonald, D. A., & Holland, D. (2002). Examination of the psychometric properties of the temperament and character inventory self-transcendence dimension. *Personality and Individual Differences, 32*, 1013–1027.

Macleod-Morgan, C. (1979). Hypnotic susceptibility, EEG theta and alpha waves, and hemispheric specificity. In G. D. Burrows, D. R. Collison, & L. Dennerstein (Eds.), *Hypnosis 1979*. Amsterdam: Elsevier/North-Holland.

MacLeod-Morgan, C., & Lack, L. (1982). Hemisphere specificity: A physiological concomitant of hypnotizability. *Psychophysiology, 19*, 656–672.

Maltby, J., & Day, L. (2003). Religious orientation, religious coping and appraisals of stress: Assessing primary appraisal factors in the relationship between religiosity and psychological well-being. *Personality and Individual Differences, 34* (7), 1209–1224.

Maltby, J., Garner, I., Lewis, C. A., & Day, L. (2000). Religious orientation and schizotypal traits. *Personality and Individual Differences, 28*, 143–151.

Maltby, J., & Lewis, C. A. (1997). The reliability and validity of a short scale of attitude towards Christianity among U.S.A., English, Republic of Ireland, and Northern Ireland adults *Personality and Individual Differences, 22* (5), 649–654.

Maltby, J., Lewis, C. A., & Day, L. (1999). Religious orientation and psychological well-being: the role of the frequency of personal prayer. *British Journal of Health Psychology, 4*, 363–378.

Martindale, C. (1977–1978). Creativity, consciousness and cortical arousal. *Journal of Altered States of Consciousness, 3*, 69–87.

Martindale, C. (1989). Personality, situation, and creativity. In J. Glover, R. Ronning, & C. Reynolds (Eds.), *Handbook of creativity* (pp. 211–232). New York: Plenum Press.

Martindale, C. (1991). *Cognitive psychology: A neural network approach.* Pacific Grove, CA: Brooks/Cole Publishing Company.

Martindale, C. (1995). Creativity and connectionism. In S. Smith, T. Ward, & R. Finke (Eds.), *The creative cognition approach* (pp. 249–268). Cambridge, MA: MIT Press.

Martindale, C. (1999). Biological bases of creativity. In R. Sternberg (Ed.), *Handbook of creativity* (pp. 137–152). Cambridge: Cambridge University Press.

Martindale, C., Anderson, K., Moore, K., & West, A. (1996). Creativity, oversensitivity and rate of habituation. *Personality and Individual Differences, 20,* 423–427.

Martindale, C., & Armstrong, J. (1974). The relationship of creativity to cortical activation and its operant control. *The Journal of Genetic Psychology, 124,* 311–320.

Martindale, C., & Greenough, J. (1973). The differential effects of increased arousal on creative and intellectual performance. *Journal of Genetic Psychology, 123.* 329–335.

Martindale, C., & Hasenfus, N. (1978). EEG differences as a function of creativity, creative process and effort to be original. *Biological Psychology, 6,* 157–167.

Martindale, C., & Hines, D. (1975). Creativity and cortical activation during creative, intellectual and EEG feedback tasks. *Biological Psychology, 3,* 91–100.

Martindale, C., Hines, D., Mitchell, L., & Covello, E. (1984). EEG alpha asymmetry and creativity. *Personality and Individual Differences, 5,* 77–86.

Maslow, A. (1964). *Religions, values and peak experiences.* Cleveland: Ohio State University Press.

Maslow, A. (1971). *The further reaches of human nature.* New York: Viking.

Mason, A. A., & Black, S. (1958). Allergic skin responses abolished under treatment of asthma and hay fever by hypnosis. *Lancet, 1,* 877–880.

Mason, O., Claridge, G., & Jackson, M. (1995). New scales for measurement of schizotypy. *Personality and Individual Differences, 18,* 7–13.

Mason, O., Claridge, G., & Williams, L. (1997). Questionnaire measurement. In G. Claridge (Ed.), *Schizotypy: Implications for illness and health* (pp. 19–37). New York: Oxford University Press.

Masters, K. S., Spielmans, G. I., & Goodson, J. T. (2006). Are there demonstrable effects of distant intercessory prayer? A meta-analytic review. *Annals of Behavioral Medicine, 32,* 21–26.

Matheson, S., & Langdon, R. (2008). Schizotypal traits impact upon executive working memory and aspects of IQ. *Psychiatry Research, 159,* 207–214.

Mavromatis, A. (1987). Creativity. In A. Mavromatis, *Hypnagogia: The unique state of consciousness between wakefulness and sleep* (pp. 186–218). New York: Routledge and Kegan Paul.

Mavromatis, A. (1987). *Hypnagogia: The unique state of consciousness between wakefulness and sleep.* London: Routledge and Kegan Paul.

May, E. C., Paulinyi, T., & Vassy, Z. (2005). Anomalous anticipatory skin conductance response to acoustic stimuli: Experimental results and speculation about a mechanism. *Journal of Alternative and Complementary Medicine, 11,* 695–702.

Mayer, J., & Geher, G. (1996). Emotional intelligence and the identification of emotions. *Intelligence, 22,* 89–114.

McCallum, M., & Piper, W. (2000). Psychological mindedness and emotional intelligence. In R. Bar-On and J. Parker (Eds.), *The handbook of emotional intelligence: Theory, development, assessment and application at home, school and in the workplace* (pp. 118–136). San Francisco: Jossey-Bass.

McClenon, J. (1994). *Wondrous events: Foundations of religious belief.* Philadelphia, PA: University of Pennsylvania Press.

McClenon, J. (2002). *Wondrous healing: Shamanism, human evolution, and the origin of religion.* Dekalb, IL: Northern Illinois University Press.

McCormack, K., & Gruzelier, J. H. (1993). Cerebral asymmetry and hypnosis: A signal detection analysis of divided visual field stimulation. *Journal of Abnormal Psychology, 102,* 352–357.

McCrae, R. (1987). Creativity, divergent thinking, and openness to experience. *Journal of Personality and Social Psychology, 52,* 1258–1265.

McCrae, R. (1994). Openness to experience: Expanding the boundaries of factor V. *European Journal of Personality, 8,* 251–272.

McCreery, C. (1997). Hallucinations and

arousability: Pointers to a theory of psychosis. In G. Claridge (Ed.), *Schizotypy: Implications for illness and health* (pp. 251–273). New York: Oxford University Press.

McCreery, C., & Claridge, G. (1996). A study of hallucination in normal subjects: II. Electrophysiological data. *Personality and Individual Differences, 21,* 749–758.

McCreery, C., & Claridge, G. (2002). Healthy schizotypy: The case of out-of-body experiences. *Personality and Individual Differences, 32,* 141–154.

McCullough, M. E., Hoyt, W. T., Larson, D. B., Koenig, H. G., & Thoresen, C. E. (2000). Religious involvement and mortality: A meta-analytic review. *Health psychology, 19,* 211–222.

McDougal, W. (1950). *An introduction to social psychology.* London: Methuen.

McGorry, P., Nordentoft, M., & Simonsen, E. (2005). Early psychosis: A bridge to the future. *British Journal of Psychiatry, 187 (Supplement 48).*

McNair, D., Lorr, M., & Droppleman, L. (1971). *Profile of mood states manual.* San Diego: Educational and Industrial Testing Service.

McWhirter, L. (1983). Growing up in Northern Ireland: From aggression to the Troubles. In A. P. Goldstein & M. H. Segall (Eds.), *Aggression in a global perspective* (pp. 367–400). New York: Pergamon.

Mednick, S. (1962). The associative basis of the creative process. *Psychological Review, 69,* 220–232.

Mednick, S., & Mednick, M. (1967). *Examiners manual for the remote associates test.* Boston: Houghton Mifflin.

Meier, C. A. (1989). *Healing dream and ritual: Ancient incubation and modern psychotherapy.* Einsiedeln, Switzerland: Daimon Verlag.

Mercante, M. S. (2004). *Miração and healing: A study concerning spontaneous mental imagery and the healing process.* Paper presented at the Toward a Science of Consciousness Conference, Tucson, AZ.

Mercante, M. S. (2008). *Consciousness and spontaneous mental imagery.* Unpublished manuscript, Saybrook Graduate School and Research Centre, San Francisco, CA.

Merleau-Ponty, M. (1962). *The Phenomenology of Perception.* (Trans. by C. Smith). London: Routledge. (Original 1945).

Merton, T., & Fischer, I. (1999). Creativity, personality and word association responses: Associative behavior in forty supposedly creative persons. *Personality and Individual Differences, 27,* 933–942.

Meszaros, I., Crawford, H. J., Szabo, C., Nagy-Kovacs, A., & Revesz, M. A. (1989). Hypnotic susceptibility and cerebral hemisphere preponderance: Verbal-imaginal discrimination task. In V. Ghorghui, P. Netter, H., & R. J. Miller (1975). Response to the Ponzo illusion as reflection of hypnotic susceptibility. *International Journal of Clinical and Experimental Hypnosis, 23,* 148–157.

Metzinger, T. (1993). *Subjekt und selbstmodell: Die perspektivität phänomenalen bewusstseins vor dem hintergrund einer naturalistischen theorie mentaler repräsentation.* Paderborn: Schöningh.

Metzinger, T. (2003). *Being no one: The self model theory of subjectivity.* Cambridge, MA: MIT Press.

Meyer, P. (1994). Apparent communication with discarnate entities induced by dimethyltryptamine (DMT). In T. Lyttle, *Psychedelics* (pp. 161–203). New York: Barricade Books.

Miller, W. R., & Rollnick, S. (1991). *Motivational interviewing.* London: Guildford Press.

Milner, M. (1950). *On not being able to paint.* London: Heinemann.

Mindel, A. (1993). Long-term clinical and psychological management of genital herpes. *Journal of Medical Virology, Supp 1,* 39–44.

Moerman, D. E., & Jonas, W. B. (2002). Deconstructing the placebo effect and finding the meaning response. *Annals of Internal Medicine, 136,* 471–476.

Mohr, C., Graves, R., Gianotti, L., Pizzagalli, D., & Brugger, P. (2001). Loose but normal: A semantic association study. *Journal of Psycholinguistic Research, 30,* 475–483.

Mohr, C., Krummenacher, P., Landis, T., Sandor, P. S., Fathi, M., & Brugger, P. (2005). Psychometric schizotypy modulates levodopa effects on lateralised lexical decision performance. *Journal of Psychiatric Research, 39,* 241–250.

Mohr, C., & Leonards, U. (2005). Does contextual information influence positive and negative schizotypy scores in healthy individuals? The answer is maybe. *Psychiatry Research, 136,* 135–141.

Mölle, M., Marshall, L., Lutzenberger, W., Pietrowsky, R., Fehm, H. L., & Born, J. (1996). Enhanced dynamic complexity in the human EEG during creative thinking. *Neuroscience Letters, 208,* 61–64.

Mölle, M., Schwank, I., Marshall, L., Klöhn A., Born, J. (2000). Dimensional complexity and power spectral measures of the EEG during functional versus predicative problem solving. *Brain and Cognition, 44,* 547–563.

Monastra, V. J., Lynn, S., Linden, M., Lubar, J. F., Gruzelier, J., & LaVaque, T. J. (2005). Electroencephalograpic biofeedback in the treatment of attention-deficit/hyperactivity disorder. *Applied Psychophysiology and Biofeedback, 30,* 95–114.

Montinelli, D. G., & Parra, A. (2000). Conflictive psi experiences: A survey with implications for clinical parapsychology, In *Proceedings of the 43th Annual Convention of the Parapsychological Association,* 178–191.

Montinelli, D. G., & Parra, A. (2004). A clinical approach to the emotional processing of anomalous/paranormal experiences in group therapy. *Journal of the Society for Psychical Research, 68,* 129–142.

Moore, A., & Malinowski, P. (2009). Meditation, mindfulness and cognitive flexibility. *Consciousness and Cognition, 18,* 176–186.

Moore, D. L., Sanders, B., & Ramsay, B. (2004). Differences in inferred hemispheric organization associated with hypnotizability and gender: A study of lateralized dual-task performance. *International Journal of Clinical and Experimental Hypnosis.* In press.

Moreira-Almeida, A., Neto, F. L., & Koenig, H. G. (2006). Religiousness and mental health: A review. *Revista Brasileira de Psiquiatria, 28,* 242–50.

Morgan, A. H., Macdonald, H., & Hilgard, E. R. (1974). EEG alpha: Lateral asymmetry and related to task and hypnotizability. *Psychophysiology, 11,* 275–285.

Morris, R. L. (1986). What psi is not: The necessity for experiments. In H. L. Edge, R. L. Morris, J. Palmer & J. H. Rush (Eds). *Foundations of parapsychology.* Boston: Routledge & Keegan Paul.

Morrison, A. P. (1998). A cognitive analysis of the maintenance of auditory hallucinations: Are voices to schizophrenia what bodily sensations are to panic? *Behavioral and Cognitive Psychotherapy, 26,* 289–303.

Morrison, A. P. (2001). The interpretation of intrusions in psychosis; an integrative cognitive approach to hallucinations and delusions. *Behavioral and Cognitive Psychotherapy, 29,* 257–277.

Morrison, A. P., & Peterson, T. (2003). Trauma, metacognition and predisposition to hallucinations in non-patients. *Behavioral and Cognitive Psychotherapy, 31,* 235–246.

Morrison, A. P., Wells, A., & Nothard, S. (2000). Cognitive factors in predisposition to auditory and visual hallucinations. *British Journal of Clinical Psychology, 39,* 67–78.

Mullis, K. (1998). *Dancing naked in the mind field.* New York: Pantheon Books.

Murphy, C. (2009). The link between artistic creativity and psychopathology: Salvador Dali. *Personality and Individual Differences, 46,* 765–774.

Nachman, G. (2009). Clinical implications of synchronicity and related phenomena. *Psychiatric Annals, 39,* 297–308.

Nadon, R., Laurence, J. R., & Perry, C. (1987). Multiple predictors of hypnotic susceptibility. *Journal of Personality and Social Psychology, 53,* 948–960.

Naitoh, P, Kales, A., Kollar, E. J. Smith J. C., & Jacobson, A. (1969). Electroencephalographic activity after prolonged sleep loss. *Electroencephalography and Clinical Neurophysiology, 27,* 2–11.

Naito, A., Laidlaw, T. M., Henderson, D. C., Farahani, L., Dwivedi, P., & Gruzelier, J. H. (2003). The impact of self-hypnosis and Johrei on lymphocyte sub-population at exam time: A controlled study. *Brain Research Bulletin, 62,* 241–253.

Naranjo, C. (1967). Psychotropic properties of the harmala alkaloids. In D. Efron (Ed.), *Ethnopharmacologic search for psychoactive drugs: Proceedings of symposium held in San Francisco, January 28–30, 1967* (pp. 385–391). Public Health Service Publication No 1645. Washington, DC: U.S. Department of Health, Education, and Welfare.

Naranjo, C. (1973). *The healing journey: New approaches to consciousness.* New York: Ballantine Books.

Naranjo, C. (1987). "Ayahuasca" imagery and the therapeutic property of the harmala alkaloids. *Journal of Mental Imagery, 11* (2), 131–136.

Narby, J. (1998). *The cosmic serpent, DNA, and the origins of knowledge.* London: Tarcher/Putnum.

Narby, J. (2004). Shamans and scientists. In J. Narby and F. Huxley (Eds.), *Shamans through time: 500 years on the path to knowledge* (pp. 301–305). London: Thames and Hudson.

Narby, J. (2006). *Intelligence in nature: An inquiry into knowledge.* New York: Jeremy P. Tarcher/Penguin.

Nash, C. B. (1982). Hypnosis and trascendental meditation as inducers of ESP. *Parapsychology Review, 13*, 19–20.

Nelson, L. D., & Cantrell, C. H. (1980). Religiosity and death anxiety: A multidimensional analysis. *Review of Religious Research, 21*, 148–157.

Neppe, V.M. (1988). Psychopathology of psi: I. A perspective. *Parapsychology Review, 19*, 1–3.

Neppe, V. M. (1988). Psychpathology of psi, part II: A new classification system for psi experience. *Parapsychology Review, 19*, 8–11.

Neppe, V. M. (2009). *Phenomenological anomalistic psychology: Ensuring homogenous data collection for present and future research on possible psi phenomena by detailing subjective descriptions using the Multi-Axial A to Z SEATTLE classification.* Abstract of paper presented at the 52nd Annual Convention of the Parapsychological Association, 17–18.

Nettle, D. (2006). Schizotypy and mental health amongst poets, visual artists, and mathematicians. *Journal of Research in Personality, 40*, 876–890.

Nettle, D., & Clegg, H. (2006). Schizotypy, creativity and mating success in humans. *Proceedings of the Royal Society of London B: Biological Sciences, 273*, 611–615.

Neveu, P. J. (1993). Brain lateralisation and immuno-modulation. *International Journal of Neuroscience, 70*, 1917–1923.

Nielsen, T. (2007). Felt presence: Paranoid delusion or hallucinatory social imagery? *Consciousness and Cognition, 16*, 975–983.

Nielsen, N. C., Hein, N., Reynolds, F. E., Miller, A. L., Karff, S. E., Cowan, A. C.,

McLean, P., & Erdel, T. P. (1988). *Religions of the world.* New York: St. Martin's Press.

Noll, R. (1985). Mental imagery cultivation as a cultural phenomenon: The role of visions in shamanism. *Current Anthropology, 26*, 443–461.

Noll, R. (2004). Shamans, "spirits," and mental imagery. In J. Narby and F. Huxley (Eds.), *Shamans through time: 500 years on the path to knowledge* (pp. 248–250). London: Thames and Hudson.

Norlander, T. (1999). Inebriation and inspiration? A review of the research on alcohol and creativity. *The Journal of Creative Behavior, 33*, 22–44.

Norlander, T., Bergman, H., & Archer, T. (1998). Effects of flotation rest on creative problem solving and originality. *Journal of Environmental Psychology, 18*, 399–408.

Norlander, T., & Gustafson, R. (1996). Effects of alcohol on scientific thought during the incubation phase of the creative process. *Journal of Creative Behavior, 30*, 231–248.

Norlander, T., & Gustafson, R. (1997). Effects of alcohol on picture drawing during the verification phase of the creative process. *Creativity Research Journal, 10*, 355–362.

Norlander, T., & Gustafson, R. (1998). Effects of alcohol on a divergent thinking figural fluency test during the illumination phase of the creative process. *Creativity Research Journal, 11*, 265–274.

Norlander, T., Kjellgren, A., & Archer, T. (2002–2003). Effects of floatation- versus chamber- restricted environmental stimulation technique (REST) on creativity and realism under stress and non-stress conditions. *Imagination, Cognition and Personality, 22*, 343–359.

Nott, K. H., Vedhara, K., & Spickett, G. P. (1995). Psychology, immunology, and HIV. *Psychoneuroendocrinology, 20*, 451–74.

O'Connor, D. B., Cobb, J., & O'Connor, R. C. (2003). Religiosity, stress and psychological distress: no evidence for an association among undergraduate students. *Personality and Individual Differences, 34*, 211–217.

O'Reilly, T., Dunbar, R., & Bentall, R. (2001). Schizotypy and creativity: An evolutionary connection? *Personality and Individual Differences, 31*, 1067–1078.

Oertel, V., Rotarska-Jabiela, A., van de Ven, V., Haenschel, C., Grube, M., Sangier, U.,

Maurer, K., & Linden, D. E. J. (2009). Mental imagery vividness as a trait marker across the schizophrenia spectrum. *Psychiatry Research, 167,* 1–11.

Ogalde, J. P., Arriaza, B. T., & Soto, E. C. (2008). Identification of psychoactive alkaloids in ancient Andean human hair by gas chromatography/mass spectrometry. *Journal of Archaeological Science, 36*(2), 467–72.

Olness, K., Culbert, T., & Den, D. (1989). Self-regulation of salivary immunoglobulin A by children. *Pediatrics, 83,* 66–71.

Oshmann, J. (2000). *Energy medicine — the scientific basis.* Edinburgh: Churchill Livingstone.

Osis, K., & Bokert, E. (1971). ESP changed states of consciousness induced by meditation. *The Journal of the American Society for Psychical Research, 65,* 17–65.

Ospina, M. B., Bond, T. K., Karkhaneh, M., Tjosvold, L., Vandermeer, B., Liang, Y., Bialy, L. Hooton, N., Buscemi, N., Dryden, D. M., & Klassen, T. P. (2007). *Meditation practices for health: State of the research evidence report/Technology assessment No. 155.* Rockville, MD: AHRQ Publication No. 07-E010.

Ossoff, J. (1993). Reflections of Shaktipat: Psychosis or the rise of Kundalini? A case study. *The Journal of Transpersonal Psychology, 25,* 29–42.

Ots, T. (1994). The silenced body — the expressive Leib: On the dialectic of mind and life in Chinese cathartic healing. In T. J. Csordas (Ed.), *Embodiment and experience* (pp. 269–290). Cambridge: Cambridge University Press.

Pahnke, W. N. (1966). Drugs and mysticism. *The International Journal of Parapsychology, 8* (2), 295–313.

Palmer, J. (1979). A community mail survey of psychic experiences. *Journal of the American Society for Psychical Research, 73,* 221–251.

Palmer, J. (2003). ESP in the Ganzfeld: Analysis of a debate. *Journal of Consciousness Studies, 10,* 51–68.

Palmer, J., Khamashta, K., & Israelson, K. (1979). An ESP Ganzfeld experiment with trascendental meditators. *The Journal of the American Society for Psychical Research, 73,* 333–348.

Palmer, J., Simmonds-Moore, C., & Bau-mann, S. (2006). Geomagnetic fields and the relationship between human intentionality and the hemolysis of red blood cells. *Journal of Parapsychology, 70,* 275–302.

Panells, T., & Claxton, A. (2008). Happiness, creative ideation, and locus of control. *Creativity Research Journal, 20,* 67–71.

Pargament, K. I. (1997). *The psychology of religion and coping: Theory, research, and practice.* London: Guilford Press.

Parker, A. (1975). *States of mind: ESP and altered states of consciousness.* London: Malaby Press.

Parker, A. (2000). A review of the Ganzfeld work at Gothenburg University. *Journal of the Society for Psychical Research, 64.1,* 1–15.

Parra, A., & Espinoza Paul, L. (2009). Exploring the links between nocturnal hallucinatory experiences and personality characteristics. *European Journal of Parapsychology, 24.2,* 139–154.

Passie, T. (2007). Contemporary psychedelic therapy: An overview. In M. J. Winkelman and T. B. Roberts (Eds.), *Psychedelic medicine: New evidence for hallucinogenic substances as treatments* (vol. 1) (pp. 45–68). Westport, CT: Praeger.

Pekala, R. J. (1991). *Quantifying consciousness: An empirical approach.* New York: Plenum Press.

Pekala, R. J., & Nagler, R. (1989). The assessment of hypnoidal states: Rationale and clinical application. *American Journal of Clinical Hypnosis, 31,* 231–6.

Peniston, E. G., & Kulkosky, P. J. (1989). Alpha-theta brainwave training and beta endorphin levels in alcoholics. *Alcoholism: Clinical and Experimental Research, 13,* 271–279.

Peniston, E. G., & Kulkosky, P. J. (1991). Alpha-theta brainwave neurofeedback for Vietnam veterans with combat-related post-traumatic stress disorder. *Medical Psychotherapy, 4,* 47–60.

Perkins, S. L., & Allen, R. (2006). Childhood physical abuse and differential development of paranormal belief systems. *Journal of Nervous and Mental Disease, 194,* 349–355.

Perry, M. (1987). *Deliverance.* London: SPCK.

Persinger, M. A. (1989). Psi phenomena and temporal lobe activity: The geomagnetic factor. In L. A. Henkel and R. E. Berger (Eds.), *Research in parapsychology 1988* (pp. 121–156). Metuchen, NJ: Scarecrow.

Persinger, M. A. (1996). Hypnosis and the brain: The relationship between subclinical complex partial epileptic-like symptoms, imagination, suggestibility, and changes in self identity. In R. G. Kunzendorf, N. P. Spanos and B. Wallace (Eds.), *Hypnosis and imagination* (pp. 283–305). New York: Baywood.

Persinger, M. A., & Makarec, K. (1987). Temporal lobe epileptic signs and correlative behaviors displayed by normal populations. *The Journal of General Psychology, 114, 179–195.*

Persinger, M., & Makarec, K. (1992). The feeling of a presence and verbal meaningfulness in context of temporal lobe function: Factor analytic verification of the muses? *Brain and Cognition, 20, 217–226.*

Persinger, M. A., Tiller, S. G., & Koren, S. A. (2000). Experimental simulation of a haunt experience and elicitation of paroxysmal electroencephalographic activity by transcerebral complex magnetic fields: induction of a synthetic "ghost"? *Perceptual and Motor Skills, 90, 659–674.*

Persinger, M., & Healey, F. (2002). Experimental facilitation of the sensed presence: Possible intercalation between the hemispheres induced by complex magnetic fields. *Journal of Nervous and Mental Disease, 190,* 533–541.

Peters, E. R., Day, S., McKenna, J., & Orbach, G. (1999). The incidence of delusional ideation in religious and psychotic populations. *British Journal of Clinical Psychology, 38,* 83 – 96.

Peters, E. R., Joseph, S., Day, S., & Garety, P. A. (2004). Measuring delusional ideation: The 21-item Peters et al. Delusions Inventory (PDI). *Schizophrenia Bulletin, 30,* 1005–1022.

Phillips, R., Clarke,I., & Wilson, H. (in submission). What is real and what is not. Evaluation of an inpatient group CBT for psychosis program designed to address the stigma of diagnosis. *Psychology and Psychotherapy: Theory, Research and Practice.*

Piaget, J. (1967). *The language and thought of the child.* New York: Basic Books.

Piedmont, R. L. (2001). Does spirituality represent the sixth factor of personality? Spiritual transcendence and the five-factor model. *Journal of Personality, 67,* 985–1013.

Pine, F., & Holt, R. (1960). Creativity and primary process: A study of adaptive regression. *Journal of Abnormal and Social Psychology, 61,* 370–379.

Pizzagalli, D., Lehmann, D., Gianotti, D., Koenig, T., Tanaka, H., Wackermann, J., & Brugger, P. (2000). Brain correlates of strong belief in paranormal phenomena: Intracerebral EEG source and regional Omega complexity analyses. *Psychiatry Research, 100,* 139–154.

Platt, B. (2007). Presence, poetry and the collaborative right hemisphere. *Journal of Consciousness Studies, 14,* 36–53.

Plucker, J., & Dana, R. (1999). Drugs and creativity. In M. A. Runco & S. Pritzker (Eds.), *Encyclopedia of creativity* (pp. 607–611). San Diego, CA: Academic Press.

Plucker, J., & Renzulli, J. (1999). Psychometric approaches to the study of human creativity. In R. Sternberg (Ed.), *Handbook of creativity* (pp. 35–61). Cambridge: Cambridge University Press.

Posey, T. B., & Losch, M. E. (1983). Auditory hallucinations of hearing voices in 375 normal subjects. *Imagination, Cognition and Personality, 3,* 99–113.

Poulton, R., Caspi A., Moffitt T. E., Cannon M., Murray R., Harrington, H. (2000). Children's self-reported psychotic symptoms and adult schizophreniform disorder: A 15-year longitudinal study. *Archives of General Psychiatry, 57,* 1053–1058.

Prentky, R. (2000–2001). Mental illness and roots of genius. *Creativity Research Journal, 13,* 95–104.

Price, L. H., & Lebel, J. (2000). Dextromethorphan-induced psychosis. *American Journal of Psychiatry, 157* (2), 304.

Quekelberghe van, R., Alstotter-Gleich, C., & Hertweck, E. (1991). Assessment schedule for altered states of consciousness. *The Journal of Parapsychology, 55,* 377–390.

Raab, J., & Gruzelier, J. H. (1994). A controlled investigation of right hemispheric processing enhancement after restricted environmental stimulation (REST) with flotation. *Psychological Medicine, 24,* 457–462.

Radin, D. (2006). *Entangled minds.* New York: Pocket Books, Simon & Schuster.

Radin, D. (2008). Testing nonlocal observation as a source of intuitive knowledge. *Explore: The Journal of Science and Healing, 4,* 25–35.

Radin, D., & Lobach, E. (2007).Toward understanding the placebo effect: Investigating a possible retrocausal factor. *The Journal of Alternative and Complementary Medicine, 13,* 733–739.

Radin, D., Stone, J., Levine, E., Eskandarnejad, S., Schlitz, M., Kozak, L., Mandel, D., & Hayssen, G. (2006). Effects of motivated distant intention on electrodermal activity. *The Parapsychological Association 49th Annual Convention. Proceedings of Presented Papers* (pp. 176–188). Stockholm, Sweden.

Rainville, P., Hofbauer, R. K., Bushnell, M. C., Duncan, G. H., & Price, D. D. (2000). Hypnosis modulates activity in brain structures involved in the regulation of consciousness. *Journal of Cognitive Neuroscience, 14,* 887–901.

Rainville, P., Hofbauer, R. K., & Paus, T. (1999). Cerebral mechanisms of hypnotic induction and suggestion. *Journal of Cognitive Neuroscience, 11,* 110–25.

Ram Dass. (1971). *Be here now.* New York: Crown.

Rand, W. L. (2000). *The spirit of reiki.* 6th ed. Twin Lakes, WI: Lotus Press.

Rao, K. R., Dukhan, H., & Rao, P. V. K. (1978). Yogic meditation and psi scoring in forced-choice and free-response tests. *Journal of Indian Psychology, 1,* 160–175.

Rao, K. R., & Puri, I. (1978). Subsensory perception (SSP), extrasensory perception (ESP) and trascendental meditation (TM). *Journal of Indian Psychology, 1,* 69–74.

Rao, P. K., & Rao, K. R. (1982). Two studies of ESP and subliminal perception. *Journal of Parapsychology, 46,* 185–207.

Rawlings, D. (1985). Psychoticism, creativity and dichotic shadowing. *Personality and Individual Differences, 6,* 737–742.

Rawlings, D., & Locarnini, A. (2008). Dimensional schizotypy, autism, and unusual word associations in artists and scientists. *Journal of Research in Personality, 42,* 465–471.

Rawlings, D., & Toogood, A. (1997). Using a "taboo response" measure to examine the relationship between divergent thinking and psychoticism. *Personality and Individual Differences, 22,* 61–68.

Rawlings, D., Williams, B., Haslam, N., & Claridge G. (2008). Taxometric analysis supports a dimensional latent structure for schizotypy. *Personality and Individual Differences, 44,* 1640–1651.

Raymond, J., Sajid, I., Parkinson, L., & Gruzelier, J. (2005a). Biofeedback and dance performance: A preliminary investigation. *Applied Psychophysiology and Biofeedback, 30,* 65–73.

Raymond, J., Varney, C., & Gruzelier, J. H. (2005b). The effects of alpha/theta neurofeedback on personality and mood. *Cognitive Brain Research, 23,* 287–292.

Reed, G. (1988). *The psychology of anomalous experience.* New York: Prometheus Books.

Rees, A. (2004, August 8). Nobel Prize genius Crick was high on LSD when he discovered the secret of life. *Mail on Sunday.* http://www.hallucinogens.com/lsd/francis-crick.html.

Rein, G. (1998). Biological effects of quantum fields and their role in the natural healing process. *Frontier Perpectives, 7,* 16–23.

Renouz, G., Biziere, K. Renoux, M., Guillaumin, J., & Degenne, D. (1983a). A balanced brain asymmetry modulates T-cell mediated events. *Journal of Neuroimmunology, 5,* 227–238.

Renouz, G., Biziere, K. Renoux, M., & Guilluamin, J. (1983b). The production of T-cell inducing factors in mice is controlled by the brain neortex. *Scandinavian Journal of Immunology, 17,* 45–50.

Richards, R. (2010). Everyday creativity: Process and way of life—four key issues. In J. Kaufman & R. Sternberg (Eds.), *The cambridge handbook of creativity* (pp. 189–215). Cambridge: Cambridge University Press.

Richardson, A., & Gruzelier, J. (1994). Visual processing, lateralisation and syndromes of schizotypy. *International Journal of Psychophysiology, 18,* 227–240.

Richards, R., Kinney, D., & Lunde, I. (1988). Creativity in manic-depressives, cyclothymes and their normal first-degree relatives: A preliminary report. *Journal of Abnormal Psychology, 97,* 281–288.

Rinaldo, C. R., Jr., & Torpey, D. J. (1995). Cell mediated immunity and immunosuppression in herpes simplex virus infection. *Immunodeficiency, 5,* 33–90.

Robinson, G., Heenan, D., Gray, A. M., & Thompson, K. (Eds.). (1998). *Social attitudes in Northern Ireland: The seventh report.* Hants: Ashgate Publishing.

Rock, A. J. (2006). Phenomenological analysis of experimentally induced visual mental imagery associated with shamanic journeying to the lower world. *International Journal of Transpersonal Studies, 25*, 45–55.

Rock, A. J., Casey, P. J., & Baynes, P. B. (2006). Experimental study of ostensibly shamanic journeying imagery in naïve participants II: Phenomenological mapping and modified affect bridge. *Anthropology of Consciousness, 17*(1), 65–83.

Rock, A. J., & Krippner, S. (2008). Some rudimentary problems pertaining to the construction of an ontology and epistemology of shamanic journeying imagery. *International Journal of Transpersonal Studies, 27*, 12–19.

Rodriguez, M. A. (2007). A methodology for studying various interpretations of the N,N-dimethyltryptamine-induced alternate reality. *Journal of Scientific Exploration, 21*(1), 67–84.

Roe, A. (1946). Alcohol and creative work. *Quarterly Journal of Studies on Alcohol, 6*, 415–467.

Roll, W. G., Krippner, S., Montagno, E. de A., Siegel, C., Solfvin, S., Isaacs, J., & Stewart, J. L. (1986). Clinical parapsychology. In D. H. Weiner & D. I. Radin (Eds.), *Research in parapsychology 1985: Abstracts and papers from the twenty-eighth annual convention of the Parapsychology Association, 1985* (pp. 168–177). Metuchen, NJ: Scarecrow.

Romme, M., & Escher, S. (1989). *Accepting voices.* London: Mind Publications.

Romme, E., & Escher, A. (1989). Hearing voices. *Schizophrenia Bulletin, 15*, 209–216.

Rominger, R. A. (2009). Exploring the integration of near-death experience aftereffects: Summary of findings. *Journal of Near-Death Studies, 28*, 3–34.

Roney-Dougal, S. M. (1991). *Where science and magic meet.* London: Element Books.

Roney-Dougal, S., & Solfvin, J. (2006). Yogic attainment in relation to awareness of precognitive targets. *Journal of Parapsychology, 70*, 91–117.

Roney-Dougal, S., & Solfvin, J. (2008). Meditation attainment in relation to precognition. (Abstract). *Poster presented at Bial Foundation 7th Symposium Behind and Beyond the Brain.* Fundaçao Bial, Portugal, March 26–29, 2008.

Ros, T., Moseley, M. J., Bloom, P. A., Benjamin, L. Parkinson, L. A., & Gruzelier, J. H. (2009). Optimizing microsurgical skills with EEG neurofeedback. *BMC Neuroscience, 10*, 87.

Ros, T., Munneke, M. A. M., Ruge, D., Gruzelier, J. H., & Rothwell, J. C. (2010). Endogenous control of waking alpha rhythms induces neuroplasticity. *European Journal of Neuroscience, 31*, 770–778.

Rose, R. (1987). *Northern Ireland: A time for choice.* London: MacMillan.

Rosenthal, R. (1994). Parametric measures of effect size. In: H. Cooper & L. V. Hedges (Eds.), *The handbook of research synthesis* (pp. 231–244). New York: Russell Sage Foundation.

Ross, C. A. (1985). Problems in diagnosing partial forms of Multiple Personality Disorder. *Journal of the Royal Society of Medicine, 75*, 933–936.

Rossi, E., Rossi, K., Yount, G., Cozzolino, M., & Iannotti, S. (2006). The bioinformatics of integrative medical insights: Proposals for an international psychosocial and cultural bioinformatics project. *Integrative Medicine Insights, 2*, 1–19.

Rothenberg, A. (2001). Bipolar illness, creativity and treatment. *Psychiatric Quarterly, 72*, 131–147.

Rowan, J. (1988). *Ordinary ecstasy: Humanistic psychology in action.* London: Routledge.

Rubic, B., Brooks, A. J., & Schwartz, G. E. (2006). In vitro effect of Reiki treatment on bacterial cultures: Role of experimental context and practitioner well-being. *Journal of Alternative and Complementary Medicine, 12*, 7–13.

Rubinstein, G. (2008). Are schizophrenic patients necessarily creative? A comparative study between three groups of psychiatric inpatients. *Personality and Individual Differences, 45*, 806–810.

Runco, M. (1994). Creativity and its discontents. In M. Shaw & M. Runco (Eds.), *Creativity and affect* (pp. 102–123). Norwood, NJ: Ablex Publishing Corporation.

Russ, S. (1999). Play, affect and creativity: Theory and research. In S. Russ (Ed.), *Affect, creative experience and psychological adjustment* (pp. 57–75). Philadelphia, PA: Brunner/Mazel.

Russ, S. (2001). Primary process thinking and creativity: Affect and cognition. *Creativity Research Journal, 13*, 27–36.

Ryan, R. M., & Frederick, C. (1997). On energy, personality and health: Subjective vitality as a dynamic reflection of wellbeing. *Journal of Personality, 65* (3), 529–565.

Ryle, A. (1995). *Cognitive Analytic Therapy.* Chichester: Wiley.

Saß, H., Wittchen, H.-U., & Zaudig, M. (2003). *Diagnostisches und statistisches manual psychischer störungen. (DSM-IV-TR.) textrevision.* Göttingen: Hogrefe.

Sanderson, S. K. (2008). Adaptation, evolution, and religion. *Religion, 38,* 141–156.

Santarcangelo, E. L., & Sebastiani, L. (2004). Hypnotizability as an adaptive trait. *Contemporary Hypnosis, 21,* 3–13.

Sarà, M., & Pistoia, F. (2010). Complexity loss in physiological time series of patients in a vegetative state. *Nonlinear Dynamics, Psychology and Life Sciences, 14,* 1–13.

Sass, L., & Schuldberg, D. (Eds.). (2000–2001). Special issue: Creativity and the schizophrenia spectrum. *Creativity Research Journal, 13.*

Sayer, A. G. (2000). Design therapy. In L. E. Luna and S. F. White (Eds.), *Ayahuasca reader: Encounters with the Amazon's sacred vine* (pp. 127–132). Sante Fe, New Mexico: Synergetic Press.

Schedlowski, M., Jacobs, R., Stratmann, G., Richter, S., Hadicke, A., Tewes, U., Wagner, T. O., & Schmidt, R. E. (1993). Changes of natural killer cells during acute psychological stress. *Journal of Clinical Immunology, 13,* 119–126.

Schlitz, M., Radin, D., Malle, B. F., Schmidt, S., Utts, J., & Yount, G. (2003). Distant healing intention: Definitions and evolving guidelines for laboratory. *Alternative Therapies in Health and Medicine, 9,* A31-A43.

Schmeidler, G. (1970). High ESP scores after a Swami's brief instruction in meditation and breathing. *Journal of the American Society for Psychical Research, 64,* 100–103.

Schmeidler, G. (1994). ESP expriments 1978–1992: The glass is half full. In S. Krippner (Ed.), *Advances in parapsychological research 7* (pp. 104–197). Jefferson, NC: McFarland.

Schmidt, S. (2003). Direct mental interaction with living systems (DMILS). In: W. B. Jonas & C. C. Crawford (Eds.), *Healing, intention and energy medicine: Research and clinical implications* (pp. 23–38). Edinburgh: Churchill Livingstone.

Schmidt, S. (2008). Aristotle's fly: Remarks on anomaly research and a review on the relationship between meditation and psi. *Behind and Beyond the Brain. 7th Symposium of the Bial Foundation 2008.* Emotions. Proceedings (pp. 73–95). Fundaçao Bial, Portugal, March 26–29, 2008.

Schmidt, S. (2009). *Mindfulness in east and west: Is it the same?* (Unpublished).

Schmidt, H., & Schlitz, M. (1989). A large-scale pilot PK experiment with prerecorded random events. *Research in Parapsychology 1988* (pp. 6–10). Metuchen, NJ: Scarecrow.

Schmidt, S., Schneider, R., Utts, J. M., & Walach, H. (2004). Distant intentionality and the feeling of being stared at: Two meta-analyses. *British Journal of Psychology, 95,* 235–247.

Schofield, K., & Claridge, G. (2007). Paranormal experiences and mental health: Schizotypy as an underlying factor. *Personality and Individual Differences, 43,* 1908–1916.

Schooler, J., & Melcher, J. (1995). The ineffability of insight. In S. Smith, T. Ward, & R. Finke (Eds.), *The creative cognition approach.* Cambridge, MA: MIT Press.

Schredl, M., Schafer, G., Hofmann, F., & Jacob, S. (1999). Dream content and personality: Thick vs. thin boundaries. *Dreaming, 9,* 257–263.

Schuldberg, D. (1992). Ego-strength revised — A comparison of the MMPI-2 and MMPI-1 versions of the Barron Ego Strength Scale. *Journal of Clinical Psychology, 48,* 500–505.

Schuldberg, D. (1994). Giddiness and horror in the creative process. In M. Shaw & M. Runco (Eds.), *Creativity and affect* (pp. 87–101). Norwood, NJ: Ablex Publishing Corporation.

Schuldberg, D. (2000–2001). Six subclinical spectrum traits in normal creativity. *Creativity Research Journal, 13,* 5–16.

Schultes, R. E., & Hofmann, A. (1992). *Plants of the Gods: Their sacred, healing, and hallucinogenic powers.* Rochester, VT: Healing Arts Press.

Schupp-Ihle, C. (2010). Post-counseling interviews of the IGPP counseling clientele. In D. Vaitl (Hrsg.), *Tätigkeitsbericht — Biennial Report 2008–2009* (p. 70). Freiburg: Institut für Grenzgebiete der Psychologie und Psychohygiene e.V.

Schupp, H. T., Lutzenberger, W., Birbaumer, N., Miltner, W., & Braun, C. (1994). Neurophysiological differences between perception and imagery. *Cognitive Brain Research, 2,* 77–86.

Schwartz, S., & Dossey, L. (2010). Nonlocality, intention and observer effects in healing studies: Laying a foundation for the future. *EXPLORE: The Journal of Science and Healing, 6,* 295–307.

Schweinle, A., & turner, J. (2006). Striking the right balance: Students' motivational experiences and affect in upper elementary mathematics classes. *Journal of Educational Research, 99,* 271–293.

Scott, W. C., Kaiser, D., Othmer, S., & Sideroff, S. I. (2005). Effects of an EEG biofeedback protocol on a mixed substance abusing population. *American Journal of Drug and Alcohol Abuse 31,* 455–469.

Segal, J. Z. (2005). *Health and the rhetoric of medicine.* Carbondale: Southern Illinois University Press.

Segal, Z. V., Gemar, M., & Williams, S. (1999). Differential cognitive response to a mood challenge following successful cognitive therapy or pharmacotherapy for unipolar depression. *Journal of Abnormal Psychology, 108,* 3–10.

Segal, Z. V., Williams, J. M. G., & Teasdale, J. D. (2002). *Mindfulness-based cognitive therapy for depression: A new approach to preventive relapse.* New York: Guilford Press.

Sessa, B. (2008). Is it time to revisit the role of psychedelic drugs in enhancing human creativity? *Journal of Psychopharmacology, 22,* 821–827.

Seto, A., Kusaka, S., & Nakazato, S. (1992). Detection of extraordinary large biomagnetic field strength from human hand. *Acupuncture and Electro Therapeutic Research International Journal, 17,* 75–94.

Sewell, R. A., & Halpern, J. H. (2007). Response of cluster headache to psilocybin and LSD. In M. J. Winkelman and T. B. Roberts (Eds.), *Psychedelic medicine: New evidence for hallucinogenic substances as treatments* (vol. 1) (pp. 97–123). Westport, CT: Praeger.

Shadish, W. R., & Haddock, C. K. (1994). Combining estimates of effect size. In: H. Cooper & L. V. Hedges (Eds.), *The handbook of research synthesis* (pp. 261–281). New York: Russell Sage Foundation.

Shames, V., & Bowers, P. (1992). Hypnosis and creativity. In E. Fromm & R. Nash (Eds.), *Contemporary Hypnosis Research* (pp. 334–363). New York: Guildford Press.

Shankman, R. (2008). *The experience of samadhi. An in-depth exploration of Buddhist meditation.* Boston: Shambala.

Shanon, B. (2002). *The antipodes of the mind: Charting the phenomena of the ayahuasca experience.* Oxford: Oxford University Press.

Shanon, B. (2003). Hallucinations. *Journal of Consciousness Studies, 10* (2), 3–31.

Shapiro, D. (1982). Overview: Clinical and physiological comparison of meditation with other self-control strategies. *American Journal of Psychiatry, 139,* 267–274.

Shapiro, D. H. (1992). A preliminary study of long-term meditators: Goals, effects, religious orientation, cognitions. *The Journal of Transpersonal Psychology, 24,* 23–39.

Shapiro, S. L., Carlson, L. E., Astin, J. A., & Freedman, B. (2006). Mechanisms of mindfulness. *Journal of Clinical Psychology, 62,* 373–386.

Sherwood, S. J. (2002). Relationship between the hypnagogic/hypnopompic states and reports of anomalous experiences. *Journal of Parapsychology, 66,* 127–150.

Sherwood, S. J., & Roe, C. A. (2003). A review of dream ESP studies conducted since the Maimonides dream ESP programme. *Journal of Consciousness Studies, 10,* 85–109.

Shevlin M, Dorahy M, Adamson G. (2007). Childhood traumas and hallucinations: An analysis of the National Comorbidity Survey. *Journal of Psychiatric Research, 41,* 222–228.

Shiah, Y-J. (2009). Can ESP abilities be trained? A model for ESP training. *Journal of the Society for Psychical Research, 73,* 231–242.

Shor, R. E., & Orne, E. C. (1962). *Harvard Group Scale of Hypnotic Susceptibility: Form A.* Palo Alto, CA: Consulting Psychologists Press.

Shulgin, A. T, & Shulgin, A. (1997). *TIHKAL: The continuation.* Berkeley, CA: Transform Press.

Siegal, A. B. (2010). Dream interpretation in clinical practice: A century after Freud. *Sleep Medicine Clinics, 5,* 299–313.

Simeonova, D., Chang, K., Stong, C., & Ketter, T. (2005). Creativity in familial bipolar disorder. *Journal of Psychiatric Research, 39,* 623–631.

Simmonds, C. A. (2003). *Investigating schizo-typy as an anomaly-prone personality.* Unpublished doctoral thesis: University College Northampton.

Simmonds-Moore, C. A. (2009). Sleep patterns, personality and subjective anomalous experiences. *Imagination, Cognition and Personality, 29,* 71–86.

Simmonds-Moore, C. A. (2010). Personality variables in spontaneous psi research: Contextualising the boundary construct in its relationship to spontaneous psi phenomena In C. A. Roe, W. Kramer, & L. Coly (Eds.), *Proceedings of an International Conference Utrecht II: Charting the future of parapsychology* (pp. 151–215). New York: Parapsychology Foundation.

Simmonds-Moore, C. A., & Connell, C. (in preparation). Exploring sleep interjection theory: Do reduced sleep quality and gender impact on hallucinatory experiences in the general population?

Simmonds, C. A., & Fox, J. (2004). Note: A pilot investigation into sensory noise, schizotypy and extrasensory perception. *Journal of the Society for Psychical Research, 68,* 253–261.

Simmonds-Moore, C., & Holt, N. (2007). Trait, state and psi: An exploration of the interaction between individual differences, state preference and psi performance in the Ganzfeld and a waking ESP control . *Journal of the Society for Psychical Research, 71,* 197–215.

Simonton, O. C., Matthews-Simonton, S., & Creighton, J. (1978). *Getting well again.* Los Angeles: J. B. Tarcher.

Sinclair-Geiben, A. H., & Chalmers, D. (1959). Evaluation of treatment of warts by hypnosis. *Lancet, 2,* 480–482.

Singh, N. N., Lancioni, G. E., Wahler, R. G., Winton, A. S. W., & Singh, J. (2008). Mindfulness approaches in cognitive behavior therapy. *Behavioral and Cognitive Psychotherapy, 36,* 659–666.

Sio, U., & Ormerod, T. (2009). Does incubation enhance problem solving? *Psychological Bulletin, 135,* 94–120.

Skirda, R. J., & Persinger, M. A. (1993). Positive associations among dichotic listening errors, complex partial epileptic like signs, and paranormal beliefs. *Journal of Nervous and Mental Disease, 181,* 663–667.

Sladeczek, I., & Domino, G. (1985). Creativity, sleep and primary process thinking in dreams. *Journal of Creative Behavior, 19,* 38–46.

Smart, N. (1996). *Dimensions of the sacred.* London: HarperCollins.

Smith, D. J. (1987). *Equality and inequality in Northern Ireland part 3: Perceptions and views.* London: Policy Studies Institute.

Smith, B. R. (2007). Body, mind and spirit? Towards an analysis of the practice of yoga. *Body and Society, 13* (2), 25–46.

Smith, D. (2007). *Muses, madmen and prophets: Hearing voices and the borders of sanity.* New York: Penguin.

Snoyman, P. (1985). Family therapy in a case of alleged RSPK. *Parapsychological Journal of South Africa, 6,* 75–90.

Snyder, T., & Gackenbach, J. (1988). Individual differences associated with lucid dreaming. In J. Gackenbach, & S. LaBerge (Eds.), *Conscious mind, sleeping brain: Perspectives on lucid dreaming* (pp. 221–259). New York: Plenum Press.

Solé-Leris, A. (1986). *Tranquility and insight. An introduction to the oldest form of Buddhist meditation.* Boston: Shambala.

Solfvin, J. (convenor) (1995). Clinical parapsychology: A panel discussion. In N. J. Zingrone (Ed.), *The Parapsychological Association 38th Annual Convention of Presented Papers,* 461–467.

Solfvin, J., Morris, R. L., Busch, M., Bennett, V., Klimo, J., & McRae, B. (1995). Clinical parapsychology: A panel discussion. In *Proceedings of Presented Papers from the Parapsychological Association 38th Annual Convention,* 461–467.

Spanos, N., & Moretti, P. (1988). Correlates of mystical experience and diabolical experiences in a sample of female university students. *Journal for the Scientific Study of Religion, 27,* 105–116.

Spiegel, H. (1972). An eye-roll test for hypnotisability. *The American Journal of Clinical Hypnosis, 15,* 25–28.

Spiegel, D., Bloom, J. R., Kraemer, H. C., & Gottheil, E. (1989). Effect of psychosocial treatment on survival of patients with metastatic breast cancer. *Lancet, 2,* 888–891.

Spielberger, C. D., Gorsuch, R. L., & Lushene, R. E. (1970). *Manual for the state-trait anxiety inventory.* Palo Alto, CA: Consulting Psychologists, 65.

Spitz, H. (2005). Emotionsregulation bei außergewöhnlichen erfahrungen: Eine fallstudie über ratsuchende mit außergewöhnlichen erfahrungen. Unveröffentlichte Diplomarbeit: Universität Freiburg.

Srinivasan, N., &. Baijal, S. (2007). Concentrative meditation enhances pre-attentive processing: A MMN study. *Neuroreport* 18, 1709–1712.

Stace, W. (1960). *The teachings of the mystics.* New York: New American Library.

Stanford, M. S., Mathias, C. W., Dougherty, D. M., Lake, S. L., Anderson, N. E., & Patton, J. H. (2009). Fifty years of the Barratt Impulsiveness Scale: An update and review. *Personality and Individual Differences, 47,* 385–395.

Stanford, R. G., & Palmer, J. (1973). Meditation prior to the ESP task. An EEG study with an outstanding ESP subject. *Research in Parapsychology 1972* (pp. 34–36). Metuchen, NJ: Sass, L. (2000). Schizophrenia, modernism, and the "creative imagination": On creativity and psychopathology. *Creativity Research Journal, 13,* 55–74.

Steel, C., Fowler, D., & Holmes, E. A. (2005). Trauma related intrusions and psychosis. *Behavioral and Cognitive Psychotherapy, 33,* 139–152.

Steinkamp, F., Milton, J., & Morris, R. L. (1998). Meta-analysis of forced-choice experiments comparing clairvoyance and precognition. *Journal of Parapsychology, 62,* 193–218.

Sternberg, R. (2005). Creativity or creativities? *International Journal of Human-Computer Studies, 63,* 370–382.

Storm, L., Tressoldi, P. E., & Di Risio, L. (2010). Meta-analysis of free-response studies, 1992–2008: Assessing the noise reduction model in parapsychology. *Psychological Bulletin, 136,* 471–485.

Strassman, R. (2001). *DMT: The spirit molecule: A doctor's revolutionary research into the biology of near-death and mystical experiences.* Rochesta, VT: Park Street Press.

Strassman, R., Wojtowicz, S., Luna, L. E., & Frecska, E. (2008). *Inner paths to outer space: Journeys to alien worlds through psychedelics and other spiritual technologies.* Rochester, VT: Park Street Press.

Stuckey, H., & Nobel, J. (2010). The connection between art, healing, and public health: A review of the current literature.

American Journal of Public Health, 100, 254–264.

Suedfeld, P., Metcalfe, J., & Bluck, S. (1987). Enhancement of scientific creativity by flotation REST (Restricted Environmental Stimulation Technique). *Journal of Environmental Psychology, 7,* 219–231.

Suedfeld, P., Steel, G., & Wallbaum, A. (1994). Explaining the effects of stimulus restriction: testing the dynamic hemispheric asymmetry hypothesis. *Journal of Environmental Psychology, 14,* 87–100.

Suler, J. (1980). Primary process thinking and creativity. *Psychological Bulletin, 88,* 144–165.

Sumich, A., Kumari, V., Gordon, E., Tunstall, N., & Brammer, M. (2007). Event-related potential correlates of paranormal ideation and unusual experiences. *Cortex, 44,* 1342–1352.

Taft, R. (1969). Peak experiences and ego permissiveness: An exploratory factor study of their dimensions in normal persons. *Acta Psychologica, 29,* 35–64.

Taft, R., & Gilchrist, M. (1970). Creative attitudes and creative productivity: A comparison of two aspects of creativity among students. *Journal of Educational Psychology, 61,* 136–143.

Targ, R. (1994). Remote viewing replication evaluated by concept analysis. *Journal of Parapsychology, 58,* 271–84.

Targ, E., Schlitz, M., & Irwin, H. (2000). Psi-related experiences. In E. Cardeña, S. Lynn, & S. Krippner (Eds.), *Varieties of anomalous experience: Examining the scientific evidence,* pp. 219–252. Washington, DC: American Psychological Association.

Tart, C. T. (1972). States of consciousness and state-specific sciences. *Science, 176,* 1203–1210.

Tart, C. T. (2000). Investigating altered states of consciousness on their own terms: A proposal for the creation of state-specific sciences. *International Journal of Parapsychology, 11* (1), 7–41.

Tarrier, N, Beckett, R, Harwood, S, Baker, A, Yusupoff, L, & Ugarteburu, I. (1993). A trial of two cognitive-behavioral methods of treating drug-resistant residual psychotic symptoms in schizophrentic patients: I. Outcome. *British Journal of Psychiatry, 162,* 524–532.

Teasdale, J. D. (1988). Cognitive vulnerability

to persistent depression. *Cognition & Emotion, 2,* 247–274.

Teasdale, J. D. (1999). Emotional Processing: Three modes of mind and the prevention of relapse in depression. *Behavior Research and Therapy, 37,* S53–S77.

Warner, R. (2003). *Recovery from schizophrenia: Psychiatry and political economy* (3d ed.). London: Routledge.

Teasdale, J. D., & Barnard, P. J. (1993). *Affect, cognition and change: Remodelling depressive thought.* Hove, UK: Lawrence Erlbaum Associates.

Teasdale, J. D., Moore, R. G., Hayhurst, H., Pope, M., Williams, S., & Segal, Z. V. (2002). Metacognitive awareness and prevention of relapse in depression: Empirical evidence. *Journal of Consulting and Clinical Psychology, 70,* 275–287.

Teasdale, J. D., Segal, Z. V., & Williams, J. M. G. (1994). How does cognitive therapy prevent depressive relapse and why should attentional control (mindfulness) training help? *Behavior Research and Therapy, 33,* 25–39.

Teasdale, J. D., Segal, Z. V., Williams, J. M. G., Ridgeway, V. A., Soulsby, J. M., & Lau, M. A. (2000). Prevention of relapse/recurrence in major depression by mindfulness-based cognitive therapy. *Journal of Consulting and Clinical Psychology, 68,* 615–623.

Tellegen, A., & Atkinson, G. (1974). Openness to absorbing and self-altering experiences ("absorption"), a trait related to hypnotic susceptibility. *Journal of Abnormal Psychology, 83,* 268–277.

Thalbourne, M. A. (1998). Technical note: The level of paranormal belief and experience among psychotics. *Journal of Parapsychology, 62,* 79–81.

Thalbourne, M. A. (1998). Transliminality: Further correlates and a short measure. *Journal of the American Society for Psychical Research, 92,* 402–419.

Thalbourne, M. A. (2000a). Transliminality: A review. *International Journal of Parapsychology, 11,* 1–34.

Thalbourne, M. (2000b). Transliminality and creativity. *The Journal of Creative Behavior, 34,* 193–202.

Thalbourne, M. (2000c). Relation between transliminality and openness to experience. *Psychological Reports, 86,* 909–910.

Thalbourne, M. A. (2003). *A glossary of terms used in parapsychology* (2nd ed.). Charlottesville, VA: Puente Publications.

Thalbourne, M., Bartemucci, L., Delin, P., Fox, B., & Nofi, O. (1997). Transliminality: Its nature and correlates. *The Journal of the American Society for Psychical Research, 91,* 305–332.

Thalbourne, M. A., Crawley, S. E., & Houran, J. (2003). Temporal lobe ability in the highly transliminal mind. *Personality and Individual Differences, 35,* 1965–1974.

Thalbourne, M., & Delin, P. (1994). A common thread underlying belief in the paranormal, creative personality, mystical experience and psychopathology. *Journal of Parapsychology, 58,* 3–38.

Thalbourne, M., & Houran, J. (2000). Transliminality, the mental experience inventory and tolerance of ambiguity. *Personality and Individual Differences, 28,* 853–863.

Thalbourne, M., Keogh, E., & Gerke, W. (2005). Transliminality and the Oxford-Liverpool Inventory of Feelings and Experiences. *Psychological Reports, 96,* 579–585.

Thalbourne, M., & Maltby, J. (2008). Transliminality, thin boundaries, unusual experiences, and temporal lobe lability. *Personality and Individual Differences, 44,* 1617–1623.

Thayer, R. E. (1967). Measurement of activation through self-report. *Psychological Reports, 20,* 663–78.

Thompson, T., Steffert, T., & Gruzelier, J. H. (2009). Effects of guided immune imagery: The moderating influence of openness to experience. *Personality and Individual Differences, 47,* 789–794.

Thompson, T., Steffert, T., Steed, A., & Gruzelier, J. H. (2010). A controlled trial of 3D virtual reality animation to assist training in creative immune-visualisation with self-hypnosis with mood and salivary cortisol assessment. *International Journal of Clinical and Experimental Hypnosis,* in press.

Tien, A. Y. (1991). Distributions of hallucinations in the population. *Social Psychiatry and Psychiatric Epidemiology, 26,* 287–292.

Tierney, I. (1993). The experience of significance. In L. Coly & J. D. S. McMahon (Eds.), *Psi and clinical practice.* New York: Parapsychological Foundation.

Tierney, I. (2007). Psychotherapeutic style and the MPI. Paper presented at Euro-PA Conference, Paris.

Tierney, I. (*in press*). Lessons from a case study: An annotated narrative. In W. H. Kramer, E. Bauer & G. H. Hoevelmann (Eds), *Clinical aspects of exceptional human experience*. Utrecht: Stichting Het Johan Borgman Fond.

Tierney, I., Coelho, C., & Lamont, P. (2007). Distressed by anomalous experience: Early identification of psychosis. *Clinical Psychology Forum, 170*, 37–39.

Tölle, P. (2003). *Typische planstrukturen von menschen mit aussergewöhnlichen erfahrungen*. Unveröffentlichte Diplomarbeit: Universität Freiburg.

Tononi, G., Sporns, O., & Edelman, G. M. (1994). A measure for brain complexity: Relating functional segregation and integration in the nervous system. *Proceedings of the National Academy of Sciences of the United States of America, 91*, 5033–5037.

Torrance, E. (2000). *Research review for the Torrance tests of creative thinking figural forms A and B*. Bensenville, IL: Scholastic Testing Service, Inc.

Travis, F., & Arenander, A. (2006). Cross-sectional and longitudinal study of effects of transcendental meditation practice on interhemispheric frontal asymmetry and frontal coherence. *International Journal of Neuroscience, 116*, 1519–1538.

Trubshaw, B. (1995). Dream incubation. *Mercian Mysteries, 23*, 30–33.

Tsakanikos, E., & Claridge, G.S. (2005). More words, less words: Verbal fluency as a function of "positive" and "negative" schizotypy. *Personality and Individual Differences, 39*, 705–713.

Tsuang, M. T., Stone, W. S., & Faraone, S. V. (2000). Toward reformulating the diagnosis of schizophrenia. *American Journal of Psychiatry, 157*, 1041–1050.

Turner, D. M. (1995). Exploring hyperspace. *Entheogen Review: The Journal of Unauthorized Research on Visionary Plants and Drugs, 4* (4), 4–6.

Twemlow, S. W., Gabbard, G. O., & Jones, F. C. (1982). The out of body experience: A phenomenological typology based on questionnaire responses. *American Journal of Psychiatry, 139*, 450–455.

Ullman, M., Krippner, S., & Vaughan, A. (1989). *Dream telepathy: Experiments in nocturnal ESP* (2d ed.). Jefferson, NC: McFarland.

Ullman, M., Krippner, S., & Vaughan, A. (2002). *Dream telepathy: Experiments in extrasensory perception* (3rd ed). Charlottesville, VA: Hampton Roads Publishing.

Unterrainer, H-F, Ladenhauf, K. H., Moazedi, M. L., Wallner-Liebmann, S. J., & Fink, A. (2010). Dimensions of religious/spiritual well-being and their relation to personality and psychological well-being. *Journal of Personality and Individual Differences, 49*, 192–197.

Utts, J. M. (1995a). An assessment of the evidence for psychic functioning. *Journal of Parapsychology, 59* (4), 289–320.

Utts, J. M. (1995b). Response to Ray Hyman's report of September 11, 1995, "Evaluation of program on anomalous mental phenomena." *Journal of Parapsychology, 59* (4), 353–6.

Utts, J. M. (1996). An assessment of the evidence for psychic functioning. *Journal of Scientific Exploration, 10*, 3–39.

Vaitl, D., Birbaumer, N., Gruzelier, J., Jamieson, G., Kotchoubey, B., Kübler, A., Lehmann D., Miltner, W. H. R., Ott, U., Pütz, P., Sammer, G., Strauch, I., Strehl, U., Wackermann, J., & Weiss, T. (2005). Psychobiology of altered states of consciousness. *Psychological Bulletin, 131*, 98–127.

Vaitl, D., Gruzelier, J., Jamieson, G., Lehmann, D., Ott, U., Sammer, G., Strehl, U., Birbaumer, N., Kotchoubey, B., Kübler, A., Miltner, W., Pütz, P., Strauch, I., & Wackermann. J. (2005). Psychobiology of altered states of consciousness. *Psychological Bulletin, 131*, 98–127.

Valentine, E. R., & Sweet, P. L. G. (1999). Meditation and attention: A comparison of the effects of concentrative and mindfulness meditation on sustained attention. *Mental Health, Religion & Culture, 2*, 59–70.

Van de Castle, R. L. (1977). Sleep and dreams. In B. B. Wolman (Ed.), *Handbook of parapsychology* (pp. 473–499). New York: Van Nostrand Reinhold.

Verdoux H, Maurice-Tison S, Gay B, Van Os J, Salamon R. (1998). Bourgideation in primary-care patients. *Psychological Medicine, 28*, 127–134.

Vernon, D. (2005). Can neurofeedback training enhance performance? An evaluation of the evidence with implications for future research. *Applied Psychophysiology and Biofeedback, 30*, 347–364.

Verwoerd, J., Wessel, I., & de Jong, P. (2009). Individual differences in experiencing intrusive memories: The role of the ability to resist proactive interference. *Journal of Behavior Therapy and Experimental Psychiatry, 40,* 1–13.

Wackermann, J., Putz, P., Buchi, S., Strauch, I., & Lehmann, D. (2002). Brain electrical activity and subjective experience during altered states of consciousness: Ganzfeld and hypnagogic states. *International Journal of Psychophysiology, 46,* 123–146.

Wade, J. (1996). *Changes of mind: A holonomic theory of the evolution of consciousness.* Albany, NY: State University of New York Press.

Walach, H., Jonas, W. B., & Lewith, G. T. (2003). The role of outcomes research in evaluating complementary and alternative medicine. *Alternative Therapies in Health and Medicine, 8* (3), 88–95.

Walach, H., Schmidt, S., Schneider, R., Seiter, C., & Bosch, H. (2002). Melting boundaries: Subjectivity and intersubjectivity in the light of parapsychological data. *European Journal of Parapsychology, 17,* 72–96.

Walker, L. G. (1999). Psychological factors can predict the response to primary chemotherapy in patients with locally advanced breast cancer. *European Journal of Cancer, 35,* 1783.

Wallace, B. (1986). Latency and frequency reports to the Necker Cube illusion: Effects of hypnotic susceptibility and mental arithmetic. *Journal of General Psychology, 113,* 187–194.

Wallace, B. (1988). Hypnotic susceptibility, visual distraction, and reports of Necker Cube apparent reversals. *Journal of General Psychology, 115,* 389–396.

Wallace, B. A. (2006). *The attention revolution.* Boston: Wisdom Publications.

Wallace, B., Knight, T. A., & Garrett, J. B. (1976). Hypnotic susceptibility and frequency reports to illusory stimuli. *Journal of Abnormal Psychology, 85,* 558–563.

Wallas, G. (1926). *The art of thought.* New York: Harcourt, Brace.

Waller, N., Putnam, F., & Carlson, E. (1996). Types of dissociation and dissociative types: A taxometric analysis of dissociative experiences. *Psychological Methods, 1,* 300–321.

Walsh, R. (1990). Shamanic cosmology: A psychological examination of the shaman's worldview. *ReVision, 13* (2), 86–100.

Walsh, R. (2005). Can synaesthesia be cultivated? Indications from surveys of meditators. *Journal of Consciousness Studies, 12,* 5–17.

Ward, J., Thompson-Lake, D., Ely, R., & Kaminski, F. (2008). Synaesthesia, creativity and art: What is the link? *British Journal of Psychology, 99,* 127–141.

Watson, D. (2003). To dream, perchance to remember: Individual differences in dream recall. *Personality and Individual Differences, 34,* 1271–1286.

Watt, C. A., & Baker, I. S. (2002). Remote Facilitation of attention focusing with psi-supportive versus psi-unsupportive experimenter suggestions. *Journal of Parapsychology, 66,* 151–168.

Watt, C. A., & Brady, C. (2002). Experimenter effects and the remote facilitation of attention focusing: Two studies and the discovery of an artifact. *Journal of Parapsychology, 66,* 49–71.

Watt, C. A., & Ramakers, P. (2003). Experimenter effects with a remote facilitation of attention focusing task: A study with multiple believer and disbeliever experimenters. *Journal of Parapsychology, 67,* 99–116.

Weber, R. (1995). Philosophical and foundations for healing. In D. Kunz (Ed.), *Spiritual healing: Doctors examine therapeutic touch and other forms of holistic treatments.* (pp. 21–43). Wheaton, IL: Quest books.

Weinstein, S., & Graves (2002). Are creativity and schizotypy products of a right hemisphere bias? *Brain and Cognition, 49,* 138–51.

Weisberg, R. (1989). Problem solving and creativity. In R. Sternberg(Ed.), *The nature of creativity* (pp. 148–176). Cambridge: Cambridge University Press.

Weisberg, R. (2006). *Creativity: Understanding innovation in problem solving, science, invention and the arts.* Hoboken, NJ: John Wiley.

Weiss, G. (1998). *Body images: Embodiment as intercorporeality.* London: Routledge.

Weitzenhoffer, A. M., & Hilgard, E. R. (1962). *Stanford Hypnotic Susceptibility Scale, Form C.* Palo Alto, CA: Consulting Psychologists Press.

West, D. J. (1993). Reflections on the investigation of spontaneous cases. In L. Coly &

J. D. S. McMahon (Eds.), *Psi and clinical practice.* New York: Parapsychological Foundation.

Wetzel, W. (1989). Reiki healing: A physiologic perspective. *Journal of Holistic Nursing, 7*, 47–154.

Whitehouse, W. G., Dinges, D. F., Orne, E. C., Keller, S. E., Bates, B. L., Bauer, N. K., Morahan, P., Haupt, B. A., Carlin, M. M., Bloom, P. B., Zaugg, L., & Orne, M. T. (1996). Psychosocial and immune effects of self-hypnosis training for stress management throughout the first semester of medical school. *Psychosomatic Medicine, 58*, 249–263.

Wilber, K. (1980). The pre/trans fallacy. *Re-Vision, 2*, 51–72.

Williams, L. M. (1994). The multidimensional nature of schizotypal traits, a cluster analytic study. *Personality and Individual Differences, 16*, 103–112.

Williams, C. (2008). Xie qi in the Ling Shu: Balance, harmony and the possibility of invasion. *Journal of Chinese Medicine, 85*, 52–56.

Williams, R. L., & Cole, S. (1968). Religiosity, generalised anxiety, and apprehensions concerning death. *Journal of Social Psychology, 75*, 111–117.

Williams, J. M., Duggan, D. S., Crane, C., & Fennell, M. J. (2006). Mindfulness-based cognitive therapy for prevention of recurrence of suicidal behavior. *Journal of Clinical Psychology, 62*, 201–210.

Williams, C., Dutton, D., & Burgess, C. (2010). Communicating the intangible: A phenomenological exploration of energy healing. *Qualitative Research in Psychology, 7*, 45–56.

Williams, J. D., & Gruzelier, J. H. (2001). Differentiation of hypnosis and relaxation by analysis of narrow band theta and alpha frequencies. *International Journal of Clinical and Experimental Hypnosis, 49*, 185–286.

Williams, L. M., & Irwin, H. J. (1991). A study of paranormal belief, magical ideation as an index of schizotypy and cognitive style. *Personality and Individual Differences, 12*, 1339–1348.

Wilson, R., & Cairns, E. (1992). Troubles, stress and psychological disorder in Northern Ireland. *The Psychologist, 5* (8), 347–50.

Wilson, R., & Cairns, E. (1994). *Psychological consequences of the remembrance Sunday explosion in Enniskillen: A community survey.*

Wilson, R., & Cairns, E. (1996). Coping processes and emotions in relation to political violence in Northern Ireland. In G. Mulhearn & S. Joseph (Eds.), *Psychological perspectives on stress and trauma: From disaster to political violence* (pp. 19–28). Leicester: British Psychological Society.

Winkelman, M. J. (2007). Shamanic guidelines for psychedelic medicine. In M. J. Winkelman and T. B. Roberts (Eds.), *Psychedelic medicine: New evidence for hallucinogenic substances as treatments* (vol. 2) (pp. 143–167). Westport, CT: Praeger.

Wolfradt, U., Oubaid, V., Straube, E. R., Bischoff, N., & Mischo, J. (1999). Thinking styles, schizotypal traits and anomalous experiences. *Personality and Individual Differences, 27*, 821–830.

Wolfradt, U., & Pretz, J. (2001). Individual differences in creativity: Personality, story writing, and hobbies. *European Journal of Personality, 15*, 297–310.

Wood, J., Sebba, D., & Domino, G. (1989–90). Do creative people have more bizarre dreams? A reconsideration. *Imagination, Cognition and Personality, 9*, 3–16.

Woody, E. Z., Bowers, K. S. (1994). A frontal assault on dissociated control. In S. J. Lynn & J. W. Rhue (Eds.), *Dissociation: Clinical and theoretical perspectives* (pp. 52–79). New York: Guilford Press.

Woody, E., & Claridge, G. S. (1977). Psychoticism and thinking. *British Journal of Clinical Psychology, 16*, 241–248.

Woody, E., & Sadler, P. (1998). On reintegrating dissociated theories: Comment on Kirsch and Lynn (1998). *Psychological Bulletin, 123*, 192–7.

Wulff, D. M. (1997). *Psychology of religion: Classic and contemporary.* New York: Wiley.

Wulff, D. (2000). Mystical experience. In E. Cardeña, S. Lynn, & S. Krippner (Eds.), *The varieties of anomalous experience* (pp. 397–440). Washington DC: American Psychological Association.

Wunthrow, R. (1978). Peak experiences: Some empirical tests. *Journal of Humanistic Psychology, 18*, 59–75.

Wuthrich, V., & Bates, T. (2001). Schizotypy and latent inhibition: non-linear linkage between psychometric and cognitive markers. *Personality and Individual Differences*, *30*, 783–798.

Yardi, N. (2001). Yoga for control of epilepsy. *Seizure, 10*, 7–12.

Young, E., & Mason, O. (2007). Psychosis-proneness and socially relevant reasoning. *Psychiatry Research, 150*, 123–129.

Zahradnik, F. (2007). *Irritation der wirklichkeit*. (Psychologie des Bewusstseins, Band 8). Hamburg: LIT.

Zanes, J., Ross, S., Hatfield, R., Houtler, B., & Whitman, D. (1998). The relationship between creativity and psychosis-proneness. *Personality and Individual Differences, 24*, 879–881.

Zha, P., Walczyk, J., Griffith-Ross, D., Toba-cyk, J., & Walczyk, D. (2006). The impact of culture and individualism–collectivism on the creative potential and achievement of American and Chinese adults. *Creativity Research Journal, 18*, 355–366.

Zhang, X.S., Roy R. J., & Jensen, E. W. (2001). EEG complexity as a measure of depth of anesthesia for patients. *IEEE Transactions on Biomedical Engineering, 48*, 1424–33.

Zimmerman, W., & Guildford, J. (1963). *The Zimmerman-Guildford interest inventory.* Beverley Hills, CA: Sheridam Supply

Zollman, C., & Vickers, A. (1999). ABC of complementary medicine: What is complementary medicine? *British Medical Journal, 319*, 693–696.

About the Contributors

Eberhard **Bauer** is a psychologist (DipPsych). A former assistant to Hans Bender (1907–1991), founder of the Institut für Grenzgebiete der Psychologie und Psychohygiene (IGPP) in Freiburg, he is now a council member of the IGPP in charge of the Counseling and Information and Historical Studies, Archives and Library departments. For many years he has edited the German *Zeitschrift für Parapsychologie und Grenzgebiete der Psychologie* with Walter V. Lucadou. Among his interests are counseling work with persons reporting exceptional experiences and research into biographical and cultural-historical aspects of paranormal phenomena.

Martina **Belz** holds a Ph.D. in psychology and studied psychology, cultural anthropology and classical archeology. She works as a research fellow in psychology at the University of Bern and as a licensed psychotherapist and supervisor in her own private practice. Her research has centered on the study of the psychological functioning of people claiming ExEs, case conceptualization and emotion regulation, subjective health concepts and gaining expertise in psychotherapy. Since 1998, she has been a clinical supervisor and research advisor at the counseling unit of the Institut für Grenzgebiete der Psychologie und Psychohygiene (IGPP) in Freiburg.

Eve **Binks** is a senior lecturer in psychology at Liverpool Hope University where she contributes to the Desmond Tutu Center for War and Peace Studies. She received a Ph.D. from the University of Liverpool in 2007, and her research focused on the "psychosocial dimensions of the Irish and Northern Irish diaspora." She has published invited contributions to books on "Responding to Traumatized Children" and "Conflict and the Reconstruction of Civil Society," and has co-authored a number of cross-national research articles with international research teams. Her most recent research focuses on the readiness for reconciliation in Israel and Northern Ireland.

Chris **Burgess** is an energy healer who facilitates stress management for the corporate world, industry, commerce and the individual through his company, Alterity. He has a M.A. Dip. in hypnosis and is also Deputy National Councilor in Merseyside and Cheshire (UK) for the Federation of Small Businesses. He worked with Carl Williams and Diane Dutton in their recent research.

Isabel **Clarke** is a consultant clinical psychologist, working in acute mental health in the National Health Service as psychological therapies lead in Woodhaven — a psychiatric inpatient hospital. She has published and organized symposia at national and international conferences on how therapy can be delivered in the inpatient setting as well as on the psychology of spirituality. In 2001, she edited a book, *Psychosis and Spirituality; Exploring the New Frontier*, and has organized three conferences on this theme. Her recent book, *Madness, Mystery and the Survival of God* (O-Books), brings together these themes in an accessible form.

Diane **Dutton** received a Ph.D. in psychology in 2001 from the University of Liverpool. Her doctorate focused on chimpanzee social relationships and personality, also exploring how people construct and interpret personality in animals. She is currently a senior lecturer in psychology at Liverpool Hope University, teaching a range of subjects including parapsychology, applied psychology and research methods. As well as continuing work on conceptions of energy, she is exploring phenomenological accounts of human-animal relationships and has recently completed a project reviewing the role of animals in parapsychological research.

John **Gruzelier** is a professor of psychology and a professorial research fellow working to further research on self-hypnosis and energy medicine, and in creativity in the arts and humanities using neurotechnology, notably EEG-neurofeedback. His 250+ publications span schizophrenia, psychosis-proneness, psychophysiological measurement, brain lateralization, hypnosis and energy medicine. From 1984 to 2004 co-editor of the *International Journal of Psychophysiology*, he has since 2001 edited *Contemporary Hypnosis*. He has been president of the British Psychophysiology Society and vice-president of the Federation of European Psychophysiological Societies, is a governor of the International Organization of Psychophysiology, and recently established the Society of Applied Neuroscience.

Nicola J. **Holt** is a lecturer in psychology at the University of the West of England, Bristol. Following an M.Sc. in consciousness studies and transpersonal psychology at Liverpool JM University, she conducted doctoral research at the University of Northampton, exploring the relationship between creativity and both altered states of consciousness and psi. Her post-doctoral work includes experimental work on schizotypy, paranormal belief, creativity and attentional disinhibition, as well as research using conversational analysis to assess the dynamics of the stream of consciousness (with Robin Wooffitt at the University of York). She is interested in individual differences in conscious experience.

David **Luke** is a senior lecturer in psychology at the University of Greenwich where he coordinates and teaches an undergraduate course on the psychology of exceptional human experience. He has a Ph.D. from the University of

Northampton where he studied beliefs about luck and the paranormal in relation to precognition task performance. He is a past president of the Parapsychological Association and is a research associate at the Beckley Foundation, Oxford, an organization dedicated to the study of consciousness and its altered states.

Stefan **Schmidt**, a trained psychologist, received a Ph.D. from the University of Freiburg, Germany, in 2002, with a thesis on distant intentionality experiments. He is the head of the Academic Section for Evaluation of Complementary Medicine at the University Medical Center, Freiburg, and is also leading the Center for Mindfulness, Meditation and Neuroscience Research at the Institute of Environmental Health Sciences. He is conducting research on the interface of health, spirituality and consciousness and is the principal investigator of several projects on the neurophysiologic and behavioral effects of mindfulness meditation.

Christine **Simmonds-Moore** earned a Ph.D. in psychology from the University of Northampton. She is an assistant professor of psychology at the University of West Georgia. She is adjunct faculty at Atlantic University and research associate at the Rhine Research Center. She has worked on a variety of Bial (and other) funded research projects, including anomalous healing, ganzfeld research, virtual reality and ESP, and gender role and anomalous experiences and beliefs, and is working on a book about schizotypy as a "psychic personality" and co-writing a text book on anomalistic psychology.

Ian **Tierney** is a chartered clinical psychologist and associate fellow of the British Psychological Society. In 2003, he retired from the position of clinical director of the Keil Centre, Edinburgh, which he founded in 1983. He completed his first degree in psychology at the University of Wales, his Ph.D. at the University of Stirling, and his clinical training during his post-doctoral fellowship in the Department of Psychiatry, University of Edinburgh. With Caroline Watt, he is organizing the "Europsi Study"—a pan-European test of Von Lucadou's Model of Pragmatic Information involving nearly 50 individuals with an academic interest in parapsychology in 30 centers throughout Europe.

Carl **Williams** received a Ph.D. from the University of Edinburgh in 1997. His research examined the role of cognitive style on the construction of anomalous experiences, and also explored the relationship between mental health and unusual experiences. He is a senior lecturer in psychology at Liverpool Hope University, teaching parapsychology, research methods, applied psychology and philosophy of science at both undergraduate and postgraduate levels. His research interests include the philosophy and psychology of science and especially the role of conceptual frameworks in constructing and explaining marginal phenomena, such as those in parapsychology and more recently in alternative healing practices such as Oriental medicine.

Index

absorption 27, 28, 33, 43- 45, 48, 62, 100, 114, 135, 136, 139, 140, 141, 143, 148, 164, 167, 169; Johrei 3, 11, 27, 29, 46–54, 56–60, 62, 63; Reiki 3, 11, 12, 27, 29, 46, 53, 54–56, 60, 62, 63; states 135, 136, 139–143, 148, 164, 167; traits 169
acupressure 83, 85, 89–90
acupuncture 83, 87, 89–91
adaptive novelty 132, 169; *see also* creativity
advanced training courses for mental health professionals 212–214
alcohol 144, 147, 151–152; *see also* drugs
alexithymia 157
alternative medicine 82, 211; *see also* complementary medicine
ambicognitivity 154; *see also* creativity
American Center for the Integration of Spiritually Transformative Experiences (ACISTE) 21
animated visualization 42–43
anomalous beliefs 173
anomalous cognition 173
anomalous experiences (AEs) 19, 21, 22, 23, 29, 131–169, 242, 171–194, 196, 200, 242, 243, 244, 248, 252; control of 8, 24, 160, 168, 171, 172, 174, 182, 183, 186–194; controllability 200; definition 132–133; distress 14, 16, 17, 18, 20, 22, 166, 169, 180, 181, 199, 210–221, 223–224, 234, 239, 241, 242–252; healthy anomalous experiences, 186–191; manipulation of 173, 183–186, 191-194; measurement 133–135; mental health 162–169, 171–195; multidimensionality 136–140; mystical and oneiric 140–144; personality 144–152; *see also* anomaly-proneness; exceptional experiences
anomalous healing 1, 297; *see also* energy; psychic healing
anomalous sensations/sensory perceptions 173, 175–177
anomaly-prone personality 8, 173, 186, 187, 194
anomaly-proneness 140, 152, 156, 160, 161,

165, 167, 169, 172–174, 177–179, 184, 189; state 140, 152, 156, 160, 161, 165, 167, 169, 172–174; trait 177–179, 184, 189
anxiety 29, 35, 36, 40, 41, 44, 47–48, 50,-52, 55–56, 78, 79, 87, 95, 118, 119, 146, 148, 157–158, 164, 166, 179, 182, 205, 209
Appraisals of Anomalous Experiences Interview (AANEX) 200; *see also* Brett, Caroline
artistic creative personality 130, 140–144, 149, 152, 156–170, 233
Asclepions 64, 65, 66; *see also* Asclepius; dreaming; klínè
Asclepius 64, 65, 68; *see also* Asclepions; klínè
attention 113, 115–117, 122, 125–129, 132, 145, 148, 153–158, 160, 165–166, 175–176, 179, 182, 185–188, 192–195, 222, 224
attention allocation 187–188
Attention Focusing Facilitation Experiment (AFFE) 122, 125, 128, 129; *see also* DMILS; meditation
Autoimmune disorders 34
automatic processing 188
ayahuasca 67–78; constituents of 68; history of usage 68; miração 70; ordeal and catharsis 70; revelation 70; simple vision 70; *see also* shamanism

Bial Foundation 13
bioenergy 3, 12, 56; *see also* biofield therapies; biomagnetic fields; Johrei; Reiki
biofield therapies 27, 29, 46, 54;*see also* Johrei; Reiki
biomagnetic fields 60
bipolarity of exceptional experiences 14, 23; *see also* anomalous experiences; distressing exceptional experiences; exceptional experiences
boundary thinness 138–140, 169, 174–175, 183–188, 194; boundary thickness 191, 194; correlates of 138–140, 174–175, 183–188; creativity 138–140; definition 138; manipulation of 183–185; *see also* anomaly

www.ingramcontent.com/pod-product-compliance
Lightning Source LLC
Chambersburg PA
CBHW031403270326
41929CB00010BA/1301